The Greenback

The Greenback

Paper Money and American Culture

HEINZ TSCHACHLER

McFarland & Company, Inc., Publishers
Jefferson, North Carolina, and London

LIBRARY OF CONGRESS CATALOGUING-IN-PUBLICATION DATA

Tschachler, Heinz.
The greenback : paper money and American culture / Heinz Tschachler.
p. cm.
Includes bibliographical references and index.

ISBN 978-0-7864-4973-6
softcover : 50# alkaline paper ∞

1. Paper money—United States—History. 2. Dollar,
American—History. I. Title.
HG591.T834 2010 332.4'0440973—dc22 2010006529

British Library cataloguing data are available

Front cover ©2010 Shutterstock

Manufactured in the United States of America

*McFarland & Company, Inc., Publishers
Box 611, Jefferson, North Carolina 28640
www.mcfarlandpub.com*

For Gerhild

Acknowledgments

This book would not have been possible without the help of a great many people, though responsibility for it lies entirely with its author. With that said, special thanks go to my colleagues Eleonore Wildburger and Franz M. Kuna, who made time from impossible schedules to comment on drafts. Among my extended support group, the late Johann Köberl, Gerda Elisabeth Moser, Maureen Devine, Simone Puff, Petra Strohmaier, Dagmar Wernitznig, Stefan "Steve" Rabitsch, Helga Klopcic, Manuela Bernhardt, and Christina Obermann helped me in various stages of this project.

A particular thank-you goes to the staff of the library and interlibrary loan desks at the Alpen-Adria-Universität Klagenfurt, to Eva Muhm from the American Reference Center in Vienna, the New Orleans Public Library, and the Princeton University Library. I also thank Joseph E. Boling, Joyce Corbett, Herbert Emmerig, Winfried Fluck, Walter Grünzweig, Dennis R. Hall and Susan Grove Hall, Jörg Helbig, Gene Hessler, the late Robin Hoople, Glen A. and Rhoda Love, Daniel Shanahan, Marc Shell, Julia Watson, Judy Bolton and Gayle Campbell, and Irene Wainwright.

In addition, I thank the anonymous readers for the *Journal of American Studies of Turkey* and for the *Journal of the American Numismatic Association*, all of whom made comments cautionary and supportive. From their remarks, I have made all the use I could.

Invaluable support has also come from Douglas A. Mudd, Andrew Dickes, Lane Brunner, Sharon Thomas, Jane Colvard, and Joyce Wohlfert (all from the American Numismatic Association), Richard G. Doty (Smithsonian Institution), Fred Reed (Society of Paper Money Collectors, Dallas, Texas), Mark D. Tomasko and Leena Akhtar (Museum of American Finance), Jan Ferguson (Federal Reserve Bank of San Francisco), Elaine Grublin (Massachusetts Historical Society), the NOAA's library reference staff, David Greg Harth, as well as Nadejda Kisseleva, Olga Brown and students from my Research Forum graduate seminar and, not to forget, the wonderful people from *H-AMSTDY* and *Cultstud-L* who graciously responded to my various calls for help. They are, in alphabetical order, Charlie Bertsch, Elizabeth Bishop, Martyn Bone, Megan Brown, Ben Chappell, Juliette Kristensen, Josh Lauer, Anthony McCann, Murray Forman, Emily Gilbert, Jonathan P. Gill, Kevin Hearle, Joseph Heathcott, Roger Hecht, Mary Kaplan, Andrew McMichael, Kevin R. McNamara, Susan Nance, Cynthia Patterson, Nancy A. Pope, Michael Sappol, Jeffrey Sklansky, Martha Starr, Carolyn Tyjewski, Annette L. Varcoe, with her father John R. Varcoe, and Shirley Wajda.

Most recently, I have been able to profit from speakers and participants at the *Almighty Dollar* Conference of October 2008, in particular from Stephen Mihm, a true fellow scholar of the dollar, Nadja Gernalzick, Eva Boesenberg, Veronika Timpe, and Kathleen Loock.

I gratefully acknowledge a grant from the dean of the School of Humanities and Culture Studies at Alpen-Andria-Universität Klagenfurt to help cover the costs of reproductions and rights.

Special thanks go to Richard G. Doty, David Greg Harth, Fred Reed, and Mark D. Tomasko for generously contributing images. I am also grateful to the New Orleans Public Library and the NOAA (National Oceanic and Atmospheric Administration/Department of Commerce) photo library. The American Numismatic Association and the Massachusetts Historical Society provided additional images.

Table of Contents

—Money ... ? in a voice that rustled.

—Paper, yes.

—And we'd never seen it. Paper money.

—We never saw paper money till we came east.

—It looked so strange the first time we saw it. Lifeless.

—You couldn't believe it was worth a thing.

—Not after father jingling his change.

—Those were silver dollars.

—And halves, yes and quarters, Julia. The ones from
his pupils. I can hear him now...

Sunlight, pocketed in a cloud, spilled suddenly broken
across the floor through the leaves of the trees outside.

—William Gaddis, *JR* 3

Preface

GONZALO: "When every grief is entertain'd that's offer'd, Comes to th' entertainer —

SEBASTIAN: "A dollar."

GONZALO: "Dolour comes to him, indeed: you have spoken truer than you purpos'd."

— William Shakespeare, *The Tempest*, 2.1.18–21

By a cunning of history, this book was being finished at the very time that the United States and world economies were plunging doomward. Of course, they had it coming and so the book's working title, "Beyond Face Value," inadvertently became a commentary on the high rollers of Wall Street and the gnomes of Zurich who were and, of course, are still playing a confidence game, with all the ambiguities that attend the word "confidence." Everything from abusive lending to unregulated derivatives has unleashed what Jonathan Duchac, the Director of the Program in Risk Management at Wake Forest University, called "the perfect storm."[1] Indeed, the numbers are truly staggering. When subprime mortgage lenders began declaring bankruptcy in August 2007, the Federal Reserve and other financial authorities believed that the losses would peak around $100 billion. Instead, the crisis spread with amazing rapidity to other markets. In October 2008, the entire financial system melted down. Attempts to resuscitate it cost the Federal Reserve some $1,000 billion in a couple of weeks. The federal takeover of Fannie Mae and Freddie Mac added more than $5 trillion to the national debt. Big European banks were forced to write off almost as much money as their American brethren. Taking the U.S. and Europe together, banks and other financial institutions had, by that time, written off roughly $450 billion in subprime-related charges. Many institutions, a financial expert wrote then, "are sitting on losses that they haven't yet declared. Estimates of the total losses that will eventually result range from $1 trillion to $2 trillion."[2]

Such figures probably are enough to put anyone into a gloomy mood, including Alan Greenspan, the former Federal Reserve chairman and not usually known as a man for superlatives,[3] Nobel-prize winning economist Paul Krugman, who has come forth with sober suggestions of what to do,[4] and, not to forget, the cartoonists who altered George Washington's portrait on the one-dollar bill to images of the founding father with his hands over his eyes or with a clinical thermometer in his mouth. The use of visual images to illustrate the magnitude of the crisis is at the same time surprising and not surprising. It is surprising to see visual images drawn on the lowly one-dollar bill since today money exists

This Berlin woman, realizing that fuel costs money, is starting the morning fire with marks "not worth the paper they are printed on" (Library of Congress, Prints & Photographs Division, LC-USE6-D-009361).

mostly as a metaphysical order: not only is the vast bulk of monetary transactions made by checks based on bank deposits or by credit cards; nearly all dollars now exist electronically.[5] Yet to explain the crisis with the help of pictorial representations is far more effective than to translate it into verbal symbols, that is, into words.

Although the dollar may have metamorphosed into a symbol of debt—from "dollar" to "dolour"—I still carry a one-dollar bill in my wallet, for good luck. I also look at it from time to time, noticing that it speaks to me in a voice that is more familiar and more reassuring than that of the new euro currency. Why should that be so? Am I just another hapless victim of the relentless pressure to modernize? Is it true, then, that the acceptance and legitimacy even of modern currencies depend on their ability to symbolize a community based on a political territory and, at the same time, to transcend social contradictions? If the appeal of a currency that grounds value in "sacred" symbols reveals this author's somewhat sentimental relationship to money, this is not merely contingent upon almost a lifetime spent under rather straitened circumstances. A great deal of it is owed to my grandmother, who once gave me a stash of old bank notes. The notes were worthless, but not "bogus," which they would have been had the stash consisted of fantasy bills and had she or I lived in America in the early 1800s. The notes my grandmother gave me were emergency issues—"*Notgeld*"—from the inflation-plagued 1920s. Billions of those old bills— Austrian crowns and German reichsmarks alike—together were probably worth less than "ten bucks." By contrast, my late uncle Erich's coin collection, always the object of my youthful fascination, must have been worth quite a few "grand." Telling these youthful recollections to a colleague earned me the designation "pecuniast." (The word is not in the dictionary, though its meaning should become sufficiently clear as this book progresses.)[6]

I could also think of another reason for choosing the lowly paper dollar as the subject matter for my analysis. Again, the reason would be personal, but on a deeper level. It is not always easy to summon the energy that is necessary for researching a subject. However, once I had as it were taken the first fateful step, there was no stopping the voices. Why was I doing all this? Why didn't I just remain in some kind of splendid isolation? One of the demons plaguing me even assumed the shape of Dr. Freud, who would insist that what kept me going was any one of the following five expectations: recognition by my peers, power, wealth, glory, and the love of women. Recognition by my peers? Didn't I have that already? Alternatively, if I didn't, was not the only thing between me and success myself? The love of women, then? My unconscious is of no concern here, but I will admit that I am sometimes troubled by the idea that whatever I creatively do is forever compromised by my inability to bear children. Power and glory were hardly less troubling, as they might make me unpopular with my ancestors, to whom the pursuit of them would have appeared sinful or, if they had read the philosopher, "unnatural." Maybe I could get away with money or "dough," to use the American colloquialism. Everyone "kneads dough," and let no one claim that it does not matter in the academy. Gaius Cornelius Tacitus, in his *Germania*, may have counted the Germanic tribes lucky for caring so little about gold and silver. The sentiment is echoed in Hegel, who likewise spoke admiringly about the contempt his compatriots allegedly had for money. However, coming as I do from Austria, I rather sympathize with Johann Nestroy, who complained that the Phoenicians may have invented money, "but why so little?"

The French writer Jules Renard once said that the key to distinguishing humans from animals was that only humans worried about money. I myself also worried about the fact that my project was to be text-centered only in a very loose sense of the word. For anyone from a continental European English department to forsake the world of words for the world of material culture involves risks. Of course "literature" can be stretched to an extreme, making it encompass cultural forms like TV sitcoms or hip-hop; even so, the study of it would not be cultural automatically. Studying forms and objects culturally involves how and why such work is done, not just what. It is the study *through* cultural objects and forms of the values, assumptions, ideas, attitudes, and beliefs of a particular community or society at a given time. It explores, not just a body of texts, but historical forms of consciousness in their relation to practical activity. The term culture study thus refers at the same time to the subject matter of the study, cultural forms and objects, and to its purpose, the understanding of culture.[7] The unease, even discomfort, that such an enterprise has caused and to an extent still causes in the academy appears to stem from an unconscious ordering that attaches a higher value to anything abstract, intellectual, or spiritual than to material and physical things.[8]

The present study does not stop at representations of paper dollars *in* texts. Nor does it treat them as if they were texts, that is, as material or aesthetic artifacts *analogous to* "texts." To do so may be limiting, leading to a mere restaging of New Critical practices. In their stead, an "anti-idealist" conception of paper dollars as symbols of values was deemed appropriate.[9] Such a conception acknowledges that pieces of currency not merely *are* "living history."[10] They *have* history in that they are representations of how people saw themselves and how they wanted to be seen. To look at paper dollars in this way opens a view on what the British historian E. P. Thompson called meaningful social change "over a considerable historical period."[11] It allows us to see that the identities generated by the paper dollar not only bind people together but also leave them bound, often by quite narrow notions. As unappreciated as this point may be, it is a corroboration of academic trends. For the past decade or so, scholars in American Studies have increasingly argued that the United States be understood, not as an island, separate and distinct from the rest of the world, but as a nation among nations.[12]

Indeed, the dollar seems to compel us to engage in a transnational approach to culture studies. The dollar may be a symbol of and proxy for the power of the American nation, but it is at the same time an object whose significance transcends the national borders. Even now, at the height of a global economic crisis, the dollar remains the lingua franca of the global monetary system, much as the close to a trillion dollars' worth of paper dollars in circulation in the world continue to pass from hand to hand in almost every nation. Nor is this transnational quality of the dollar a matter of the present only: the dollar has always transcended national boundaries. The convoluted path from its origins in the colonial era to its present status is a journey that, following the historian Stephen Mihm, "has always taken place within a transnational frame of reference, and in fact, can best be understood in terms of the relations between nations, empires, and regions of the world."[13]

These relations are not simply constituted by economic forces. Money is more than a commercial convenience; it is also always a document of culture. Within this frame, the difference between the American and the European experiences becomes more salient: Americans united politically before they created a monetary union and integrated economically. By contrast, the introduction of the euro effectively undid many of the monetary standardizations that had been undertaken in the name of the nation. These standardizations had created the political differences that then would compete with other such differences. If the loss of difference that followed the introduction of the euro bred resistance, this only revealed the complex relations between national and other allegiances. Eventually, however, most Europeans did "learn to think in a new language."[14] At least in the realm of the currency, people in Europe appear to have stopped lamenting the loss of diversity, which in the American context has been framed by the ideological struggle between states' rights and federal rights. All this is to say that the paper dollar of course is an American product, albeit one that is of considerable interest also to the student who is not in or of that culture. The distance that this position entails, a distance that is one of neither hostility nor uncritical adulation, should also make the present book a foreign product that American readers might want to use for further processing.

A Note on Illustrations

I have not referenced individual currency notes or coins in the text. It is easy to identify them in standard reference works such as Newman (*Early Paper Money*), or Friedberg and Friedberg (*Paper Money of the United States*). Similarly, coins can easily be identified in Yeoman.

All U.S. notes in this book are reduced to less than 75 percent of their actual size. This is done to comply with Treasury Department regulations regarding reproductions of U.S. currency, specifically with the Counterfeit Detection Act of 1992, Public Law 102–550.

Images of coins and currency can also be viewed online at a variety of sites, including *www.bep.treas.gov/* (Bureau of Engraving and Printing), *www.usmint.gov* (United States Mint), *www.frsbsf.org* (Federal Reserve Bank of San Francisco, American Currency Exhibit), *www.americanhistory.si.edu* (National Numismatic Collection), *www.coins.nd.edu* (University of Notre Dame Special Collections), and *www.ana-museum.org* (the Beebee Collection at the American Numismatic Association). The Library of Congress Business Reference Services division maintains a section on money that provides valuable links to other sites (*www.loc.gov/rr/business/money*).

Introduction

Where money has not been introduced, men are brutish and savage and nothing good has been cultivated.
— Cotton Mather, *The Christian Philosopher*, 1721

For an American Studies analyst to write about the paper dollar may seem natural. Although in light of the present plunge doomward of the United States and world economies any such study is in danger of becoming a dithyramb of old, not all hands have been called. In the United States at least, everyone is still handling dollar bills for a variety of reasons, though this goes largely unexamined. Dollar bills do not draw looks. Perceiving them evokes neither distance nor foreignness, which would define them as noteworthy. Dollar bills ordinarily draw inattention or interaction, created by the perception of familiarity or sameness, a perception that initially, of course, also involves looking. Nevertheless, very few people are actually aware of the images that grace the notes that they handle daily, though they may be very aware of the *kinds* of images that appear on them, and are certainly capable of telling one note from another.

It seems safe to say that the lowly paper dollar is one of those everyday, self-evident things that are most taken-for-granted but that for that very reason may well be the most important ones for revealing an understanding of American culture.[1] Yet what *do* we learn about American culture by studying what everyone there has in his or her pockets, what everyone has to hand, and whose use, physical character, and value everyone knows? Is it, as Stephanie Faul claims, that Americans think that not only time but also everything is money? According to Faul, this is because of the egalitarianism of a society in which other signs of distinction are of no use, such as a noble family, a cultured mind, even clean hands and a pure heart. Americans are said to think that everything is money because "money can be quantified. In the game of life, money is the most effective way to keep score." Small wonder, then, that Americans are "quite open about their obsession with money. They cheerfully ask and tell each other what possessions cost and how much they earn (though the latter figure is often inflated for public consumption), and have conversations like, 'How much did your lawyer charge you for your divorce? Really? Wow, I guess I got a better deal than I thought.'"[2]

To say, as Faul does, that Americans think "everything is money" suggests that there are certain shared understandings among Americans, as well as among non–Americans.[3] Shared understandings are crucial for a definition of culture. They convey a sense of identity, of who we are and with whom we belong. Shared understandings connect to questions of how culture is used to mark out and maintain identity within and difference between groups. The principal argument of the present book thus is that paper bills are more than mere commercial conveniences, performing their proper function by encouraging trade and investment. They are also documents of culture, cultural products that speak to the identity of a group of people, a place, and a time. Typically, we distinguish denominations not just by numerical symbols of perceived worth, but also by images that convey messages to and from the society that gives rise to them. The political scientist Eric Helleiner has found that these non-monetary articulations are organized in at least five different ways. One concerns the verbal and visual images on monetary tokens. Another concerns their function as a common medium of social communication. Yet another one concerns the creation of collective monetary experiences among a currency's transactors. Still another one concerns its ability to provide a sense of popular sovereignty. Finally, there is the ability of a currency to strengthen the quasi-religious faith associated with nationalism. The same ability belongs to anthems, flags, slogans, and other phenomena. Currency notes (and coins) are special. In modern times, they have come to reinforce what Michael Billig calls "banal nationalism," that is, the collection of ideological habits of practice and belief that reproduce the nation as a nation on an *everyday* level.

Overall, the present project studies America's *paper* money. Aspects concerning *coins* therefore will be discussed much more briefly than those concerning bank and government notes and other types of paper money. Of course, in terms of the national symbolic alone, coins are of considerable interest. Alexander Hamilton recognized coins as "vehicles of useful impressions" as early as 1791.[4] Already the United States' very first official coin was emblazoned with the inscription "We Are One." Moreover, as of 1792, all coins would have one side devoted to a representation of Liberty, while the other side would show an eagle. This is owed largely to George Washington's objection to having his name and portrait placed on the nation's coinage, considering this a "monarchical" practice. On the other hand, the new coins did not monopolize the coinage in the first decades of the republic so that their symbolic messages were at first heavily diluted by the presence of foreign or localized coins. It was not until the 1850s that domestic coins came into dominance and the attachment to nationalist images became stronger, symbolizing sentiments of nationality.

Paper money, we can say by way of hypothesis, is quintessentially American. This is not to assert any innate quality — neither in the material itself nor by way of ascribing certain character traits to all Americans — so much as it is to acknowledge that paper money has been bound up with questions of sovereignty to a degree unmatched by coins. The beginnings must be sought in historic contingency. Although from the start of European settlement in North America metal was the undisputed basis for most of the colonies' money, not enough coins of any kind were available ever, and there was an almost complete absence of precious metals in what is now the United States of America — gold was not discovered in any usable quantity until 1848 and silver even later. These facts left the colonists little choice. Like it or not, they had to make do with paper money, which developed early and increased rapidly. Massachusetts led the way in 1690, and by 1750, every single one of the thirteen colonies was using paper money. On the eve of the Revolution, Eric Newman points out, "the money supply in America consisted of one-fourth specie and three-fourths paper money."[5] Altogether, Richard Doty is right in his estimate that paper money alone would give the United States "the peculiar capital elasticity" it required for its development as a nation. "Had there been no paper, we would now be speaking of the numismatic history of a much smaller, and a much lesser country."[6]

Presumably, in such a country people would still be seen biting on a coin to see if it is real. Today, that gesture still works in films. Everyday language too has preserved some interesting things: "It ain't worth a plug nickel" is a reference to counterfeit coins or else to coins whose metallic content is inferior to what it is supposed to be or that are otherwise defective. "He's an old moneybags" too suggests coin, not paper. The expression, which appears to go back to the late sixteenth century, unfolds economic transactions resting on personal ties. By contrast, to bite on a coin to see if it is real is a practice that belongs to an organization of society characterized by economic anonymity. One does not usually bite on a paper bill, though paper money enables an even greater level of economic anonymity than other forms of money, including personal checks, book credits, and promissory notes. All these financial instruments work best in transactions between people who already know each other. In other words, they rest "on the trust and confidence of familiars." Paper money or, more specifically, bank and government notes are different. They usually originate with distant institutions in far-away places, completely detached from the legal fictions that had enable their circulation. Anyone can use them, in particular people who are strangers to one another, and for whom they soon became the preferred instruments of payment.[7]

Paper, if it was to be accepted as a substitute for "real" money, thus required confidence, especially confidence in people's relationships to one another. Such confidence, the Englishman Thomas Churchyard in a discourse appended to his *A Sparke of Friendship and Warme Goodwill* of 1588 wrote, was inherent in paper: "For paper still from man to man doth go, / when parchment comes in few mens hands, you knowe."[8] If Churchyard saw the potential of paper — its efficiency, its ability to cover great distances, its democratizing effects — when it came to paper money functioning in a largely anonymous setting, confidence did not come about naturally but required backing by trustworthy institutions. Private institutions, like banks or businesses, only had limited success in establishing confidence. In the long run, confidence came to rest upon governmental institutions. Prior to the American Revolution, these were all colonial governments, which at least technically were under the jurisdiction of the Crown. However, the Crown did not look favorably upon the monetary schemes in the colonies, and gradually confidence in the currency became linked with issues of political sovereignty. The colonial experiments with paper money, from the Massachusetts bills of credit on, thus constituted a series of struggles over sovereignty or, to use the words of economic historian Alexander Del Mar, "acts of defiance so contemptuous and insulting to the Crown that forgiveness was thereafter impossible."[9]

Whereas the Continental Currency can still be seen as an expression of the sovereignty of the colonies as a whole — of the United Colonies — the history of paper money thereafter followed a path marked by policies that betrayed a deeply felt suspicion about paper. This changed when, following the Civil War, the Department of Treasury brought about the consolidation of the currency as a truly national one. In this context, which has been referred to in terms of the currency's *territorialization*, that is, in terms of becoming "homogeneous and exclusive within the territorial boundaries of a state,"[10] the currency's value no longer seemed to disappear into an endless series of anonymous hands, each issuing paper promises that depended on yet more paper promises. Instead, value came to rest on the nation-state, constituted by the reference of a signifier (e.g., the verbal and visual images on a piece of paper money) to a transcendental signified (e.g., gold, silver, or a nation's economic power), which became the general equivalent without which exchange is impossible.[11] Traditional forms of money such as wampum, cowrie shells, buckskin, Indian corn, or simple nails, which are themselves commodities, can never be "the cement of societies."[12] Only the "imagined" value of paper money will play a significant role for individuals recognizing their membership in the equally "imagined" political community of the nation.[13]

A few words regarding terminology are in order here. First, there will be clarification of the term "culture." This will be followed by clarification of terms like "money," "currency," "paper money," and "bank and government notes." As regards the word "culture," it is undoubtedly one of the most complex words in the English language and there are many different ways of using it. Traditional concepts define "culture" as "simply the best that has been thought and said in society." Culture thus is the sum total of a society's greatest ideas, as they are represented in the classic works of literature, music, philosophy, and the fine arts. Defined in this way as "high" culture, it also refers to its opposite, "low" or "popular" culture, from popular music and literature to all kinds of activities and entertainment that make up the everyday lives of "ordinary" people. A more recent way of describing "culture" is to see it as a "whole way of life" of a group of people, together with their "shared values."[14]

As regards the second clarification, an important distinction is between "money" and "currency." "Money" is really anything people can use to buy something else with; thus, "money" concerns the measure of value. "Currency" usually refers to the medium of exchange and may as well refer to paper money. The term "paper money," however, refers to a wide range of circulating media, including bank and government notes, but also merchant bills and other private money, checks, letters of credit, bills of exchange, and traveler's checks.[15] This book will frequently use the term "paper money" in a rather loose sense, though the focus is really on bank and government notes, that is, on those slips of paper that are recognizable as a species by shape, color, size, and engraved work. Such pieces of paper have been the most prevalent medium of exchange since the creation of the United States of America and, to an extent, since the colonial era.[16] These objects will be studied culturally, that is, in terms of their belonging to the symbolic domain within American society. To do so requires an eye on how paper dollars speak, on what they do, on how they affect the inner world of real people, the ways they feel about life, the relations between individuals, or culture in general.

The material itself — paper — gave rise to many prejudices and anxieties. André Blum in his classic study on the origin of paper cites a twelfth-century account by Peter the Venerable, abbot of Cluny, of copies of the Talmud made, not from papyrus or parchment, but "from old rags or from some other vile material." Some three centuries later, a German Benedictine by the name of Johannes Trithemius commented that despite the obvious differences in durability between a manuscript written on parchment and a printed book — the former "will last a thousand years" whereas the latter will not exceed "two hundred"— there are "many who think they can entrust their works to paper. Posterity will judge."[17] Anxieties about the degenerative or ephemeral character of paper doubled when the material was used to represent value, as in paper money. The paper money form thus created problems of acceptance from the beginning and spawned the most vigorous debates. Some of the debates centered on the notes' redeemability or, failing that, on their being backed by something else. Either way, the combination of representation and value — its ideal or mental form — stems from the signature of the authority issuing it, just like the combination of representation and value in the Christian Eucharist stems from its being backed by God.

Both religious and secular forms of authentication require faith. However, the authenticating signatures on paper bills, like the serial number or the name of the original bearer, only seemingly represent the personal accountability they suggest. Although they are usually marked in quite idiosyncratic handwriting, the bills themselves register personal absence, recalling the *Deus absconditus* that Pascal tragically pursued in his *Pensées*. Once a piece of paper money changes hands, all access to and accountability of the individual (or institution) who issued and passed it disappears as well, making the ground that underlies this system of exchange extremely unstable. The problem cannot be solved, which is why the issuers of paper money have never ceased to harness specific iconographies to support their social and political agendas, from creating faith in their notes to constituting their users as national subjects. Thus, though people take the notes for granted, their very success makes the images they carry so important.

A currency speaks to us through the images it carries, which constitute its rhetoric of endearment. A good example is the current one-dollar note, which is often called an icon of America or of the United States. With George Washington's portrait on the face and the two sides of the Great Seal of the United States on the back, it is an object that codifies, condenses, and anchors America's national memory. Indeed, the note is so loaded with national symbols, both visual and verbal, that when we hear the word "dollar" we can, in a favorable context, visually and mentally picture America or the United States. Literally, as an icon the one-dollar note is produced and put into circulation as capturing something sacred and honored with a relative worship—the American nation. The one-dollar note does not therefore stand for something else but rather is a form that enables a singular meaning. Thus, it serves as a sign of immortality within America's cultural memory, even though historically it is specifically located and has meant different things in different times.

An important distinction is the one between money per se, that is, between the form that money can take—shells, wampum, deerskin, tobacco, nails, copper or bronze tokens, gold or silver coins and, not to forget, paper—as opposed to what money has come to represent. In itself, the dual nature of money has been recognized in theoretical terms—respectively described as symbol and essence, symbol and thing, idea and application, or, implicitly following Aristotle, as a store of value and a medium of exchange. When it comes to actual analyses, however, they for the most part deal only with money's symbolic character, as if money was something objective, unrelated to the culture and society in which it functions as a circulating medium. Yet to focus exclusively on money's symbolic character "takes the money form for granted, overlooking the ways in which it is also a social and cultural construct."[18]

The thought is not new. In an 1860 essay titled "Wealth," Ralph Waldo Emerson wrote that the "value of the dollar is social, as it is created by society."[19] The statement was insightful. If the value of a given monetary token is not absolute, but the product of all kinds of social negotiations, the meaning of a word is also not found in some natural correspondence with the world, but rather in social consensus and use. Thus, neither paper bills or coins nor words have any value beyond the contexts in which they circulate. Coins and bills may become worthless through inflation; words may be debased into stereotypes and clichés, or worse. As Kevin Jackson emphasizes, the notion of a purely private language is an impossibility; the notion of a private currency is equally empty.[20] Given these and other resemblances, we can say that the uses both of words and of money constitute signifying practices. Some such practices use highly sensual impressions and images—hands, pockets, and eyes—that point to all kinds of political and social relations and contacts. Hence, we talk about bucks passing, money changing hands, dirty money, laundered money, or money sent from heaven.

For James Buchan, money, though it means different things to different people, is "incarnate desire. Money takes wishes, however vague or trivial or atrocious, and broadcasts them to the world."[21] A similar thought is evident from the authoritative guidebook to United States paper money, which discusses dollar notes in terms of "living history." While they may be disappointing as communicators of historical fact, they nevertheless are excellent indexes of culture, embodying memory and past experience.[22] History of course imparts validation, which is why dollar notes are not only useful in preserving the culture and heritage but may also be a good investment. Earlier dollar notes, that is, such as a $1000 "Grand Watermelon" Treasury (Coin) note of 1890, which set the current world's paper money record when in December 2006 it sold at auction for $2,255,000.[23]

Auction catalogs or numismatic works understandably are interested mostly in objects that display "discernible differences" or, more important still, objects that are graced by the "attractions of rarity and age."[24] Possibly the combination of difference, rarity and age is the reason that handbooks or catalogs of American paper money often ignore current dollar notes. Tellingly, the Friedbergs' *Paper Money of the United States* includes a lavish appendix, with color reproductions of notes from the collection of the American Numismatic

Top: $1000 "Grand Watermelon" Treasury (Coin) Note, face. *Above:* $1000 "Grand Watermelon" Treasury (Coin) Note, back (courtesy National Numismatic Collection, Smithsonian Institution).

Association, yet this part of the book does not go beyond the first Federal Reserve notes and a Gold Certificate of 1922. Tellingly also, no current note is among the "100 greatest American currency notes" compiled by Bowers and Sundman, though a few small-size notes made after 1929 are included. Still, auction catalogs or numismatic works are useful in that they usually contain overview backgrounds on currency and more or less complete listings and prices for the currency they cover. Attempting to meet the needs of collectors and dealers, these sources at least recognize the materiality of culture, acknowledging paper money as a central symbol and medium of modern cultures in general.

Things mean something only within specific contexts. Likewise, dollar bills may be produced well or badly, depending on printing and/or engraving technologies, as well as on the quality of the paper that is available. Alternatively, they may be issued by large-scale central institutions such as the Bureau of Engraving and Printing or by small private banks serving local populations. However, the creators of dollar bills also are subject to influence and suggestion, and they cannot always predict how the notes will be received. People also give them meaning—by being indifferent to, interested in, or passionately assured of the economic, political, or even aesthetic importance of the bills they are handling. So depending both on the nature of the performance and on the context within which it is set, the meaning of what is ostensibly the same "text" may fundamentally change. No analysis restricted to the "text" that ignores the nature of the performance (the production of meaning at different sites, past and present, and usually in connection with power) can hope to offer a convincing explanation of the "meanings" of dollar bills.

The present study draws on a theoretical model developed by the British sociologist Paul du Gay and his associates. Called "circuit of culture," the model brings together five interlinked cultural processes through which any analysis of a cultural text or object should pass if it is to be adequately studied. Each moment can be seen either as a site where meaning is produced or as a process or practice through which these meanings are circulated. Each depends on the others and answers to the whole. Each involves distinctive changes or transformations of form. Following the precept, it has been deemed necessary to analyze the paper dollar in terms of how "it is represented, what social identities are associated with it, how it is produced and consumed, and what mechanisms regulate its distribution and use."[25] The six chapters of the present study reflect the various processes that relate to paper dollars as cultural objects as well as the practices involving them.

Chapter One begins with questions of meaning. Meanings do not directly rise from paper dollars, but from the ways in which they are represented through signs such as words, gestures, sounds, expressions, and visual images. Representation means that things do not carry fixed and unchanging meanings on their backs. People give meaning to things, by using them, or by saying, thinking, imaging, or feeling and telling stories about them — in short, by creating little worlds about them. In doing so, people also achieve a sense of identity, which is the reason that this chapter is not exclusively concerned with representation. It also raises the question of how various groups and types of people come to be associated with paper dollars. In short, a second moment is added to questions of representation, that of the construction of identities on different levels—national, ethnic, religious, class, sex, and gender.

Chapters Two, Three, and Four focus on the production of American paper money as cultural objects. Cultural objects require to be produced, though we tend to see only the results of this process. The act of producing them, especially of producing them cultur-ally — making them meaningful, encoding them with particular meanings—disappears in the objects. The way "production" is used here, it refers both to enhanced printing technology and to "soft" production factors such as monetary and financial policies. The mechanisms of forging a national political consciousness through the visual images and promises of negotiability conveyed on paper money from early on likewise are "soft" production factors, as are challenges to these mechanisms, for instance from notes issued by private banks or even private individuals. Concern with the question of production will take us back once again to questions of representation and identity, as well as forward to questions of consumption.

The idea of cultural consumption goes beyond a narrow understanding of consumption as the mere purchase of goods, extending it to include both the physical act of consuming or handling bills, and what they may come to mean for those using them in their everyday lives. Chapter Five thus treats meaning making as an ongoing process that does not just end at a pre-ordained point. While designers attempt to encode a note with particular meanings and associations, this is not the end of its cultural work. Meanings are made as well in consumption, from using the dollar sign in renderings of $crooge McDuck to creating personalized ID cards.

Chapter Six highlights the role and impact of the paper dollar in transforming America at the level of everyday life by setting the rules, norms, and conventions by which people in society order and govern their lives. Of particular importance in this matter is the question of trust, without which neither the legal tender clause nor the promise to pay the bearer on demand clause on a variety of notes would make much sense. If contestations over cultural meanings have accompanied the history of the paper dollar from the beginning, they were made worse by forgery. Hence, we will look closely at attempts towards curbing counterfeiting, which the authorities habitually considered as transgressions of the boundaries between the public and the private spheres. Also of importance is the rejection of the paper dollar, in the years following the Civil War, for its symbolic value of racial equality. Thus, we will deal with greenbackism, silverism, and defenses of the gold standard. Recent efforts, both by the Treasury and by the Justice Departments, to defend against challenges to using the national motto also are matters of cultural regulation. Like other regulatory measures, these efforts serve to reproduce a cultural pattern so that it appears "natural" or "normal."

In the Conclusion, we will return to the question of what we learn about American culture by studying the cultural work of its paper money. The stereotypical saying that Americans do not only think time is money, they think everything is money, helps us see that the national currency is both a symbol of the cohesiveness of the United States as a nation and a prime object of reverence in what we might call the "religion of capitalism." Either way, paper dollars appear to perform some kind of alchemy that invests in pieces of paper values that they do not possess of their own accord. The transformation attributes timelessness and universality to the paper dollar, though neither is possible without the mutual complicity of producers and consumers in the exaltation of the iconic image. The complicity is folded into a contract governing the relations between the public and the private, that is, between the state and the citizens. This contract derives its legitimacy from God, which is enshrined in the phrase "In God We Trust" on current dollar notes.

ONE

Making Sense of the Buck

Cultural Representations and
Signifying Practices

> How do we know whether we have faculties fit to perceive the truth in its unity
> and in the simplicity of its precepts? In some countries the people think that it
> resides in symbols, hieroglyphics, splendid ornaments.
> — Crèvecoeur, "Sketches of Eighteenth-Century America" 322

Introduction: Questions of Meaning

Things in themselves do not have meanings. It is by our use of them and by what we say, think, or feel about them that we give them meanings. Take for instance Salmon P. Chase, Secretary of the Treasury under Lincoln, who in 1863 began to solicit bank note designs that were to be "national in their character."[1] In doing so, Secretary Chase created a little world about the new notes. His saying, thinking, or feeling about them effectively transformed neutral pieces of paper into symbols of national cohesiveness at a time when the nation's unity was in jeopardy. In this instance, someone acting within a network of power brought the pieces of paper into meaning. This insight connects meaning back to the social dimension of culture. However, to represent the paper dollar as the *national* currency is only one way (albeit a major one) of bringing it into meaning. Quite different meanings have been established at other times. During the American Revolution, the paper dollar was rather a symbol of sovereignty from Britain. By contrast, the paper dollars of the fledgling republic were a liability rather than an asset, and will be remembered forever for the rapidity with which they became worthless. Each representation in its particular way fixed the meaning of the paper dollar.

Meanings are not just produced and exchanged for their own sake. They also give people a sense of identity, of who they are and with whom they belong. In other words, people are positioned as subjects through processes of representation, though the signifying practices and symbolic systems surrounding things create only *possibilities* of what people are and what they may become. Not everyone sees in a dollar bill the national money icon, but only those people to whom it has a special appeal and to whom it provides images with which they can identify as patriotic citizens. This chapter is thus not exclusively concerned with representation. It also raises the question of how various groups and types of people come to be associated with the national currency, while others would prefer being associated

15

with local or regional currencies, or even with currencies that no longer bear any traces of belongingness, such as debit or credit cards. In short, a second moment is added to questions of representation, that of social *identities*. Adding that moment is to acknowledge that in complex societies there is never only one monolithic culture that reflects, mirrors, and expresses its social and institutional relations. Instead, there are a variety of places from which individuals can position themselves and from which they can speak.

Representations

Michel Foucault, writing about seventeenth-century coins, contends that although any object may be used for money, for coins and bills to be accepted as currency they must possess "peculiar properties of representation." For this reason, Foucault continues, "money does not draw its value from the material of which it is composed, but rather from its form, which is the mark or image of the prince."[2] The phrase "mark or image of the prince" is a useful reminder that coins and, by extension, paper currencies function as representatives of a sovereign territory and speak to their origins. Coins, paper currencies, and their iconography thus work symbolically to define the boundaries between the public and the private. Today, the formation and dissemination of monetary texts is enabled by the fact that a territorial currency is the *only* medium of exchange authorized by a state, so that citizens *must* encounter it in any public transaction. Consequently, citizens will recognize themselves and each other in precisely the terms specified by the state. This recognition is a — largely unconscious— mechanism, which has been termed "interpellation or 'hailing.'" By this mechanism, individuals are recruited into subject positions through recognizing themselves—"yes, that's me."[3]

Not among the notes being transported in the following image would have been the current one-dollar note, though by taking a look at it we can see to what extent the paper dollar has become an important means by which nationality is represented and through which citizens identify themselves. The current one-dollar note is truly unique in that no other piece of paper money, American or non–American, communicates such abundant information about the nation's history, the structure of the nation, and its highest goals and aspirations. The face or front (sometimes also called "recto" or "obverse") most prominently features a portrait of a mutton-jawed George Washington, the first president of the United States. Other iconographic details include the numeral "1" (which stands for the bill's nominal value, its denomination) and the seals of the Treasury Department and of the Federal Reserve Bank (for the two institutions guaranteeing its value). In addition, there are the facsimile signatures of the Treasurer of the United States and of the Secretary of the Treasury (the note shown below bears the signatures respectively of Rosario Marin and John W. Snow).

Also on the face is a serial number with a prefix and suffix letter to identify it (in our case this letter is an "F," which indicates that the note was issued by the Federal Reserve Bank in Atlanta).[4] Furthermore, on the face is indicated the series of which the note is a part (in our case the series year is 2003, which indicates that a change in the Office of the Secretary of the Treasury had occurred in that year).[5] The phrase "Federal Reserve Note" signifies the issuing institution as well as the decree authorizing its production, hence the "kind" or "class" of the note. The sentence, "This note is legal tender for all debts, public and private" summarizes the dominant fiscal theory.[6] In addition, just to make sure there

Transporting the new small size currency (Library of Congress, Prints and Photographs Division, LC-USZ62-106969)

is no mistaking the semiological relation, there is again the phrase "The United States of America." Thus, the presence of the United States of America as a fiscal and/or monetary community is established in words and in image. The final stamp of approval is the Treasury Seal, which has appeared on every piece of paper money issued by the Treasury Department since 1862.

The back ("verso" or "reverse") of the current one-dollar note repeats both the nominal value and the phrase "The United States of America." The famous phrase "In God We Trust" gives the note a divine imprimatur. It encodes the conviction that the contract governing the relations between the state and the citizens derives its legitimacy from God. In plain English, it means that the people of the United States should trust that God has empowered the state to fulfill the promises and obligations articulated on the note, in particular the paying back of debts. However, the phrase "In God We Trust" means all this specifically to people who know that it is the national motto and who value it. Similarly, the two circles (the one featuring a picture of a pyramid capped by an eye, the other featuring a stylized bald eagle) are also meaningful primarily to people who know that they represent the two sides of the Great Seal of the United States.

The current one-dollar note is undoubtedly the most familiar denomination among

Top: $1 Federal Reserve note, Series 2003, face. *Above:* $1 Federal Reserve note, Series 2003, back.

United States notes. This is hardly a surprise, as about sixty percent of the nation's paper bills are of this denomination.[7] It is also the most widely produced note: forty-five percent of all notes printed each year are one-dollar notes. One possible reason for this is that their approximate life span is only some eighteen to twenty months, though other denominations, from twenty up, last relatively longer.[8] Some notes seem to last a great deal longer, especially those stuffed under mattresses, both within the United States and abroad. I am saying "abroad" deliberately here because according to recent estimates the grand total of United States currency held outside the United States is some $700 billion (about the amount the war in Iraq has already cost). The great majority of these dollars exist electronically, but almost a third is printed.[9] For this reason alone we may reasonably assume that most people worldwide will know something about dollar bills.

How does meaning making work? Partly we give things meaning by the way we *represent* them, and the principal means of representation in culture is *language*. Using language is to use a set of signs to represent things and exchange meanings about them. In order to fix the meaning of the one-dollar note we can therefore use a familiar language to describe or represent it. For instance, Richard Doty in his chronicle of American money

$1 Silver Certificate, Series 1923, face

puts the one-dollar note in a series of other notes that as of 1929 were likewise produced "on a new, smaller module," following a general "standardization of design."[10] Here Doty uses language in a plainly descriptive sense to create a little world for the one-dollar note. However, his description only works if one already knows what "smaller module" and "standardization" mean in the context of American numismatic history. One needs to know that prior to the 1930s American bank and government notes were much larger (7⅜ by 3⅛ inches as opposed to 6 by 2⅝ inches).

Meaning making also works by mapping new things in terms of, or by extension or analogy from, things we already know. Mapping the supposedly strange phrases and unmistakable lettering of the one-dollar note, the two seals, the facsimile signatures and the serial number to what we already know, we might say for instance that large, rectangular pieces of paper with numerals, phrases, and images on it have served as paper money at least since the beginning of the modern era. This takes us back, perhaps, to the phrase "Federal Reserve Note." Together with the stolid aesthetics, lapidary floral and animal patterns of the one-dollar note, the phrase gives us an important clue to the time period of the design's origin — the Great Depression. The architects of the period, most notably Franklin D. Roosevelt, were convinced that they too had been called upon to design and implement a new order of the ages— the *Novus Ordo Seclorum*.

The idea of a new order of the ages might take us back, in turn, to the portrait of George Washington, the most revered and idealized of the Founding Fathers of the American republic, and its first President. Each meaning leads us back to another meaning, in an infinite chain. We already know that currencies often depict people in charge. As regards the images now appearing on dollar bills, we may or may not know that around 1929 a special committee appointed by the Secretary of the Treasury determined that "portraits of the Presidents of the United States have a more permanent familiarity in the minds of the public than any others."[11] So once again we can bring together "Dollar" and "American money," which we can then map to the phrase "The United States of America." In addition, we can map the phrase "In God We Trust," together with the image of the bald eagle, to "The United States of America."

There is really no beginning or end to the chain of meanings that we can build. However, if we want to map the full range of meanings, associations, and connotations that the current one-dollar note has acquired over time, we have to move well beyond the so-called literal or descriptive meanings. Since its introduction as a Silver Certificate beginning in 1929 (the current one-dollar note is a Federal Reserve note), the one-dollar note has acquired a much richer set of meanings—what are called "connotations"—than is captured in the lapidary phrase "One Dollar." Its range of references and representations has expanded enormously. Let us take at random a French commentator, Jean-Joseph Goux, who said "an emblematic power emanates from [the one-dollar note] and transforms it into a potent political symbol."[12] Political symbolism connects the one-dollar note to the —fairly recent — phenomenon of the modern nation-state. Issued by the state, the note's validity is set within well-defined boundaries.

The one-dollar note, like a language spoken by a nation marks the national limits of monetary exchange. At the same time, the note conjures up an association for the national currency with the world of rivaling political powers, fierce economic competition, territorial expansion, domestic challenges to rule, and the vital role of invented traditions in the creation of "imagined political communities." Benedict Anderson's famous phrase refers to a time when authorities, in order to maintain legitimacy, embarked upon various projects of instilling in citizens a sense of collective identity which centered around nationalist images of a common past and culture. Conceived thus, the one-dollar note serves to bind together all Americans, as well as to introduce them to all non–Americans, though as a piece of paper money it mediates a relationship in which buyers and sellers remain anonymous.

The paper dollar, we might say, is firmly located on maps of meaning that make up the cultural knowledge of Americans. However, the bills are not only part of a given culture. They also have a distinct "culture" of their own. This means that around them has developed a distinctive set of *meanings* and *practices*. The very word "dollar" conjures up an image or an idea of a piece of paper money. This image or idea — a concept, such as wealth, empowerment, success, universal acceptance, America itself, but also poverty and blood, sweat and tears, governmental deception and dishonesty, corruption, crime and illegality, and money-laundering — is then used to think about it. Thus, the word (or the piece of paper) can be used as a sign that people can communicate about to other people in a variety of different contexts. It is rare for people in these days of rising prices to keep one-dollar notes in their wallets, or if they do, they might keep just one, for good luck. Contrariwise, people continue to stuff wads or bundles of one-dollar notes in their pockets, to be used as tips or gratuities or, on occasion, as bribes. Of course, people might refuse to be bribed, like the woman in a song by Clarence Ashley who, disappointed in her lover, rejects his "greenback dollar," wanting only to shoot out his "dirty brain."[13] These examples tell us that paper dollars belong to American culture because people have constructed for them little worlds of meaning. These meanings help and have helped the bills' holders interpret their world, classify it in meaningful ways, make sense of things and events and, as well, of objects in the real world.

Social Identities

Thanks to the embodiment of associated ideas, paper dollars can deliver meanings beyond their utilitarian function as a means of payment into every text and context in which they appear. These meanings are essential for buttressing and sustaining a community of common purpose. Possessing dollar notes may make one an American, much as it may represent one as an American. A good example are the words of a congressional representative from Michigan, in 1874: "As surely as our flag represents ... the unity of these States, just so surely, sir, do the United States Treasury Notes represent the cost of life and blood and treasure, the priceless value of that unity of States."[14] The congressman's words not only speak of the working of elites in the employ of the nation-state; they also echo the triumphalist rhetoric of the victorious Unionists, much as they resonate with the economic problems (and successes) that were characteristic of post–Civil War America. Finally, the words illustrate the precarious state of paper money as *fiduciary* or *fiat* money, that is, as monetary paper backed by neither gold nor silver.

Greenbackers like our congressman formulated a theory of value and identity drawn from nationalism and patriotic labor.[15] Public response to their efforts was favorable, at least in the Northern press. In a typical dispatch, the *New York Herald* in 1862 spoke of the "general joy and satisfaction" with which people hailed a currency standing on the good faith of the nation. The greenbacks were cited as "a currency as secure as the nation itself" and thus as a proxy for the "patriotism of the people, who, under no circumstances, will depreciate them."[16] A century and a half later, a quite different theory of value and identity emerges from the words of Treasury Secretary John W. Snow. Nationalism and patriotic labor may still be present, but they are drowned out by economic anxieties. For many years, American policy-makers and administrators had been notorious for refusing to modernize the currency. Finally, in the mid–1990s, the overhaul began. With the Series 2004, background colors were added. When in September 2004, the new $50 note was officially unveiled, the Bureau of Engraving and Printing's press release quotes Secretary Snow as saying, "in addition to keeping our currency safe from counterfeiters, the President's economic policies are ensuring that more of those dollars stay in the pockets of American families."[17]

It is easy to see how a particular concept or identity position is set up here, that of an American middle-class citizen, loyal and patriotic but nonetheless haunted by the very real possibility of social decline. Put another way, we can see Secretary Snow creating a particular target audience for the new $50 note. This connects Secretary Snow to the congressional representative from Michigan, even though the two men are separated in time by more than a century. Each man, by virtue of his direct involvement in the production of particular representations and thus in controlling the effect of the sign in the minds of the users, is somehow superior to the people at large. This takes us on to yet another moment in the circuit of culture, that of power. Clearly, each man is a member of the political and cultural elite and may well be in a position to encode the national money icon in their preferred way. In the following, we will look at an example of the voluntary consent of the non-dominant. That consent is essential if hegemony is to assume the dominance of a particular ideology.

Here, then, is the story about an American businessman who when traveling abroad allegedly opens his wallet, takes out a dollar bill, and thus has his sense of identity confirmed. Of course, it would seem only "natural" for the good man to seek, when stranded overseas, some confirmation of his own identity, and he may just as well do so by flipping through his wallet. Class and gender identity may make him dig out pictures of his wife and children, club membership cards, his driver's license, maybe a library card. However, there is something else that makes him "take comfort in the sight of the American money he kept

in reserve — greenbacks, legal tender, cold hard cash." American money, the story continues, "will look much more solid and dependable than the funny money he has been spending on his trip."[18] Clearly, our businessman is "spoken by" the language of the national
symbolic rather than merely speaking it. Moreover, since the businessman is an invention,
we can also say that his creator, Brian Burrell, is "spoken by" it.[19] To the extent that our
businessman (like Burrell himself) is "spoken by" the national symbolic, dollar bills mean
something very specific for him, and that meaning gives him a sense of his own identity.
What the American businessman is doing when stranded overseas — opening his wallet and
taking out a dollar bill — is therefore a symbolic practice which gives meaning to the idea
of belonging to a specific national culture, or identification with that culture. It is part of
the language of national identity or, in Stuart Hall's words, of the "discourse of national
belongingness."[20]

The Dollar: How American Is It?

It is quite possible to say that the pound symbolizes British monetary sovereignty, and
that the franc used to be recognized as the French sign, and the peseta as Spanish. Similarly, it is possible to say that the dollar is the American sign, though there are some thirty
other countries worldwide using the dollar as their currency, and though originally the
word "dollar" did not even refer to American money. The word "dollar" first appeared in
the English language as early as 1553. It was then usually spelt "daler" or "daller." This type
of spelling is a reminder that the word began as the anglicized form of the German "Thaler"
or "Gulden of Joachimsthal" in Bohemia, where coins of one ounce of silver were minted
beginning in the first decades of the sixteenth century.[21]

The Dutch introduced the word "dollar" in the North American colonies. Since at least
1581 and thus long before the Pilgrims set sail for their Promised Land across the Atlantic,
"dollar" also has been the English name for the Spanish peso or *piastre*, as it was rendered
in French. Readers of Robert Louis Stevenson's classic of 1883, *Treasure Island*, might recall
that the peso also was called Spanish Piece of Eight. "Pieces of eight, pieces of eight,"
screamed the old pirate's parrot aboard the *Hispaniola*, referring to a large silver coin of
eight *reales* denomination and weighing 423.7 grains each. The coins were struck at any of
the Spanish colonial mints in Mexico or South America and are therefore also known as
"Mexican Dollars" or "Spanish Milled Dollars."[22]

The Spanish silver dollar may not have been America's first dollar, though its reverse
has been connected to the origin of the dollar sign ($). Beginning in 1661, that side was
graced with the two Pillars of Hercules at the mouth of the Mediterranean, flanking two
globes, and rendered in astonishing detail. Around the two pillars were draped two scrolls
or ribbons, each with a motto in Latin. Hence the term "pillar dollar." For a number of
commentators, the dollar sign took its origin from the left-hand pillar, as its scroll or ribbon is in the form of an S, possibly signifying the Seville mint through which all Spanish
silver originally had to pass. The dollar sign is written either with one stroke (the more
common variant) or with two strokes (the less common variant). The two strokes have been
explained as coming from the two pillars on the Spanish silver dollar. There are many more
explanations, with varying degrees of plausibility.[23]

Whatever their origin, dollar signs were widely used even before the adoption in 1785
of the dollar as official unit of value. These signs had evolved as a response to the very real

need of a practical symbol for the primary coin used in commercial transactions in colonial America. That coin was indeed the Spanish milled dollar, and the Spanish were using "ps," "pS," "Ps," or "PS" for their pesos. These abbreviations consisted of two letters of the alphabet and were written in script or capitals in both upper and lower case, often with flourishes and rubrica, and involving more than one horizontal level of writing. To use any form of these abbreviations as a symbol for the English word "dollar" was somewhat "confusing and

Silver peso of Felipe V, México, 1739 (Wikimedia Commons)

cumbersome. Calculations needed a monetary symbol like the British £ (Libra) which was entirely distinctive and did not have to be repeated when extensively used." Such a symbol, Newman found, was already developed, and it had come from the "S" gradually written over the "P," but often as a superscript "S" ("P^S"), a way of writing that gradually developed into a close equivalent to the "$" mark.[24]

It has been said that the dollar sign first appeared in print in a 1797 book titled *American Accomptant*, in which the author, Chauncey Lee, suggested four symbols for the federal currency created by Act of Congress in 1786, including a symbol using strokes, slashes, and curved S-like shapes across them. The symbol has been interpreted as the dollar sign, though Eric Newman found that Lee used it rather for the dime.[25] A surer bet for a symbol to stand for dollar is a squiggle a bit like "$" that was found in the account books of 1768 of a trader from the Louisiana Territory named John Fitzpatrick. Other early examples are a memo from New York in 1776, and a letter the trader and patriot Oliver Pollock wrote to George Rogers Clark in 1778. Use of the dollar sign was perpetuated when Congressman and financier Robert Morris, upon receiving a billing record from Pollock, as it were gave his blessing to the "S" with two vertical strokes through it. The first printed conventional $ sign appeared in a pamphlet to be submitted to the Pennsylvania House of Representatives in early 1799. The United States government for its part was rather reluctant to accept the $ sign on formal or official documents. "It was not until U.S. obligations were privately designed and printed by Rawdon, Wright & Hatch," Newman concludes, "that the use of the printed $ sign on some of the formal U.S. obligations was commenced and continued at convenience."[26] That was in 1837. Today the pesos theory has also been adopted by the Treasury Department. We therefore might refer to it as the United States' "official" theory; this will put to rest all other theories, or myths.

The word "dollar" is not just a signifier of national belongingness. Often it is embedded also in the rich discourse of national stereotypes. One of the earliest persons to comment on the idolization of money in America was Isaac Weld, Jr., in an account of his travels through North America published in 1799. Alexis de Tocqueville likewise did so in *Democracy in America*. "I know of no country," the worthy Frenchman pontificated, "where the love of money has taken stronger hold on the affections of men." In America, we learn from an early chapter of the second volume, "everyone finds facilities unknown elsewhere for making or increasing his fortune. The spirit of gain is always eager, and the human mind [...] is there swayed by no impulse but the pursuit of wealth." The passion for or love of money that is said to characterize Americans serves an important function, Tocqueville explains in a later chapter in volume two. When "the reverence that belonged to what is old has vanished [...] hardly anything but money remains to create strongly marked differences between [people] and to raise some of them above the common level. The distinction originating in wealth is increased by the disappearance or diminution of all other distinctions," in particular the distinctions of a noble family.[27]

Nineteenth-century Americans knew that if the distinctions of a noble family no longer offered a marker of identity, possession of money and the virtues it implies offered a substitute. However, what if the money itself had no fixed character? What if it represented only social convenience, like trust in future prosperity, that is, paper promises? The answer was the gold (and silver) fetish, the nineteenth-century obsession with a specie economy and the intrinsic value of precious metal. Yet if gold (or silver) could not be had, and if local banks, especially but not exclusively in the West, would issue paper notes in excess of actual specie deposits, the answer was often satire. A famous case is Washington Irving, who will be remembered for the expression "Almighty Dollar," which inimitably enshrines its creator's conviction that as a result of the speculative fever that had gripped the United States money was elevated to the status of a deity.

Irving coined the term "Almighty Dollar" for the sketch "The Creole Village," which originated from his frontier notebooks, begun in 1833. The sketch was first published in Henry Herbert's annual, *The Magnolia*, in 1837, at the height of the financial crisis following President Andrew Jackson's war on the Second Bank of the United States. At the time, not even the federal government would accept paper dollars for the payment of debts, though paper dollars were plentiful, if worthless. A severe shortage of hard money had led to the suspension of specie payment in May of 1837. As a result, banks, businesses, and municipalities began to issue fractional currencies or scrip in lieu of coin. The illustration on the following page, which depicts Jackson's treasure hunt for the gold that "real" notes (the "gold humbug") are supposed to represent, is a parody of these worthless "shinplasters."

Shinplasters are unknown in Irving's "Creole Village." The sketch, which is subtitled "A Sketch from a Steamboat," describes one of the villages of French and Spanish origin in Louisiana that seem to have been bypassed by modernization and thus were spared the monetary turbulences of the time. Typically in those villages, the ancient trees are still standing, "flourish[ing] undisturbed; though, by cutting them down, [the villagers] might open new streets, and put money in their pockets. In a word, the *almighty dollar*, that great object of universal devotion throughout our land, seems to have no genuine devotees in these peculiar villages." In 1855, "The Creole Village" was republished in *Wolfert's Roost*, with one major addition in the form of a footnote, which reads as follows: "This phrase [the almighty dollar] used for the first time, in this sketch, has since passed into current circulation, and by some has been questioned as savoring of irreverence. The author, therefore, owes it to his orthodoxy to declare that no irreverence was intended even to the dollar itself; which he is aware is daily becoming more and more an object of worship."[28]

Irving may have been a burned child, having seen the Liverpool branch of the family business go bankrupt in 1818, though he was by no means the only American to chastise money for the damage it was inflicting on civic mores. Other guardians of public morality came forth with equally damning indictments of money and its effects on people. One was Ralph Waldo Emerson, who in "The American Scholar" of 1837 characterizes Americans as "a people too busy to give to letters any more." To prove his point, Emerson continues in the following way: "The tradesman scarcely ever gives an ideal worth to his work, but is ridden by the routine of his craft, and the soul is subject to dollars."[29] Henry David Thoreau, Emerson's close friend and disciple, would continue in the same spirit. Writing

Fifty cents. Shinplaster (Library of Congress, Prints and Photographs Division, LC-USZ62-1582)

some sixty years after Jefferson, Thoreau had no illusions about the present-day husband-man. The land, he suggests in *Walden,* has become an investment like any other and the farmer a willing participant in the marketplace, a "serf of the soil" who spends his life in a parody of self-reliance by "buying and selling." In a celebrated image in this chapter, which is appropriately titled "Economy," Thoreau envisions the farmer as "creeping down the road of life," pushing before him "a barn seventy-five feet by forty [...] and one hundred acres of land, tillage, mowing, pasture, and wood-lot!"[30] A half-century later, labor leader Eugene Debs came to bemoan the "mad chase for the 'almighty dollar.'" In its stead, he wanted to revive the "spirit of fraternity abroad in the land." Later still, the cultural critic Van Wyck Brooks felt compelled to chastise the "catchpenny opportunism" of "low-brow" America.[31]

Given the damning indictments, on the part of America's intellectual elites, of money and its effects on social life, it is revealing to see how Charles Dickens, another foreign observer, dealt with the subject matter. Dickens's commentaries can be found in the travel book *American Notes* (1842) as well as in the novel *Martin Chuzzlewit* (1843–44). In the novel, the young hero, fresh from England, learns that there is really only one form of aristocracy in America, namely one of dollars. Even a dinner party he is asked to attend "may be summed up in one word. Dollars." For young Martin, then,

All cares, hopes, joys, affections, virtues, and associations, seemed to be melted into dollars. Whatever the chance contributions that fell into the slow cauldron of their talk, they made the gruel thick and slab with dollars. Men were weighed by their dollars, measures gauged by their dollars; life was auctioneered, appraised, put up, and knocked down for its dollars. The next respectable thing to dollars was any venture having their attainment for its end. The more of that worthless ballast, honour and fair-dealing, which any man cast overboard from the ship of his Good Name and Good Intent, the more ample stowage-room he had for dollars.[32]

Although many Americans at the time did not take well to having reflected back to them the tyranny of the "omnipotent" dollar, in general Dickens's attitude towards Americans was generous and well meaning. Dickens consistently presented himself as a faithful supporter of republican government, and he repeatedly mentioned the good will, generosity, and hospitality of his many American friends. He even attached to later editions of *Martin Chuzzlewit* the observations he made at a dinner given in his honor by representatives of the press in New York City in April 1868. He did the same with later editions of *American Notes*. Dickens's dinner observations are interesting in that they are full of admiration of the "amazing changes" which had taken place since his first visit in 1842.[33]

The relation to the United States of other foreign commentators was considerably more troubled, though visitors from Britain tended to sound like the proverbial cousin from the other side of the Atlantic. Among German-speaking artists and intellectuals, however, the interest in America was in steady decline. Take the Austrian poet Nikolaus Lenau, who in 1832 fled to the United States from Europe's depravations. Once he tried to build a new life, though, his attitude took a dramatic turn toward soberness. After a brief experiment as a backwoodsman, plowing his fields with glacé kid gloves, Lenau quickly returned to old Europe with its familiar "culture." Lenau's writings became the basis for Ferdinand Kürnberger's 1855 novel *Der Amerikamüde* (*The Man Weary of America*), which is but another instance of the sober and increasingly hostile outlook on the United States by German-speaking intellectuals. One rather extreme example is Oswald Spengler, the author of the infamous book *Untergang des Abendlandes* (*Decline of the West*), published between 1918 and 1922. Spengler was a typical representative of the educated German bourgeoisie. Hatred of modernity and modernization had led this social group to identify "civilization" (as opposed to "culture") with the West in general and with the United States in particular. Indeed, in a later book Spengler without irony or subtlety wrote that in the vastnesses of the United States one encounters merely a restless people of trappers, always and forever in grim pursuit of the dollar, callous and footloose, and in utter contempt of the law.[34]

Spengler's hostility towards anything American resulted both from the vicissitudes of German nation building and from the rivalry among nations that began in the late nineteenth century. Then the United States also began to make a forceful presence in the global arena. "American" thus became a discourse that represents the dollar as the undisputed leading currency of the western world. This recalls "dollar diplomacy," that is, all kinds of strategies to secure opportunities for employment of American capital abroad. It also recalls the Bretton Woods conference of 1944, which established fixed parities to the dollar for all currencies under the IMF, the International Monetary Fund, and left the United States the only nation that promised to redeem its currency in gold. Of course, those days of glory are long gone, swept away by the dramatic weakening of the dollar beginning in the 1960s, by an even more dramatic decline in the gold stocks, and by an exploding national debt. Yet the dollar is still the dominant currency of international finance and export trading. "American" is thus also a discourse that reflects pride in the United States' success story. It conjures up the country's pre-eminence in the global economy, its highly effective financial sector and its almost unlimited purchasing power. These may be myths, but they help to construct for the dollar an image very different from, say, the Austrian schilling, or "Alpine dollar."[35]

The discourse of "greenbacks" our American businessman uses so fondly also connects the paper dollar to the world of recognizable and reliable items, and, by association, to the world of familiar things and popular culture.[36] To this world belong fictional characters such as "buckaroo" (a known alias for Scrooge McDuck), as well as other terms for dollar bills that have or have almost made it into Standard English. These terms include "green," "folding green," and "long green" (all of which suggesting how deep-seated the connection between is money and the green ink that has been used on the back of U.S. currency since the Civil War). Other terms are "buck," "dough" (which means money because everyone "kneads" it), or "single" (for the $1 bill), "grand," "G," and "K" (each meaning a thousand, as in "ten grand," "10G," or "10K," from "kilo," and pronounced "kay"). A number of terms seem to have outlived their life-span—terms like "spondulicks," "rutabaga," "wad," "ready," "boodle" (which in the nineteenth century was used for counterfeit money or, later, for money used in corrupt dealings in politics), "beans," "dinero," "moola" or "moolah," "tin," or "simoleon."

Still other terms could be mere literary inventions—terms like "berries," "bones," "dead presidents," or "scratch." There are plenty more, including the term "C-note," for a hundred-dollar bill, the C of course being the Roman numeral C, which appeared on hundred-dollar bills in the nineteenth century. *Zveri buksy*, or "beastie bucks," is a derisive term reserved by Russians for the troubled local currencies of the post–Soviet states in Central Asia.[37] Hip-hop has likewise valorized money throughout its existence, from Jimmy Spicer's "Money (Dollar Bill Y'all)" in 1981 to Puff Daddy's "It's All About the Benjamins" (meaning the $100 notes emblazoned with Benjamin Franklin's portrait)[38] in 1997. In 2003, the American rapper Curtis Jackson renamed himself 50 Cent and took as his motto for life the sentence "get rich or die tryin."

Should Mr. Cent succeed in his efforts, he might no longer have to burn "hell money" for good luck; nor would he have to "squeeze every dollar till the eagle shits." Instead, he might be measuring his wealth in terms of "ducats," "cheddar," "cheese" or "c.r.e.a.m." ("Cash Rules Everything Around Me"), all of which are likewise terms for money in hip-hop. These references and metaphors are standard facets of a modern subcultural parlance, whereas "queer as a three-dollar bill" is an American idiomatic expression describing someone as obviously or positively homosexual. One needs to enter the world of bank note collectors and dealers—invariably called "syngraphists" or, more colloquially, "ragpickers"—for recognition of terms like "horse blanket," "pocket change," or "paper mills." A "horse blanket" note is any large-size paper currency, whereas the term "pocket change" is used for small-size notes issued after 1929. "Paper mills" may seem clear enough, yet among numismatists the term refers to pre–Civil War banks that did no real business but ordered large quantities of bills to be shipped off to brokers in distant cities and sold at large discounts, in the hope that few of these notes would ever find their way back home for redemption. One other term should be mentioned here—"bogus." In the nineteenth century, the word implied that a note was a fantasy bill intended for circulation with the same destructive effect as a counterfeit, which had been the word's meaning during the early republic.[39] There have been other expressions for counterfeits, but it may no longer be advisable to use them all. "Shoving the queer" might get one in serious trouble today, whereas in mid-nineteenth century America it meant passing counterfeits.[40]

A "Bungtown copper" was once a phony cent, enshrining the original meaning of Bungtown as "Shitsville," though it is doubtful whether our businessman (or anyone else, for that matter) would refer to coppers as "cold hard cash," and never mind that that is what the word "cash" originally meant.[41] More likely than not, the phrase draws our attention to the fact that coin or "hard money" was an integral element of the national currency once and, with the Susan B. Anthony and the Sacagawea dollar coins in circulation, is arguably even today. Yet the unpopularity of the latter two makes one doubt whether the phrase "cold hard cash" would actually be conferred upon them. That phrase refers us back to the days when there were coins in circulation whose denomination was equal to their value in gold or silver. But since the status as legal tender of foreign gold and silver coins was repealed in 1857, and since the metallic value of all older coins now exceeds by far their nominal value, it is not very likely for someone traveling today to carry pieces of gold or silver in their wallet. The phrase "cold hard cash" therefore also conjures up the long-standing contest in the United States between coin and paper currency, a contest that was effectively decided because of the Civil War, whose uncertainties instantly drove gold and silver coins into hiding.[42]

Signifying Practices

The complex of values, associations, and imaging practices that serve to flesh out the paper dollar's meaning as a cultural object only constitute its immediate cultural significance. People also do all kinds of things with dollar bills, which likewise gives them significance and meaning in cultural life. People use cash when buying something or bribing someone, or when paying taxes or donating to charity. Another practice associated with dollar bills is to stuff them under mattresses, in the hope that to do so would preserve their value. On occasion, people even get hurt using paper money, which allegedly claims nearly as many victims as scissors.[43] Given the — hypothetical — combination of folding money and a subsequent trip to the ER, presumably it is wise not to use dollar bills at all. That precaution seems to apply especially to the two-dollar note, though the bill's unpopularity rather stems from its association with bad luck or even impropriety.

Colonial paper usage patterns included the practice of endorsing the notes. Buyers in commercial transactions would sign their names on the backs of the currency paid to a seller. Sellers hoped that with this safety net in place, a counterfeit note could be traced back to its scandalous source. Other practices involved using dollar bills to wallpaper rooms with or to fashion into a makeshift garment, which was done when the "Continentals" became worthless in the 1790s. In the nineteenth century, it was customary to spindle or stitch new notes together. This was done for safekeeping or for hiding them within a coat's lining; banks also shipped notes for redemption in bundles sewn together with needle and thread.[44]

A great many practices belong to the vast area of "earmarking" money, that is, the creation of distinctions among the uses and meanings of currencies. "Earmarking" thus may refer to the artful creations of gift monies. It may also refer to the use of all sorts of domestic containers (labeled envelopes, colored jars, socks and stockings, boots, mattresses, piggy banks) as well as to the keeping of dollar bills out of circulation by tacking them to the wall or to the counter of a new store. Similarly, it may refer to designating a child's income for specific appropriate purchases, or reserving income earned by the wife for her children's education while her husband's income pays the mortgage.[45]

Still other practices have evolved around using representations of dollar bills as game or toy money, on ID cards, or in the form of personalized notes, usually of $1 million denomination or more, and as chocolate bar gift-wraps. As of the late 1980s, the ANA, the American Numismatic Association, began to issue "Collector Currency" in denominations of $1, $2, and $5. The notes, which are produced by the American Bank Note Co., are almost

Money washing machine at the Treasury Department, 1912 (Library of Congress, Prints and Photographs Division, LC-USZ62-90450)

the size of genuine notes, and they have "the look and feel of real currency."[46] Make-believe dollar notes serving as teaching instruments for inculcating patriotic values in students likewise have the look and feel of real currency, as do the millions of imitation dollar bills burned every year at celebrations of Chinese New Year.[47]

Although all these practices involve bodily and physical movements, it is not their physical or biological character that makes them culturally significant. Simply moving the hand to dig into one's wallet is not in itself culturally distinctive; nor is flashing a dollar bill. What matters for culture is that these practices, too, are organized, guided, and framed by meaning. We therefore call them "signifying practices." As onlookers, observing them, they do not puzzle us because, unlike the proverbial alien from outer space, we know how to "read" them. We do not say, "Look at the funny thing that person is doing — using his hand to flip through a bundle of large, rectangular pieces of paper he keeps in a flat leather container. What is he up to?" We are able to make sense of what that person is doing by de-coding the meaning behind the action, by locating it within some interpretive framework that the person doing it and we share. Shared meaning, we might say, makes the physical action "cultural."

The process by which meaning translates mere behavior into a cultural practice is also reversible. When money becomes increasingly dematerialized, many of the practices described above — like paying cash or stuffing dollar bills under mattresses — will again become mere behavior. It is also possible that the same denominator refers to quite different behaviors. In the early twentieth century, the expression "money laundering" did not yet refer to the altering of bank and commercial transactions for the purpose of making income from illegal or questionable operations appear to be legitimate. On the contrary, it quite literally meant the cleansing of paper money by removing dirt and grease, and it was undertaken by the United States Treasury Bureau of Engraving and Printing. In February 1911, an article by Thomas D. Gannaway, of the Treasury Department, appeared in various American magazines. The article, which was appropriately (and quite unironically) titled "The Government Money Laundry," reported that by washing and ironing soiled and dirty greenbacks the government was saving considerable expense, "equal to an annual interest of almost 1 percent on the $1 notes, which have an average life of only 14 months."[48]

The following chapters will focus on the production of the paper dollar as a cultural object. We will be considering a number of different narratives and representations of the "facts" that have become associated with the paper dollar, past and present. Dealing with this kind of subject matter is a way of demonstrating that the production of the paper dollar involves not only technical aspects such as printing technology and safety features. It also involves the question of how dollar bills are encoded with particular meanings. Concern with the question of production will take us back once again to questions of representation and identity, as well as forward to questions of consumption.

Two

The Production of the Paper Dollar

Green is the color of prosperity, and black is a good thing, too—it shows we're sound and solid and in the black.
— Mary Ellen Withrow, former United States Treasurer, in Goodwin 294.

Introduction: The Many Origins of the Paper Dollar

Current dollar bills only appear to be paper, but they are not: they are a fabric, composed of seventy-five percent cotton and twenty-five percent linen, with blue and red synthetic fibers woven through it. Possibly, it is a good thing that they are not paper. One-dollar bills in particular are left in pockets and thrown in the wash more than any other notes. This is not really a catastrophe, as a special ink is used and the notes are starched after the pictures are printed on them. However, when American paper money was consolidated in the eighteenth and nineteenth centuries, the notes were indeed paper. There also were a great variety of them. For instance, the Province of Massachusetts Bay in December 1690 issued £7,000 of Bills of Credit that would circulate as money. Other issues were to follow respectively in February and May 1691, to an aggregate of £40,000. Though printed to pay for soldiers and supplies for a military expedition to Canada during King William's War, the preamble to the law justified the venture by referring to "the present poverty and calamities of the country, and through a scarcity of money, the want of an adequate measure of commerce." Since the notes constituted the first authorized paper money issued by any government in the western world, the entire move has been described as "one of the most important events in monetary history."[1]

Other reasons for ascribing an exalted position to American paper money abound. American currency, Arthur and Ira Friedberg claim, is absolutely "unique in the annals of world finance," as no nation past or present "can point to such a long, unbroken series of currency issues, the integrity of which has so surely and confidently been maintained." Some representations reach much further, like Arthur Nussbaum's, which has America's monetary history appear as forever "ascendant," a romantic quest for democracy that eventually gathered a large number of nations under its beneficial fold. Writing at the height of the Cold War, and from the standpoint of a political refugee from Hitler's Germany, Nussbaum's intention is to cull from the history of the dollar "a fuller understanding of the spirit of this great, free, and hospitable country."[2]

By contrast, Doty's *America's Money* represents an epic struggle between national, regional, and local interests, with little sympathy for the shift of authority to the central government, while Goodwin's *History of the Greenback* comes to us as a heroic story shaped by larger-than-life individuals who as it were "invented" America. The mode of the moral drama also informs, at least in part, Friedman and Schwartz's analytical narrative of post–Civil War monetary developments in the United States, especially in the section about the Great Depression, which the authors claim could have been averted if the Fed's leading men had shown more leadership and courage. Last but not least, there are even examples of the satirical mode. One is Standish's book on *The Art of Money*, in which the deterioration of aesthetic standards since the late nineteenth century is described with grim humor.

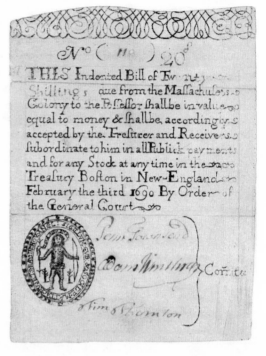

20s, Indented Bill, Massachusetts, 1690 [1691], 13.7 × 10.3cm (courtesy of the Massachusetts Historical Society)

Wars and Other Mighty Events

Probably the most important devices for constructing narratives of America's monetary history have been wars and other emergencies, colonial or national. The Province of Massachusetts Bay came first, paying in 1690 for a military expedition to Canada during King William's War with bills of credit. Next came South Carolina, which in 1703 printed paper money to finance a military foray against Spanish-held Saint Augustine. The costs of Queen Anne's War, lasting from 1702 to 1713, prompted New Hampshire, Connecticut, New York, New Jersey, and Rhode Island to print their first paper money, respectively in 1709 and 1710, all to finance expeditions into Canada to protect the colonies' northern borders. In 1713 came North Carolina's first paper money, also to finance a war — against the Tuscarora Indians. When in 1755 the French and Indian War began, Virginia too would resort to paper, primarily to finance the effort of controlling the Ohio valley.

Technically speaking, the paper issued during these ventures was not money, as most of these issues were designated "bills of credit" or IOUs, in today's parlance. They were meant to be short-term loans *to* the various colonial governments to be able to fulfill their obligations, and England, which would send out silver to help a colony "retire" its notes, guaranteed their value. During most of the colonial period, then, people could exchange paper money into specie if necessary because the mother country stood behind the currency being issued. The end of the wars against France in Canada and the freewheeling over-issuing that many colonies indulged in pushed inflation to a point that made Britain step in. In 1764, four years after the French formally surrendered in Montreal, a proclamation issued by the Parliament in London forbade the use of paper money as legal tender in payment of debts in all British colonies in North America. This piece of legislation only extended to *all* colonies a situation that had been in force in New England since 1751, and in Massachusetts since 1727, when, following the French experience of the Great Mississippi Bubble, the English government suppressed the circulation of the bills of credit of 1690.

Other acts, declarations, and bills were to follow. Since each somehow touched upon the money question, they frustrated and angered the colonists to the point of rebellion. As Alexander Del Mar pointed out more than a century ago, all these acts constituted a "series of repressive measures which furnished the first distinctive provocation to the American Revolution."[3] Once that Revolution was under way, everything changed. It was unthinkable that England would stand behind a colonial paper currency during the Revolutionary War, "unless Americans succeeded in invading, defeating, and occupying it, extracting such payment by force. Not even the most ardent patriot could have expected this scenario to take place."[4] If Britain would no longer guarantee the value of the currency, the colonial governments themselves were incapable of doing so for the simple reason that they did not have enough gold or silver. Robert Morris, the "Financier of the Revolution," obtained loans from France, Spain, and the Dutch. Yet these amounts—altogether a little over eight million dollars—were "more symbolic than real."[5]

When the Continental Congress assembled in Philadelphia in May 1775, it had no authority to impose taxes, while the states were unwilling to do so in any measure that would have been adequate to financing the revolution. A finance committee took four days to recommend that Congress issue bills of credit, and beginning in June the "Continental Currency" was issued. The currency notes essentially were the earliest symbols of the sovereignty of the United States, yet the meanings surrounding them were conflicted during the entire Revolutionary period and the early republic until their demise in 1789. Building national identity made up one semantic network, while other such networks were constituted by the desire for economic and political stability. Whereas the former became a true success story, the latter became a disaster. Legally, the "Continentals," as the bills came to be known, were money that had the form of debt. They were printed in such excessive numbers that the result was hyperinflation.[6]

Overall, the monetary practices of the pre-revolutionary and Revolutionary periods have been read from two perspectives. From one perspective, of which the clearest example is the work of Alexander Del Mar, they have been regarded as a series of struggles over political sovereignty. From another perspective, exemplified for instance by the work of Charles J. Bullock, the entire period is regarded as scandalous. For Bullock, who was a staunch defender of the gold standard, the paper money schemes of the entire period were a "curse" that largely contributed to the era's "carnival of fraud and corruption." The Continental currency in particular opened the doors to the "most shameful frauds upon all who were so unfortunate as to be in the position of creditors. Dishonest debtors were enabled to pay their debts in worthless currency."[7] Even more sympathetic commentators like Samuel Breck and Henry Phillips, Jr., viewed the era's monetary experiments with shame. More recently still, Arthur Nussbaum termed the period the "least satisfactory" in America's monetary history. "The effects of the breakdown of the colonial regime had not been overcome at the beginning of this period; authorities and sound policies were widely lacking." Indeed, the United States Mint, established in 1792, was unable to provide a steady and reliable supply of coins, so that all kinds of foreign coins continued to be in circulation. In particularly short supply were small denomination coins, which were partly needed to pay the increasing number of laborers. Importing these coins in bulk was hardly a practicable solution and, for Americans with a nationalistic turn of mind, it also was not a desirable one. What had been done during the Revolution again was being done now: public and private groups and merchants taking up the slack on the local level and issuing small change notes, called fractional currency or scrip.[8]

There was also a new money supply, in the form of paper notes from private commercial banks, especially from the First and Second Banks of the United States, which until 1837 made up a large part of the paper currency in circulation.[9] However, these particular financial instruments would pull America's money away from the direction the drafters of the Constitution, steeped in their suspicions about paper money, had sought to channel it into, and the two banks were duly abolished. Thereafter, the federal government showed that it no longer needed a central bank to implement monetary policy and to act as a lender of last resort. Thus, the Treasury would manage payments and raise funds by selling notes and securities directly to investors. The government from time to time also issued its own paper money, in the form of Treasury notes. In doing so, they were following James Madison, who during the Federal Convention of 1787 had cautioned that bills of credit "may on some emergencies be best." Some of these bills were interest bearing, and were redeemed as quickly as possible. Others circulated as money for a brief period. Among the events that brought forth these notes were the War of 1812, the Mexican War of 1846, the hard times of 1837–1843, the Panic of 1857, and the situation just prior to the Civil War.[10]

The Civil War, commentators are in agreement, was the defining experience of American history, a true watershed, and it made the United States an entirely different country. The same estimate, Richard Doty suggests, "might be equally applied to its money." Indeed, in the four years of the Civil War, America's currency would begin "in familiar modes, be constantly altered under pressure, and emerge with fundamentally new identities, identities which they still maintain today with minor modifications." Put simply, an increasingly powerful national government would "acquire a monopoly on the making and circulation of *all* money within the United States of America."[11] What happened in the 1860s was the precise opposite to what had taken place in the early years of the republic. During the 1770s and 1780s, people were disillusioned with public currency, thus forcing the emergence of private currency. Now that another war was raging, people became disillusioned with private currency; this would lead to the re-introduction of public currency, and to the ultimate demise of private currency.

Once the first shots had been fired at Fort Sumter on April 12, 1861, *both* sides were in desperate need for money for the war effort.[12] The Confederacy at first left the money business to the private banks, then to the states, and finally took it over itself. However, the exigencies of the war proved disastrous to the private banks, which in the end took to typesetting notes, sometimes overprinting older paper. State banks and the Confederacy instantly took to issuing paper money. While they were accustoming the people to public rather than private notes, both were issuing only paper *promises*. The problem arose in part because of a constitutional clause that allowed both the southern states and the Confederate government to issue paper, while neither could make them legal tender. The combined result was a flood of worthless paper, made worse by counterfeiting.

The situation became so bad that the Confederate government even decided to honor counterfeits as genuine. Most of these counterfeits came, not from counterfeiters in the South but from legitimate printers and engravers in the North who sought to undermine the Southern currency while turning a profit. The strategy seems to have worked, as the

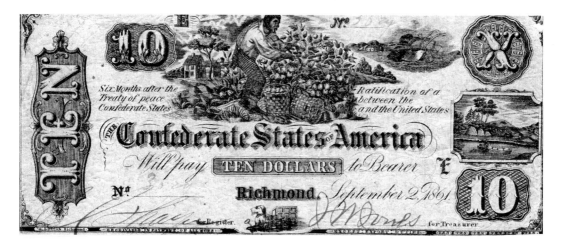

$10, Confederate States of America, 1861 (courtesy National Numismatic Collection, Smithsonian Institution)

greenbacks, the enemy's money, were much sought after; they were exchanged, at first clandestinely, then quite openly, at a ruinous discount on Confederate notes. At General Lee's surrender at Appomattox, the currency was worthless; its use value, if it had any, was in serving as wall insulation in homes. John Kenneth Galbraith's observation is quite to the point: "The miracle of the Confederacy, like the miracle of Rome, was not that it fell but that it survived so long."[13]

The Union, which was bound by the Independent Treasury Act of 1846 to pay all expenditures in gold or silver, at first experimented with bond sales, then with a variety of taxes, at first on the states, then on income. A year later came taxes on alcohol and tobacco, playing cards and billiard tables, carriages and yachts, medicines and advertisements, manufactured goods and farm produce, licenses and stamps, dividends and inheritances. Tariffs were also raised, and the conversion of paper notes into gold or silver was suspended. Although all these measures helped keep the Union economy from overheating, much as they signaled the government's seriousness about paying for the war effort by honest means rather than by turning on the paper mills, in the long run none of them proved enough. Consequently, and all the bad experiences in the past with paper money notwithstanding, the Treasury Department was authorized to print and circulate paper money to the extent of $60 million, which was about twice the amount of gold and silver coins struck in one year. Plainly a wartime expedient, the notes were printed on a cotton/linen paper, using cheap green ink, which quickly earned them their lasting nickname, "greenbacks."[14] Their official name was "Demand Notes," as the bearer was given the right to have the notes paid at any time, "on demand," although it was not always clear what the bearer would be paid.

The Demand notes were only a first step in the complete nationalization of the currency. When gold and then silver coins disappeared from circulation and the need for a widely accepted high-denomination paper currency became more acute with a war that was not going anywhere, Congress in February 1862 authorized a new type of notes. Before their constitutionality had been secured, they were called "Treasury Notes." Once Congress had declared them "lawful money" (again because many people and institutions refused to accept and pay them), they were called "Legal Tender Issues." Thereafter the term "United States Notes" was exclusively used.[15] These notes, which were likewise called "greenbacks," are considered the first genuinely national paper currency. It was "a bold new step for the government," J. Earl Massey concludes, as the paper money field previously had been left to the private commercial banks.[16]

Since the greenback type notes were acceptable as lawful money simply because the government said so, their value fluctuated, as did the war effort. When the Union was winning, the notes rose in value, as in August 1863, after Gettysburg and Vicksburg, when they hit eighty-two cents a dollar. By June 1864, when the war was costing the Union over two million dollars per day, they were valued at thirty-five cents on the dollar. Their value rose again in spring of 1865, as the Union forces seemed more certain of winning the war.[17] When the war was over, Wall Street "bulls" like Jay Gould and Jim Fisk would speculate on the performance of the greenbacks against gold. At one point, they drove the premium for the latter up to 150 (meaning that 150 paper dollars were required to purchase $100 in gold), which was up more than 20 points from the "normal" rate and so high that gold was literally sucked out of banks, many of which became insolvent. At the height of the crisis, President Ulysses Grant stepped in, ordering the sale of $4 million in federal gold. In no time, the price of gold fell to 135 and the bubble burst, ruining any number of people.[18]

Altogether, it would take ten more years for the greenbacks being once again accepted at face value. The Resumption Act, which John Sherman helped steer through Congress in 1875, had gone into effect: the Act held that the United States would be paying out gold in exchange for greenbacks as of January 1, 1879. Consequently, the monetary situation became stabilized, $1 and $3 gold pieces were dropped from mintage, and the greenbacks came to greatly contribute to economic expansion. What also greatly contributed to economic expansion were notes from private banks, though the conditions under which these notes could be issued had changed dramatically during the Civil War.

As of 1863, private banks were encouraged to apply for federal charters under which they would become "National Banks" and were then permitted to issue "National Bank notes." Private commercial banks would use their funds to purchase Union bonds. The bonds would be deposited with the United States Treasurer, who would then give the banks permission to issue national bank notes against up to ninety percent of the value of the bonds they had just deposited. This was a good deal for the government, which through selling bonds was able to raise money for the war effort. Likewise a good deal for the government was the creation of low denomination subsidiary coins; in the 1860s, producing them left over a million dollars per year in the public coffers. Authorities had recognized that a more homogeneous and exclusive currency would greatly augment the state's ability to extract resources directly from the people it governed.[19]

Wars continued to be important in the monetary and economic history of the United States. Because of World War I, the available resources and money supplies of the major European powers were badly upset. Although the war was also costly for the United States, it nevertheless catapulted the nation into the position of a world power. Its European allies paid for their much needed supplies and materials in gold, which led to an unprecedented increase in the nation's gold holdings. By the end of 1918, the country's stocks of gold "equaled about 40 per cent of the world's known gold reserves."[20] Fifty years earlier, this would have been unthinkable to the world's leading nations. In addition, while most European nations had to abandon the gold standard because of substantial losses and depleted reserves, the United States continued on the gold standard until the 1930s. By then, the dollar had become the world's leading currency, backed by ever-growing reserves and a newly attained strong credit position. The United States no longer had to import money. Instead, it was able to help the Allies to maintain their weakened monetary systems with some $10 billion in loans. The expansion of business and employment and the necessity of making possible the government's war loans also brought forth and into dominance a new form of paper currency, the Federal Reserve notes.

Federal Reserve notes are a direct obligation of the United States government. Originally, they were to be secured by commercial paper and, as well, a reserve of not less than forty percent in gold.[21] Under the Constitution, the power to create all forms of currency belongs to Congress, yet it delegated this power to the Federal Reserve System. The Fed had been created in December 1913, under the leadership of President Woodrow Wilson, and in belated reaction to the financial panics of 1893 and 1907. The notes created under this system, together with the "circulating notes" to be issued by the banks under the system, were intended to regulate the quantity and flow of the national currency for greater economic stability, thus furnishing an "elastic currency."[22] The term "elastic currency" means that money is subject to quantitative changes over short periods. An example is when the public shifts from deposits to currency, which without expanding supply would lead to crisis and panic. For the first few years, the Fed had little power to contract the money stock. Once that power was granted, they refused to make use of it, sitting idle as the stock market went out of control.[23]

Whereas the Federal Reserve remained inactive during these years of crisis, the Treasury Department at the same time put into circulation a new small-size currency. More strategically planned measures were to follow. For instance on March 9, 1933, the day when legislation was enacted to provide relief in the banking emergency that had developed, President Roosevelt directed the Bureau of Engraving and Printing to proceed with the physical production of new Federal Reserve Bank notes. When confidence had been restored, normal currency came back and issuing Federal Reserve Bank notes was curtailed later in the year. Within the next two years, other types of paper money were being curtailed as well. Moreover, all United States currency was made redeemable "in lawful money" rather than spelling out precisely what sort of coin might be received for each note.

All these measures only strengthened the Federal Reserve notes, and beginning in the mid–1930s, this type of currency would "reign supreme."[24] Indeed, the monetary disturbances that appeared during the Great Depression and that occasioned the growth to dominance of Federal Reserve notes were absent in World War II. This period was twice as long as that of American participation in World War I and it cost the lives of almost 300,000 men and women, yet for the United States it was one of incredible monetary and financial vigor. As this was largely the result of a stupendous rise in domestic production, the circulating currency rose from $6 billion in 1939 to $27 billion in 1945, of which no less than $23 billion consisted of Federal Reserve notes. There were no serious disturbances, and of the few changes in the nation's money, none was permanent.[25]

By the end of 1945, the monetary situation was back to its prewar mold. Paper money was again printed in its normal seal colors, and coins resumed their normal alloys. World War II thus did not greatly affect the production of American paper money, though its aftermath did. It all began in 1955, at the height of the Cold War, when President Eisenhower signed into law a bill providing that the phrase "In God We Trust" appear on all United States paper currency and coins. One-dollar Silver Certificates bearing the inscription were first made available to the public beginning October 1, 1957. The reason given for the adoption of the phrase was to set the godly United States off from the atheist or ungodly Soviet Union. The story has it that Matthew H. Rothert, a past President of the American Numismatic Association, presented the suggestion to Secretary of the Treasury George W.

Humphrey in November 1953. Rothert is thus credited with the ultimate adoption of the idea.[26] The interventions of people like Rothert remind us of the fact that decisive but unforeseen events such as wars or economic crises are not in themselves agents. So it does make sense that some of the stories or representations of the production of the paper dollar focus on the activities of inspired individuals. Some of these individuals will concern us in the following section.

Money's Heroes (and Anti-Heroes)

One of the earliest "heroes" is John Hull, whose Boston mint in 1652 was authorized by the Massachusetts Colonial Legislature to strike Pine Tree Shillings in denominations of 12, 6, and 3 pence (and, as of 1662 also of 2 pence). The measure was adopted because of the severe shortage of money in the colony. Striking these coins continued through 1686, when they were suppressed by order of the English king, who considered the practice a breach of a royal prerogative. It was this suppression of the Pine Tree Shillings that led to the emergence of the first paper money in America, where in 1690 the bills of credit were printed in Massachusetts. John Hull was doubtless remarkable, though also remarkably overlooked, relegated by economic historians into the shadow of the single most widely discussed of money's heroes, Benjamin Franklin. Franklin is often seen as the "father" of the quasi-religious belief associated with capitalism. This may be a judgment on hindsight, put into circulation in order to get even with at least one of the Founding Fathers. Indeed it is a vague charge, which thinly disguises an anti-capitalist reflex, and we may even trace its origin to Hawthorne's condemnation of the Poor Richards proverbs from Franklin's *Almanack* as being "all about money or getting it."[27] From another perspective, Franklin appears as a lifelong friend and defender of paper money. Paper money, Franklin said, makes people associate one with another. It enlivens and quickens social intercourse, turns over products and ideas, encourages the poor, and ensures that the rich spread their wealth about them by buying things and employing people. Last but not least, its presence acts as a magnet to new settlers.

Many of Franklin's ideas about money were laid down already in a 1729 pamphlet entitled "A Modest Enquiry into the Nature and Necessity of a Paper-Currency." Its purpose was to allay the fears and reservations of colonial Americans, who had been plagued with a shortage of money from the beginning of settlement. Franklin therefore welcomed the first Pennsylvania issue of £150,000, which for him meant that finally there was more paper money around. The future seemed safe for Franklin. A "plentiful Currency" would produce low interest rates. In turn, this "will be an Inducement to many to lay out their Money in Lands, rather than put it out to Use, by which Land will begin to rise in Value and bear a better Price: And at the same time it will tend to enliven Trade exceedingly, because People will find more Profit in employing their Money that way than in Usury." Furthermore, Franklin argued, those who are already wealthy might dread a "plentiful Currency" but it would help the poor advance, as they "will be encouraged to borrow Money; to trade with, when they have it at a moderate interest." Ultimately, a "plentiful Currency" would be an inducement to immigration, whereas a "want of money" would rather discourage "Labouring and Handicrafts Men (which are the chief Strength and Support of a People) from coming to settle"—because they could not make a decent living.[28]

"A Modest Enquiry" was well received in America. It got printed all through the colonies; and within a decade Franklin had secured contracts to print paper money for at least three of them — his home colony of Pennsylvania; the colonies of Delaware and New Jersey; and, finally, an entire country, the United States of America. His printing press — Franklin had had previous experience as a printer in Massachusetts and London — became the undisputed leader for the next half century. Franklin also became the man who almost single-handedly established the matrix of land, debt, and paper money that was to shape American life for more than a century. Moreover, he was the one to go before a British parliamentary committee in 1767, trying to convince the colonial masters of the advantages of paper money for the colonies. Paper money, Franklin argued, had swept away "the inconvenient method of barter ... gave new life to business, [and] promoted greatly the settlement of new lands."[29] The British were unconvinced. For them, using paper money to bolster colonial economies made no sense. Not only was the point of having colonies to provide raw materials cheap to the mother country; the British also suspected that paper money would release unruly and uncontrollable ambitions among the colonists. It turned out that they were right on this point. Twenty-some years after the British Parliament put a ban on paper money the War of Independence had been won — by the unruly and uncontrollable American colonists.[30]

For many commentators Franklin is the personification of monetary technology (the "father" of America's paper money, who single-handedly built something like a United States Mint), of an institution (the government, at first colonial and, later, national), and of the nation (first the colonies, then the United States). Yet Franklin was not building any of these alone, least of all America's paper money. He also was not simply starting from scratch. Although he broke with tradition, he at the same time was drawing upon the experience, knowledge, and capital that he had gained. Moreover, given the absence of precious metal on American territory, Franklin had little choice but to rely on paper money. Paul Revere must have known this when he printed the Massachusetts issue of August 1775, in which he engraved on the back plate the motto "Issued in Defence of American Liberty." He later designed and printed the first revolutionary Massachusetts paper currency and the first official seal of the United Colonies. After a brief (and undistinguished) military career, Paul Revere returned to business.[31]

Alexander Hamilton likewise served in the Revolutionary army, though his career *was* distinguished. He was twenty-one when, as a lieutenant colonel, he became Washington's aide-de-camp. He left camp during one of the General's rages, and would lead a night attack at Yorktown, under heavy fire. When the War was over, he married rich, settled in New York, and established himself a reputation as an able and successful lawyer. In 1786, Hamilton, deeply worried about the constant clashes and arguments among the states, called together a congress at Annapolis. A year later, delegates from the states would meet to work on a proper federal constitution. They would also debate what sorts of money would be allowed and be created by whom. Hamilton was on his way to becoming one of those leading figures of American history that shaped the country's monetary institutions, to paraphrase Arthur Nussbaum.[32] As Secretary of the Treasury under Washington, Hamilton contributed a great deal towards the creation of a national currency. The first federal Congress met in 1789. On January 14, 1790, Hamilton delivered his "Report on the Public Credit." The news must have been sobering: foreign nations were owed $12 million; the states were some $25 million in the red; and the federal debt amounted to almost $42.5 million. Hamilton was unperturbed. The public debt, he explained to Congress, was actually a "national blessing," and could actually answer "most of the purposes of money."[33] All the government needed to do was to pay regular interest on it, in hard coin accrued from import duties and the selling off of public land. If there were any money left over, it would go to pay for the principal.

Hamilton' scheme also saw to the funding of all war debts, not only those incurred against foreign nations but also internal war debts incurred by the Confederation as well as by the individual states. This policy (the technical term for which is "assumption") was a decisive step in the shift of balance between the states and the national government. As one of Hamilton's supporters explained in the House, "if the general government has the payment of all the debts, it must of course have all the revenue, and if it possesses the whole revenue, it is equal, in other words, to the whole power."[34] Not only did the assumption of the war debts strengthen the credit of the new government, in favorable contrast to the old one. In Richard Doty's estimate it would also cause an "inevitable *shift of loyalty* on the part of the business community (which held most of the depreciated paper) away from the locality, and toward the new national polity."[35] Loyalty had its price, though, for it greatly favored the many speculative holders of old debt certificates bought cheaply from former soldiers or merchants who had patriotically supplied the army. Hamilton may have regretted this, but he could see no other way forward. He pointed out that the assistance of the rich was essential for the frail government, and deep down he may have considered wealth a substitute for aristocracy — an attitude that earned him the nickname "the monarchist"; it also proved to be disastrous for him in the end, in the duel with Aaron Burr.

Burr shot Hamilton on July 12, 1804. By that time, the Bank of the United States had been established under Hamilton's guidance, and Hamilton had steered into law the Coinage Act of 1792, which established the dollar as the nation's official unit of account. Both acts were decisive steps towards the creation of a federal monetary system, the bank charter perhaps more so than the Coinage Act. For, the bank was authorized to issue paper money, the "lively sort" of money, as Hamilton called it, in contrast to "dead" gold and silver, which rather than being paid in at one address and withdrawn at another tended to be lugged about in chests or hoarded in bank deposits. Hamilton was too shrewd and troubled a politician to suggest that the government itself issue paper money. That, he thought, would only be a temptation to multiply debts in order to print more paper — as had been done in the past.

Hamilton proposed a privately owned national bank, modeled on the Bank of England (though he prudently remained silent about that fact). He invited people to buy shares in it, which they did in a rush. He also offered shares to the government. Since the government did not have the money, it was allowed to borrow it from the bank, upon the promise to pay it back in installments — and with import duties and federal land as collateral. With all the shares sold, the bank was earning interest on the government securities, which in turn were used to back a currency issue — printed on paper and with a six percent interest when loaned out. Once again, Jefferson and the anti–Federalists were "apoplectic," and the whole plan of the bank might have collapsed if the President had not finagled another deal — Congress would pass the bank bill in return for the siting of the new capital city.[36]

When President James Monroe had taken office in Washington, he offered the position of president of the Bank of the United States to Nicolas Biddle. Biddle was a Pennsylvania state legislator, a patrician of Philadelphia, a true wit, a literary man who edited the first printed edition of Lewis and Clark's journals, and of an "impossibly unbankerly" temperament.[37] Still, in 1823 he accepted the bank job, with the intention of giving the country better money. Better, meaning a single paper currency that would be valid anywhere in the United States. Notes from the Second Bank were sound, and people could exchange them for real gold and silver at any of the bank's branches, upon demand, as the bank kept a high reserve for doing so. The government too did business with the bank, letting it handle its proceeds from land sales and import duties. As these earnings were often paid in notes from the private banks, Biddle had an opportunity to supervise these banks too, by promptly presenting them with their own notes for redemption. If they were defaulting, they were soon found out, and the banks increasingly became more cautious in giving out loans. Thanks to Biddle, then, the country was on the road to a transparent financial and fiscal system. It never occurred to him that anyone would want anything else. Biddle paid no attention to people who thought there was too much control and who suspected "money power" accruing. When he incautiously let it be known that he could destroy any bank in the country if he wanted to, this was altogether too much for quite a few people, chief among them Andrew Jackson, who had suspected something like that all along.

Andrew Jackson, who came from poor tenant farmers in the Carolinas, was Biddle's exact opposite. With no prospect at home, Jackson left for the West at age seventeen. Before long, he was appointed a judge of the Superior Court of Tennessee. In 1802, Jackson was elected major general of the state's militia. In the Creek War of 1813, he wiped out Indian opposition to white settlement. Asked to shift his commission to the regular army, Jackson complied, and defeated the British in the Battle of New Orleans in 1815. Eight years later, he ran for the presidency, with a result so close it was decided in the Electoral College. The decision, against Jackson and for John Quincy Adams, galvanized Jackson into a "capital hater," in Goodwin's apt term.[38] Jackson would later confess that he did not really hate banks but, in light of what he had learned from history, was simply afraid of them. Indeed, it may have been a deep-seated fear that led to Jackson's "war" against the Second Bank of the United States, which he called "a monster" and "a hydra of corruption." Yet by seizing on the money question Jackson, who had been elected President in 1828, also put himself at the head of a large segment of the American people, those less affluent ones who felt alienated and alarmed by the growth of banks and the uncertainties of paper money. Jackson united everyone against the "power of the moneyed interest" of the Northeast that, derived from the paper currency they were able to control, threatened to undermine his western republic of "the planter, the farmer, the mechanic, and the laborer."[39]

In Jackson's rhetoric, Thomas Jefferson's doubts became exaggerated and vulgarized. Banks, Jefferson had said, serve "to enrich swindlers at the expense of the honest and industrious part of the nation." For Jackson it was clear that his political opponents—men like Henry Clay or John Quincy Adams—wanted to "convert our government into a heartless aristocracy, in which the people are to be transferred, cheated, taxed, and oppressed, that a few may revel on the spoils of many."[40] That message, which accompanied Jackson's veto of a bill the Whigs under Henry Clay had pushed through Congress to renew the Second Bank's charter, was probably enough for people to vote for him again in the elections of 1832. The facts admitted to no such thing, though. The Second Bank of the United States, that "great monetary tie of the Union," as Tocqueville had called it, paid interest to holders of unredeemed bills, at a rate of twelve percent per annum. This made its bills worth slightly more than bills from the private banks. The private banks therefore resented the Second Bank's strength, though they remained quiet about this.

Jackson and the popular press vehemently attacked the Second Bank, levying charges of mismanagement and the disruption of the banking system. In addition, Jackson went ahead with his plan to withdraw all government deposits from the bank and redistribute them to private banks.⁴¹ This was to be done gradually, though Biddle started a policy of massive curtailment. Biddle would shovel the money out of the bank and pull in money and loans, as he was convinced that "nothing but the evidence of suffering abroad will produce any effect on Congress." It did not, and the Second Bank in 1836 had to liquidate its affairs. Jackson's promise, made on his way home after the election of 1832, that there would be "no more paper-money [...] if I can only put down this Nicholas Biddle and his monster bank," had been fulfilled.⁴²

For the time being, the contest between the less affluent, as represented by the Jacksonians, and the moneyed classes, had been decided. Never again would there be anything like a central bank in America. Moreover, from 1836 (the year Jackson abolished the Bank of the United States) to 1861 (the year the United States Treasury and its equivalent in the CSA were authorized to issue paper money) the United States government stayed out of the note-issuing business altogether. By the time it entered it again, another hero had stepped onto the stage, Salmon P. Chase. Chase was a former governor of Ohio, an antislavery leader who ran unsuccessfully against Lincoln for the Republican Party nomination in 1860. At the Chicago Convention, he eventually released his delegates to Lincoln, giving him the needed votes. As a reward, Lincoln, who had come to know Chase well, named him Secretary of the Treasury. Secretary Chase became the architect and guiding force in legislating into existence both the Demand notes and the United States notes. Hence the honor of his appearance on the $1 United States note of 1862. (It was not unusual at the time to have living persons portrayed on bank and government notes, but Chase clearly had his portrait put on the bill in an effort to further his own political career.) Chase might have deserved this honor also for creating the Treasury Department's Bureau of Engraving and Printing.

Another of Chase's lasting achievements—probably his greatest—was the attempt to regulate the country's chaotic banking system through the establishment of a national one. Chase suggested the idea, worked out all the principles, and guided it through Congress, which passed the National Bank Acts of 1863 and 1864.⁴³ These Acts created a structure for setting up national banks in the various states. These banks would be permitted to issue notes—the National Bank notes. As a uniform national currency differing only in the names of the individual banks they carried, the National Bank notes became an important step in the direction of a homogeneous and territorially exclusive currency. They opened a market for government bonds and stabilized the currency, performing their duty until the creation of the Federal Reserve notes in 1913. Chase would not live to see that, as he died of a stroke in 1873. In June 1864, he resigned from the Treasury. In December of the same year, he was appointed as Chief Justice of the Supreme Court. In 1869, he defended the "death tax" on state bank notes in *Veazie Bank v. Fenno*, a ruling that did much to consolidate the National Bank notes.

In 1868, in *Hepburn v. Griswold*, Chase delivered a decision that ruled that the Acts authorizing the Legal Tender issues were unconstitutional. Since Chase had been Secretary of the Treasury when the first greenbacks were issued, the ruling would both disqualify him and convict him of having been responsible for an unconstitutional action in his capacity as Secretary of the Treasury. Chase, who has been described as "a man with unbounded ambition,"⁴⁴ never gave up hankering for office. In 1868 and in 1872 he ran again for president, for the Democrats and then for the Liberal Republicans, though just as unsuccessfully as before. Chase had more success with posterity: his portrait came to grace the $10,000 Federal Reserve note, which was printed from 1928 to 1946. The Chase Manhattan Bank is also named after him, or rather, its predecessor was, the Chase National Bank, formed in 1877.

A place in the pantheon of America's monetary heroes is usually reserved also for Leslie M. Shaw, whom Friedman and Schwartz describe as a "vigorous and explicit advocate of using Treasury powers to control the money market and [who] had great confidence in the Treasury's ability to do so."[45] Treasury interventions in the money market had become customary, partly in response to the growth in relative importance of non-national banks, particularly of loan and trust companies, in the period of monetary stringency at the end of 1899, and again in mid–1901. Under Shaw, who was appointed Secretary of the Treasury in 1902, Treasury intervention reached its peak. In fact, though, the Treasury's powers were not as great as Shaw would have wished them to be. Had they been expanded as he requested, the Treasury's power clearly would not have been inferior to that later assigned to the Federal Reserve System — especially the power to control note issues, by varying the limit on the amount of lawful money that banks could deposit, or by requiring banks to increase their reserves.[46]

A similarly heroic status has been accorded to Benjamin Strong, who was governor of the Federal Reserve Board from 1914, but became inactive in 1928 (he also died that year). Strong had had tremendous experience but more importantly, "more than any other individual, [he] had the confidence and backing of other financial leaders inside and outside the System, the personal force to make his own views prevail, and also the courage to act upon them."[47] Once Strong was removed from the scene, a leadership crisis followed. As one contemporary remarked, "I thoroughly believe that if [Strong] had lived and his policies had been continued, we might have had the stock market crash in a milder form, but after the crash there would *not* have been the great industrial depression."[48] Strong's biographer adds that the Governor's death "left the System with no center of enterprising and acceptable leadership."[49] Not surprisingly, therefore, Strong's successor is unflatteringly described as "an able administrator" or, worse, as simply lacking "the personal qualities and the standing within the System to exercise the required leadership." As a result, there were "tendencies of drift and indecision" once Strong had left.[50] Small wonder, then, that on inaugurating a particular policy a member of the Board worried whether the Federal Reserve System "could retain the confidence of the public."[51]

The Federal Reserve System during the Depression years clearly did not retain the confidence of the public. Instead, the public would turn to President Roosevelt. This only confirms a point made by Friedman and Schwartz, that the "detailed story of every banking crisis in our history shows how much depends on *the presence of one or more outstanding individuals* willing to assume responsibility and leadership." In light of this sweeping generalization, it is quite a surprise that the two authors continue, not with the President but with the New Deal or, more precisely, with the New Deal "atmosphere."[52] Obviously these distinguished economists are no friends of the "big government" generally associated with Roosevelt, who as an advocate of the Keynesian revolution would "make money the instrument of public rather than of private purposes."[53]

Roosevelt was inaugurated on March 4, 1933. In his address, he boldly declared that the "money changers" had shamefully betrayed the United States. Fortunately for America, however, they had now fled "from their high seats in the temple." Roosevelt had found in Jackson's war against Biddle and the Second Bank of the United States a precedent for the battles he waged against the moneylenders in the temple. So in a letter written in November 1933 Roosevelt stated that "a financial element in the larger centers has owned the government ever since the days of Andrew Jackson [...] The country is going through a repetition of Jackson's fight with the Bank of the United States—only on a far bigger and broader basis."[54] Arthur Schlesinger would use the letter to defend the President against conservative attacks, which were denouncing the New Deal as un–American. Holding up the connection to Jackson, this distinguished historian argued that Roosevelt had been acting in a robust American spirit and tradition.

Friedman and Schwartz, whose book is steeped in free-market doctrine and monetarism, have little to say on the American spirit and tradition in Roosevelt's thinking.[55] Their emphasis is rather on the measures that were adopted by the President's administration after the collapse of the banking system and the economic crisis of the 1930s—most notably on measures that would effect changes in the banking structure. The changes began with Roosevelt's proclamation of a national banking holiday. That move, a contemporary and close ally of Roosevelt would later remember, marked the "revival of hope."[56] A month later, on April 5, 1933, the President forbade the "hoarding" of gold. All gold, including the gold held in the country by foreigners, was to be delivered to one of the Federal Reserve banks for an equivalent amount of lawful money—a way of "nationalizing" the country's gold, as it were.[57] Furthermore, under the authority of the Gold Reserve Act of 1934 Roosevelt specified a fixed buying and selling price of $35 an ounce for gold. This measure greatly devalued the gold dollar; gold coins were to be withdrawn from circulation, and further coinage discontinued.

Although gold would continue to play an indirect role in the money supply for several more decades, the legislation made confidence in the currency synonymous with confidence in the federal government. The right to make money was now firmly in the hands of the federal government alone, and from the beginning it would put this state of affairs to its advantage. Since the Treasury had formerly valued its own gold hoardings at just over $20 an ounce, it realized a substantial "paper" profit from the devaluation of the dollar. Consequently, the Treasury could print additional paper money, which they did — nearly $3 billion in *fiat* money, in addition to the $3 billion in greenbacks already explicitly authorized by an earlier act. After 1945, a number of currencies were retired in favor of Federal Reserve notes, so that in the end these notes had a quasi-monopoly among United States paper money, rising from 51 percent of the currency in circulation in 1932 to 84 percent in 1960. This development, in the words of Friedman and Schwartz, is indicative of the "continuing centralization of monetary authority" in the United States.[58] It will concern us in the following section on the tug-of-war between local, regional, and national interests.

Local, Regional, and National

Before the American Revolution, the monetary situation was one of relative values. Financial assets ranged from bonds and notes to gold and silver coins, the local paper money issued by each particular province, English pound sterling notes, as well as a variety of foreign coins, particularly of Portuguese, Spanish, and French origin. Yet there was almost always a scarcity of money of any kind. This situation, together with economic problems such as falling prices or a scarcity of imported goods, put many of the early settlers into what John Winthrop in his journal called "an unsettled frame of spirit." As a result, many settlers accordingly "began to hasten away, some to the West Indies, others to the Dutch, at Long island [...] and others back to England." Among those who remained, in-kind payments at accepted valuations in local money became a preferred mode of settling one's debts. In Maryland and Virginia, for instance, taxes and other debts were settled in pounds of tobacco beginning in the 1620s.[59] Altogether, the monetary situation befitted a country of small villages and cities with a total population of 1.6 million that was living somewhere between the Atlantic seaboard and the Appalachian Mountains. Philadelphia was British North America's largest city with some 18,000 people, followed by Boston with 15,000 and New York with 14,000. There was no major urban center with a wealth of capital and a strong economy. In 1774, the amount of cash held by Americans classified as freemen (excluding slaves and indentured servants) amounted to a mere £1.50 per capita.

The American Revolution brought some changes, but not too many. Characteristically, it was not until the Civil War that Americans switched from referring to the United States in the plural (the United States "are") to using the third person singular (the United States "is"). This usage gives an indication as to how the name that expressed and reinforced the union of the nation—"United States of America"—was invariably contradicted by local power and, accordingly, also had to serve as an antidote to what it claimed had been overcome in the act of naming, division. Overcoming "division" was also a key moment in the introduction of "one dollar" as the monetary unit of the United States. (It also made the United States the first national government to adopt the dollar as official unit of money.) Delegates to the Philadelphia convention and the ensuing federal constitution agreed that the money supply had to be brought under control and that different monies should not compete with one another. Alexander Hamilton in *Federalist Number 30* wrote about a single currency as "the vital principle of the body politic; as that which sustains its life and motion, and enables it to perform its most essential functions. *A complete power therefore to procure a regular adequate supply of it ... may be regarded as an indispensable ingredient in every constitution.*"[60]

The framers of the Constitution complied with Hamilton's ideas. The Coinage Act of 1792, guided into law by Hamilton, was a measure to lead to greater consolidation. The Act, which was officially named "An Act Establishing a Mint and Regulating the Coins of the United States," also defined the dollar as a "unit of account."[61] Since this was done in terms of gold as well as of silver, the American monetary system became bimetallistic. Likewise, the decimal system was accepted with the denominations of "cent" (for the hundredth part of a dollar) and "dime" (for the tenth part, from *dixième*, and originally spelt "disme"). Even greater was the symbolic meaning of the Act, for it led to what Nussbaum termed the "definite separation of the American dollar from its Spanish forerunner, in other words, *the establishment of a new monetary unit of the United States.*"[62]

Symbolic meanings notwithstanding, the primary criterion for societies to employ paper money on a wider scale is the government's willingness to guarantee the value of paper money. Whatever willingness there may have been, at first the Bank of North America, set up in 1781 and chartered by both the Continental Congress representing the united colonies and later by the state of Pennsylvania, failed because the money deposited in it had to be withdrawn. Monetary experience likewise stood in the way of employing paper money on a wider scale and from early on. The Articles of Confederation were found to be bad for business by the Federalists, as they provided for strong states that, through issuing fast-depreciating paper money, seemed to be increasingly privileging poor farmers. Therefore, the Federalists strove for a shift of the balance of monetary authority from the "wicked states" to the federal government.[63] However, as the Federalists were also dedicated to the idea of making precious coin the mainstay of the national currency, they would remain silent over federal paper money. Once the United States Constitution was adopted, the national government thus would have the authority only to "coin Money, regulate the Value thereof, and of foreign Coin."[64]

Another instance of shifting the balance of monetary authority from the states to the federal government was the creation of the First Bank of the United States, which Congress, under Hamilton's guidance and against Madison's fierce opposition, chartered in February of 1791.[65] The bank's objectives were manifold. On one hand, it was to boost the economy by making loans to encourage business and farming. On the other hand, it was to serve the federal government by handling federal funds, taking taxes, and furnishing federal salaries. It also took care to ensure that the paper dollars printed by the smaller private banks could be redeemed in gold and silver, as promised. Overall, the B.U.S. became the largest money-printing operation in the country, and it provided something like a uniform currency. Its notes enjoyed a high reputation both at home and abroad, buying the entire Louisiana Territory from Napoleon in 1803. Still, the B.U.S. was never as successful as its proponents would have wished. It was also not a truly "national" institution, even though the government owned a fifth of the shares, and even though it was authorized to issue notes receivable in payment to the government. Always under attack by the Anti-Federalists led by Jefferson, who believed that the bank was unconstitutional, its end came in 1811, when Congress refused to renew the bank's charter.

The lawmakers' refusal was a give-in to the national mood of financial free enterprise and state power. It also marked a victory to hard-money advocates who regarded the bank as merely another "paper mill" that, rather than hold other banks in check, actively encouraged them in their "pernicious activity of issuing a paper currency" that would inevitably depreciate.[66] The mood received additional fuel through the idea of a national debt (which had been set at a modest three percent) and, perhaps even more so, by the recognition that a substantial portion of the bank's shares had been bought by British investors.[67] So, almost all of the bank's notes were redeemed, which makes them excessively rare today; at the time it whisked more than $7 million in hard cash out of the country to refund the stockholders. The result was a national shortage of gold and silver, which led many banks in the country to stop redeeming their notes.

The situation was of increasing concern to the federal government, which expected

$30, First Bank of the United States, 1791 (courtesy National Numismatic Collection, Smithsonian Institution)

and depended on prompt payment of debts, taxes, and tariffs. Only a national bank, Secretary of the Treasury James Alexander Dallas wrote in December 1815, could "relieve the country and the Government from the present embarrassments."[68] Congress came round, and in 1816 another central bank was chartered, the Second Bank of the United States. Ironically, Republicans renewed Hamilton's bank.[69] The Bank's capital was originally set at $35 million, with $7 million of this stock held by the federal government, which paid for it in obligations. Of the remaining $28 million, a quarter had to be paid in specie, and the balance in specie or government bonds. Within a year of the bank's incorporation, however, $41 million in loans were added to the ante, on the scanty base of a bare $2.5 million in specie that it held in its vaults.

By 1819, the bank's specie reserves had reached a dramatic low, its notes fallen to an ever-increasing discount to specie. A few years later, the B.U.S. had issued over $100 million of notes, or about 20 to 25 percent of paper money in circulation. (By contrast, a typical state bank would have issued $100,000 to $200,000 of notes.)[70] In 1834, the United States government deliberately overvalued gold by reducing the gold content of coins. This was done mainly to bring back into circulation coins that had not been seen since 1820. As Thomas Hart Benton, who was largely responsible for the legislation, explained, "gold goes where it finds value, and that value is what the laws of the great nations give it [...] we must place the same value upon gold that other nations do, if we wish to gain any part of theirs, or regain any part of our own."[71] The Gold Coin Act of 1834 thus marks yet another attempt to nationalize value and to value nationalism. It did not have the desired effect, though, and the financial and economic crisis following Jackson's war against the bank put an end to it in 1836. Like the Bank of North America, the Second Bank was turned into a local institution under a Pennsylvania charter. President John Tyler vetoed a bill that called for the re-establishment of the Second Bank on August 16, 1841.

The veto only made worse the country's financial crisis, which had been triggered mainly by yet another overexpansion of business, combined with the extension of loans to many persons who could not pay them, and over-speculation in public lands sold in the West. When Andrew Jackson became President, he ordered that public lands be sold only for gold and silver, not paper. The decree was a direct outcome of the demise of the B.U.S., at Jackson's own hands, which had freed the privately owned state banks of the oversight of the central bank. These banks now began to issue notes in excessive numbers, producing speculative bubbles all around them. Jackson could do nothing about most of the speculation, though he could curb the one in land, through the "specie circular."[72] The strategy backfired: with specie being transferred from the East, where it was most wanted, to the West, where it was least wanted, the land boom collapsed, banks called in their loans at the same time as they stopped redeeming their notes in gold and silver, interest rates were raised, and the price of state bonds collapsed. Former President John Quincy Adams was horrified at the suspension of specie payments by the nation's banks. The only difference between a bank director and a counterfeiter, he thundered in the August 5, 1837, issue of *The New-Yorker*, was that the counterfeiter showed "evidence of superior skill and superior modesty. It requires more talent to sign another man's name than one's own and the counterfeiter does at least his work in the dark, while the suspenders of specie payments are brazen in the face of day, and laugh at the victims and dupes, who have put faith in their promises."[73]

By 1843, about a third of the nation's banking capital had been lost; a great number of the established banks had been liquidated or closed entirely. Among them was the Bank

of the United States of Pennsylvania, the former Second Bank.[74] The future had boded ill
to contemporary observers as early as 1819. Washington Irving, during a prolonged trip to
Europe, unearthed an earlier incident, the 1719 bailout by John Law, which ushered in the
downfall of this father of modern paper money. Irving turned this historic event into a
timely moral fable of financial hubris, "The Great Mississippi Bubble," published in *The
Crayon Papers* in 1820. Irving's vivid description of the background of Law's folly makes
history but a pretext to the contemporary drama unfolding across the Atlantic.[75] However,
the great writer's moral fable was not much heeded, and while the "panic" of 1819 added a
new word to the dictionary, after a brief interlude of *sauve qui peut* the economy expanded
again, ushering in the great land boom of the 1830s.[76] This boom clearly was even more
dramatic than the one preceding it: in 1834, some five million acres of public land were
sold; a year later, the figure had more than doubled, and by 1836, it had reached the twenty
million mark. The proceeds of a land auction went to the Land Office; from there they would
go on deposit in the local bank. If there were no local bank before, one would spring up
just to receive the money.

The increase in the number of banks is truly astounding. Banking expansion had begun
in 1780, with the founding of the Bank of Pennsylvania. It continued with the Bank of North
America, which was incorporated by the Continental Congress in 1781. In 1790, there were
only four banks. The number was up to twenty-nine by 1800, and ninety by 1811. Only five
years later, in 1816, there were 260 of them; in 1835, banks numbered 704 as compared to
330 in 1830; by 1859, there were 1,365 of them, and most of them were issuing notes. By
1861, the number of banks totaled 1,601 throughout the United States, with $207 million
in circulating notes, up from $62 million in 1813 and $120 million in 1836.[77] These figures
roughly correspond to the growth of the nation's population, which by 1850 was nearing
25 million, and to the extension of the national boundaries from coast to coast.[78] All of the
new territories were shortly seeing settlement and, as well, a proportionate number of note-
issuing banks and similar institutions—usually about a decade before the territory became
a state.

Between 1790 and 1865, some eight thousand fiscal entities issued paper notes in the
United States. Most of them were banks, though insurance companies, railroads, turnpikes,

$5, Second Bank of the United States, 1830 (courtesy National Numismatic Collection, Smithson-
ian Institution)

factories, hotels, churches, and other institutions also were in the paper money business. Most of these entities put into circulation notes in a wide range of — often quite unusual — denominations. The average bank, Richard Doty explains, "issued currency in half a dozen different values." Some of the notes from this era were of great beauty of design and color and are therefore widely collected today. Good examples are the "DIX" notes issued by the Citizen's Bank of Louisiana in New Orleans. The notes bore the denomination, ten, as well as other details in English and in French. If we are to believe the stories woven around them, from these notes stems the word to describe the American South — "Dixieland."[79] To contemporaries, however, there was often "an element of flimflam, of fraud." Hence, the entire era is often disrespectfully called the era of "broken bank notes" or even "rag notes."[80]

The private banks operated under state law, that is, without regulation by federal authorities, laws, or uniform policies. At least in theory, all the paper money the private banks issued was backed by the amount of gold or silver in the bank, though some banks

$10, Citizens Bank, obsolete, c.1860, face (American Numismatic Association Money Museum)

$10, Citizens Bank, obsolete, c.1860, back (American Numismatic Association Money Museum)

were reluctant to have their notes redeemed. The destruction of the B.U.S. further contributed to eroding the boundaries between legitimate and illegitimate banking. Indeed,
once the B.U.S. ceased to exercise any significant control over the state-chartered banks,
few of them were willing to make common cause against counterfeiting. In response to the
situation, the New Hampshire legislature in 1803 passed an act that made it illegal to give
any place of payment other than the town in which the bank was situated. Certain states
also set up safety funds, or deposit accounts, which were contributed to by individual
banks. Their purpose was to repay holders of paper bills from banks that failed. Most states
required at least annual reports. They also appointed bank inspectors to verify the banks
did have a reserve of hard cash, and they placed individual banks under the supervision of
a Board of Currency.[81] None of all this sufficed the political faction that from the beginning
had favored management of money and banking by the federal government. These people
worked hard to discredit the local banks with stories about banks going broke or of bankers
whose reserves of precious coins consisted of little more than nails, broken glass, or lead
ingots. Based on such anecdotal evidence they would push for the federal chartering of
banks, a measure that would considerably increase federal power over the notes that the
private banks were putting into circulation.

In recent years, researchers have been able to perform detailed empirical analyses of
the records of the private banks. Their findings are truly astonishing. For, despite contemporary observations about the system of "free banking" being the "principal cause of social
evil in the United States," most private banks managed the business of paper money quite
responsibly. The final stripping of these banks of their power to issue money came, not
because the freedom they enjoyed had degenerated into lawlessness but because of political movements to centralize power in Washington. Financier Jay Cooke might grumble
about annual losses of $50 million growing out of "broken banks, counterfeits, altered
notes, and cost of exchange between different points," yet until the Civil War, the incon-
venience was not so great as to cause Congress to overrule the money men. In addition,
"Free-banking laws" really did make a difference, as before this time, most state-chartered
banks were set up only after petitions had been submitted, reviews had been made, and
political considerations had been weighed. Thus, their introduction marks both the country's removal of the fetters of tradition and its embrace of free market capitalism. The
conflict itself, which can be reduced to the question whether the creation and management
of currency should be under the direction of elected officials or private entrepreneurs,
would linger on, taking ever-new forms and eventually spawning new mores and institutions. During the Civil War, the proponents of increased federal power finally found their
opportunity to move against the private banks. The "death tax" on state bank notes once
and for all established the federal government's monopoly in providing circulating paper
money.[82]

The look of the new notes issued by the federal government was different from anything that people had seen before. Gone were the colorful notes of the era of free banking,
when banks would personalize their notes with elaborate designs of individuals, scenes, or
other details meaningful for their locality. Gone also were plans for making the currency
system more secure by mandating local or regional designs that would indicate "the locality of the bank, or of the town, or state, at least, the section of country, to which they
belong."[83] Instead, there were notes "bearing a common impression," as they were all issued
and controlled by the federal government. Also of importance for the creation of a single
homogeneous currency were initiatives to remove foreign coins from domestic circulation

and to eliminate old and worn money, as well as "thalers" and other "foreign inscriptions" on currency. Just as important were attempts to stamp out counterfeiting, which during mid-century had been so rampant that, some writers estimate, at times roughly forty percent of the money in circulation was counterfeit.[84]

Decisions concerning the amount of money in circulation required the establishment of a national banking system. The legal basis was to have been provided by the National Bank Acts of 1863 and 1864. Yet as Richard Doty argues, these acts were "primarily intended as a money-raising scheme for the Union war effort," with numerous opportunities for the advertising genius of America's first "celebrity banker," Jay Cooke.[85] As a measure towards regulating the country's chaotic banking system, the attempt was at best half-hearted. While it did not permit the creation of a central bank, it empowered the federal government to grant charters for setting up national banks in the various states. The arrangement only perpetuated the American public's limited tolerance for central banking. On the other hand, the policy of securing by attrition the privilege of note issuing for the federal government was extremely successful. "There are already 25 National Banks in New England alone," an account in the *Portsmouth* (New Hampshire) *Herald* of April 23, 1865, stated, "*i.e.*, banks which issue United States bills, founded on public credit, the capital for security being in United States bonds, deposited in the public Treasury. The United States new loan [...] is likely to have a complete success."[86]

The statement was hardly prophetic. Greenbacks had outnumbered private bank notes two years before. By 1866, the private note — what Secretary Chase in 1864 had called "unnational circulation" — had passed out of America's monetary history. If they were not redeemed, they would become worthless. By 1867, over ninety percent of the total currency held by the public and the banks was of Civil War origin, that is, of types of money that had not existed only six or seven years earlier — National Bank notes, United States notes (the "greenbacks"), other United States currency (such as interest-bearing Legal Tender notes), and fractional currency.[87] The Union government emerged victorious from the Civil War not only because it had defeated the South but also because it had managed to assert control over all of the states' and the nation's money. Henceforth, the boundaries within which American paper money circulated corresponded to an ever-increasing degree with the national boundary.

A record of sorts was set by the new First National Bank of Richmond, Virginia, which received its charter on April 24, 1865, less than a month after the city had fallen to the North.[88] Other banks followed its lead, so that by 1874, every state in the former Confederacy was represented in the system and the South could slowly return to economic life. As it did so, both the local spaces of notes issued by private banks and the regional space inhabited by the Confederate currency were fundamentally reshaped by the spatial regime imposed by the national government.[89] Within that regime, a single form of money now existed that would facilitate economic relationships in a horizontal sense across the entire territory of the expanding United States, and that would enable Americans to communicate using the same "monetary language" within the new homogeneous national fiscal order.[90]

The idea of a national fiscal order met with renewed popularity at the end of the nineteenth century. Among the strongest advocates were the leaders of the Progressive movement, in particular Herbert Croly, whose 1909 book *The Promise of American Life* boldly attacked the modern-type Jeffersonians, with their emphasis on free competition and a weak federal government. Croly fervently believed that only a strong national government was capable of solving the problems of growing inequality in America. He thus wrote that the traditional trust in individual freedom "has resulted in a morally and socially undesirable distribution of wealth [...] in the hands of a few men." Among the politicians who most ardently listened to Croly's message was Theodore Roosevelt, who shocked the conservatives in the Republican Party by declaring that private property was "subject to the general right of the community to regulate its use to whatever degree the public may require it."[91]

Roosevelt's declaration came just prior to the 1912 elections. Roosevelt had already served two terms as president, had bowed to the third-term taboo, but was now back in the political arena, espousing a "New Nationalism" of strong government and domestic reform. For, Roosevelt was convinced that the "American people have but one instrument which they can effectively use against the colossal combinations of business—and that instrument is the government of the United States."[92] Roosevelt was not elected, though. The Republicans chose Howard Taft as their candidate; Roosevelt founded his own party; and the Democratic candidate, Woodrow Wilson, won. However, the controversy between Taft and Roosevelt irreparably split the Republican Party into reactionary and reformist wings. More importantly perhaps, Republicans and Democrats changed roles, the Republicans dedicating themselves to conservative values and the Democrats to government activism and reformist idealism. Therefore, in the end Franklin Delano Roosevelt's New Deal fulfilled the promise of Theodore Roosevelt's "New Nationalism" of 1912.

A beginning had been made already with the creation of the Federal Reserve System in 1913, a year into the presidency of Woodrow Wilson. Wilson had been elected by a movement that wanted domestic reforms and that was ready and eager to address the problems that the unfettered capitalism of the Gilded Age had created or worsened—especially the problems of the big trusts, including the "money trust" that had been uncovered by a congressional committee chaired by Louisiana representative Arsène Pujo in 1912. The "peril," the report said, was "manifest," and enough to outrage anyone.[93] By the time of Wilson's inauguration, public opinion was vociferously demanding a dismantling of the "money trust" or at least its containment by the federal government. One way to keep the octopus in bounds might be by exerting a greater federal control over the banking system, in particular by controlling the paper money employed in its operation. Congress had been active before Wilson assumed office. When he did, on March 4, 1913, he would find the "Aldrich plan," named after the influential Republican Senator Nelson W. Aldrich, who had proposed it in 1912.

In its final form, the Federal Reserve Act was different from the original plan on one important count—it attempted to entrust financial leadership and direction to the federal government rather than to private bankers. The Act stipulated that the Board of Governors was to be appointed by the federal government. However, under the law of 1913 the power of the Board was still limited. It was to appoint only a third of the directors of each district bank as representatives of the public at large. The remaining two thirds were elected by the member banks, which were therefore in a position to select the governors of the Federal Reserve Banks.[94] With the governors being the dominant figures in the system, the Fed is at best a substitute for a central bank, the more so as it was set up not with one but altogether twelve banks of issue, over which the Central Board in Washington exercises only limited control. Still, never before in American history had there been a centralized banking authority so actively and ambitiously concerned with fostering a flow of credit and money in order to "facilitate orderly economic growth, a stable dollar, and long-run balance in our international payments."[95]

With the creation of the Federal Reserve System, the integrating power of monetary policy reached a climax. The particularities of its structure — the allocation of power to form a system of "regional federalism" — have made it possible for the system to be used, if necessary, as an instrument of activist monetary management.[96] The policy of activist monetary management also fostered a sense of national identity in that more and more citizens experienced a greater sense of participation in the national economy. This must have been good news for Franklin Roosevelt, who knew that he and his administration were expected to give inspiration to a Depression-demoralized nation. The President's remark, in his first inaugural address of 1933, that "the only thing we have to fear is fear itself," is particularly poignant in this context. There was indeed much to be feared, from inflation to the inability, following the abandonment of the gold standard in 1933, to redeem currency in specie. The national currency therefore had to be made popular with a people who, Roosevelt declared, had been shamefully betrayed by the "money changers." Popularity may as well have been a function of newness, which is especially true of the one-dollar note, whose design Roosevelt signed into law in 1935.[97] That design included both sides of the Great Seal of the United States, which thus appeared for the first time ever in the full light of day. The following section deals with how the redesign came about.

Happy Accidents: Enter the New $1 Note and Other Quirks of Fate

The impetus for creating a new one-dollar note was a routine organizational change, which then led to a rather happy accident. Former Vice President Henry A. Wallace may have been the originator for the new design, which put both sides of the Seal of the United States on the back of the note.[98] Wallace made the claim in his behalf in two letters written in, respectively, 1951 and 1955. As he remembers, he had accidentally stumbled upon a reproduction of the Seal. "In 1934 when I was Sec. of Agriculture I waited in the outer office of Secretary [of State Cordell] Hull and as I waited I amused myself by picking up a State Department publication which was on a stand there entitled 'The History of the Seal of the United States.'" Secretary Wallace appears to have been so impressed by the phrase *Novus Ordo Seclorum* as meaning the New Deal of the Ages that he took the publication to President Roosevelt, suggesting that a coin be put out with the Seal stamped upon it. The President, it seems, was struck the most with the image of the All-Seeing Eye, a Masonic rendering of God as the Great Architect of the Universe. He also quite liked the idea that the foundation of the new order of the ages "had been laid in 1776 but that it would be completed only under the eye of the Great Architect." However, being the "great stickler for details" that he was, Roosevelt pressed that the Seal be put out on a dollar *note* rather than on a coin.[99]

When the new design was ready, the President at first hesitated over using the Great Seal, in all likelihood because the suggested design offended his aesthetic sense. Consequently, he suggested that the positions of the reverse and obverse be switched: the reverse should appear on the left, over the words "The Great Seal," and the obverse on the right, over the words "of the United States." Reversing the positions of the reverse and obverse was quite a breach with accepted heraldic practice. However, Roosevelt was also responsible for introducing the word "Great" in the phrase "The Great Seal" as it is now found under the left circle on the back of the one-dollar note. What followed is legend: since 1935, the Great

Seal has been printed in its entirety on the backs of one-dollar notes, at first on the $1 Silver Certificates and, beginning in 1963, on the $1 Federal Reserve notes. Thus, if it had not been for Secretary Wallace's amusing himself while waiting in the outer office of Secretary of State Cordell Hull, the one-dollar notes would look quite different, and the mottoes would have been virtually forgotten — "but for one of those quirks of fate."[100]

Other quirks of fate occasioned the appearance on paper money of what eventually became the national motto. Altogether, the motto's making is owing to "the well-timed efforts of a few well-connected men. And it did not happen all at once." In 1861, Treasury Secretary Salmon P. Chase received a letter from the Reverend M. R. Watkinson of Ridleyville, Pennsylvania. In the letter Watkinson, who was deeply concerned about the fate of the Union in those days of the Civil War, proposed that God be invoked on the country's coinage. "What if our Republic were now shattered beyond reconstruction? Would not the antiquaries of succeeding centuries rightly reason from our past that we were a heathen nation?" Secretary Chase took the suggestion seriously enough to send a directive to the director of the United States Mint. "No nation," Chase wrote, "can be strong except in the strength of God, or safe except in His defense. [Therefore, the] trust of our people in God should be declared on our national coins." The Director of the Mint, James Pollock, was a prominent member of the so-called National Reform Association, a group of radical Protestant denominations that was petitioning Congress to "reform" the Constitution to indicate that the United States was created as and remained a Christian nation. Pollock leapt at this chance, though Secretary Chase did not like any of the suggestions he received — "God, Liberty, Law" (Watkinson's suggestion), "Our Country, Our God," "God, Our Trust," "Our God, and Our Country" — and came up with his own suggestion, "In God We Trust."[101]

The religious inscription was authorized in 1864. The new two-cent piece, which was the first coin to bear it, remained in circulation until 1873. The motto lasted much longer, and was a standard feature on many coins by the early twentieth century. Still, it was not mandated by law, and it appeared on paper money only on the Florida state seal of the National Bank notes issued in Florida, original series, series of 1875 and 1882, and on the silver dollar shown on the back of the $5 Silver Certificate of 1886, the "Silver Dollar Note."[102]

In the nineteenth century, having "God" written on the government's money may have had the additional advantage of serving as a palliative against the pains of the newly

$5, Silver Certificate of 1886, back (American Numismatic Association Money Museum)

introduced income tax. In the long run, however, the legality and, in particular, the propriety of a reference to God on currency never ceased to be a sticky issue, with the public as much as with the authorities. For example, President Theodore Roosevelt's decision to leave the motto off two new coins because to him it came "dangerously close to sacrilege" provoked a heated debate in Congress. In the end, the pro-motto faction won, and the motto was restored to all coins on which it had previously appeared.[103]

After a period of relative quiet, the motto question resurfaced again in the 1950s, when a renewed religious fervor met with the specter of a Communist threat. As Burrell recounts, in 1953, while attending a service at a Christian Science church in Chicago, an Arkansas businessman noticed that the phrase "In God We Trust" appeared on the coins in the collection plate, but not on the paper money. The pious man appears to have been scandalized by the fact that the nation's paper currency did not carry this important message. He was also apparently well connected, including to Senator William J. Fulbright, and he used his connections to get his suggestion worked into a bill that was passed by the 84th Congress and signed into law by President Eisenhower in July 1955. Under this law, the United States Department of Treasury was to gradually work the motto—it was established as the national motto by an Act of July 30, 1956—into all new currency plates. The $1 Silver Certificate of 1957 became the first note on which the motto was used. These notes were first released on October 1, 1957.[104]

Of course, the accidental story may be just as partial as the idea of dollar bills coming from the minds of inspired individuals. For, despite all accidents, there is much evidence to suggest that a great deal of effort goes into the production of dollar bills, including some very careful planning on the part of financial institutions. The representation of the Great Seal's appearance on the one-dollar note as the result of some kind of happy accident therefore needs to be placed alongside the more rational and calculated aspects of the production process. Finally, there are consumer activities, which likewise are crucial to the introduction, modification, and subsequent redevelopment and marketing of paper money.

Making the Paper Dollar Sell: Connecting Production and Consumption

Consumption and production interrelate and overlap. This is an important issue, which keys into discussions of the paper money form and, by extension, into questions of money and value. "Money's reproduction as an institution," Carruthers and Babb argue, "depends on how unproblematically it is taken for granted. If people perceive it as 'natural,' that reproduction can become almost automatic."[105] Thus, as long as paper money is not taken for granted, its circulation depends upon its successful redemption, which in turn depends upon the tacit acceptance of notes by the population or, at the very least, by a dominant majority. In other words, a dollar bill that nobody uses is only potential money. For it to be fully realized, for it to have any social meaning, production has to be connected to consumption.

Let us begin with Secretary Chase, who following the National Bank Act of 1863 instantly began to solicit designs that were to be "national in their character." For this reason, the notes had to engage their holders' confidence in many ways. Of course, they had to engage confidence in the soundness of the currency as well as in the issuing institution's stability. Beyond that, they had to engage people in confidence in the greatness of the nation and a distinctive cultural identity. Tellingly, Secretary Chase expressed the hope that the new notes would encourage "the stimulation of patriotism of the people which would arise from their closer touch with national affairs."[106] Clearly, then, the notes in question were produced with a specific target audience in mind. They were aimed at people who, to slightly modify an observation made by Tocqueville, took pride in the glory of the nation, boasted of its success, to which they conceived themselves to have contributed, and rejoiced in the general prosperity by which they profited.[107] By experiencing monetary phenomena — such as changes in the money supply, devaluations, or interest rate alterations — together, these people would have an enhanced sense of being members of the shared community of values that characterizes a modern nation.

No design element serves better to stimulate patriotism than portraits. Bureaucrats at the Treasury department saw it in this way in the late 1920s, determining that presidential portraits would be more permanently familiar in the minds of the public than any others.[108] In a more general sense, the choice of images is guided by assumptions about a particular identity that they are to signify — national strength and dignity, and personal status translated into public glory. Thus, a particular imagined consumer guides the process of production and the manufacturing schedule. With this consumer in mind, the aim is to bring together production and consumption. The way to do this is to "market" the product. A good example is the Sacagawea dollar, in whose behalf the United States Mint in 1999 launched a costly, $67.1-million marketing campaign. Yet despite the three-year campaign, estimates say people use dollar coins in just one percent of dollar transactions. People "just aren't buying the idea," an article in the *Sacramento Bee* was headlined.[109] Did public opinion, then, bring about the General Accounting Office's recommendation that no money be spent on marketing the coin, even though the government could potentially save up to $500 million annually, mostly on production, shipping and on account of the greater durability of coins?[110]

It appears the situation was complicated. In the early 1990s, a move towards putting into circulation dollar coins had come from a special interest group called "The Coin Coalition." The group lobbied to have all one-dollar Federal Reserve notes replaced with one-dollar coins, purportedly to cope with the rising prices of transit fares.[111] Although the Coin Coalition claimed that the unwillingness of the government to phase out the dollar bill prevented the Sacagawea dollar from becoming popular, it seems rather that they had found a match in "Save the Greenback," an organization of Bureau of Engraving and Printing employees and paper and ink suppliers opposed to phasing out the paper dollar. "Save the Greenback" successfully prevented a dollar bill phase-out with the help of legislators such as Virginia Representative Thomas M. Davis, who introduced the Save the Greenback Act, Mississippi Senator Trent Lott, and Massachusetts Senator Ted Kennedy. We can hardly say that the worthy senators acted entirely disinterestedly. Senator Lott's constituency included the powerful cotton industry, which produces fabrics used in the paper dollar, and Senator Kennedy's constituency included the Crane Paper Company, which produces American banknote paper.[112]

For now at least, the clash of interests has receded into the background, as the United States Mint quit circulating the new dollar coin while the Treasury abandoned its plans to phase out the one-dollar note.[113] The plans had coincided with the general currency overhaul of the 1990s. Curiously, though, when the prototypes the designers came up with reached the White House, they were not well received. Tinkering with the dollar, many politicians thought then, was pretty much the same as redesigning the flag — un–American. Moreover, when the pieces of cotton fabric were finally altered more than ten years later, the greenback stayed. As the Treasurer of the United States under President Clinton, Mary Ellen Withrow, told the *New Yorker*, "Green is the color of prosperity, and black is a good thing, too—it shows we're sound and solid and in the black."[114] This statement will surprise anyone who is even remotely familiar with current budget figures. However, at the end of Clinton's presidency there was indeed an annual surplus. Hence "sound and solid and in the black" is correct.

The changes on the redesigned notes were subtle, with all the basic features remaining in place. Still, once again not everyone was happy. One commentator even derided the enlarged portraits on the bills as "hydrocephaly on money."[115] However, for the Treasury Department what mattered was not aesthetics so much as considerations of monetary security. The introduction of new currency designs, it was announced on the Department's website, is "part of an ongoing effort by the United States government to stay ahead of currency counterfeiting and to protect the economy and [people's] hard-earned money." So on notes of the Series 1996 the security thread embedded in the paper and running from top to bottom through the note also runs through the micro-printing around the border of the portrait; it is also visible from both sides when held up to the light, and spells out the denomination in tiny print. The portraits were enlarged to make them easier to identify, and they were placed off-center, thus providing room for a watermark over to the side that reduces wear and tear on the portrait. Another important new feature is what the Treasury calls "color-shifting ink," which appears black when held at an angle but green from directly above.[116]

When the notes of the Series 1996 were put into circulation, the Treasury announced that the new designs would not be as long-lived as their predecessors would (there had been no significant design changes between 1976 and 1996). Instead, redesigns would occur much more frequently, mainly in order to protect the currency from counterfeiters. Consequently, a new round of newly designed paper currency began with the issuance of the $20 note in October 2003. It was continued with the $50 note in April 2004 and the $10 note in March 2006. The new $5 note debuted on March 13, 2008, when it was ceremoniously spent in the newly opened gift shop of President Lincoln's Cottage at the Soldiers' Home in Washington, DC. The redesigned $100 note is expected to follow some time later. There are no plans to redesign the $1 and $2 notes, and all older-design notes will remain legal tender even after the new notes have been issued.[117]

Because the features on the redesigned notes are difficult for counterfeiters to reproduce well, they often do not try. If they do, they hope that cash-handlers and the public will not check their money closely. In light of the government's most recent strategies in behalf of the currency, however, the counterfeiters' hopes should be in vain.[118] When in April 2004 the new $50 note was unveiled with much fanfare at the Bureau of Engraving and Printing's Western Currency Facility (WCF) in Fort Worth, Texas, the occasion was also used for the grand opening of the WCF's new Visitor Center.[119] The Center, which plans to welcome 500,000 guests annually, offers free tours to the public five days a week, providing a much-anticipated tourism draw to the Dallas-Fort Worth community. At the Visitor Center, guests may enjoy tours of the production facility, learn about the technology and history of United States currency through interactive displays, and purchase money-themed items and souvenirs in the gift shop.

A more recent promotional tactic involves making available a wide selection of free educational materials for previously released redesigned currency, including posters, "take one" cards, training videos and CD-ROMs. These materials are targeted at businesses, financial institutions, trade and professional associations, and citizen groups and individuals to prepare cash handlers and consumers to recognize the new design and protect against counterfeits. Materials are available in twenty-four languages to order or download online.[120] Yet another strategy concerns the Bureau's email subscription list. One email message directed customers to a website containing, *inter alia*, materials to download, an interactive note, educational material, and a video in which Anna Escobedo Cabral, who was then Treasurer of the United States, is heard explaining the "wonderful, user-friendly security features" on the new $10 note.[121]

It is tempting to see these tactics as *advertising*. Advertising is generally employed in attempts to encode and fix the meanings of a product in a particular way. Advertising must address the consumer, and it must create identification between the consumer and the thing. Somehow, it must get consumers to see themselves as the potential buyers of a product — the "sort of person who buys and uses this kind of thing." Advertising is part of the repertoire of marketing methods that are used in attempts to sell a product. However, when the Bureau developed its launch strategy for the redesigned dollar bills, making maximum use of media channels, it engaged less in advertising than in *publicity*. Unlike advertising that is paid for and controlled by a company, publicity is not "bought" in the same way. It is generally harder to identify but still very effective, in particular since the Bureau could trust that the media would pick the launch up as "news." (Indeed they did, as there were frequent public service announcements for instance on CNN such as, "Ben Franklin's face shifted slightly to the side.") The Bureau could also trust that other monetary authorities would pitch in, such as the Federal Reserve, which even set up an office in Moscow with a telephone hotline to field questions.[122]

Finally yet importantly, the Bureau could be sure that there would be regular visits to their website, where people are able to listen to the voice of C. Danny Spriggs, deputy director of the United States Secret Service, the law enforcement agency responsible for combating counterfeiting. According to Spriggs, "The combined efforts of public education, aggressive law enforcement, and improved currency security features have increased public awareness and have helped in the fight against counterfeiting."[123] Therefore, by now it should be clear that the Treasury *is* planning their promotional and marketing activities very carefully. In referring to the complex process of promoting and marketing the new currency, we come to a significant contribution to the success of paper money that is even further removed from the idea of inspired heroes and happy accidents. This contribution comprises the eagerness, aptitude, and even dedication of those responsible for launching the national money icon into a "cult" as well as the routine, rigidly organized, of protecting the national currency.

Technical Aspects of Production

Protecting the currency was important already in earlier times, although to do so was far from easy. One reason was that technology was much less sophisticated in producing the various types of paper money that were in use in all of the American Colonies while they were still under British rule. The copper plates used for these issues were soft and wore unevenly, and often needed re-engraving. The resulting bills bore inconsistent printing variations, which instantly invited the skills of counterfeiters. The problem did not go away any time soon. By the mid-eighteenth century several of the colonies were issuing very attractive notes, yet there was as yet no transfer process available, so all plates had to be re-cut or newly engraved by hand. This made it impossible to have printing plates bearing two identical designs. All of this made counterfeiting easy and greatly practiced, despite the severe penalties for it.[124]

Colonial authorities were aware that their products were vulnerable, and they did what they could. They would employ the best artists they could find to engrave the plates. A special paper would be used. Notes were indented (which means that in order to make redemption safer, a wavy line was cut between a numbered note and its stub kept in a book at the site of issuance), and borders were cut in a particular way. In addition, there were Benjamin Franklin's nature prints, introduced in 1739 and a real godsend. No counterfeiter ever caught on to Franklin's method, which was not discovered until the 1960s.[125] Other types of currency also existed through the early republic, but they were much easier to counterfeit. Americans could be much more comfortable about the bills they carried in their pockets when one Jacob Perkins invented a method of punching lettering and designs into the walls of steel cylinders and crossing them with engraved intersecting lines. These were then rolled into copper plates, and multiple intaglio impressions of exact fidelity were produced. This particular invention, which dates to 1804, has been said to mark the beginning of the "mass-production of unforgeable paper currency."[126]

Until the late eighteenth century, banknote printing remained in the hands of relatively few individual printers, like the Greens, who for several generations were the first family of American printers, and of course Benjamin Franklin. The next step were local printing companies or partnerships, such as Hall and Sellers of Philadelphia, which produced both the Continental currency and notes for some of the colonies; Murray, Draper, Fairman, and Co., which produced the Treasury notes of the War of 1812, or Burton & Edmonds of New York. By the mid-nineteenth century larger, more professional banknote companies emerged from the amalgamation of smaller ones. These companies were the first to achieve the vertical and horizontal integration characteristic of the modern industrial system, and they operated nation-wide. They had names like Columbian Bank Note Company, National Banknote Company (NBNCo), and Continental Bank Note Company. The foremost of these companies was the American Bank Note Company (ABNCo), the owners of the green ink used on the greenbacks and the prime contractor for federal and fractional currency through the mid–1870s, when it controlled more than ninety percent of the market. Indeed, so dominant did the ABNCo become that, as a journalist observed in 1861, it "begins to hold the same relation to the paper currency of the country, as the United States Mint holds to the specie currency."[127]

From 1863, the "Big Four" also produced National Bank notes. More specifically, they produced the notes in part, for the Treasury Department reserved the right to print the Treasury seal and serial numbers. A more striking example of governmental jealousy is the attempt to have American and National turn over dies and plates from which federal currency was printed. According to Secretary Chase, they belonged to the U.S. government. While the request met with no resistance from National, ABNCo declined, retaining the hardware the Bureau of Engraving and Printing in Washington, DC, needed so badly. Nevertheless, in 1875 banknote and security printing began to be moved to the Bureau. By October 1877, the entire production of National Bank notes had been assigned permanently to the Bureau. This measure, together with the move, in July 1880, of all operations for processing paper money to the new Bureau building, was yet another decisive step towards the consolidation on the monetary level of the modern nation-state.[128]

Also a crucial year for production technology had been 1812, when a certain Asa Spencer patented a device with a stationary point tracing or cutting an endless design of perfect regularity. Spencer's geometric lathe was instantly recognized as an effective deterrent against counterfeiting.[129] Jacob Perkins purchased the rights to the device in 1815 and it was subsequently introduced to the banknote business. The result, known as "Patent Stereotype Steel Plate" style, came in several variations, mostly with backgrounds of tiny lettering in italic type, such as *Twenty Dollars*, repeated hundreds of time on the face.

Other experiments were done with color, which brings us to the most frequently asked question at the Bureau of Engraving and Printing—"Why did the government select green for our currency?" It appears that choice of a second color was largely determined by efforts to bust counterfeits, especially after the invention of photographic methods in the 1840s. Different colors were tried, with red and orange long enjoying great popularity—until it was discovered that green was much more of a challenge to photographers than any other tint. Still, counterfeiters could remove the colored tints, make any number of copies, and then restore an imitation of the colored parts. However, in 1857 an ink was developed that could not be erased without destroying the paper. The company of Rawdon, Wright, Hatch and Edson first used this ink—the Patent Green Tint—on state bank bills. Thanks to the promotional efforts by its subsequent owner, the American Bank Note Company, the ink has been in use on American paper money ever since.[130]

When in 1861 the New York banknote companies printed the first greenbacks, the Treasurer and the Registrar of the Treasury personally signed them. Signing bills was a purgatorial task, according to a contemporary, whose "self-imposed limit was a thousand sheets (four thousand signatures) a day. For a single day ... this would not be a hard task; but to follow it for weeks and months, as I did ... would, if it were a punishment, be too inhuman to be inflicted upon the most guilty of criminals."[131] Congress had enough consideration in this matter, and authorized signing by proxy. It did not take long until, as we learn from an account published in 1883, "70 clerks at $1,200 a year were kept busy in writing their own in lieu of these officers' names." The problem was not public expense so much as the fact that "so many different hands destroyed all the value of signatures." The signatures, which were to guarantee the trustworthiness of the notes, being

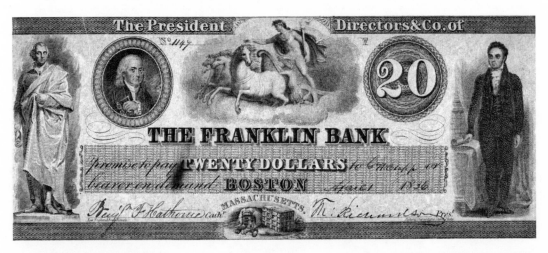

$20, Franklin Bank, Boston, MA, Perkins's "Patent Stereotype Steel Plate" (American Numismatic Association Money Museum)

those of clerks, were no protection against fraud, and the Secretary was "in sore perplexity."[132]

At this point a Mr. Spencer M. Clark, who was then Superintendent of Constructing the Public Buildings, proposed facsimiles of the signatures, and also of the Treasury seal, to be engraved and printed on the notes in special ink, and by a special process. The proposal was accepted by Secretary Chase and was given official sanction by Congress. This considerably speeded up production, though there was one sticky issue left. The trimming and separation of the notes was still done by hand, or rather by female hands armed with shears—until Clark came up with a machine that mechanically did just that. That feat, the account concludes, was "the origin of the Printing and Engraving Bureau of the Treasury Department." Spencer M. Clark became its first director.[133]

This marks the end of our discussion of the *production* of American paper money. Studying dollar bills culturally did not mean to ignore technical aspects of production, though the emphasis clearly was on how the bills have been produced culturally — that is, on how they have been made meaningful. However, the processes of cultural production only provide a series of possibilities that have to be realized in and through *consumption*. This is why the authorities responsible for issuing paper dollars constantly seek to take account of and respond to the ways in which consumers are "appropriating" the products. In the following chapter, we will focus on design as the site where production is articulated to consumption in order to ensure that the notes are accepted as a medium of circulation.

THREE

Designing the Paper Dollar

Articulating Production and Consumption

'If you don't mind my asking, Robert, how did you get involved with the Illuminati?' Langdon thought back. 'Actually, it was money. [...] Money as in *currency*.' He reached in his pants pocket and pulled out some money. He found a one-dollar bill. 'I became fascinated with the cult when I first learned that U.S. currency is covered with Illuminati symbology.'

— Dan Brown, *Angels and Demons* 134–35

Introduction

What gives paper money its authority — what distinguishes a bank or government note from a piece of paper torn from a magazine — is its backing by a trustworthy individual or institution. Such backing contributes to a community's strength and identity politically and economically. There is, however, also a symbolic contribution, which lies in the imagery on paper money, in its look and feel. Both the visual "look" (of monetary iconographies) and the tactile "feel" (of paper as opposed to metal) are a crucial means of communicating with consumers, not simply about function or basic "use" but at the same time about identity and meaning. Paper money thus is inscribed with *meanings* as well as uses. We may even say that it is "design-led." The importance of design is evident from an article published in *Harper's New Monthly Magazine* in February 1862: "In designing a note there are several points to be considered. The various denominations must all be different in appearance, and none of them must resemble any note of any other bank. Each must combine the various kinds of work adopted as securities against frauds, and must, moreover, present a handsome appearance."[1]

Designers are not artists. They do not create their own worlds so much as they fit existing worlds in the things that they design. For that reason alone, designers need to stay close to the cultural practices and preferences of target groups of consumers, "translating" them into design. In their symbolic work of making objects "meaningful," designers articulate production and consumption. Today designers are found most frequently in the media, fashion, advertising, and design industries. However, in the field of currencies designers have been around from the beginning, as the potential importance of imagery on currencies has always been recognized by the powerful. Well before the advent of the modern nation-state, monarchs and emperors around the world sought to advertise their power and authority by having their seal or head stamped on the money that they issued. The tradition of having coins and notes bear the mark or image of the sovereign continued in America, where the first printing press was installed by Stephen Daye in Cambridge, Massachusetts, in 1638, and where Joseph Jenckes cut the crude punches for the New England coinage of 1652. Designers have also played crucial roles in the production of paper bills since they were first put into circulation. Quite a few designers, including Benjamin Franklin, became famous, and proudly left words like "Printed by B. Franklin" on notes. Most, however, had to augment their income by doing peripheral work.[2]

Banknote engravers frequently worked in different media including books and art journals, or in entirely different fields such as silver- or blacksmithing. Additionally, many of the scenes, portraits, and allegories on bank notes came from sources as varied as sketches, engravings, paintings, statues and sculptures, medals and stamps, postcards and, later, photographs. There was also a hierarchy concerning the recognized degrees of engraving. Low in the hierarchy were book illustrations and similar work. Intermediate in status, but ever increasing in volume, was banknote engraving. Highest in status was the reproduction of paintings; this would take the most time but would also bring the most money. More precisely, it made a living for the engraver and money for the painter. For, the engraver's business was to follow the painter. Given this nexus, it was not uncommon for American banknote companies to commission well-known artists—F.O.C. Darley, Asher B. Durand, Alfred Jones, or James Smillie—to create the designs that after one to twelve months of intense labor would become banknote vignettes.[3]

The name of the engraver who did the Massachusetts Colony notes of 1690 is not known. What is known is that John Foster, who had the first printing press in Boston, engraved a portrait of the Reverend Richard Mather in wood as early as 1670. The paper had to be imported, though, as the first paper mill in colonial America was not established until 1690. The first engraving of a portrait in copper was done in 1701. In 1702, another Bostonian, John Coney, engraved plates for paper money that had a different state seal. They were also a bit more artistic, but not very much so, as designers did not enjoy a great deal of liberty in those days. In Massachusetts in particular, both civil and ecclesiastical rulers kept a watchful eye on the press, fearful that, "if [printing] was not under wholesome restraints, contentions and heresies would arise among the people."[4] Consequently, in 1662 licensers of the press were appointed and two years later a law was passed that allowed printing only in Cambridge, and printing only what the government permitted. Eventually the art of engraving advanced even under those conditions, connected with the likes of Nathaniel Hurd, Henry Dawkins, Robert Aitken, James Smither, Amos Doolittle, and Paul Revere.

Paul Revere began his career as a watercolorist, developing an interest in copperplate engraving only later. Upon the advent of the American Revolution Revere, who was then a member of the Sons of Liberty, desperately wanted to enlist, but was more needed as a printer of Massachusetts notes. He stayed at the job from May 1775 to October 1787. It is said that he also built the presses to print these notes, including the issue of August 1775, in which he engraved on the back plate the motto "Issued in defence of American Liberty." Another designer who used his skills as an engraver for the fostering of patriotism was David Rittenhouse. The New Jersey £6 issue of March 25, 1776, which achieved a certain prominence in the Revolutionary War, bears his name in the border of the notes. At age sixty, Rittenhouse became the first director of the United States Mint, which started its operations in Philadelphia in 1794, in a new building on Chestnut Street.[5]

By the time operations started in what was the nation's very first federal building, the name of James Smither may well have been forgotten, but in 1778, Smither had been accused of counterfeiting Continental currency for the British. It is doubtful whether Smither ever honestly worked on the currency, but Henry Dawkins certainly did — after he had served his sentence for counterfeiting Continental currency and other paper money. The record of Elisha Gallaudet is straighter, and he will be remembered for engraving the sundial MIND YOUR BUSINESS cut and the thirteen links cut for the fractional denominations of the Continental currency issue of February 17, 1776.[6]

American engravers of the early republic would establish a genre, yet they largely relied upon European guidance to achieve what were considered to be standard performance practices. One example is Gideon Fairman, who in 1819 started out as a blacksmith before he turned engraver and designer and became a member of Murray, Draper, Fairman & Co. Together with Jacob Perkins and others, Fairman went to London, where he participated in a contest for preventing counterfeiting. In 1823 he returned to New York, where he became affiliated with a variety of companies. His most famous work as a designer and engraver is the portrait of George Washington that Gilbert Stuart had painted in 1796. Fairman's rending of the portrait has been in use ever since, including on the small-size one-dollar notes since they were first issued in 1929. (It has also found its way onto T-shirts, belt buckles, chocolates, and government web sites.)

In banknote engraving, Fairman is essentially a transitional figure, like James Smither, John Norman, or Abner Reed. None of them could do without also venturing into other work, as the age of specialization was still a few decades into the future. The first artist to belong to the "golden age" of engraving is Charles Kennedy Burt.[7] Burt had learned the trade in his native Edinburgh, Scotland. In 1842, he came to New York and was employed by A. L. Dick, spending most of that time engraving Leonardo Da Vinci's *Last Supper*. Burt later engraved for several banknote companies. Among them was the American Bank Note Company, which in early 1861 hired him to do a new, bearded likeness of Lincoln for its print work. The portrait of the recently hirsute chief executive, which Burt executed from a drawing by the sculptor Luigi Delnoce, who in turn had used photographs done by C. S. German, was destined to make history. Reproduced on any number of print work — from

war bonds to the new federal paper currency, from commercial items to Republican campaign documents — it would turn the relatively obscure lawyer from Illinois into the best-known face of his time and beyond.[8] It also secured for Burt the post of chief engraver for the Treasury Department, where he remained for twenty years. In this capacity, he engraved Chapman's mural *Baptism of Pocahontas at Jamestown, 1613*, for the back of the $20 National Bank note, a piece of work that exemplifies his true genius. Burt also engraved altogether nineteen plates of the Presidents of the United States, of which at least one is still in use — the portrait of Thomas Jefferson. Completed in 1867 and first used on the $2 Treasury note, series 1869, Jefferson's portrait made a re-appearance on the $2 Federal Reserve note of the series 1976.

George Washington on $1 note, detail

Last but not least, there is George F.C. Smillie, who in Gene Hessler's estimate was one of the most prolific engravers, with some 300 portraits and 135 vignettes to his credit.[9] Smillie was educated at Cooper Union and the National Academy of Design in New York and he studied under Alfred Jones and his uncle James Smillie. He worked for the American Bank Note Company from 1871–1887, then for several other companies. In 1894, he joined the Bureau of Engraving and Printing as Chief Engraver. One of Smillie's best-known works is the engraving of a portrait of Chief Running Antelope for the $5 Silver Certificate of 1899.[10] Other well-known works are an allegorical group showing Electricity as the dominant force in the world (for the $5 Silver Certificate of 1896), and Science presenting Steam and Electricity to Industry and Commerce (for the $2 Silver Certificate of 1896). Less well known but just as important is the engraved portrait of Woodrow Wilson, on the $100,000 Gold Certificate of 1934, the bank transfer note.

The Organization of Design

In America, few if any banks ever printed their own notes. At first, individual printers did the job. When banknote printing became more elaborate and therefore more costly, private companies stepped in, which in turn would combine to become larger organizations such as the American Bank Note Company or the National Bank Note Company, both of New York City. These companies would keep the plates, and they would gladly fill additional orders as they were received. In the early days, printers would use whatever designs were available, though individual bankers would try to satisfy their personal tastes and private companies would try to develop a distinctive style of their own. Beginning in the Civil War period, banknote design more and more became a matter of large-scale governmental institutions such as the United States Treasury Bureau of Engraving and Printing, the USBEP. The Bureau would follow its own policies. Although it often made use of earlier designs, once the new Bureau building had been completed in 1880, staff engravers and artists would be encouraged to come up with their own ideas. A good example is the $5 National Bank note in the Series of 1882, which is famous among collectors for the "circus poster" style of the lettering. The note also marks the end of nearly two decades of contracting out design work, usually to the American Bank Note Company and the National Bank Note Company.

At first only a few men and women would be found separating and trimming one- and two-dollar Legal Tender notes that had been printed by private banknote companies.[11] This small operation was done in the First Division of the National Currency Bureau, which was located in the attic of the west wing of the Treasury Building. In 1863, an additional seventy women were hired to perform the job, which included adding serial numbers and Treasury seals to bills printed by private contractors. By the fall of that year, the Engraving and Printing Bureau of the Treasury Department was printing currency of all denominations. The next year, Treasury Secretary Salmon P. Chase submitted the Bureau for official recognition.

On March 3, 1869, President Andrew Johnson signed an Appropriations Act giving recognition to the agency. This marks the beginning of the federal government's move towards ferreting bits and pieces of the production process away from the private banknote printing companies. Although the companies soon after began lobbying Congress to regain their lucrative contracts, in 1877 John Sherman, who had been appointed Secretary of the

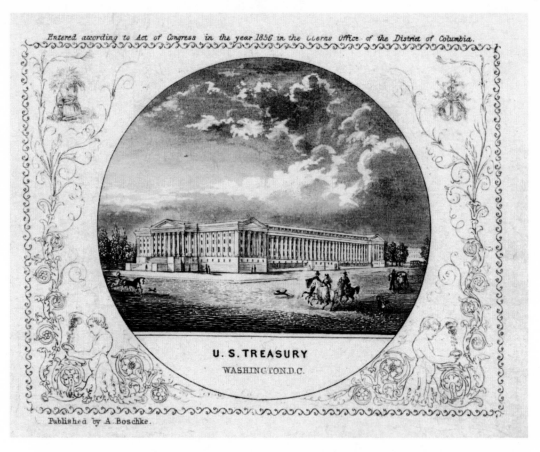

Entered according to Act of Congress in the year 1856 in the Clerks Office of the District of Columbia.

U.S. TREASURY

WASHINGTON, D.C.

Published by A. Boschke.

Treasury Building image 1856 (National Oceanic and Atmospheric Administration/Department of Commerce, <http://www.photolib.noaa.gov/aboutimages.html>)

Treasury the previous year, gave the Bureau total control over all aspects of the country's currency production. On October 1, 1887, the name of the agency finally was changed to Bureau of Engraving and Printing. The Bureau then handled the printing, separation, and trimming of all United States currency. In 1888 the majority of Bureau positions was placed under the Civil Service; by 1908 all jobs were included — a further measure in the complete monopolization of the making of currency at all levels. In 1991, a Bureau facility was established in Fort Worth, Texas. Today there are about 2,500 employees in both Washington and Fort Worth. The production of notes averages thirty-five million a day, with a face value of approximately $635 million.[12]

At the Bureau, there are a number of ways in which subjects and meanings beyond the ones that communicate information about a note as a means of exchange are manufactured. One is exemplified by the special committee that in 1929 decided to use portraits of the Presidents of the United States because of their purportedly more permanent familiarity in the minds of the public than any others. Another example concerns United States Treasurer Mary Ellen Withrow's proclamation that green and black should stay because of the symbolism, green for prosperity, and black for sound fiscal and monetary politics, which also shows to what extent politicians are implicated in the cultural production of the paper dollar. As regards the selection of designs, in 1862 it became the responsibility of the Secretary of the Treasury. However, the Secretary is to act with the advice of responsible Bureau heads, including the Bureau's Director and the Treasurer of the United States. The first Secretary to be in a position to determine the design of the United States paper currency was Salmon P. Chase.

During the planning stage for the Legal Tender notes, Spencer M. Clark, head of the National Currency Bureau, advocated the use of panoramic scenes extending across the face of notes, similar to W. L. Ormsby's "Unit System." Q. David Bowers has found a Treasury Department proof, mounted on cardboard, of a proposed design for a $1 Legal Tender note, August 4, 1862. The artwork, *Surrender of General Burgoyne at Saratoga, New York, October 1777,* by John Murdoch, is from a John Trumbull painting of the same name, now in the Frick Museum.[13] The scene did not come to pass. In its stead, Secretary Chase in a rare act of "institutional narcissism" had his own portrait put on the new note. With this rare bit of chicanery, Chase sought to achieve "what thousands of the same notes could not buy — recognition."[14] As he had designs for the presidency, he would see the dissemination of millions of copies of his likeness as good for future prospects. Chase would be mistaken, though he had his portrait reproduced on two more notes, a Compound Interest Treasury note and an Interest Bearing note, both of 1863. A minor instance of institutional narcissism may also be seen in the selection of the Treasury Building for the $100 Interest Bearing Note of 1863. Although in 1877 the selection of designs became the responsibility of the Bureau, strange incidents continued to occur in the selection of portraits, as in the case of the $2 Silver Certificate of 1891, for which a portrait of former Treasury Secretary William Windom was chosen. "It would seem," Gene Hessler found, "that everyone in Washington knew of Windom's opposition to the silver lobby. However, the person or persons who selected Windom's portrait for this honor either were oblivious to the fact or had a sense of humor that apparently went unnoticed."[15]

At present, the responsibility for design selection is shared between the Treasury Department and the Department of Justice, perhaps to ensure against such happenings. So today, when a new currency note is to be issued, designs — often in the form of "proof notes"[16] — are first discussed with a variety of government officials before they are sent to the designers of the Bureau, who prepare a final model. The Secretary of the Treasury must

$1, Legal Tender, 1862, face, portrait of Samuel P. Chase (American Numismatic Association Money Museum)

approve the final model. Photocopies of the approved model then go to the engravers, who reproduce the currency designs—such as the portrait, the vignette, the ornaments, and the lettering—in pieces of soft steel, known as "dies," by working with steel cutting instruments, called gravers, and powerful magnifying glasses. When the engraved dies have been completed, they are cleaned and hardened. The design of each die is then transferred to a cylinder of soft steel, creating an exact duplicate in relief. All cylinders are passed separately over the master roll, thereby uniting the different portions of the engraving. At the end of the entire process, a steel master plate is made from the master roll bearing all designs necessary to make up one currency note.[17]

There are two distinct kinds of design features on modern currency. Firstly, there are those that are purely ornamental or have security implications. Secondly, there are those that have historical or idealistic significance, such as the Great Seal, pictures of famous buildings, monuments, or paintings, and portraits of Great Americans or, in O'Donnell's more formal language, of "deceased statesmen whose places in history are well known to the American people."[18] The phraseology implies that selection of design features that have symbolic significance is done "by tradition," though it is not clear when or why this tradition began. In fact, the custom of selecting only portraits of deceased persons originated from a scandal under Secretary Chase, when Spencer M. Clark, who had been advanced to Superintendent of the National Currency Bureau, had his own portrait placed on a 5¢ Fractional Note in 1864.[19]

Most people who saw and handled the note thought it was William Clark of the Lewis and Clark expedition, who was being thus honored. The worthy superintendent himself was already under investigation for fraud, embezzlement, and sexual harassment when the note bearing his portrait appeared. The scandal led to the congressional ruling of April 1866 that no representation of a living person was to appear on United States notes.[20] Superintendent Clark was not removed from office, though "Treasury woman" became a code word for prostitute. Secretary Chase also remained uncensured, free to pursue his political ambitions. Only the man who had brought the scandal to light—Lafayette Baker, the Union's first secret agent and the founder of the National Detective Force, aka Secret Service—was later convicted of a rights violation.[21] In addition, the portraits on subsequent fractional notes— in denominations of 5, 10, 25, and 50 cents—respectively became those of Washington, Lincoln, Jefferson, and Grant.

Preparing the engraved plate for the new small size paper currency (Library of Congress, Prints and Photographs Division, LC-USZ62-137249)

These notes may be seen as a preview of what was to come. For when in 1929 small-size currency notes were introduced, the portraits used on the faces of the notes were those of America's grand old men who had in one way or the other played a role in the drama of the nation's life.

Generally in industry, the development of a product begins with requirements determined by basic mechanisms as engineers specify them. Only after these people have done their work may designers incorporate their ideas into design development. At the Bureau, design development is turned upside down: the engineers, as well as printers and engravers are required to work within the parameters specified in advance by designers, whose work is in turn under the control of government officials and politicians. This way of organizing production indicates the importance of design for the national currency, an importance that is by no means limited to the look and feel of the notes. Indeed the whole concept of a national currency — how it is to be marketed and advertised, from its appearance in the specimen or presentation books of the late nineteenth century to the educational outreach of the present — is developed at the Bureau. In this way, design does not merely add value to existing notes (for instance by making them safer), but is a fundamental element of product innovation, linking production and consumption.

That today American currency design is not simply concerned with creating functionally apposite (counterfeit-proof), intelligible ("American"), and stylistically pleasing notes but is specifically concerned with creating a target group of patriotic Americans can be seen from the "new symbols of Freedom" that have been added to the latest generation of dollar notes. These symbols represent icons of Americana, like the flag, the eagle, or the torch carried by the Statue of Liberty. For instance, on the new $50 note the traditional stars and stripes in blue and red can be seen behind the portrait of President Ulysses S. Grant. A field of blue stars is located to the left of the portrait, while three red stripes are located to the right of the portrait. A small metallic silver-blue star is located on the lower right side of the portrait. On the face of the new $10 note there are two images of the torch carried by the Statue of Liberty and printed in red. A large image of the torch is printed in the background to the left of the portrait of Alexander Hamilton, while a second, smaller metallic red image of the torch can be found on the lower right side of the portrait. Appearing on the face of the new $20 note are two American eagles. The large blue eagle in the background to the left of Andrew Jackson's portrait is representative of those drawn and sculpted during his period. The smaller green metallic eagle to the lower right of the portrait is a more contemporary illustration, using the same "raised ink" intaglio process as the portrait, numerals and engravings. Altogether, the "new symbols of Freedom" are key points of identification, and they as it were make the notes suggest, "This dollar note is for you!" By getting consumers to identify with the new notes, it is hoped, they will be kept on board, having built what in marketing lingo is called "brand loyalty" — not just to the national currency but to the government as well.

The notion of "brand loyalty" is evident from a variety of texts on the Treasury's website, as well as from Secretary Snow's reference to "the President's economic policies," which are said to ensure that "more of those dollars stay in the pockets of American families."[22] It is hard to see how the economic policies alluded to (presumably, tax cuts) relate to the introduction of new currency designs, except on the level of ideology. Indeed, the rhetoric of "people's capitalism" is a fitting context for Secretary Snow's claim, which reveals as its target group hard-working, middle-class Americans — the very segment that is most contested and fought over during elections and the ones who were in fact hardest hit by the past administration's economic policies.[23] If Secretary Snow's words invoke a specific social identity, most people would assume that this is so because the Treasury Department's biggest "market share" by far comes from hard-working, self-reliant Americans, and so all the publicity work the government is doing is giving a fairly accurate reflection of who in fact does acquire and use those bills. This is of course true, but only up to a point.

Representation does not work by simply assuming that Americans have their fixed cultural and social identities, outside of and apart from the product and advertising. It is too simplistic to say that Secretary Snow's words are merely reflecting the social world of real users of dollar bills. Identification works through the imaginary and on our desires. Therefore, if the dollar bill publicity work is successful in forging an identity for itself with these groups and lifestyles, then after a time it comes to stand for or symbolize them. The new dollar bills become metaphors, signifiers, of hard-working, self-reliant Americans, and they will in turn have an influence on the way these people think, behave, and act, producing a culture-specific classification of the world, that is to say, a specific way of structuring areas of knowledge and social practices through language. In order to be a hard-working, self-reliant American, therefore, one should be using those newly designed bills. They are constructed as part of the identity of hard-working, self-reliant Americans. People can enter this group, identify themselves with the crowd, and take on this particular identity by using the newly designed bills and thereby acquiring the meanings and cultural characteristics that they represent. Phrased differently, people can claim membership of a specific identity because the language of advertising and publicity is also about telling them what kinds of identities they can become.

Neither the changes in currency design nor the trend in coinage are accidental. The Presidential Coin Program in particular is proof that what Franklin could only dream about in 1785, has now come true — that America place images of her honored great on the money, thus creating "monuments against perishing and being forgotten."[24] Indeed, since the days of Franklin the currency has undergone a profound shift in its cultural work — from denotation to connotation, that is, from symbolizing a real environment (grounded in the present or in timelessness) to memory work. Borrowing a term coined by the French historian Pierre Nora, monetary tokens have become "*lieux de mémoire*," sites "where memory crystallizes and secretes itself." Their imagery serves to stabilize the community through remembering, its grand old men as well as other iconic things, including public buildings of national significance. Current dollar bills in particular provide retrospective assurance, which may be much needed when times are experienced as ever accelerating, when the cultural roots are eroding, and when historical identities are becoming blurred. The urge to review (and renew) on the currency one's national history and a usable past serves an identical function as when other national icons come into play. They defend what is threatened; otherwise there would be no need to hang on to them. All such icons thus share in a nostalgic dimension that makes them bastions of old, marking group membership in a society that, following Nora, no longer provides a genuine environment of memory and thus seeks validation in the retrospective perusal of its origins.[25]

The Only True American Contribution to the Arts?

American currency design has been much more complex and culturally hybrid than it might appear at first sight. While the imagery on dollar bills has been of tremendous importance in the construction of the idea of the American nation, it has played other roles as well. Social factors like the existence of specific authorizing institutions also have determined what images were used to represent key values such as financial stability, wealth, and wellbeing. Other important influences have been printing technology and the diversification of note issuing. For example on early notes, often the spaces for the date and signatures were left blank, to be completed by bank officials. Other early notes were only partially printed with minimal images and text, and with spaces left blank for the inclusion of specific details by hand. A number of these notes were only redeemable after a certain lapse of time, and this date was written on the notes themselves. On occasion, notes were made out to a specific person, although this was made more flexible with the addition of the words "or to the bearer."

There were other considerations as well, which affected the visual look of paper money. One was the use of notes as a form of advertising by whoever issued them. This was an essential strategy at a time when fear of counterfeits was widespread. Great emphasis therefore was placed on a variety of authenticating marks: there were images suggesting fiscal trustworthiness (it appears that the dog enjoyed the greatest and longest vogue), depictions of coins, "real" money, on the notes that stood for it, or images of reassuringly grand bank buildings, the homes of the notes that people were expected to use. Bankers also sought credibility through a judicious choice of the bank's name ("State Bank" was a particularly popular choice), through personal signatures, and through portraits of bank officials. By the mid-nineteenth century, these portraits were often rendered in a style "more usually associated with the monarchy and other heads of state," thus testifying "both to this locus of control and to a desire to convey a bank's reliability and economic solidity."[26]

Banks that opened after the Civil War were more likely to use portraits on their notes than well-established banks, though many larger institutions such as the Bureau of Engraving and Printing did so too. One reason is that established banks already had an identifiable iconography, but it can equally be attributable to new banks' need to establish a solid reputation for the institution and its personnel. In addition, it may be attributable to "institutional narcissism," as in Salmon P. Chase's case. Either way, the implications for preferring to have transactions with people of known reputation seem clear: few people were content to rely on some form of generalized morality or unstable institutional arrangements to guard against trouble. Such caution had been appropriate already during the early republic, when distrust of paper money issued by the federal government led to currency being issued by private banks. It became appropriate again from the 1830s onward, when there was a rapid expansion of banking, accompanied by territorial expansion, few if any laws to protect note holders, a bank management that was not particularly strong or else dated and, not to forget, the bane of America's monetary history, counterfeiting.

The problem with all kinds of authenticating imprints was that visible resemblance had to provide the grounds for conveying both a note's power to circulate and its authenticity. In other words, all attempts to make people take paper money for granted leaned alternately (and sometimes simultaneously) on personal marks and on the power of the notes' mechanical reproduction as security against fraud. Opinions on how to solve the problem were divided. Some currency experts continued to invoke the notion of personal marks as guarantors of authentic value. Thus, W.L. Ormsby in a book on banknote engraving saw security "in proportion to the ingenuity of design, the talent of the Artist, and the amount of labor bestowed upon it."[27] Others sought to link the notes' authenticity with modern technology or what the age called "scientific principles." However, at the time none of these currency experts was able to solve the distressing paradox that any "genuine" bill was at the same time an original and a replica. In other words, for a note to be "genuine," the notion of the original must disappear altogether. Thus, the only true "original" notes are counterfeits, fake notes, or spurious, bogus, altered, and raised ones.[28]

The issue of original and replica did not trouble a cashier of the Michigan State Bank. "Get a real furioso plate — one that will TAKE with all creation," the man wrote in October 1837. Such a plate would be "flaming with cupids, locomotives, rural scenery, and Hercules kicking the world over!"[29] The mention of locomotives is telling. From about 1820, the United States had come under the spell of "civilization," which left its imprint everywhere, though most notably in areas west of the Appalachians. Projects to "civilize" America involved the building of canals, toll roads (called "turnpikes"), bridges, and railroads. The railroad turned out to be the most popular image on nineteenth-century paper money, more important even than the steamboat, which contemporaries also got excited about. While steamboats were "confined to the routes God had created," railroads could go "wherever human will, human strength, and the capitalist imagination collaborated to direct them." Thanks to the railroad, by mid-century it became possible — and economically necessary — to talk about national markets. The railroad alone was progress promised and personified, though as the century progressed it also acquired connotations of destructiveness, culminating in the trope of the "machine in the garden."[30]

The earliest note with a railway vignette probably dates from 1831. The Susquehanna Bridge & Bank Company of Port Deposit, Maryland, issued it.[31] Especially noteworthy is a one-dollar note from the Tallahassee Rail Road Company, printed around 1860, which shows a group of people gathering to watch the coming of a train. Other companies also issued notes of their own. One was the Delaware Bridge Company of Lambertville, along the border between New Jersey and Pennsylvania. Crossing the Delaware River by a bridge became a vital step in the expanding westward movement. Surprisingly, though, the imagery on the company's notes did not include the new bridge. In its stead, there are images of two women — "fetching, diaphanously-clad damsels," as David Standish describes them — and one token cherub. Indeed, allegorical figures abounded on notes of the period. They clearly embodied the classicist spirit and ethos of the time, which sought to give dignity and originality even to mundane things such as factories.[32]

Overall, an enormous range of images was used on American paper money prior to the Civil War.[33] In Richard Doty's *Pictures from a Distant Country*, we find urban vistas as well as icons of empire, such as the eagle. We also find portraits of presidents and other leaders, of bank and government officials, bucolic landscapes and images of mining and heavy industry. There were likewise local streetcars, and any number of trains, steamships, and riverboats. Finally, there were Native Americans looking with awe at the onslaught of civilization, African Americans seemingly happy in their lowly lives as plantation slaves, barely clothed buxom women, and innocent children. Depictions of the latter often shared in the romantic and idealized view of women, though a few notes showed "real" children engaged in "real" activities, including work, on farms, in homes, and in factories. On occasion, these images display features that we know from contemporary photographs. While the emerging technology of photography provided new possibilities of "realism," other images of children were portrayed in a manner that was adapted from contemporary paintings, thus preserving a more conservative, genteel trend in portraiture.

More characteristic of the age were images related to work. Work was not simply a necessity, but gave meaning and status to people's lives. Many notes from the era depict pride in work, no matter how humble. If the bills bear true testimony, Doty suggests, the "apotheosis of the working man and woman was celebrated in these times rather than in our own." Work was represented in a variety of segments: professions and trades were there, in the shape of boot makers, coopers, surveyors, builders and carpenters, mariners and shipbuilders, all testimony to the sometimes feverish pace that characterized the age. Also represented were mills and mines, from spinning and glassmaking to metalworking, from quarrying to coalmining, pointing the way to the future. Last but not least, there were representations of work on the land, which was then the most important segment, both from the numbers engaged and from the value of production.[34]

The land's importance had been enshrined on private notes from early on. The message was always the same: land is the foundation of the nation's prosperity. A scene on a bill from the Newark Banking & Insurance Company makes the point in simple but forceful terms: a farmer plows by the riverside, while an abundance of farm produce is ready to honor his work. In the foreground, a pole with a liberty cap leans against a half-felled tree, the iconic representation of Jefferson's empire of liberty founded on the farmer's labor. This image, which dates from 1815, as well as later images, denoted "healthful country. Not wild. Not wilderness at all: only the new country learning to make sense of itself, applying 'civilized' notions of order and purpose to a near-frontier situation that would unroll from one state to the next for the entire century."[35] Projecting hope and plenty was especially important for a time when paper dollars from the private bank paid for the opening of the West. Investors and settlers alike needed to be reassured that the wilderness had no terrors. Thus, the bills sometimes would offer a measure of whimsicalness, as when they depicted dogs chasing birds, or elephants. Indeed, most bills would tell stories that the people who handled the money could readily understand. Like the new immigrant, westward bound, receiving in his change the very picture of his hope. Or like an eastern farm boy seeing all his dreams made visible on a dollar bill. Or again like the investor seeing a land that could be measured out, bought and sold, and turned into something tame, like a landscape patterned by houses, fields, crops, animals, churches, stores, hotels, and factories.

Essentially such dreams were also those of the great landscape painters of the nineteenth century — Thomas Cole and his successors, Frederic Church, Alfred Bierstadt, Asher

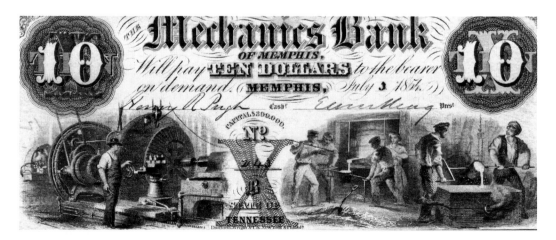

$10, Mechanics Bank of Memphis, 1854, work scenes (courtesy National Numismatic Collection, Smithsonian Institution)

Durand, and others. These artists may have been awed by the wild grandeur of America's unclaimed wilderness, and were often desperate because they could not find a moral code that would do justice to what Cole termed the "undefiled works [of] God the creator." But, had not God made a promise? If so, the wilderness *was* the Promised Land, to be made over by the chosen people. The promise would give direction, not to the past but to the present and future. This is how Cole expressed his vision: "Where the wolf roams, the plough shall glisten, on the gray crag shall rise temple and tower — mighty deeds shall be done in the now pathless wilderness: and poets yet unborn shall sanctify the soil."[36] On occasion, farmsteads would be projected into the paintings, where no farmsteads yet existed; or else, a lonely house would appear, with a few acres of tree stumps in a field, set against the grandeur of a distant peak and the magnificence of an old growth forest. Banknote art moved in the same artistic space, trying to summarize in fine lines on a cramped steel plate what the painted canvas could suggest in light and shape and size. "Where the painters dreamed, the engravers bustled," a commentator concludes, "Sometimes they were the same men."[37] Like Asher Durand, who began as an engraver before he became a painter.

The era of paper dollars issued by private banks ended with the Civil War. When it came, "the sensible blanket of the greenback" replaced the early "crazy-quilt of currencies." In terms of art on United States money, David Standish found, "it's been downhill ever since."[38] Not everyone would agree. Following the Civil War, improvements in printing technology made printing cheap, fast, and flexible, and they permitted strikingly detailed imagery to be placed on notes. National Bank notes especially of the first charter period today are greatly appreciated by collectors for their beauty. Contemporaries too became aware that banknote engraving had reached new and unprecedented heights. In February 1862, an article in *Harper's New Monthly Magazine* assured its readers that "bank notes executed in America [are] superior to any others in the world."[39] Lest this be written off as so much jingoism, here is what a writer, addressing the merits of the work of F.O.C. Darley, had remarked in the *London Art Journal* in October 1860: "This is the first time that we have ever heard of bank-note engraving being considered applicable, and pre-eminently so, to illustrations professing to have a high Art character."[40] One visitor to the United States even called banknote-engraving "the only true American contribution to the arts."[41] Given the prejudices of the European educated bourgeoisie, this may have been faint praise. In the world of paper currency, however, it must be seen as a true compliment, like the words of James Harvey, a contemporary critic for whom these notes constituted "the money of civilization."

People often understand "civilization" as the technological side of social life, the opposite of "culture," and in the reproductions of the famous Americana paintings on National Bank notes of the first series this is all too obvious. Superintendent Clark's choice deployed on National Bank notes a number of artworks in the Rotunda of the United States Capitol — *Baptism of Pocahontas, Landing of the Pilgrims, Washington Crossing the Delaware, Jefferson presenting the Declaration of Independence to John Hancock at the Continental Congress,* and *Embarkation of the Pilgrims.* Reproductions of artworks on bank notes repeat and amplify the epistemological confusions that plagued the people concerned with the notes' security. The visible resemblance to other notes had to provide the grounds for assuring both a note's power to circulate and its authenticity. For notes that carry art, the disappearance of the original is particularly disturbing, as "art" is customarily connected with originality. Walter Benjamin's classic essay on the work of art in the age of mechanical reproduction can help us in distinguishing paper money art from other art forms.

Benjamin's "mechanical reproduction" perspective has played an important part in

$50, National Bank note, series 1863, back, Embarkation of the Pilgrims (American Numismatic Association Money Museum)

structuring public debate about the social and cultural significance of paper money. Two recurring themes are worth recording. The first concerns questions of value. Among numismatists, for example, the criteria to determine a note's worth are rarity and age, as well as "discernible differences."[42] On these grounds, nineteenth-century notes have become extremely popular with collectors, whereas current bills are often ignored, perhaps because they are too closely linked to what Emily Gilbert has termed the "democratization" of their reception.[43] The second theme concerns the notion of capitalism as religion. "Nowhere more naively than in these [nineteenth-century notes]," Benjamin wrote in an earlier essay, "does capitalism display itself in such solemn earnest. The innocent cupids frolicking about numbers, the goddesses holding tablets of the law, the stalwart heroes sheathing their swords before monetary units, are a world of their own: ornamenting the façade of hell."[44] Let us examine each of the two themes in turn, to see if we can delineate within them the presence of any of the key arguments and assumptions of the "mechanical reproduction" perspective.

As regards the "rarity, age, and discernible differences" theme, it clearly entails a moral critique of contemporary culture. Real is opposed to false, authenticity to inauthenticity. Validation is conferred by pastness, not by a note's function as legal tender or by its modern design, regardless of how tasteful it is. This logic can also be found in the "mechanical reproduction" perspective measuring a work of art's worth in terms of its uniqueness, or else of its enduring quality, which is unrepeatable and gives it its aura or claim to the status as a work of art. The artwork's aura (which corresponds to the aureole or halo in Christian iconology) developed into the gilt frame corresponding to and defining the artwork and, from there, into the frames on paper bills.[45] These frames would hold portraits of "great men" as well as images of signal moments in a nation's history. The choice of subject matter may have helped to "secularize" both persons and events—though *not* in the sense that Benjamin says that photography destroyed the aura of so-called "original" things. The camera, Benjamin argues, annihilated the ontological status of the origin and its imitation: "The technique of reproduction detaches the reproduced object from the domain of tradition. By making many reproductions it substitutes, apparently miraculously, a plurality of copies for a unique existence. In addition, in permitting the reproduction to meet the beholder in his particular situation, it reactivates the object reproduced. These two processes lead to a tremendous shattering of tradition."[46]

Benjamin mentions money only once in his essay relating artistic reproduction to economic production. Nevertheless, money — paper as well as coin — serves better than photography to highlight the relation between reproduction and production. From a photographic negative, Benjamin wrote, "one can make any number of prints; to ask for the 'authentic' print makes no sense."[47] Although one can also make any number of prints from a currency plate or any number of strikes from a die, the matter is somewhat more complicated: a piece of currency is at the same time a copy and unique, both artful reproduction and active participant in the relations of production. The "original" plays no role, except as something that is kept from the public by the authorizing institution. Thus ritual, the basis of art, gives way to politics. As a result, the aesthetics of currency design does not demand metaphorical reference to superstructural and substructural levels. Coins as well as notes, Marc Shell has pointed out, are things "ontologically equal to each other" as products of the same die or plate; and money, which notes and coins symbolize, potentially equalizes all other things.[48]

It was not the invention of paper money per se, but its mass production, which became a sign of capitalist expansion. The accumulation of capital expanded, and with it those new forms of money whose value depends less on precious metal backing it than on the promise of growth, the regaining of values. Thus, the ornaments on bank and government notes were not only a way of legitimating capitalism; the notes themselves had to be charged with guardian spirits representing happiness, prosperity, economic health, fertility, and so on. Classical and allegorical images on American paper money became more rare towards the end of the nineteenth century. If they prevailed — as on the notes of the Educational Series— they were transformed into symbols of the sovereignty of the state, the pastoral idyll usurped by a Wagnerian constellation of power. Yet then as later, the importance of classical and allegorical figures lay in lending a measure of dignity to the newly emerging financial institutions and instruments. Additionally, these figures served as ways and means to cope with or even conceal economic and social instability. They would help appease white males' racial anxieties, their fears for their traditional prerogatives as well as their unease over Eastern and Southern European immigration.

There were other anxieties, too, such as discontent over the mass production of consumer goods, which blurred the line between genuine art and mere imitation. Moreover, there were complaints against the allegedly devastating effects of paper money on culture and society, especially at times when the gold standard and other categories that resisted change or renegotiation were out of reach. A special case is a vignette called "Concordia" on the one-dollar National Bank note of 1865, whose two maidens in classical garb symbolized the hopes for peace of a nation still engaged in a bloody civil war. Overall, despite the innovations of the monetary form, classical and allegorical images maintained continuity with the representations on coins that had always had such figures placed on them. What the writings of a Longfellow, a Holmes, or a Lowell, by representing and speaking to a genteel morality achieved in the realm of literature, the allegorical images on bank notes achieved in everyday life, evoking an era *before* the widespread circulation of the paper dollar, an era when "civic personality was grounded in real property and endowed with classical virtue."[49]

If the classical and allegorical figures ornamented on paper money belonged to a "religion of capitalism," that religion was truly radical: it was a religion exclusively for those possessing the money. Those without it must also do without the gods and goddesses. The

$5, Bank of East Tennessee, 1855, female allegories (courtesy National Numismatic Collection, Smithsonian Institution)

logic is a simple one: money protects only to the extent it is possessed. The more notes, the more protection. Thorstein Veblen knew this well. Writing in 1899, he dryly observed that wealth was then "the most easily recognized evidence of a reputable degree of success as distinguished from heroic or signal achievement. It therefore becomes the conventional basis of esteem."[50] Veblen portrayed the pursuit of wealth at all costs as shameful, and the accompanying way of living — by the laboring classes — as parasitic. A still life by Victor Dubreuil, which stacks dollar bills high next to a bottle of champagne and a cigar, visually expresses conspicuous consumption and the excesses of the rich.[51]

Indeed, in post–Civil War America the coarseness and money-grubbing of the rich stood in stark contrast to the ideals espoused on an official level — including on bank and government notes. The growing power of a few industrialists, especially in the oil, steel, and railroad business, only deepened the division between the rich and the rest of society, a division underscored by such events as the railroad strikes of the 1870s and the labor disputes of the 1880s. By that time, Mark Twain and Charles Dudley Warner had already created the epoch-defining name with a novel titled *The Gilded Age*. The title, Richard Doty found, "could not have been more pointed, or apt. This was *not* a golden age [but] an age which posed as something solid and worthy, but whose plating was thin, soon revealing the bigotry and brass beneath."[52] In the face of the perceived absence of morality, allegorical and classical images on paper money would be the perfect ornaments on "the façade of hell," to use Benjamin's trope one more time. Eventually, though, these images would give way to historical figures representing the nation's great sons (and, on occasion, daughters). Allegory thus came to be replaced by collective memory. Which goes to show that the "religion of capitalism," as a religion without dogma, is perfectly capable of absorbing, under a humanistic guise, even ancestor worship.

Gender, Race, and the Paper Dollar

The wide range of images used on American paper money raises the question of who selects them. Selection of images has always been solidly in the hands of elites, often but

not always the state, and, from the nineteenth century, their actual production the responsibility of ever fewer and highly specialist banknote companies. Moreover, those who were
producing, bringing into circulation, and using paper money were predominantly white
males. Consequently, the representation of others on paper money would be filtered through
the dominant group's perception of the "truth." So would representations of themselves.
For instance, the fact that Hamilton was also an immigrant from the West Indies does not
appear to have played a role in selecting his portrait for a variety of bank and government
notes. At the very least, Hamilton is never marked as an immigrant. The point is that
Hamilton *was* part of the monetary economy represented by the notes. By contrast, women,
Native Americans, and African Americans generally were *not*. The latter were often persons
in service; insofar as they were also slaves, they had "masters." Native Americans, who were
considered children, had "guardians." Women had what John Adams called the "masculine
system"—though if we are to believe Abigail Adams, they rather had "tyrants."[53] All of
them — masters, guardians, and tyrants alike — would make payments with notes bearing
pictures of women, Native Americans, and African Americans, the currency of domination.

Let us first look at women. Of the three groups, women have appeared on paper money
the most frequently. Women have traditionally symbolized fertility and thus became the
perfect embodiment of the very qualities the issuers of notes wanted to suggest, financial
stability and wealth. However, most of the female figures are anonymous and represent an
idealized beauty; in Virginia Hewitt's memorable words, they constitute "soft images to
give hard currency a good name."[54] Thus, the symbolic representation of women at the same
time conceals and enshrines women's exclusion from the material world of markets and
capital. Since the effects resulting from the enforcement of these separations are elided, use
of women as money icons becomes problematic only when attempts are made to supplant
the position occupied by the ideal woman for the real, as for example when Susan B.
Anthony's portrait was placed on the one-dollar coin beginning in 1979.[55]

"Real," that is, historical women have appeared on paper money with a certain degree
of regularity. Most of the women chosen had better-known husbands or were connected
with more famous men. The fact that this was "an obvious criterion for their inclusion on
the currency,"[56] underlines the gendered nature of monetary practices, for it was not for
their deeds but for their being that women were thus honored. Martha Washington fell into
this category and a portrait of her, designed by Thomas F. Morris and engraved by Charles
Burt, was put on the $1 Silver Certificate, Series 1886 and 1891. Tellingly, the same portrait
turned up on the $1 Silver Certificate of 1896, alongside George W., in an engraving by Alfred
Sealey. On this note the many truly dissolve into one—*E pluribus Unum*—, though in a
cruelly ironic reworking of a passage from William Blackstone's *Commentaries on the Laws
of England*: "By marriage, the husband and wife are one person in law: that is, the very being
or legal existence of the woman is suspended during the marriage [...] incorporated and
consolidated into that of the husband."[57]

Pocahontas, whose baptism was depicted on a $20 National Bank note, and who
appeared in a number of guises on other notes, may also qualify as a "real" woman. However, the mode of her representation is never far from the mythic and allegorical. Safer bets
for realism are Rachel Jackson, Catherine (Kate) Sevier, Dolly Madison, Maria Knox Innes
Todd Crittenden, the "Belle of Kentucky," and Lucy Holcombe Pickens. Mrs. Pickens's portrait was chosen for a number of Confederate notes, as she personified the very essence of
the best Southern qualities—also, significantly, she was the wife of the governor of South
Carolina, and she graced more paper bills than any other woman in American history did.[58]

$1 Silver Certificate, 1896, back, portraits of Martha Washington and George Washington (American Numismatic Association Money Museum)

Of the few females who arrived on the notes "by their own merit," the Swedish opera singer Jenny Lind (actually Johanna Maria Lind) was one. Others were Henriette Sontag, another opera singer who made the first of several American tours in 1852, and was immortalized on a Connecticut note not long thereafter, and Florence Nightingale, whose portrait appeared on note from banks in Virginia and in Georgia in 1861.[59] That is *it* for real women on American paper money. For, most "real" women depicted on the currency enjoyed a subordinate reality, and they were placed there to represent an activity, or point out a moral, like the Pilgrim women who appeared on vignettes respectively called *Embarkation* (after Weir's painting) and *Landing* (in an engraving by Charles Burt).[60]

The earliest depictions of women on American paper money had been as small black-and-white engravings, rendered in a neo-classical style, of goddesses of European extraction, Juno, Diana, Liberty (usually in a state of clothing approaching the pornographic, and

Portrait of Lucy Holcombe Pickens on $5, Winnsboro, SC, 1855 (courtesy National Numismatic Collection, Smithsonian Institution)

occasionally dressed as Columbia), or Justice (with her scales, fittingly blind). Private commercial banks might feel that by choosing a figure representing Plenty or Agriculture they could successfully advertise the prosperity of local trade and, of course, of the bank itself. What probably also influenced the decision was that bankers and their engravers knew that these female figures were not *supposed* to be fully clothed: "semi- or total nudity was part of the story."[61] By the 1840s, a seemingly more believable depiction of women set in. Women were shown involved in quite normal pursuits, such as child rearing, work on the farm, factory work, or even taking a walk with a special young man. Looking at these notes now makes the realism dwindle and shrink, though, disclosing their hidden agenda of identifying a happy domestic and working life with the solid foundation of a bank in a local community.

Farm life is usually depicted as idyllic, harvesting grain, occasionally even tobacco or hop, caring and feeding livestock and fowl, churning. Nowhere, however, is the need to idealize and romanticize women more forcefully expressed than in images of milkmaids. Based on the testimony of the notes, Richard Doty observes, "milking cows must have been *the* growth industry of the nineteenth century." In fact, these sweet-faced maidens were put on the notes to represent innocence, youthfulness, and purity, qualities that must have had a special appeal to the bankers and engravers, not the least because these qualities seemed at risk as the beginning industrialization began to change the nation. Nevertheless, factory work as we can see it on pre–Civil War notes also does not have any of the degrading qualities we have come to associate with the dark, satanic mills of the coming industrialization. Especially on notes issued in the aftermath of the War of 1812, factory work even has a tinge of patriotic labor, as the war had forced the United States to become more self-reliant for manufactured goods. Women are seen making thread, weaving it into cloth, and even doing piecework at home, along with their men.[62]

What these representations of women also show is that those who so frequently appeared on the country's currency were at long last "beginning to achieve the means of earning it, and spending it." At least some of them, for most women in antebellum America were still employed in that oldest form of female labor, motherhood. Images of mothers graced a large number of notes, and always engaged in nurturing, protecting, educating — apt symbols of creation, including the creation of wealth. Of course, that was also the manner by which those in power could keep women within safe, traditional bounds. At times, the quality of the imagery is of mushy treacle, as on a note from Medford, New Jersey, which features a seated woman tenderly cradling her child, Madonna-like, and oblivious to her surroundings. Other images likewise reinforced the status quo and the popular perception of reality in the relation between the sexes. Especially popular were images that romanticized wives and daughters as delicate flowers needing the protection of their husbands and fathers. So were images that portrayed women as temptresses, which lent a kind of pin-up quality to the notes, at the same time as they would allude to the equation of women with untamed nature, or as incipient consumptives for whom male protection might come too late.[63]

The gap between appearance and being, between perceived and photographic reality, did not close with the advent of National Bank notes. Allegorical images of women in particular continued to be a major visual motif on the currency until the introduction of Federal Reserve notes in 1915. It is as though there was a strong desire to make the Gilded Age more romantic by making abstractions such as Liberty, Victory, Justice, and Peace take the forms of attractive young women, often clothed in classically inspired gowns. Hence we have Liberty dressed as Columbia on the $50 Legal Tender note of 1874. On the $500 note stands proudly a bare-breasted Victory, now in recognizably nineteenth-century dress. That she is to symbolize the outcome of the Civil War is obvious from her sharing the stage with a portrait of Major General Joseph King Mansfield, killed in the battle of Antietam in 1862. Allegorization also was extended to a variety of human pursuits. These pursuits included Art (on the face of the $10 Legal Tender note of 1869, together with Abraham Lincoln); Transportation (on the $500 Interest Bearing note of 1861), Architecture (on the $100 Legal Tender issue, Series 1869 and 1875); Navigation (on the $10 and $50 National Bank notes of 1902); Mechanics and Agriculture (on the $20 Silver Certificate of 1886); and Agriculture (on the $2 Silver Certificate issued in 1886, along with a male figure representing Industry).

$50, Legal Tender (United States note), 1874, face, at right, Liberty dressed as Columbia (American Numismatic Association Money Museum)

The tendency to allegorize women reached a kind of apotheosis with the 1896 issue of three Silver Certificates known as the Educational Series. The notes were crucial in the designing of the national money icon, though they are also the last notes to date on which any women are depicted. Yet these women were not always well liked. For instance the $5 entry, which showed an allegorical motif, Electricity Presenting Light to the World, caused uproar among several Boston society women, who were scandalized by the uncovered bosoms of certain of the figures in the scene. Although the symbolic association between a woman's breast and nourishment from a fertile nation should have been clear enough (and had been intended by the note's designer, Walter Shirlaw, the co-founder of the Chicago Institute of Art), some banks also refused to take the notes. Thus originated the idiom "banned in Boston," and thus the "Indian Chief" ("Oncpapa") notes soon replaced them.[64]

Native Americans may have been distorted the most on American paper money. Richard Doty describes images of them in terms of "the people in the way," for that was precisely who they were for many white people.[65] The earliest instance of a figure said to represent a Native American is on the famous 1690 charter bill from the colony of Massachusetts. Text notices take up most of the space on these bills, which was typical of early paper money. The main "art"—the colony's seal—features a human figure rendered in what has been described as "a decidedly down-home folk art design."[66] The figure, though labeled by numismatists as "Standing Indian" or "Indian on the colony Seal," bears an undeniable similarity to the figure on the popular late sixteenth century European "Wildman" or "Wildermann" thaler. This could have been deliberate. The colony's seal was printed on the bill from an engraved copper plate, modeled from a 1675 woodcarving by John Foster. The original, however, was produced in 1629 by a London silversmith, who in all likelihood would have been familiar with "wildman" figures.[67]

Images recalling "wildman" figures also appeared on other denominations issued by the colony of Massachusetts—of 10 and 20

Wildermann thaler, Germany 1629 (Wikipedia)

shillings, and of five pounds. Later notes issued by the colonies respectively of New Hampshire, New York, and Georgia, and on revolutionary war issues of New York carried images bearing a closer similarity to actual Indians, that is, with headdress and all. Yet all of these images, Doty found, are suggestive of "how truly 'pastoral' America must have been"— and of how desperate for some form of currency, which is understandable, given the absence of a minting facility and the prohibitions, imposed by the British government in 1751 and, more extensively in 1764, against printing paper money.[68]

When the Revolutionary War began, the Continental Congress began to authorize the issuance of currency to finance the war. As the ideological goal of the currency was to formulate and perform a national identity, Native Americans understandably were *not* selected for representation on them. Generally speaking, in all of the early period of American paper money there were a few images of Native Americans, but not too many. This is interesting, as Indians were present everywhere in early America. A half-century or so later, everything had changed. Article 1 of the United States Constitution had excluded them from political representation, leaving it to Congress to have power over them, as "children." By the 1830s, they had disappeared from the lives of most white Americans, except in the West and in the countryside, though representations of them abounded in this period. Reduced to what Gordon Wood has termed "rare curios and exotic specimens,"[69] they appeared on paintings, in Cooper's Leatherstocking novels— and on notes issued by private commercial banks. For one thing, this was occasioned by the iconographic freedom these banks enjoyed. Additionally, improved artistry and technological advances such as steel engraving made possible the creation of more ambitious vignettes in the 1840s and 1850s. A good example is a one-dollar note of 1858, which portrays Native Americans as participants in real history. The scene, which was probably engraved by Charles Burt and created by Toppan, Carpenter & Co. of New York, shows a group of Indians meeting up with the Pilgrims for the first time — and looking awed or intimidated, the contemporary collision of cultures elided through an assumed historical distance.[70]

A slightly earlier note from a New York bank recorded a similar encounter, between two warriors and an American sailor.[71] More typical, however, is a state bank note issued in Tecumseh, Michigan, in 1838, which features a standing Indian warrior in a pose rem-

$3, Tecumseh, MI, 1838 (American Numismatic Association Money Museum)

iniscent of Cooper's Last of the Mohicans, if not of a hero from a Walter Scott novel.[72] The historic Tecumseh (the name is also rendered as Tecumtha or Tekamthi) spent much of his life attempting to rally disparate Native American tribes in a mutual defense of their lands. One of his major antagonists was William Henry Harrison, who in 1809 negotiated the Treaty of Fort Wayne. The two men's fates could not have been more different. Whereas Harrison completed his governorship of the Indiana Territory and was elected President of the United States in 1840, Tecumseh was killed during the War of 1812, on the side of the British.

It is not known whether Tecumseh ever claimed bounties offered by the British for American scalps, though reports of the practice provoked William Charles into creating cartoons bitterly denouncing it. The War of 1812 also brought back memories of the British stirring up the native tribes against the Americans during the Revolutionary War. American history books of the time were full of accounts of British misdeeds, and anti–British feeling was running high. For instance, J. Olney in 1836 wrote that, "The conduct of the British in stirring up the cruel savages to ravage the American frontiers, was altogether unworthy of a great and civilized nation. The Creeks and Cherokees at the south, and the Six Nations at the north, were excited by British agents to deeds of horrid barbarity."[73] The murder of Jane McCrae by Indians is probably the most frequently cited example of such deeds; nineteenth-century history books use the episode, as does John Vanderlyn in his 1804 painting *The Death of Jane McCrae.*

William Charles, *A Scene on the Frontiers*, 1812 (Library of Congress, Prints and Photographs Division, LC-USZC2-597)

Anti-British feelings, combined with memories of the frontier wars, died hard. Thus, fighting Indians allied with them was widely claimed as an act of patriotic virtue in the aftermath of the War of 1812. So by what logic is Tecumseh depicted as a noble savage rather than as an ignoble demon? For one thing, at the time Native peoples were not so much depicted as victims than as agents of history. For another, Tecumseh had died a hero's death. This not quite voluntary act was enough to valorize him as a noble savage and, furthermore, as a hero of a bygone time. By contrast, contemporary Indians were often objects of wrath and contempt, as in William Clark's description of the Teton Sioux as "[g]enerally ill-looking and not well made; their legs and arms small generally; high cheekbones, prominent eyes."[74] Indians of the past no longer posed a threat to white hegemony and thus could be accepted as geographical ancestors, which also proved that the country had a cultural history of its own, different from that of European countries.[75]

One of the most popular methods was to portray Native Americans in what white people imagined were typical activities and poses, like hunting. From the late 1830s, images of a hunter waiting in ambush, or of buffalo hunting and the horse, were replicated and manipulated in many different ways, particularly on notes from places where the memory or presence of hunter and prey were still strong. There, the hunter often was transformed into the "Native as Lurker," a potential threat less to the animal population than to the newly arrived white settlers. The importance of the canoe also attracted the attention of engravers.[76] Other images showed Native Americans encountering Progress, though on most of them they were reacting to it with poses that were predictable, and reassuring to white people. Thus, they were shown as silent observers—uncomprehending onlookers, never participants—from a lonely crag of a strange land booming with trains, shops, and beautiful buildings.[77]

On other notes of the period, Indians are made to realize the error of their way of life and to desire to remake themselves in the white man's image. Native American women were often enlisted in this service. For instance, in 1848 the Eagle Bank of Bristol, Rhode Island, issued a one-dollar note on which a Native American wife is attempting to convince her husband of the blessings of Western Civilization. The woman is shown pointing down to a busy harbor scene, one that she and her family could never be part of if they insisted on remaining Native Americans. Another example of the error-of-their-way-of-life topos can be found on a ten-dollar note issued in Petersburg, Indiana, which depicts an Indian woman pointing with a conciliatory gesture towards a plow, the symbol of domesticated life.[78]

These images are fanciful rather than realistic, in that they tend to reduce Native Americans to objects of decoration or didactics. Some representations, however, were beyond even a nodding acquaintance with reality, veering towards the vaguely erotic and the frankly surreal, as in the case of a three-dollar bill from 1861, which showed a semi-nude Native American woman while managing the same "disrespect for reality," to borrow Doty's expression. Illustrations of this kind also speak of a rather ambiguous relationship the producers and issuers of bank notes in the nineteenth century must have had with what they called the "fair sex."[79] In a more general sense, though, the point of all this imagery is that it had to be flattering to the dominant group and that it would bolster the image that the people who were making and putting into circulation such notes had of themselves. These people, it has been suggested, apparently were little concerned about Indian hostility—in a period when violent encounters raged throughout the country.[80]

Over time, Native Americans received an almost heraldic treatment, often with indigenous people on one side of a composition and whites on the other. Both were usually shown engaging in activities that tended to underscore the contrast between the idleness of the former and the industry of the latter. The impression is one of William Hogarth's mid-eighteenth-century engravings from class-biased England reappearing in a racialized New World context. On a Michigan note, for instance, a railroad train is juxtaposed to a lonely Indian, whose seated position of suggested apathy is in sharp contrast to the white drive into the West. By the 1850s, Native Americans often had become mere design elements, objects completely outside of time or place, and therefore no danger either to the producers or to the consumers of the notes. These images also suggest that the perceived balance between the indigenous population and white arrivals had shifted in favor of the latter. Consequently, new poses were coming into favor.[81]

Around 1855, the Bank of North America in New York put into circulation a note that showed, at left, a very realistically looking Native American warrior and, at right, a Native American woman with a child. In the center, occupying most of the space, were the name of the bank, the denomination — and a huge American eagle, wings spread. The man's solemn pose suggests he is offering tribute, perhaps to the women with the child, who may be his family, but more likely to the national bird that on the pictorial level is separating husband from wife and child. On the symbolic level, the note reflects the subjugation of a people that in reality was colonized. The note is an exception among pre–Civil War notes, though. Generally, females were much more popular in ideologically freighted depictions than males. For example, a note from the Mohawk Bank in Mohawk, New York, showed a standing Native woman in almost classical garb. Although the bow and arrow identify her as native, the surrounding picture frame, images of flags and other national symbols identify her with a more grandiose theme: she was "America," the "Indian Princess."[82]

After the Civil War, the project of being American "from the spring-head within our own domain," meaning including the "aboriginal period of our land," became more urgent.[83] While the metamorphosis of the "Indian Princess" was continued, on the male side the stereotypical figure of the "true native American" came into being. Let us deal with the "Indian Princess" first. Native American females had been used to symbolize the new world, the Americas, long before they were appropriated for the currency. Between 1765 and 1783, the female symbol of America stood for the thirteen colonies, after which the "Indian Princess" became identified with the sovereignty of the United States.[84] At first, these "Princesses" were curious mixtures of noble savages and classical goddesses, which the artists (who were often European) concocted out of extant depictions of nymphs and a vague understanding of what went on in the New World. Later, some more truly "native" figures were used, like Pocahontas, whose image appeared on a variety of Gilded Age notes.[85]

Pocahontas notes were issued from 1863 to 1902. When they first appeared, they undoubtedly met with established values and assumptions. In the long run, however, to identify the nation with an "other" whose inferiority had long been emphasized and had become codified within the expansionist ideology of "manifest destiny" seemed absurd to some critics. Ultimately, and probably just as Native Americans were being displaced from the American consciousness, the "Indian Princess" was metamorphosed into a Greek Goddess. Henceforth, the image was no longer an Indian but rather the allegorical representation of America with Indian attributes. On occasion, a flag was added to the figure, and a liberty cap and pole were included, replacing the grass skirt and feathered headdress. The latter was particularly inappropriate, as female Indians, regardless of tribe, never wore feathers. Thus, the image of a "Madonna-like Indian huntress" on a two-dollar bill issued by the Bank of Whitfield in Dalton, Georgia, in 1860 may be "impressive [and] idealized" but it nevertheless constitutes a "grim distortion of history."[86]

In nineteenth-century arts, allegorical styles would be used rather for representations of women, providing unambiguously uplifting moral examples, whereas stylistic "realism" was increasingly reserved for representations of men and manliness. This "division of labor" is the ideological underpinning of the numismatic emergence of the stereotypical figure of the "true native American," a realistically portrayed, dignified-looking male warrior, like the one appearing on the five-dollar Silver Certificate of 1899. Produced from 1900 to 1926, and in more than 500 million examples, the "Indian Chief" or "Oncpapa" note is the first and only issue of United States paper money put into general circulation for which a Native American was selected as the central vignette. The image may have been intended to represent a generic Indian chief, as there is no name on the note. The model at any rate is known, Ta-to-ka-in-yan-ka, the head chief of the Oncpapa or Huncpapa Tribe of the Sioux Nation.[87] His image on the note is based on a photograph taken by Alexander Gardner in 1872, when Ta-to-ka-in-yan-ka was invited to Washington to meet the president and, as well, to get a notion of the size and strength of the white population and the futility of continued Indian warfare.

There is a striking difference between the photograph and the portrait on the Silver Certificate — the war bonnet, which was added by the modeler for the Bureau of Engraving and Printing. In the original photograph, Ta-to-ka-in-yan-ka was only wearing three feathers in his hair, fur braid wraps, and earrings, and holding a wing fan and a peace pipe. Since the headdress projected too high on the first design of the note, George F. Smillie, the engraver, requested the Chief wear his war bonnet. Ta-to-ka-in-yan-ka refused, deeming it inappropriate, as it was not customary for Sioux Chiefs to dress in full ceremonial regalia except at important tribal meetings. Therefore, a war bonnet from the opposing Pawnee Nation was put on the head of an employee of the Bureau of Engraving and Printing and photographed, then cut out and added to the engraved portrait. This insensitive portrayal, though quite common in the creation of a piece of art that is not intended to be an accurate depiction of an individual, created a political scandal, as well as additional ill will between the Pawnee and the Sioux tribes.[88]

Chief Ta-to-ka-in-yan-ka died in 1896 and never saw the printed notes since the engraving was not completed until January 7, 1900. One wonders what he would have said

$5, Silver Certificate, Series 1899, face, the "Indian Chief" or "Oncpapa" note (American Numismatic Association Money Museum)

to his modeling an objectified and exoticized singular Native American chief in "traditional" dress. Would he have recognized himself as representing what Philip Deloria calls the "Indian modern"? The period of the "Indian modern" began with Buffalo Bill's Wild West show in the 1880s and continued with the widespread use of "Indian motifs" picture postcards. Yet it was not a simulation so much as a reenactment seeking authenticity, which therefore was using, "not substitutes but the original participants, the original objects, the original script."[89] Clearly it is the element of reenactment in his appearance that makes Chief Ta-to-ka-in-yan-ka stand for other Native Americans and, by extension, for the many Native peoples against whom Western "civilization" has defined itself and who were about to almost drop out of history as they were rediscovered as symbols of national pride and of the West.

At least for the period 1590–1900, there were many more representations in American art of Native Americans than there were of African Americans, enslaved or free.[90] One reason for this was the prevailing thought of the time, which identified Native Americans with the "sublime," and thus worthy of such representation. By contrast, African Americans (or blacks in general) were identified with the foolish, the unthinking, the unreasoning, the brutish, at any rate, with the less than fully human — what Kant, borrowing from David Hume, had termed "*das Läppische.*" There is a straight line from speculations on human variety in natural history to skin color as a marker of identity. The classifications based on that thinking found a lasting expression in President James Monroe's appeal, made during his famed eastern tour in the summer of 1817, to "a nation, unmixed and complete."[91]

African Americans clearly stood in the way of Monroe's vision, an embarrassment, if not the national sin, and at any rate inconsistent with the principles of the American Revolution. When that revolution was underway, of the total American population of two and a half million, one fifth — 500,000 men, women, and children — was enslaved. Although most slaves lived in the Southern colonies, slavery was also present in the North. Fourteen percent of New York's population was enslaved, eight percent of New Jersey's, and six percent of Rhode Island's. Slaves were regarded as little more than animals, chattel. Slaveholders bought them at markets and kept them as if they were livestock. That the majority of Americans took slavery for granted was made easier by the ubiquity of servitude everywhere, which included whites as well, and the similarities in treatment of slaves and servants.

It was the American Revolution and its emphasis on liberty that had made slavery a problem. Not surprisingly, Monroe's administration coincided with a number of attempts to render America unmixed. For instance, the American Colonization Society (ACS) was formed during this era, largely for the purpose of "the voluntary removal of free blacks— not slaves— beyond the geographic bounds of the United States." For many whites in antebellum America, the national problem was not slavery but, as David Waldstreicher emphasizes, the "freedom vested in a population whose equality they denied."[92] Unbound Africans, Henry Clay held (like Andrew Jackson, Clay was an elected officer of the ACS), were neither slave nor free. This status uncertainty also precluded depictions of them, including on the currency. Put more bluntly, why grace one's symbols of value with what is so clearly devalued? Indeed there was no felt need for depiction on the national currency (or on any other medium) of people whose anticipated embarkation from the shores of America, the Reverend Robert Finley pontificated, "would be celebrated as a jubilee, throughout the civilized world."[93]

Aside from allegorical depictions of African Americans on paper bills from the 1820s

$1, Central Bank of Tennessee, 1855 (courtesy National Numismatic Collection, Smithsonian Institution)

and later, only a single instance is known of an image of a free African American through 1861. The image appeared on a ten-dollar note issued by the Bank of Catasauqua, Pennsylvania, in about 1857, and was probably meant as a political comment on the compromise of 1850.[94] When African Americans did begin to appear on paper money in sizable numbers, they were usually shown as slaves, and on notes issued by Southern banks. These images visually represented the economic foundations of the South, specifically the cotton and sugar cane industry and the slave labor system on which it was built. Demand for depiction of African Americans came about suddenly, so suddenly that printers were caught off guard completely and, having no suitable images in stock, at first simply blackened white faces, recycling earlier images. For instance, a white farm worker from a New York note had his complexion darkened and re-emerged as a slave on a note issued in Virginia. In another instance, a wheat-harvesting scene from a Michigan bank was reworked into a cotton-picking vignette for a bank in South Carolina.

   "Real" African Americans soon began appearing on these notes, though in vignettes

$1, Adrian Insurance Company, Michigan, 1853, wheat-harvesting scene (courtesy National Numismatic Collection, Smithsonian Institution)

$5, Planters Bank, Fairfield, SC, 1855, cotton-picking vignette (courtesy National Numismatic Collection, Smithsonian Institution)

provided by Northern printers and with distinctive slave scenes, that is, in agricultural pursuits, especially in those related to "King Cotton." A good example is a ten-dollar note issued by the Eastern Bank of Alabama, Eufala, in the late 1850s. The image had a lasting impact, for on a fifty-dollar Confederate States note issued in 1861 and dated at Montgomery, Alabama, we also see slaves in a cotton field; on other notes of the time, slaves pick cotton, carry it to market, or load it on a wagon, or on a steamboat for shipment to New Orleans.[95] The latter scene was also used on a five-dollar Confederate note of 1861, the so-called "Indian Princess Note."

While cotton dominates, African Americans were also depicted alone or with other blacks in scenes of cane cutting, as haulers of goods, or as workers on the docks, say of Charleston. However, in each case they were depicted as slaves, for at the time that was the identity of almost every African American, men, women, or children.[96] On occasion, whites and blacks appeared together in a variety of work scenes, though there is never any question about who is in charge. That is true also of scenes that depict signal moments of Southern history, such as the "Sweet Potato Dinner" scene.[97] In order to make the slave system appear not only economically crucial but also in perfect compliance with tradition, classical figures often were imposed on scenes portraying black slaves.[98] Altogether, scenes involving African Americans are the visible expression of the theatricality of everyday life born of the necessary performances of whiteness (by the masters) and blackness (by the slaves). While they might be a fairly realistic statement of the daily life of a particular social group at a particular time, they at the same time tell us much about the white South's unapologetic reliance on the "peculiar institution" of slavery to sustain its way of life.

Southern banks asked for and obtained notes that represented their views of African Americans at a time when anti-slavery agitation was reaching a critical level. As if to deliberately counter the attacks and, in addition, to reinforce Southern convictions, the notes mostly showed blacks as the lovable incompetents, in bondage for their own good, of contemporary white folklore. We may see an Uncle Remus drowsing on a wagon, just letting the time go by, as on a twenty-dollar bill from the Manufacturers Bank of Macon, Georgia. Alternatively, as a variant of this we may see a docile young boy, helping his master sharpen a scythe, on a five-dollar note from the Bank of Hamburg, South Carolina.[99] The

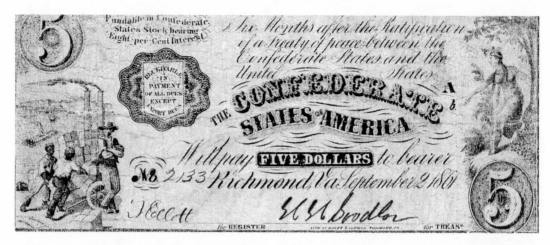

$5, Confederate States of America, 1861, loading cotton on steamboat (courtesy National Numismatic Collection, Smithsonian Institution)

apotheosis of this trend, which originated locally but was circulating nationally, in all likelihood was reached in a vignette that represents a smiling mother holding a chuckling infant on her shoulder, who in turn holds a branch from a cotton plant — the plaything that enslaves them both. Issued beginning in 1858, and appearing on bills from half a dozen banks, this vignette has justly been called "the most self-serving image of African Americans" ever to appear.[100]

By the time the notes bearing this vignette were in full circulation, the Civil War was being fought, fought also over whose view of African Americans was correct, whose view would prevail. When the conflict ended four years later, the banks that had been issuing and putting into circulation the notes depicting African Americans were no longer in business. Their notes, decorated with images that would reinforce the "natural" order of things — at least from the standpoint of the social elites of the time — began what Richard Doty describes as the "journey from private money into public memory."[101] A journey into public memory also framed the following cartoon that originally appeared in *Harper's Weekly* in 1862. The cartoon shows a "rebel planter" standing between an African American and a Confederate soldier, saying: "Yes, my Son, you must go to the War. I can't spare Pomp; he cost me Twelve Hundred Dollars, and he might get shot. Besides, you know, you couldn't stoop to work like a field-hand."

As regards the currency, following Northern victory it was on the way to a conformity of design that reflected the increased power of the nation-state. That state had uprooted in a bloody war an institution that was at the same time economic, social, and

$50, Bank of the Commonwealth, Virginia, 1858 (courtesy National Numismatic Collection, Smithsonian Institution)

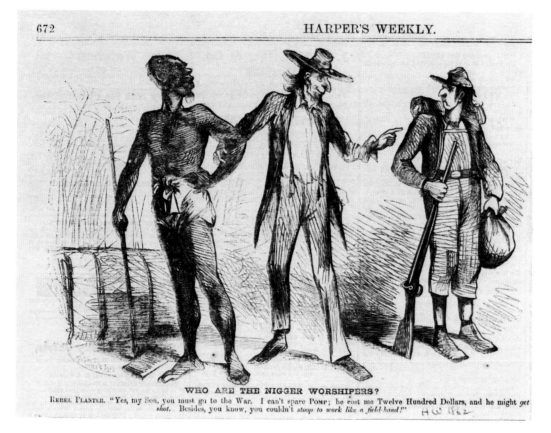

672   HARPER'S WEEKLY.

WHO ARE THE NIGGER WORSHIPERS?

REBEL PLANTER. "Yes, my Son, you must go to the War. I can't spare POMP; he cost me **Twelve Hundred Dollars**, and he might *get shot*. Besides, you know, you couldn't *stoop to work like a field-hand!*"

"Who are the nigger worshippers?" (cartoon, Civil War era) (Library of Congress, Prints and Photographs Division, LC-USZ62-65333)

racial, and it had no interest to continue to pictorialize it on the currency. For a short time, private companies such as the American Bank Note Co. would jump back into the business of serving customers in the South, and these notes would continue to depict African Americans in the same old way into the early twentieth century. Nevertheless, such orders were rare.

Even rarer were representations of freed African Americans, whose emancipation in 1863 brought up so many anxieties for those who espoused the dominant view that African Americans were pushed out of sight altogether. Thus, the only trace African Americans have left on the currency since the Civil War is through their signatures—in all, four by men and one by a woman.[102]

United States coins are notably different with respect to the representation of persons who are not Caucasian. For instance, there was an "Indian Head" one-cent coin minted 1859–1909. This coin, which was designed by James Barton Longacre, became the "most beloved and typically American" of any coin, possibly because on it America's identification myth was blossoming forth most visibly.[103] From 1907 to 1913, the United States Mint thanks to an initiative by President Theodore Roosevelt put into circulation four "Indian Head" coins. These coins were the Eagle ($10), designed by Augustus Saint-Gaudens in 1907, the Quarter ($2½) and Half Eagles ($5), designed by Bela Lyon Pratt in 1908, and the "Indian Head" or "Buffalo" nickel. The latter was created by James Earle Fraser in 1913, and so

Slavery scenes on 1872 South Carolina Revenue Bond Scrip (courtesy National Numismatic Collection, Smithsonian Institution)

called because it had a buffalo on one side and the head of a Native American on the other. Obviously, all portraits are in the tradition of the "true Native American," that is, incorporating the headdress. This, according to contemporary critics, was to give the coins a genuinely "nationalistic character."[104]

The buffalo nickel was minted through 1938, when the Jefferson nickel replaced it.[105] A more recent coin even carries a portrait of a Native American woman. Introduced in 2000, this one-dollar coin, which is gold in color and has a smooth edge, features a portrait of Sacagawea, the Shoshone Indian woman who, with her infant son, allegedly guided Lewis and Clark to the west. Meriwether Lewis and William Clark led the first national expedition across the North American continent. The introduction of the coin coincided with the bicentennial of the expedition. Not surprisingly, an American eagle was placed on the reverse of the new coin. The effect of this strategy is obvious. As in the case of the Indian-head cent or the buffalo nickel — or else of the 1929 half eagle, a five-dollar coin with the head of an Indian brave on one side and the American eagle on the other, not to mention notes featuring Ta-to-ka-in-yan-ka and other Native Americans — it reflects the subjugation of Native Americans as a colonized people.[106]

A rather more ambiguous strategy is connected with two fifty-cent commemorative silver coins produced during the late 1940s and early 1950s, which paid homage to two African Americans, Booker T. Washington and George Washington Carver. On one hand, the coins suggest that African Americans were at least beginning to receive a measure of their due on the national currency, maybe in anticipation of their progress in wider matters. On the other hand, the promotion of the Carver-Washington coin at the height of the Cold War was done expressly in order to "oppose the spread of communism among Negroes in the interest of national defense." When the real purpose of the coin issue became known, it not only cast a long-

Left: Sacagawea one-dollar coin, obverse
Right: Sacagawea one-dollar coin, reverse

lasting pall over it but also brought commemorative coinage to a halt until the Bicentennial of 1976.[107] Rehabilitation of the commemorative coin brought in its wake the Black Revolutionary War Patriots silver dollar in 1998, which carries a portrait of Crispus Attucks (1723–1770) on the obverse.

Left: Anthony dollar, obverse *Right:* Anthony dollar, reverse

In 1979, a one-dollar coin was issued to honor the noted feminist leader Susan B. Anthony. Ms Anthony's portrait was put in place of General Dwight D. Eisenhower's, which had been chosen by the incoming Nixon administration in 1971. Minting of the "Anthony" dollar began in 1979, a year after Jimmy Carter's election to the Presidency, but despite heroic efforts on the part of the United States Mint, it was never widely accepted by the public. I myself have never seen one. Alternatively, if I have, like most Americans I might have mistaken it for a quarter because of its size.

Having examined quite a motley array of paper dollars (as well as a few coins), we can clearly see how design indeed occupies a central place as a cultural intermediary at the interface between production and consumption. Design, du Gay and his associates point out, "produces meaning through embodying artifacts with symbolic significance; it gives functional artifacts a symbolic form."[108] However, currency design is effective only as long as the images and symbols on the notes are not questioned. Since the Civil War, these images and symbols have belonged to a government-issued depiction of the national self. Federal presence has been invoked to help resolve all kinds of ambiguities of value and identity. Additionally, federal presence has helped shape (and was shaped by) the dominant ideologies of the time. The "meanings" of and representations on the currency thus cannot be separated from the formative factors of American culture such as race, class, gender, ethnicity, and region. These factors have been essential elements in the fabrication of all kinds of nationalistic symbols and in the performance of nationalism since the American Revolution. This matter will concern us in the following chapter, in which we will look at how the national narratives that are conveyed on dollar bills relate to other cultural practices, especially to the ones that Eric Hobsbawm has famously labeled "invented traditions."

FOUR

The Paper Dollar and the National Symbolic

> [Nations] all bear some marks of their origin. The circumstances which accompanied their birth and contributed to their development affect the whole term of their being. [...] If we were able to go back to the elements of states, and to examine the oldest monuments of their history, I doubt not that we should discover in them the primal cause of the prejudices, the habits, the ruling passions, and, in short, of all that constitutes what is called the national character.
> — Alexis de Tocqueville, *Democracy in America* 23.

Introduction

From the colonial period, experiments with paper money in America were embroiled in struggles over political sovereignty. Following Independence, the new nation, mindful of the disaster with the Continentals, instituted policies that betrayed a deeply felt suspicion about paper money. This fear would linger on until the Civil War, driving monetary debates and policies. Thereafter, the circulation of paper money and the formation of the modern state were largely co-extensive, and the paper dollar could become a singular force in the formation and preservation of America's national political consciousness. For unlike other forces, a national currency enables citizens "not just to communicate economically but also to think in a similar way and to situate themselves in a common fashion within the national community."[1]

A sense of belonging to a national community is transmitted primarily through the images on the currency. These images have been said to constitute "the most universal form of public imagery."[2] The United States Treasury in particular has "never stinted in their use of nationalistic images on coins, paper currency [...] and various certificates." The same is true of the United States Post Office, though the paper currency is special. "With larger surfaces at their disposal, the designers of paper currency have managed to make the dollar bill and other denominations *virtual anthologies of nationalistic images*." Analyzing this imagery, especially its changes over time, therefore would contribute a great deal to a "biography of American civil religion."[3] An analysis of this kind would also have to consider the psychological impact, subliminal or otherwise, upon the American public of constant exposure to this barrage of symbols on artifacts they must handle daily. Indeed it was through the mass immersion in nationalistic iconography that the inhabitants already of the young republic "molded their identity and perceived their destiny."[4] In the section to follow, the performance of the paper dollar will be contextualized and evaluated within the symbolic consolidation of the United States.

One Nation, Indivisible?

When the Colony of Massachusetts issued its famous bills of credit, the main "art" consisted of the colony's seal, which featured a human figure wearing only a loincloth and holding a bow and arrow. Over its head is a cartoon speech balloon that says, "Come over & help us." The phrase, which was taken from the Bible (*Acts* 16:9), recalls Paul's vision of a Macedonian imploring him to help his people by spreading the gospel. In its new context it is of course ambiguous at best. Help whom? The colony? How? Or, if it is the human figure — presumed to be a Native American — saying it, help *them*? And if so, do what? Rebel? Or suffer even more from the hands of the Europeans? The issue of sovereignty is not resolved on these notes, nor was it resolved on later notes, such as the first Maryland issue of 1770, which has been described as "the earliest governmental use of the 'dollar' as an official unit of monetary value in the world."[5] Ironically, the issue consisted of indented bills in dollar denominations but were payable at the rate of 4s and 6p in London. Thus it was not until the time of the American Revolution that there was a significant shift in the look and feel of paper money. Thereafter, images on paper money came to reflect the ideas and identities about political sovereignty that were then prevalent. As one commentator put it, the first dollar notes instantly became the "earliest symbols of the United States."[6] The word "symbols" is important here, warning us not to read the images on the notes in terms of what the period actually was, but in terms of what those who produced them thought it was. If they thought that the American state of mind during the revolutionary era was homogeneous, this was simply not the case. Of course, there was rebelliousness, but the range of moods was much more diverse, including loyalism, but also indifference to the cause of the revolutionaries.

The conflicting semantic networks shaping colonial America during the first year of the revolution are evident from the Massachusetts issue of August 1775, for which Paul Revere engraved on the back plate the motto "Issued in defence of American Liberty." The note, which was still in shillings denomination, shows a Minute Man holding a copy of Magna Carta in one hand and a sword in the other, which is why among collectors it is known as "sword in hand" money. Of particular interest is the way Revere would use this figure to reflect and foster the hardening of colonial sentiment in favor of inde-

$6 Maryland Assembly, indented bill, 1770, face, 6.5 × 11.5 cm (courtesy of the Massachusetts Historical Society)

pendence. The scroll carried by the patriot on the 1775 note says "Magna Charta." This man is fighting to defend the vested liberties of *all* English people, including those in the American colonies. A year later the notes still carried the motto "Issued in defence of American Liberty," retaining the British spelling of the word "defense." However, the words on the scroll are different. They now call for "INDEPENDANCE" (sic!). Colonial sentiment, Richard Doty concludes, had changed considerably between the first and second issue of these notes, whose function was now clearly to foster popular support for seeking liberty as Americans.[7]

In order to foster commitment to the idea of popular sovereignty, anti–British propaganda was produced in mass quantities in numerous forms. Pamphlets, newspaper articles, editorials, broadsides, songs and poems, cartoons and speeches, sermons, letters, and plays were utilized. Many of those committed to independence quickly came to see the currency as an important tool that could further its realization. Indeed, there are numerous other examples of using paper money in order to communicate sentiments in a memorable fashion. For instance, a Maryland note produced by Thomas Sparrow and Frederick Green and issued without the British government's approval right after the battle of Lexington in July 1775 shows Britannia receiving a congressional petition from a female figure representing America. America is shown trampling on a scroll marked "SLAVERY" and holding a liberty cap in front of American troops. Conversely, George III is depicted trampling on the Magna Carta as he is about to set fire to the city of Annapolis under attack by a British fleet.[8]

Using paper money to finance a war was something Americans had been used to. However, using it for the war of independence was different at least on two counts: first, because unlike on previous occasions, this time England was definitely not going to back the currency. Second, because again unlike on previous occasions, this war was not going to be limited and short-lived. Ideology therefore took the place of monetary and fiscal security. As a delegate to the Continental Congress expressed the point, a paper currency backed by all the colonies together would form "a new bond of union to the associated colonies."[9] Curiously, though, at the time no one really knew what proportion of the whole each colony would have to pay. In May 1775, the Second Continental Congress convened, in secret session, agreeing upon (but not resolving until June 22) the issuance of $3 million of a new currency. The currency became known as "Continental Currency."

Benjamin Franklin designed the new currency. He began by rejecting British numismatic conventions, which, by representing the nation in the person of the king, the royal coat of arms, and a female allegory, Britannia, only perpetuated "the dull story that everybody knows, and what it would have been no Loss to mankind if nobody had ever known." Far more useful, Franklin wrote, would be to include on the currency "Some important proverb [...] some pious moral, prudential or oeconomical Precept, the frequent inculcation of which by seeing it every time one receives a Piece of Money, might make an Impression upon the Mind especially of young Persons, and tend to regulate the Conduct."[10] For motifs, Franklin turned to books in his own library — Joachim Camerarius's *Symbolorum ac Emblematum Ethico-Politicorum*, Diego Saavedra's *Idea principis Christiano-Politici Symbolis*, Weigels's *Emblematum Repositorium*. From these venerable tomes, Franklin selected several emblems that visually expressed discrete moral and political lessons.[11]

Although Franklin's designs represented some of the era's most ambitious republican propaganda, the initial issue was not a success iconographically. For instance, on the $3 bill (and on a variety of notes issued by the colonies) the main "art" consisted of an engraving showing an eagle (representing England) fighting a subdued-looking crane (representing the colonies). If the motif was not particularly encouraging, the motto was probably even less so: "*Exitus in dubio est*" ("The issue is in doubt" or "The event is uncertain"). Clearly, the motto was directed to the outcome of the War of Independence, which was indeed most uncertain, but it may also be said to include the value of the currency, which was then backed by an utterly inconsequential government power.

More uplift was provided by the motto on the $1 note, which read "*DEPRESSA RESUR-GIT*" ("Though oppressed it rises"), though neither the motto nor the note was able to stem the fiscal crisis the country was sliding into. Only two years after their adoption, ten dollars in Continental Currency bills were worth only one Spanish silver dollar; by 1781, the ratio was forty-to-one. At that point, it cost more to print than they would buy. Consequently, Jonathan Carver observed in *Travels in America*, the "Congress paper dollars are now used for papering rooms, lighting pipes, and other conveniences." The depreciation of the notes is also perpetuated in the colorful American colloquialism "not worth a Continental"—a synonym for utter worthlessness.[12]

The experience with the Continentals highlights an important point: a national currency may foster a sense of nationhood only to the extent that it is managed in accordance with the wishes of the nation. Indeed, the attempt to build national identity at the expense of economic and political stability—the production of symbolic rather than real capital—soured many Americans on the idea of a paper currency for generations to come. (Even a rebellion—Shays's Rebellion of 1786—has been connected with the problem of paper money.) James Madison, too, was disgusted, calling the current "rage for paper money" an "improper or wicked project," which only a strong federal government and a country run on republican (that is, on representational) principles would be likely to avoid.[13]

The young nation's coins are interesting in their own right, as at first they were overwhelmed by the sheer quantity of foreign coinage. Indeed, for American nationalists, the profusion of foreign coins was evidence that the United States was not fully a nation. Thomas Jefferson for instance declared, "coinage is peculiarly an attribute of sovereignty. To transfer its exercise into another country is to submit to another Sovereign."[14] Words of this kind reveal an unpleasant truth: the currency of the young republic was subordinate, derivative, one that took its cue from the currencies of other nations and empires. Was it in order to compensate for the monetary reality that it was attempting to find its iconographic and artistic identity through the imagery?

$1, Continental Currency, May 10, 1775, face, motto "**DEPRESSA RESURGIT**" ("Though oppressed it rises") (American Numismatic Association Money Museum)

The Confederatio copper of 1785 in particular has been said to be "the most iconographi-cally-loaded coin in early American history." On its obverse, we see the goddess Diana leaning against an altar, trampling on a crown. On the altar is a helmet that resembles a liberty cap, the *pileus*. Around the goddess, there is the legend, "*AMERICA INIMICA TYRANNIS*," "America, enemy of tyrants." An Englishman struck the coin.

Alexander Hamilton too was concerned about the currency. His "Report on the Estab-lishment of a Mint," delivered to Congress in January 1791, had set the agenda when it stated that, "the devices of the coins are far from being a matter of indifference, as they may be made the vehicles of useful impressions."[15] The "useful impressions" Hamilton and his fellow Federalists had in mind would include a portrait of George Washington on the coins' reverses.[16] Republicans, especially in the House of Representatives argued for motives that emphasized the union of separate states and that used an image of the Goddess of Lib-erty. They recoiled from designs that bore an "image of the Prince." President Washing-ton, mindful of Republican sensitivities, let it be known that he considered patterns with his head on them as too monarchical.

Washington's position may have been "politically correct" both in rejecting the past experience with English coins bearing the King's image and in wishing to display the code of conduct of the ancient Roman republic (depictions of Liberty had also appeared on Roman coins). However, it was neither what the elites had envisaged nor did it in the least diminish the popularity of himself as the nation's founder and savior. In fact, Washington's image continued to appear on objects of all descriptions, from works of art to common household crockery—and on bank notes.[17] In a sense, the obsession with Washington's

Washington inspecting the first money coined by the United States (Library of Congress, Prints and Photographs Division, LC-USZ62-75580)

face — the sentimental look — would replace the monarchical obsession with the king's body, helping citizens to participate in the exchange of federal feeling. "Seeing Washington's face," David Waldstreicher explains, "impressed in his audience's character the sentiments of patriotic union they saw in the hero of the Revolution."[18]

On the coinage, such sentiments were to be impressed by different means. The Coinage Act of April 2, 1792, stipulated that all United States coins were to have one side devoted to a representation of Liberty, and the other side, of an eagle, each suggesting that national authority was vested in "the people" rather than in a glorified individual. Furthermore, iconographic details like the liberty cap, representations of Liberty, and legends like "America, enemy of tyrants" indicate that inspiration for creating a new monetary system had indeed come from the Roman republic. The choice of symbols would create a clear divide between the new national identity as outlined by the Constitution and what had gone before, economically, politically, and culturally. Through their daily usage, these images would at the same time convey patriotic messages and materially signify its stability and economic strength.[19]

The combined experience of the Continentals and the Constitutional prohibition against issuance of paper currency on every level of government put the paper dollar on a different trajectory. Hamilton handled the paper debt by initiating legislation that redeemed the worthless Continentals at a magnanimous rate of 100 to 11. He also wanted the federal government to assume all state wartime debts as well. The project was so unpopular with some states that it took a great deal of compromising for it to be realized — it has been suggested that Virginia only agreed to the idea once the nation's new capital had been established on land inside its borders.[20] Other than that, the United States government stayed away from paper money for over a half century. As a result, the paper dollar did not come to be used as a federal means to educate the public, let alone as a medium for exerting control and direction, until after the Civil War. Until then, private commercial banks in every state took over the paper money business.

The insufficiency of the national interest deeply worried the nation's first President, who in his Farewell Address of 1796 explicitly pointed to "internal and external enemies" (meaning radical democrats who had taken their inspiration from France, as well as France itself). Washington therefore admonished his "friends and fellow-citizens" that it was "of infinite moment that you should properly estimate the immense value of your national union to your collective and individual happiness." Thus, he continues, "the name American, which belongs to you in your national capacity, must always exalt the just pride of patriotism more than any other appellation derived from local discriminations."[21] This is a glimpse of the Founding Father quite literally inventing a tradition. The Revolutionary War clearly had not forged a nation out of the United States. The states had histories, Jason Goodwin remarks, but "the dates Americans had to remember were mostly recent. Their battles had yet to be glorified in legend." For the present, Americans were rather quarreling among themselves, suspicious of their neighbors' motives, as when Marylanders were suspecting Virginians of wanting boundaries to the Mississippi. "People called themselves New Yorkers or Carolinians first; Columbians second; and seldom Americans."[22] A generation later, the tensions between local and regional interests, and the national interest were as unresolved as they ever had been. They also came to the attention of foreign observers such as Tocqueville, who wrote that the people's allegiance was "still directed to the state and has not passed over to the Union."[23]

The form of allegiance feared by Washington and observed by Tocqueville derives from the love of, and loyalty towards, one's immediate environs, hence from a more local attachment.[24] For Robert Crunden, the entire period of local culture lasted from the beginnings of European settlements to about 1815. The Revolution and its aftermath therefore "did much to forge a sense of national unity *at the top*, but few people were aware of themselves as anything more than citizens of Newport or Charleston on a daily basis."[25] The period of local culture or localism was followed by one characterized by sectionalism. It lasted from about 1815 until the inauguration of Theodore Roosevelt in 1901. At first there was the distinction of the North from the South and West — all taking on political meaning in the larger national context. Following the Civil War, sectionalism took the form of Northern hegemony, with Northern culture gradually metamorphosing into national culture. Beginning with Theodore Roosevelt's presidency, the United States could finally "take itself for granted and seek some place for itself in the community of nations," culturally, as well as politically, economically, and militarily.[26]

As stated, at the time of the American Revolution, a sense of national unity was forged essentially at the top. William Hedges's claim that the United States of America is different from most other nations in that it does not have a tribal past; its past is literally the word, is further evidence of this. The word, that is the famous proposition contained in the Declaration of Independence and in the United States Constitution, America's "Scripture." So in order to become an American (and at least in theory anyone can become an American), one needs to assent to this secular Bible, and thus to the myth of the republic, created roughly between 1765 and 1800. Its conceivers liked to believe that it was actually built on universally valid assumptions. It speaks of the United States as the land of liberty, buttressed by a disinterested patriotism and rationally contrived political institutions. In fact, the myth was far from universal, but was rather the cultural product of a property-owning society settling east of the Appalachians in the thirteen original colonies. In many respects, Hedges concludes, the myth of the republic was "an Americanized version of [...] the ideology of the English Whigs, which had been widely circulated in the colonies."[27]

The myth of the republic involved the colonists' traditional jealousy of their rights as Englishmen, derived ultimately from Magna Carta. Thus, it told of English freedoms having fled England to seek refuge in the New World, as well as of the patriots being called upon to resist tyrannical power reaching across the Atlantic Ocean to enslave them. Typically, for Thomas Jefferson the Declaration of Independence was a "signal" calling upon humanity to break the "chains" under which humans had lived "in monkish ignorance and superstition for so long."[28] Once independence was won, the original liberties acquired a new dimension: the government's role was no longer to secure people's rights as Englishmen but their natural rights as human beings. The Constitution, it was hoped, by enshrining these liberties would permanently secure them in a "more perfect union." Of course, the vanity of the hope was soon exposed, and the myth's falsity brought to light by the behavior of the politicians themselves, by factionalism, commercialism, westward expansion, the War against Mexico, know-nothingism, and racism.

Even Abraham Lincoln at one time would have welcomed a convenient place to send black slaves to, though eventually he freed them.[29] Lincoln's commissioner of emigration, the Reverend James Mitchell, believed, as did many others that the mere presence of blacks was the cause of war: "Our republican institutions are not adapted to mixed races and classified people. Our institutions require a homogeneous population to rest on as a basis."[30] This is probably enough to put anyone in a rather gloomy mood, which is indeed what happened to a number of American writers, artists, and intellectuals. Three of them —

Hawthorne, Melville, and Poe—later became known as the "triumvirate of darkness," in Harry Levin's apt term. "Where the voice of the majority is by definition affirmative," Melville, disgusted by the falsity in the myth of the republic, wrote to Hawthorne, "the spirit of independence is likeliest to manifest itself by employing the negative: by saying *no* in thunder."[31]

Yet notwithstanding the naysayers, the myth itself, based as it was on a revolutionary rhetoric articulating republican aspirations, became official American doctrine. "Without the myth to begin with," Hedges claims, "there would have been no United States."[32] Without the myth to begin with, there also would not have been attempts to create a standardized national language, which its champions saw as a crucial task in the creation of a new national political community. Noah Webster, the "schoolmaster of America," set out to define an American language, declaring, in the preface to his *Spelling Book* of 1783, "America must be as independent in literature as she is in politics."[33] Characteristically, Webster spoke out both against classical philology and the English tradition of linguistics, much as he also tried to set down rules for a uniform American pronunciation. By 1789 he demanded that independence must also be achieved through "order and regularity" in spelling. Webster lived up to his own demand with the *Dictionary* of 1828, which to this day survives in *Webster's Third International Dictionary*.

Also without the myth of the republic to begin with, Ralph Waldo Emerson hardly would have said, in his Commencement Address of August 31, 1837, delivered to the Phi Beta Kappa Society of Harvard University, "We have listened too long to the courtly muses of Europe."[34] Moreover, what if not the myth of the republic underlies the declaration, in the *Democratic Review* of 1839, "Our national birth was the beginning of a new history [...] which separates us from the past and connects us with the future only."[35] Ordinary people too found avenues in which they could work out what they meant by "the nation." Fourth of July celebrations became particularly popular for the preservation of the legacy of the American Revolution. There were parades, but also ballads, broadsides, orations, and newspaper reportage through which, David Waldstreicher has shown, Americans literally performed and thought themselves into nationhood. A particularly impressive set of performances can be found in and surrounding the historic Lewis and Clark expedition, which thanks to the bicentennial has received a lot of excitement.

However, by commemorating the expedition as an event of national importance, many facts have been simply glossed over, in particular the fact that the newly acquired territories were actually becoming colonies, with white Americans defining themselves as the natural and undisputed masters of the indigenous population.[36] It was of little effect that in 1791 Jefferson wrote to William Short that, "If there be one principle more deeply rooted than any other in the mind of every American, it is that we should have nothing to do with conquest."[37] Only a few years before, Jefferson had guided into law the Northwest Ordinance. Although it has often been ignored, the Ordinance of 1787 essentially is the clearest and most compelling picture of union in the period, guaranteeing the spread of republican government across the continent. Drafted by Nathan Dane of Massachusetts, the Ordinance and its provisions mandate and orchestrate the appropriate stages of development from wilderness to territory to something like colonized status to full equality in statehood. Political boundaries and land divisions thus were the first expression in material form of federal presence.

In Robert Ferguson's estimation, the Northwest Ordinance was "the cardinal achievement of Congress in the first ten years of the Republic."[38] A different kind of achievement was to draw the attention of Americans to the newly opened lands in a concerted effort to populate them. By the time of the war against England, in 1812, pictures of what was happening behind the Appalachians and over the Ohio River were gracing the notes from the private commercial banks that had sprung up in the new states and territories. The journals of the Lewis and Clark expedition likewise opened up the rich possibilities of these happy landscapes, to a reading public. Nicholas Biddle, who saw the first edition into print, in 1814, made this possible. Biddle himself appears to have learned a great deal from the journals. Three years later, he was part of a committee of Philadelphia bankers who glowingly described the United States as a banker's heaven. The gates to that heaven had been pushed open in 1803, when the First Bank of the United States financed the Louisiana Purchase, the biggest real estate deal in the history of the country, and at four cents an acre a real bargain. Without the bank, the money would not have come forward, the United States would be a different country altogether, and Lewis and Clark would never have set out on their historic journey across the continent.

When Lewis and Clark did set out on their journey, the rituals, celebrations, and public displays taking place throughout its course were starkly a matter of command and control. The national flag came to serve as a symbol that would simply and emphatically articulate at the same time the national pride of the young republic and the newly acquired sovereignty of the United States government over the native population and their lands. As the expedition "proceeded on" across the vast expanses of the American West, Lewis and Clark would assign place names, lots of them. Towards the end of July 1805, the men reached the Three Forks of the Missouri River, respectively naming them Jefferson, Madison, and Gallatin Rivers. Lewis and Clark's names for the three forks have survived. Of course, the rivers (as well as other sites) the Corps of Discovery encountered had not previously been nameless. Name giving by the Corps therefore constitutes an act of colonization in which the land is symbolically appropriated. Yet by picking Jefferson, Madison, and Gallatin, Lewis and Clark were at the same time honoring and respecting the emergent state to the degree that it embodied the loftiest national principles.[39]

Lewis and Clark were not alone in their faith in the unique virtues and transcendent mission of the Republic. Deeply internalized, this faith was inspiring the hearts and minds of a large number of men and women through the 1840s, though over time distinct differences in racial, class, and regional approaches evolved to its manifestations.[40] These manifestations included hero-worship, appropriate songs, the adoption of nationalistic names, including for the capital city, the observation of holidays, or the enjoyment of paintings, oratory, and printed matter celebrating the republic as a remarkable political achievement and defining its purpose as a nation. Nathaniel Currier's hand-colored lithograph of 1844, *The Presidents of the United States*, is a good example of this faith fueling the creative energies of artists. In this particular artwork, images of American presidents are arranged in a circle around a representation of a signal moment in American history, the signing of the Declaration of Independence, thus also quoting Trumbull's original painting.

Fourth of July orations were probably the most popular sites for celebrating the republic and defining its purpose, though in the early 1800s they were also a form of electioneering. As David Waldstreicher found, these orations "brought party workers together, identified the candidates, and informed voters about the issues, whether the voters actually attended or simply read the accounts in the newspapers."[41] Fourth of July orations were secular sermons. Regardless of whether the celebrations were staged by Federalists or by Republicans (who adopted the formers' methods), the orations were directed to their audiences in the

Nathaniel Currier, *The Presidents of the United States,* hand-colored lithograph, 1844 (Library of Congress, Prints & Photographs Division.)

same manner that the protestant clergy directed religious sermons to the community. In each instance, the oration's tenor was the renewal of the nation's covenant with God, and the country's model character, which would show the path to salvation to humankind in general. Typically, on July 4, 1800, an orator announced, "the cause of democracy is the cause of God."[42] Also typically, on July 4, 1823, James Knowles declared that God had chosen America as his instrument in the political and moral regeneration of the world. Typically again, in 1830 William E. Channing ranted that America was absolutely new and necessary. Thus on no account must it become a "mere repetition" of the Old World.[43] What we sense in all these pronouncements (and there were many more) is the conviction that Americans were a new and special breed, and that the political union they had fashioned was beyond the abilities of decadent Europeans, superstitious Roman Catholics, ignorant heathens, or colored races to imitate. God had created America and called her to establish democracy throughout the world. Americans were to teach inferior peoples the ways of Christian America.

With the passing of the revolutionary generation and the living memory of the early heroic struggles, a new phase in the biography of American nationalism set in. The deaths both of John Adams and of Thomas Jefferson on July 4, 1826, are truly symbolic in this context. By the late 1820s, Gordon Wood suggests, Americans understood the Founders less as men than as symbols, to be deployed amid flags and speeches on July Fourth and then forgotten on the fifth. Such usage was not unknown to Jefferson himself, who shortly before he passed away complained about being "left alone amidst a new generation whom we know not, and who know not us."[44] Alexander Hamilton had died in 1804, mortally wounded in the duel with Aaron Burr. Had he lived, surely he too would have felt profoundly alienated from the United States at the dawn of the age of Jackson. He would have understood Jackson's war against the Second Bank of the United States as the ultimate gesture of anti–Hamiltonianism, a radical dismissal of the idea that a national bank, along with other instruments such as the national debt and taxation, be used to making the United States capable of standing up to the great European powers of the time.

With the demise of the Second Bank, symbols of economic nationalism — the eagle, the shield, the nation's seal, and others— disappeared from the currency, though a number of national figures were used for notes issued by private banks.[45] Washington of course was everywhere, as were Jefferson and Franklin. Presumably, their presence somehow suggested that the notes were as trustworthy as they had been. Other countenances to grace the notes were those of the Marquis de Lafayette, of William Penn, Alexander Hamilton, Andrew Jackson, Zachary Taylor, DeWitt Clinton, James Polk, Franklin Pierce, James Buchanan, Lawrence Kearney, and as for Southerners, John C. Calhoun. If the selection strikes us as somewhat unusual, let us remember that portraits were used because they were available in a form suitable for the notes. The creation of a master design took a great deal of effort, Richard Doty explains, "and printers had a natural disinclination to expend efforts on more images when decent ones already existed."[46] Hence, the appearance of DeWitt Clinton at a time when few people would remember precisely what he had done — he was governor of New York when the Erie Canal was opened in 1825, and had unsuccessfully run for president in 1812. Hence also, there were portraits even of a few actual, living Native Americans, a Mohawk chief on notes from a New York bank, and a "nameless, but unquestionably real" Indian on several bills from a Vermont bank.[47]

Also to appear on American paper money before the Civil War were scenes of national remembrance. On occasion, they would make a connection with the location of a bank, as with a note issued by a bank in Norfolk, Virginia, which showed the ruins of nearby Jamestown, or another note from a Philadelphia bank, which depicted the signing of the Declaration of Independence. The Monmouth Bank of Freehold, New Jersey, chose the Battle of Monmouth, thus commemorating Washington's victory over the British under Sir Henry Clinton. Also celebrated was the Battle of Lexington, on a note from a bank in Georgia. Later history likewise received its due, especially the War of 1812, with the battles of Lake Erie and New Orleans becoming bankers' favorites. However, history was then not narrowly understood as national history, as among the almost fifty vignettes representing historical events and found on notes from private banks there are curiosities such as Wilhelm Tell's marksmanship, printed for the Western Bank of Philadelphia in the early 1830s. These notes, with inscriptions in German, were identifiably regional, characteristic of the civic isolation the Pennsylvania Germans were pursuing during the period between the Revolution and the Civil War. Their ethos— summarized by Steven Nolt in terms of regarding "true liberty [...] as freedom from intrusive agents to change"—fostered maintenance of the German language as a means of transmitting their folk wisdom. At the same time, it allowed them to consider themselves loyal Americans, but precisely because they were counting on the republic to guarantee their right to pursue and perpetuate their vision of freedom from coercion.[48]

Other constituencies would express loyalty to the young nation with the help of scenes involving ordinary citizens rather than national icons. An example cited by Richard Doty is a five-dollar bill from the Central Bank of Nashville, Tennessee, which depicts the return of a veteran from the recent war against Mexico. An image of General Washington appears at the opposite corner, stretching his hand toward the homecoming scene, as if he were blessing it, enfolding it in the ongoing American experience, the peaceable kingdom.[49] The Tennesseans, like new Westerners in general, had good reasons for their assertive celebration of nationhood. They knew that easterners viewed the volatile frontier with varying degrees of pride and worry, thanks to backcountry tax revolts, Indian wars, separatist movements, and the disloyalties of the likes of James Wilkinson and Aaron Burr. Westerners would often go out of their way to distance themselves publicly from separationists and conspirators. (In 1807, Nashville residents burned an effigy of Burr.) While certainly attuned to local partisanship, some of these western notes—legitimate and illegitimate ones alike— seem particularly designed for eastern consumption.

By mid-century, Southern banks had found a pictorial language of their own. Increasingly, events depicted on their notes were "Southern" rather than "national." A note from Charleston, South Carolina, depicted a dramatic rescue of American prisoners that had taken place in the state during the War of Independence. Other banks put on their notes "native sons," such as Generals Daniel Morgan and Andrew Pickens. A later note carried a portrait of George M. Troup, a former governor of Georgia and a leading advocate of states' rights. Southern sectionalism became even more pronounced when John C. Calhoun was chosen for the currency. His portrait, which appeared on dozens of notes issued throughout the entire South, was sending a clear message across the Mason-Dixon Line. Overall, this type of numismatic localism or sectionalism can be considered an epiphenomenon of the "dismemberment of the Union and the beginning of the Civil War."[50]

Though one would expect an increase in "Southern" imagery once the war was under way, this was not the case. The image, on an 1862 note from the Commercial Bank of Richmond, Virginia, of a Confederate soldier with battle flag, defending Southern womanhood from Yankee depredations, was an exception rather than the rule. One reason, Doty explains,

$100, Confederate States of America, 1862, at left John C. Calhoun (courtesy of the National Numismatic Collection, Smithsonian Institution.)

is that it "took *time* to create new images, and time was precisely what Southern bankers and their customers did not have."[51] Some patriotic images were indeed created in the South, but scenes of Southern heroism were to be found rather on notes from Southern states or from the Confederate government. Yet even among these notes, a great many were designed not so much to celebrate the South's white heroes as to validate a system that held blacks in perpetual slavery.[52]

The situation was somewhat different in the North, where patriotic images were much easier to obtain, at least for those willing to pay for them. The Merchants' Bank of Trenton, New Jersey, instantly came forth with an image of the North's first military leader, Winfield Scott. The bank also issued a note with an image of Abraham Lincoln, though in a much less central position — as if the relative difference was a measure of the proportionate confidence people had in their leaders. Throughout the North, patriotic images prevailed on the currency, though few notes would refer to what was actually taking place. There are a few images of Union soldiers at rest, but no image has been found of them in action, possibly because such scenes would be altogether too graphic for an audience that still considered itself genteel.

Notes issued in the South also avoided graphic scenes of violence. Typical is a Confederate note that shows, at left, Confederate soldiers at guard, an image of Lucy Holcombe Pickens, wife of the governor of South Carolina, at center, and George W. Randolph, military hero, politician, and diplomat, at right. The note was issued in 1862. Two years later, Southern nationalism peaked, and ended, with a five-hundred dollar note featuring both the Great Seal of the Confederacy and a portrait of Thomas "Stonewall" Jackson. None of the products of the Union government, Doty claims, "came close to the quiet fervor of this design."[53] The reason for this is simple. The Union, when it returned to the paper money business, had no printing facility of its own. Thus, it had to rely on companies that had been supplying the private banks. These companies, like the American Bank Note Company, at first simply "recycled" what they had in stock. Very few images were actually created for the occasion. Among them were a portrait of Abraham Lincoln (the one engraved by Burt), an image of the Statue of Freedom (from the Capitol Dome in Washington, DC), and a figure of America, complete with sword and the national shield.

There had been countervailing tendencies to sectionalism in the antebellum period, for example in the mythologies that were expected to overcome, through a symbolic representation of history, the antagonisms that were threatening to tear apart the social fabric. Among the earliest events to become mythologized were the foundation of Massachusetts Colony and the landing of the Pilgrims at Plymouth Rock. Each event was seen as an act of God's providence. Tellingly, in 1845 Charles A. Goodrich wrote in *The Child's History of the United States*, that the people "prayed much, and still trusted in God. They had come to America to serve Him; and they believed, that He would not forsake them. And He did not forsake them."[54] The glorification of the Pilgrims found a lasting expression also in Peter Frederick Rothermel's oil painting of 1854, titled *The Landing of the Pilgrims at Plymouth Rock*. The picture offers a reading of the American people as the second people of Israel, and the foundation of Plymouth as the "New Jerusalem," at the same time as it speaks of persecution and privation in Europe. Its inherent direction, towards America, is emblematic for the new freedom and opportunity, and the rebirth of humans in America.[55]

Other signal moments of American history that were mythologized at the time included the French and Indian wars. Understood as the result of the competition between Britain and France, accounts of the war introduced George Washington as a national hero who was prudent and brave, and could be relied on. Washington's counterpart was the haughty British General Braddock, who by ignoring the advice of the experienced American frontierspeople wantonly lost the battle of Fort Duquesne. "Washington and his troops," J. Olney wrote in 1836, "were the only part of the army that effectually resisted the enemy."[56] Olney's rhetoric, as well as a painting related to the event, contributed greatly to stylizing Washington as the "Father of his Country."[57] It also served to legitimize the Revolution as a political necessity, the combined result of the destructiveness of the colonial powers and the long tradition of American self-defense. Indeed, British politics was seen as the prime cause of uniting the colonies; in Olney's words, British politics gave the people "one heart and one mind, firmly to oppose every invasion of their liberty."[58] If there were ideological controversies, social tensions, or divergent interests, they did not matter. What did matter were the encounters in Lexington and Concord in April 1775, which were used as the beginning of the Revolution, creating the first martyrs. Even the battle of Bunker Hill, which the Americans lost, was reinterpreted as a victory, as British losses had been substantial.

Washington's distinguishing himself at the battles of Trenton in December 1776, and of Princeton in early January, 1777, gave rise to further glorification, again by Olney: "The bold and successful movements of Washington excited the admiration of both Europe and America. Joy and hope now began to revive the drooping spirits of the nation. The people everywhere hailed Washington as the Savior of his country."[59] Clearly, that view of Washington still speaks from Emmanuel Gottlieb Leutze's monumental oil painting *Washington Crossing the Delaware* (1851), in which the hero's apotheosis is evident from his resolute pose, erect, with one leg on the boat's rim. The general's gazing into the distance gives him resolution and optimism, at the same time as it symbolizes America's glorious future, which is underscored by the American flag behind him. There is hardly another picture better known in nineteenth-century America; at one point it even traveled through the country. After the Civil War, *Washington Crossing the Delaware*, which by then had become a public symbol of the strength and glorious future of "these United States," also appeared on the currency, on the $50 National Bank note, though in John Trumbull's more modest rendering.

Emmanuel Gottlieb Leutze, *Washington Crossing the Delaware*, 1851, original size 149 × 255 inches (The Metropolitan Museum of Art, Gift of John Stewart Kennedy, 1897 [97.34] Image © The Metropolitan Museum of Art)

Next to Washington in terms of national import was the Declaration of Independence. Although nineteenth-century historians often saw the event as a war measure in the conflict with Britain, the document was generally seen as the unanimous decision of the members of the Second Continental Congress. The fact that the decision was not reached quite so unanimously was of little account. The signers were worshipped as heroes, all of them, including the reluctant John Dickinson, and they were all looked at as the true representatives of America's exceptional status. In 1859 Charles Goodrich eulogized that "the unusual age to which the signers, *as a body*, attained, was [...] a reward bestowed upon them for their fidelity to their country, and the trust, which they in general reposed in the over-ruling providence of God."[60] Goodrich's rhetoric at the same time points forward to the motto "In God We Trust," which was to materialize only a few years later, and backward to John Trumbull's oil painting *The Declaration of Independence*, which was produced in a series of versions between 1787 and 1820. Indeed the most striking feature of Trumbull's painting is the centrality of the committee responsible for drafting the document. By positioning the committee in this way, Trumbull, who was a direct participant in the Revolutionary War and an aide to George Washington, established the model character of the Founding Fathers, who are representatives neither of themselves as historic persons, nor of their social and economic status, but rather of the collective psyche, standing in for the idea of America, "as a body," in Goodrich's words. Future generations were called upon to continue this idea. Hence, a version of Trumbull's painting was used for the back of the $100 National Bank note, put into circulation in 1863.[61]

Another version, the *Declaration of Independence in Congress*, can be found in the Rotunda of the Capitol building, together with three other paintings by Trumbull that also depict key events during the War of Independence — the *Surrender of Lord Cornwallis*, the

Surrender of Burgoyne, and *General George Washington Resigning his Commission to Congress*. These paintings, which represent the apex of America's desire to commemorate and memorialize the watershed events in American self-definition, had been completed by 1824. For the remaining four panels, which were to illustrate America's history before Independence, four different artists were commissioned, John Vanderlyn (*Landing of Columbus*), William Powell (*Discovery of the Mississippi by De Soto*), Robert Weir (*Embarkation of the Pilgrims*), and John Chapman (*Baptism of Pocahontas*). With the exception of Vanderlyn's *Landing of Columbus*, all artworks were used on the national currency in the post–Civil War years. They were used for good reason, as each visually captures the hegemony of white civilization, which by that time had become America's lasting inheritance.[62]

Invented Traditions and Related Phenomena, Civil War to 1913

The founders had formed a nation in terms of a voluntary association of defiantly individualistic citizens, who had a special sense of their being different from Europe, a transcendent mission and, not to forget, little tolerance for the idea of the state. Yet whatever the founders' wishes and ideals, the pressures of modernization asserted themselves with a force that grew each passing year. The logic of the new economics and technologies, of industrialization and, eventually, of mass immigration, began to be expressed politically through a burgeoning state apparatus. The inevitable outcome was arrived at only after many difficulties, culminating in the Civil War. When it was over, all doubts as to the supremacy of the state were dispelled. Statefulness had become the only acceptable condition for American citizens, while local and regional variants became few and far between.

The outcome of the Civil War also affected the Fourth of July: the defeated Southerners were, understandably, not much interested in continuing to celebrate the holiday, but in the North, too, interest in it declined rapidly. The centennial of the American Revolution of course brought back some of the old enthusiasm, so that there was any number of activities, yet it had no lasting effect. More and more it became an ordinary holiday. What it was supposed to celebrate had become schoolbook knowledge; some of the ideas associated with it — like virtue and equality — appeared antiquated to an ever-greater number of people. In the long run, original heroes, events, and ideals upon which the nation's creed had been grounded, were replaced by new symbols. Unlike earlier symbols like the eagle or the flag, the new symbols would simply declare "identification with the state, and nothing more."[63]

Identification with the state was also promoted by the national currency, which was becoming increasingly homogeneous and exclusive. At the beginning of 1863, Senator John Sherman had proposed that through a national currency, "Government and the people ... would for the first time become inseparably united and consolidated."[64] The monetary reforms of the Civil War era strengthened the state's territoriality *internally*, at the same time as they helped build it *externally*. The new types of notes that emerged dissolved the local and regional spatiality within which the notes from the private commercial banks circulated. The creation of forms of non-convertible money such as the greenbacks led to clear economic boundaries between the nation and the outside world. As a non-redeemable currency was not easily acceptable abroad, its exchange became "one of the more significant ways in which people began to experience the crossing of a national frontier."[65] Given these developments, the currency's cultural work became articulated in two ways: while it was to give the national culture a distinctive cohesiveness and shape, its *identity* as it were, it also was to establish its *difference* from other well-bounded cultures.

Accompanied by increasing government control and banking centralization, currency notes provided "an unparalleled opportunity for officially-sanctioned propaganda, to colour the recipient's view."[66] Senator Sherman's hopeful words that the images emblazoned on the new United States notes would promote "a sentiment of nationality" fully illustrate the degree to which authorities would see them as effective carriers of symbolic messages. With the help of these messages, they were able to at the same educate citizens about their country and endear them to the authorities responsible for issuing the notes.[67] The $5 Demand note of 1861 in particular offered nothing less than "an object lesson in economic and political nationalism."[68] The federal legislation on which the issue was based—"ACT OF JULY 17, 1861"—is set above a portrait of Alexander Hamilton, one of the earliest (and strongest) believers in a federal currency. The oversize obligation on the face—"THE UNITED STATES PROMISE TO PAY THE BEARER ON DEMAND"—was one that Hamilton clearly would have endorsed. This advocate of the unifying power of a national debt also would have agreed with the symbolism of Thomas Crawford's statue *Freedom in War and Peace*, which appears to the left. Originally designed in the 1850s, Liberty here serves as a symbol of national unity: a brooch marked "US" holds her robes in place; the shield in her left hand contains the nation's seal; and the national motto—*E Pluribus Unum*—is wrapped around the statue's base. As a piece of propaganda, the note conveyed a message of *national* unity that was aimed not just at the financiers in the North who were to underwrite the war, but also at the Southern states whose secession had precipitated the carnage.

Another example is the $1 Legal Tender note, which carried a portrait of Salmon P. Chase at left. Beyond the display of institutional narcissism, this feature marked a radical departure from existing practices in its momentous, if symbolic, expansion of federal authority. On pre–Civil War notes, citizens would rarely if ever encounter a representative of national authority. Now, Chase's confident visage and the economic nationalism he stood for circulated widely. Generally on post–Civil War notes, the newly unified interests of nation and a common currency are dominant and exclusive, loud and brash, and no longer

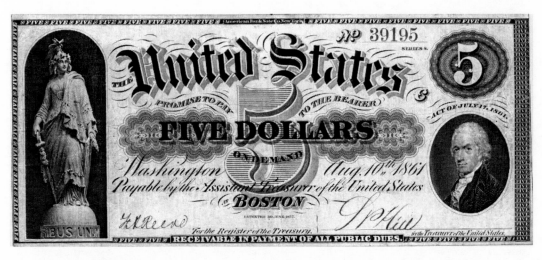

$5 Demand note, 1861, face (American Numismatic Association Money Museum)

sharing the stage with other subject matters.[69] Heroes of the nation's distant and more recent past also abound, Franklin, Washington, and Lincoln — who was alive then, but it had to be demonstrated that he was the representative of the nation, in contrast to Jefferson Davis, whose portrait had come to grace the Confederate currency. In order for people to see the new President, Treasury Secretary Chase selected an engraving that Charles Burt had executed only the previous March. The engraving captured a vibrant Lincoln, who had posed for a Springfield, Illinois, photographer hired by a sculptor needing a reference for the bust he was creating.[70] According to the historian Harold Holzer, Lincoln, who was clad in a "handsome, broadcloth suit, snug high collar, and small, neatly arranged tie [...] looked calm and elegant, though understandably distracted — his faraway stare indicating his thoughts were elsewhere."

The first known use to which the splendid, new Lincoln portrait was put was state war bonds for Pennsylvania and Massachusetts in the summer of 1861. It was through government printing contracts, however, that the portrait was brought to the attention of people on the street. Beginning August 26, 1861, Burt's image was released on the faces of the newly introduced $10 Demand notes. Lincoln was the first President to appear on federal paper money. His selection was a patriotic act, as well as a political one. Impressing the image of the ruler — what Foucault termed the "mark of the Prince" — on money had been done almost from times immemorial, yet it had never been done in the United States. Nor had it ever been done in such vast numbers. More than 2 million of these $10 notes circulated, together with almost twelve million Legal Tender notes. While their repeated use reinforced the notes' acceptance by the public and popular culture, the image also impacted on other media — like engravings, prints, *cartes de visite*, and, not forget, bogus notes. All these uses (and abuses) established an indelible image of Lincoln as the man on the $10 bill.

Also on the new federal paper money were placed events from the nation's history, like the signing of the Declaration of Independence, as well as traditional symbols like the flag and the eagle. The latter came to grace the $100 Legal Tender Note from 1863. It was the first United States note to feature the national bird, and it did so in a majesty and intensity never seen on earlier, private notes or on later, federal ones. The Civil War may be understood as a way of negotiating, through use of organized violence, the different interests between the local and regional, and the national. These differences did not just disappear with Northern victory. Authorities continued to be confronted with the necessity of maintaining legitimacy in the face of various domestic challenges to their rule. Not the least of these challenges were over territory or territorial expansion. This had far-reaching implications on currency design. Territorial expansion depended on state credit, which made paper money a condition of possibility for the fulfillment of America's "manifest destiny," at the same time as the institution of new

Photograph taken by Christopher S. German, 1861 (Library of Congress, Prints and Photographs Division, LC-USZ62-7334)

$100, Legal Tender (United States) note, the "Spread Eagle Note," 1863, face (American Numismatic Association Money Museum)

economies in the newly admitted states or newly acquired territories became an integral aspect of what in fact were acts of colonization. Beginning with the Civil War, the imagery on paper money increasingly was related to a common past and culture, thus serving to instill in citizens a sense of collective identity. Monetary authorities were aided in these initiatives by advances in printing technology, which permitted strikingly detailed imagery to be placed on paper money. Among numismatists in particular, National Bank notes rank "among the most beautiful examples of American currency."[71]

National Bank notes also displayed features that retained for them a measure of the local and regional. A measure, but not too much. They might proclaim that they were from New York, or North Carolina — or the Nevada Territory, in time. But they all looked alike. They all displayed the same scenes, and they were all coming from a single printer by the beginning of the 1880s, the Bureau of Engraving and Printing in Washington, DC. Even when the notes were still contracted out, the national was clearly identified. This had been a wartime expedient. The climate of opinion clearly was such that victory of the Union was anything but self-evident. Hence, people distrusted their money, which for the most part was not backed by anything. The only assets worth talking about were those of the private banks. In order to enlist the private banks in the war effort, the National Bank Act was passed in February 1863. On March 28, Secretary Chase received a letter from his chief clerk, Spencer M. Clark. The letter concerned the role of currency design. The new notes, Clark explained, ideally would use panoramic scenes extending across their faces, each scene providing a patriotic, uplifting imagery. "The advantage of such a currency," the letter said,

> would be that a series properly selected, with their subject titles imprinted on the notes, would tend to teach the masses the prominent periods in our country's history. The laboring man who should receive every Saturday night, a copy of the "Surrender of Burgoyne" for his weekly wages, would soon inquire who General Burgoyne was, and to whom he surrendered. His curiosity would be aroused and he would learn the facts from a fellow laborer or from his employer. The same would be true of other National pictures, and in time many would be taught leading incidents in our country's history, so that they would soon be familiar to those who would never read them in books, teaching them history and imbuing them with a National feeling.[72]

In this passage, the chief clerk not only speaks to anti–British sentiments in his reference to General Burgoyne.[73] He also identifies two central points about the potential power of imagery on paper currency in constructing a collective national identity. First, because of the pervasiveness of paper currency in the kind of market economy that was spreading across the American continent, images on paper money were guaranteed a much larger audience than images carried by other media. Images on paper money thus were particularly effective in conveying messages to the poor and illiterate with whom the state had difficulty communicating through other means such as newspapers or schooling. In contexts in which the infrastructural reach of the state was weak and transportation and communications were difficult, imagery on paper currency often provided the state with the only means to convey symbolic messages to vast numbers of such citizens. Second, images on paper currency were considered particularly effective tools of propaganda because people could not refrain from encountering them in their daily transactions. By providing a frequent reminder to people that they were members of what nationalists considered a common, homogeneous community, the currency could be expected to work as a much more effective vehicle of nationalist messages than flags or anthems.[74]

The Bureau, in its efforts to provide patriotic uplift as well as to create a common history, would deploy on National Bank notes a number of artworks in the Rotunda of the United States Capitol. These included John G. Chapman's *Baptism of Pocahontas* (engraved by Charles Burt for the back of the $20 note), Robert W. Weir's *Embarkation of the Pilgrims* (engraved by W.W. Rice for the back of the $50 note), Peter Frederick Rothermel's *Landing of the Pilgrims* (engraved by Charles Burt for the back of the $1 note), John Trumbull's *Washington Crossing the Delaware* (on the face of the $50 note), and his *Jefferson presenting the Declaration of Independence to John Hancock at the Continental Congress* (on the back of the $100 note). Other signal moments of American history making it onto National Bank notes (and onto the National Gold Bank notes of California) include, in chronological order, Columbus in sight of land; the Landing of Columbus; Presentation of an Indian Princess representing America to the Old World; De Soto discovering the Mississippi in 1541; Sir Walter Raleigh in England in 1585, exhibiting corn and tobacco from America; Franklin capturing electricity with a kite and a key; the Battle of Lexington on April 19, 1775; the surrender of General Burgoyne to General Gates at Saratoga on October 17, 1777; Washington resigning his commission; Commodore Oliver Perry leaving his flagship during the Battle of Lake Erie, September 10, 1813; and General Winfield Scott entering Mexico City in 1847 during the Mexican-American War.

Altogether, the designs sought to create a common history that would transcend not only the history of individual states but also the formal chronological boundaries of the nation itself. That so many of the earlier vignettes predated the ratification of the Constitution testifies to the need to establish a shared history between North and South that avoided the bitter debates over slavery during the antebellum period. This intent is particularly obvious from the most common of all notes—the one-dollar bill—which showed two young women shaking hands before an altar. Titled "Concordia," the vignette provided a rather unsubtle allusion to hopes of unification.[75] The images were a triumph, though taken as a whole, they represent but an imperfect attempt to paste over sectional divisions and set the stage for reconciliation between North and South.

A number of what were considered emblematic moments in American history also appeared on National Bank notes of the second charter period (1882–1902, and issued through 1922)— Benjamin Franklin drawing electricity; the Battle of Lexington; Washington crossing the Delaware; and Commodore Perry on Lake Erie. One image, Burtsch's Landing of the Pilgrims, was re-entered in different form on the $5 note of the third char- ter period (1902–1922, and issued through 1929). Still other images—Columbus in sight of land; and again, the landing of the pilgrims—even appeared on large-size Federal Reserve Bank and Federal Reserve notes, series 1918. Last but not least, images of De Soto discov- ering the Mississippi, Washington resigning his commission, and the embarkation of the pilgrims appeared on Federal Reserve notes, series 1918.

Whereas the proliferation on bank notes of politicians and bureaucrats speaks a clear language of the symbolic consolidation of the nation-state, other types of illustrations embody ideas and values that were considered important for the self-representation of America's cultural elites. These illustrations included some less familiar but more modern allegories—such as Civilization, Science, Mechanics and Navigation, Steam, Electricity, or Commerce and Manufacture. Civilization (also known as "The Spirit of the Navy") appears on the $500 National Bank note of the Original and 1875 series. Science and Mechanics, in the form of two men sitting on a bench, appear on the $100 interest-bearing Treasury note of 1864; Mechanics and Navigation, the one a male type caster, the other a bare-breasted female, appear on the back of several issues of the $50 National Bank note, Series 1902. Sci- ence presenting Steam and Electricity to Commerce and Manufacture, engraved by George F.C. Smillie after a design by Edwin H. Blashfield, appears on the face of the $2 Silver Certificate, Series 1896. That note is among the most famous of all United States currency issues—and by general consent one of the most perfectly designed.

Another engraving by Smillie, Electricity as the Dominant Force in the World, fea- tures prominently on the $5 Silver Certificate, Series 1896, the third and last of the Educa- tional series. Critics have thought that the note looks a bit overwrought, with "a touch of Wagner and Beethoven in its highly dramatic imagery,"[76] but ornate art and architecture had reached a high point in the 1890s, and the theme may have been a good choice. By 1896, Thomas Edison's bulbs were beginning to quite literally light up the world; also by 1896, the world's first hydroelectric power plant had been built on the Niagara River right above the falls. The first note in the Educational series was the $1 Silver Certificate, Series 1896.

$2, Silver Certificate, Series 1896, face, the second note of the Educational series (American Numis- matic Association Money Museum)

Known as "History Instructing Youth," the note's face, which was designed by Will H. Low and engraved by Charles Schlecht, represents History pointing out to Youth the principal sights of Washington, DC—the Washington Monument and the Capitol—and presumably telling the narratives behind them, including the story of the United States Constitution, which appears at right. Other artistic highlights include representations of the discoverers Meriwether Lewis and William Clark, on the $10 United States note, Series 1901, where they are to the left and right of a huge buffalo, and the $5 Silver Certificate of 1899, the "Oncpapa" note.

Altogether, the creation of a national currency in the years after the Civil War clearly was an epiphenomenon of the consolidation of the United States into a nation-state. Already the names of the currency—"United States Notes" or "National Bank Notes"—were an index that confidence in the currency no longer rested on the seemingly endless series of private hands that had governed the values of pre–Civil War notes, but on faith in a new abstraction—the nation. In addition, other currencies were taxed out of existence, the private issue of monies was suppressed, and their personalization by individuals stamped out. Still, the way toward a uniform legal tender was never smooth or consensual but, framed by such formative factors as race, class, gender, ethnicity, and region, was rather twisted, even torturous. Although the National Bank Act of 1863 had eliminated distinctions among currencies, allowing only the newly chartered National Banks to issue paper currency, the stock of American money remained highly diversified for some time to come. The new National Bank notes circulated alongside other Civil War currency inventions—not only greenbacks, but also interest-bearing Legal Tender notes, government Demand notes, postage and fractional currency, as well as Silver and Gold Certificates ("yellowbacks"), not to mention the more traditional gold coins and subsidiary silver.

These multiple official monies were in many cases earmarked for specified purposes. Greenbacks, for instance, were receivable in most payments, but not for duties on imports, nor for interest on bonds and notes. Gold, on the other hand, though designated largely for foreign transactions, was also accepted for certain domestic payments, such as custom duties. Limited regional variation also persisted; for example, payment in gold continued to prevail on the West Coast, where certain paper bills (the National Gold Bank notes of

$20 National Gold Bank Note of California, face (courtesy National Numismatic Collection, Smithsonian Institution)

$20, National Gold Bank Note of California, back (courtesy National Numismatic Collection, Smithsonian Institution)

California) even carried depictions of gold coins on their backs. All these differences in types of money show, in Cecilia O'Leary's words, that there was "considerable motion and flux regarding who possessed sufficient authority to speak for the nation and which memories, icons, and rituals could represent the nation's symbolic meanings."[77] The move toward a more uniform legal tender was not to be stopped, though. In a sense, it was an important achievement, as without a standardized form of money, citizens would face enormous difficulties in interacting with each other in a national marketplace that was no longer driven by land but by industry. Standardization is likewise reflected in the "company literature" of the post–Civil War. Of particular importance is a statement made in 1861 by another American supporter of a single National Bank note. Such a note, the man said, would help foster a sense of national unity not just by producing economic benefits to individuals but also by encouraging communication between citizens:

> Every citizen [...] who is supplied with such a currency—a currency which will be equal to gold through every foot of our territory, and everywhere of the same value, with which he can travel from Oregon to Florida and from Maine to New Mexico, would feel and realize, every time he handled or looked at such a bill bearing the national mark, that the union of these states is verily a personal benefit and blessing to all.[78]

These words are a good illustration of the primary motive for the creation of a territorial currency—that of bolstering the economic territoriality of the nation-state. However, what the good man did not say was that no one traveling from Oregon to Florida and from Maine to New Mexico would ever know most of the people living there, much as the people living there would also never know most of their fellow citizens. What such a traveler could take for granted was that, in Benedict Anderson's words, "in the minds of each lives the image of their communion." The notes bearing the national mark thus would achieve their cultural work within a nation that was "imagined as a *community* because, regardless of the actual inequality and exploitation that may prevail in each, the nation is always conceived as a deep, horizontal comradeship."[79]

The incompleteness and contradiction in the cultural-symbolic constitution of the United States that had marked the years of the early republic was gone by the time of Reconstruction. In the thirty or forty years before World War I, particular care was taken in the business of inventing traditions. Quite new and, as well, old but dramatically transformed social groups, environments, and social contexts called for new devices to maintain or express social cohesion and identity, and to structure social relations. At the same time, a changing society required new methods of governing or establishing bonds of loyalty. Consequently, the invention of political traditions was much more conscious and deliberate, since it was largely undertaken by institutions with political purposes in mind. It was practiced both officially and unofficially, both by the state or organized social and political movements, and by social groups not formally organized as such. Nevertheless, the state increasingly defined the largest stage on which the crucial activities determining human lives as subjects and citizens were played out. As Eric Hobsbawm expresses the point, from the mid-nineteenth century, "society ('civil society') and the state within which it operated became increasingly inseparable."[80]

In terms of national identity, the United States after the Civil War was facing a paradox. Although the country was then the most democratic and, both territorially and constitutionally, one of the most clearly defined nations, the basic political problem, once secession had been averted, was how to assimilate a heterogeneous mass of people who were Americans not by birth but by immigration. Americans, Hobsbawm found, "had to be made. The invented traditions [...] in this period were primarily designed to achieve this object."[81] For one thing, immigrants were encouraged to accept rituals commemorating the history of the nation — the Revolution and its Founding Fathers (July 4), and the Protestant Anglo-Saxon tradition (Forefathers Day, Thanksgiving Day) — as indeed they did, since these now became holidays and occasions for public and private festivity. The educational system too was transformed into a machine for political socialization by such devices as the worship of the flag, which, as a daily ritual in the country's schools, spread from the 1880s onwards. An even more effective vehicle of nationalist messages was the currency, which provided a much more frequent reminder to people that they were members of what nationalists considered to be a real community. The mass immersion in the nationalistic iconography on the currency molded people's identity, perceived their destiny, and expressed commands to them.

In actual fact, reproductions of the famous paintings of Americana tended to appear on higher denominations. Notes above $20 in face value generally were used primarily for interbank business and large transactions, such as loans. Possibly, therefore, the notes of the Educational Series provided a better means to convey symbolic messages to large numbers of citizens. They came in denominations of 1, 2, and 5 Dollars and were thus more likely to reach the hands of the average workers, who in the late nineteenth century earned somewhere around two dollars a day and who essentially constituted what Secretary Chase's clerk had called "the masses." Many of them, especially in the big cities, were new immigrants. Yet immigrants, Hobsbawm suggests, provided a body of rather "*doubtful members of the national community*; all the more doubtful because [...] they could actually be classified as foreigners." The doubts stemmed from the fact that the concept of one's national identity as an American was an act of choice (the decision to learn English, to apply for citizenship) and a choice of specific beliefs, acts and modes of behavior. Thus, identity as an American always implied the corresponding concept of "un–American," which necessarily threw a doubt on an individual's actual status as a member of the nation. The concept of "un–American" thus provided an "internal enemy against whom the good American could assert his or her Americanism, not least by the punctilious performance of all the formal and informal rituals, the assertion of all the beliefs conventionally and institutionally established as characteristic of good American."[82]

By the end of the nineteenth century, to be a good American meant to believe in and worship the achievements of a nation that had assumed its present borders with the addition of Alaska in 1867 and Hawaii in 1898. Moreover, that nation was on the threshold of becoming a world power, as the United States had assumed control over the Philippines, Puerto Rico, Guam, the Canal Zone, and Guantánamo Bay. The proud republic was now an empire, a member of a club hitherto reserved for European monarchies. Many people saw the inconsistency in this, though the new domains were popular with "the man in the street, who therefore voted for the empire-builders when election times rolled around."[83]

Voters were also served well by the United States Treasury, which obliged them by asserting institutionally established belief through the triumphalist iconography chosen for the currency. The first signs of a changeover to symbols of power and national achievement are evident from the one-dollar Silver Certificate Series 1899, which received on its face a picture of the American eagle — the "Eagle of the Capitol" — showcased prominently above the heads of Presidents Lincoln and Grant, and replacing History instructing Youth. On the face of the ten-dollar United States note, Series 1901, which is popularly known as the "Bison" note, portraits of the explorers Meriwether Lewis and William Clark to the left and right, and a bison at the center, replaced the head of Congressman and Senator Daniel Webster and a vignette of Pocahontas being presented to England's royal court. The note's new face is symbolic of the pride the nation's elites then took in the West — at a time when the bison was about to become extinct.[84]

The changeover to symbols of power and national achievement is also evident from Treasury notes, whose design originally had sought to commemorate the Civil War by using images of the various military leaders and statesmen of the period. By the end of the nineteenth century, the need to commemorate the Civil War clearly had played itself out. Similarly, Trumbull's *Jefferson Presenting the Declaration of Independence* on the $100 National Bank note had to go. In its stead was put an altar-like device consisting of an escutcheon for the obligation at the base, two male allegories supporting the shield of the United States, and a rather bellicose-looking eagle with wings spread on the top. Also of interest is the $50 National Bank note of 1902, which in lieu of *Embarkation of the Pilgrims* features an

$10, Legal Tender note, series 1901, the "Bison" note, face, portraits of the explorers Meriwether Lewis and William Clark to the left and right (American Numismatic Association Money Museum)

industrial scene from which a locomotive emerges at full tilt and, oddly, a female figure representing Navigation to the right. On the new $20 note, *Baptism of Pocahontas* was replaced by the United States Capitol, with a representation of Liberty to the left, in a pose that suggests that she is actually protecting it.

The idea of empire building is expressed more brashly on the $10 note of the same series, on which *De Soto Discovering the Mississippi* gave way to two ocean-going vessels. The two ships make reappearance on the $50 Federal Reserve note, Series 1914. However, now the ships are much larger and the allegorical figure is no longer called Liberty or Progress, but Panama, in celebration of the completion of the Canal, which was prominent in the news and minds of Americans then, and one reason for staging the 1915 Panama-Pacific Exposition in San Francisco. Finally, there is the $2 Federal Reserve Bank note of 1918. Boasting as it does of a picture of a battleship, it has been read as an expression of martiality, a "guns-and-steel assertion of American strength, an emblem of the country's contribution to winning World War I."[85] Both the "Battleship Note" and the $10 Federal Reserve Bank note of the same series (the "Green Eagle" bill, which features on its back the American eagle with the national flag grasped in its talons) appear to have been "collectors' favorites" for a long time.[86] As in the case of the Americana histories, the element of invention is patently clear, as the history that became part of the national money icon is not what has actually been preserved in popular memory, but what has been selected, written, pictured, popularized, and institutionalized by those whose function it is to do so—the representatives of the state.

There is an interesting parallel between representations on the currency of the sovereign majesty of the United States and those of public buildings. As the contemporary architect Cass Gilbert observed, public buildings should inspire "just pride in the state," and be "a symbol of the civilization, culture, and ideals of our country." Gilbert's words were occasioned by the Senate Park Commission's recommendation, in 1901, that Pierre L'Enfant's original grand plan of Washington, DC, be completed and extended. To do so, it was explained, would serve to enhance "the effect of grandeur, power, and dignified magnificence which should mark the seat of government of a great and intensely active people." The completion of the Washington Monument, the White House extension, the Union

$100, National Bank note, 1908, back, triumphalism on the banknote (American Numismatic Association Money Museum)

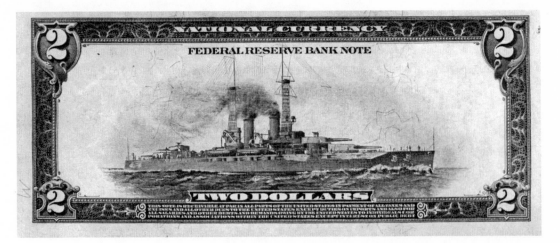

$2, Federal Reserve Bank note, Series 1918, back, the battleship note (American Numismatic Association Money Museum)

Station, the Lincoln Memorial (which had its first appearance on the $5 Legal Tender and Federal Reserve notes of the series of 1928), and the scheme for various government buildings surrounding the United States Capitol all date from this period. The sole purpose of these buildings was to overwhelm with the functional majesty of government. As the commission concluded, when these offices are completed, "the resulting architectural composition will be unparalleled in magnitude and monumental character by any similar group of legislative buildings in the world."[87]

The large-scale re-building of capital cities is undoubtedly the most visible and most ostentatious manner in which the great powers were bolstering their self-esteem in this period of extreme international competition. Another form of putting nationalism on the landscape was the creation of lavish monumental ensembles, often for commemorating historic events. The centennial of the American Revolution and the four-hundredth anniversary of Columbus's discovery of America were commemorated in this manner.[88] President Chester Arthur at the same time began to improve the ritual and ceremonial associated with the White House, and, no less significantly, Cass Gilbert's plan for Washington, DC, in 1900 included provision for "a great receiving ground for pageants and official ceremonies."[89]

Altogether during the period 1865–1914, the United States acquired the basic official institutions, symbols, and practices—capitals, flags, national anthems, military uniforms, a national literature, and a national currency—that would help ensure political obedience and loyalty and, as well, establish legitimacy. Whatever was novel in the invention of traditions during that period had to ceremonially enhance the achievements of the United States as a civilization—such as the arts and literature, and the unprecedented developments in manufacturing industry, trade and transportation, and technology. Additionally, venerated personalities like Presidents were no longer just the chief executives but were now to be seen as the heads of the nation and, in the case of Abraham Lincoln, as its savior or else, as symbols of national consensus and continuity to which all citizens might defer.

None of all this was characteristic of the United States alone. Only in one major regard did the American experience differ significantly from that of other western nations. In most countries, the efflorescence of ceremonial on paper money was centered on a living head of state. However, in the United States, while the ceremonial shadow was cast over the

Chief executive as a matter of fact, the substance lay never on the bills. The reason is extraneous, in that pursuant to a congressional ruling from the Civil War years no living person was to be portrayed on United States paper money. The precedent not to put images of living heads of state on the coinage had been established in 1792 by George Washington himself, whose refusal to have his portrait put on the new coinage marked a deliberate break with a British tradition that did just that. By using the figure of Liberty, American coinage from early on symbolized what the people had won so dearly. The twentieth century, by abandoning symbolic design in favor of real people or, rather, of the "great men of American history," broke with this tradition.

Invented Traditions and Related Phenomena, World War I through the Present

The year 1914 marked the beginning of World War I, at the same time as it marked the introduction of a new type of currency, from the Federal Reserve System. The notes were printed in Washington at the Bureau of Engraving and Printing, and their black faces and green backs were "undeniably products of the *national* government."[90] So, it seems, were the images that came to be placed on the notes. Although the United States was absent from the war scene until 1917, once it entered the conflict it was ready to flex its muscles. It also did so on the currency.[91] Appropriately, on the back of the $2 Federal Reserve Bank note of 1918 there is an intaglio image of a battleship of the dreadnought class at full steam on a run at sea.

Less martial is the $1 Federal Reserve Bank note of 1918, which is nonetheless noteworthy, firstly because the inscription "National Currency" verbally symbolizes the consolidation of the nation-state, and secondly because on the back there is depicted an eagle clamping an American flag, which reinforces the national symbolic on the pictorial level. By contrast, the $10 and $20 notes, in their emphasis on domestic affairs, are strikingly different from the two notes described above. Depicting domestic scenes undoubtedly met with the national tendency, more vibrant than ever at the dawn of World War I, to mind one's own business and, as well, to celebrate the country's achievements. Hence, the back of the $20 bill illustrates forms of transportation from the early 1900s. An automobile is seen next to a steam train, and an ocean liner similar to the *Titanic* is seen steaming past the Statue of Liberty. On the back of the $10 bill is a scene that is interesting on another count. The scene juxtaposes America's agrarian past with its industrial future. The way the farmers and the team of horses are aligned — away from the viewer — seems emblematic of the dramatic changes America had gone through, when, as Henry Adams observed, "agriculture had made way for steam; tall chimneys reeked smoke on every horizon, and dirty suburbs filled with scrap-iron, scrap-paper and cinders, formed the setting of every town."[92]

World War I had been costly also for the United States, yet it nevertheless catapulted the country into the position of a world power. The nation's gold holdings increased at an unprecedented rate as its European allies paid for their supplies and materials in gold. Backed by ever-growing reserves and a newly attained strong credit position, the dollar became the world's leading currency. As a result, its cultural work ceased to be merely one aspect of widespread competitive inventiveness, and became instead a unique expression of the convergence between the national state, monetary policy, and political issues.[93] The convergence is most obvious from the fact that in 1929 all United States currency was

$10, Federal Reserve Bank note, series 1915, back, agriculture making way for steam (American Numismatic Association Money Museum)

reduced in size and redesigned. Consequently, the new paper dollar became "the perfect ingredient in the corporation paycheck [...] an indispensable partner to Big Business." Indeed, in its capacity as the national money icon, every dollar note issued by the Federal Reserve was a kind of

> Big Business itself. Like a Model T or a Hollywood movie, a dollar was something you could have confidence in wherever you were, a reassuringly familiar quantity from coast to coast, a brand like the other brands already beginning to conquer and even define aspects of the nation. The dollar helped this happen. Uniformity drove down price: a clear price fostered uniformity.[94]

The new design was here to last, "fixed in a single, changeless pattern," as Richard Doty put it. Doty is concerned about this development, which he essentially sees from the viewpoint of collecting.[95] Indeed, bureaucrats and politicians became the main fare of the portraiture, and the Great Seal of the United States the main signifier of the nation-state. For the $1 note, George Washington was chosen, as his portrait was familiar to everyone and as this note had the greatest circulation. The original selection for the $2 note was James Garfield, possibly because of the sentiment for martyred presidents.[96] Abraham Lincoln was selected for the $5 note, as he stood next to Washington in the ranks of American heroes. The $10 note depicts Alexander Hamilton; Andrew Jackson appears on the $20 note and Ulysses S. Grant on the $50 note.

The largest denomination note now being printed is the $100 note, colloquially known as "Benjamin" for its portrait of Benjamin Franklin. All other larger notes (only Federal Reserve notes were issued) — the $500 note depicting William McKinley, the $1,000 depicting Grover Cleveland, the $5,000 note depicting James Madison, and the $10,000 note depicting Salmon P. Chase — were last printed in 1945 and, pursuant to an executive order issued by President Nixon, have not been issued since July 1, 1969. "Use of these large denominations," it was explained in a press release by the Treasury Department and the Federal Reserve System, "has declined sharply over the last two decades and the need for them appears insufficient to warrant the added cost of production and custody of new supplies."[97] The largest ever United States note, the $100,000 Gold Certificate carrying Woodrow

Wilson's portrait, in an engraving by George F.C. Smillie, was printed only between December 1934 and January 1935. It never appeared in general circulation, and was only used in transactions between Federal Reserve Banks and clearinghouses.

Back designs of the new Federal Reserve notes are closely associated in each case with the persons depicted on the faces of the notes. The $2 note has Jefferson on the face and a picture of his Monticello home on the back. The $5 note couples Lincoln and the Lincoln Memorial. The $10 note brings together Hamilton and the Treasury Building. The $20 note features Andrew Jackson and the White House, the $100 note (issued both as a Federal Reserve and a United States note) Franklin and Independence Hall. Other currency notes have plain back designs, usually the denomination, in numerals and spelt out, and implications of currency security. The exception of course is the one-dollar note, which first appeared in its familiar form, that is, with the Great Seal of the United States as the central feature of the back design, in 1935.[98]

In terms of face portraits alone, the changes in the currency's design were not nearly as radical as they have been made out to be. Already the large-size Federal Reserve notes carried center portraits, with most of them being those of former Presidents. More of a break was constituted by the anachronistic, ceremonial grandeur of the new currency design, which suited well the idiom of public symbolic discourse of the period between the wars. That idiom was more theatrical, with a tendency to foregrounding the actors rather than the stage-set. Tellingly, nationalism was also put on the landscape in Mount Rushmore, where the monumental heads of Presidents Washington, Jefferson, Theodore Roosevelt, and Lincoln were sculpted out of the granite between 1927 and 1941.[99] In 1931, the "Star-Spangled Banner" became the national anthem, and in the same year, June Fourteenth was officially recognized as a legal day for the observance of Flag Day (which had been a national holiday since 1916). The completion of the Lincoln Memorial in 1922, the Arlington Memorial Bridge in 1933, and the Jefferson Memorial in 1942 essentially showed the force of the same influence in the field of public building.

If contemporary expressions of nationalism make use of the national past, they do so in a purely nostalgic way, constructing a nationalism that has been labeled "synthetic."[100] Contemporary expressions of nationalism thus are no longer rooted in historic circumstances that bred their predecessors; additionally, there is little or no awareness of the contentious ideas that made the early republic special — the wonder for some, who found asylum in America, and the fear of others, like European aristocrats and parts of the bourgeoisie. Most importantly, perhaps, contemporary forms of nationalism are no longer at odds with statism. Conflicts that were very real in former times are now on the surface or simmering below it. As Wilbur Zelinsky found, the "symbols, rites, and other nationalistic practices in vogue today are essentially nonideological and nonethnic in character, and simply proclaim the power and glory of Uncle Sam." On occasion, observances of nationalism have become "a sometime and rather tepid thing," relegated to museums and costumed spectacles. On other occasions, the arms of the state provide spiritual refuge, such as when the flag is shown, especially during periods of international tension, at Olympic Games, or, also quadrennially, during the orgy of a presidential inauguration.[101]

On still other occasions, the principles of the Declaration of Independence are invoked, kept alive in a presidential rhetoric dedicated to restoring meaning from America's sacred text and to symbolically renewing faith in America and its role in the world. All these events and phenomena serve as the proper antidotes to doubts about purpose and identity, and the national currency is no exception. This is exemplified by the design of the one-dollar note, which has remained unchanged except for the addition of the motto "In God We Trust" to the 1935G Series in 1957. Printing of the notes began in July 1957, two years after Congress had declared "In God We Trust" the official national motto. Of that note, more than 50 million items went into circulation beginning November 26, 1957. The Bureau considered placing these notes into circulation so urgent that they were made available to the public not at Federal Reserve Banks or branches but through commercial banking channels.[102]

Although the Bureau rushed the new 1935G Series to the public, Allen Ginsberg in all likelihood did not see any of the new notes for some time, though he does focus on a one-dollar bill in his poem "American Change." The poem bears the epigraph "*S.S. United States*, July 1958," suggesting that it was probably written during the poet's voyage home from a trip to Europe. "American Change" is quite literally all about the currency, the final section offering an almost ekphrastic rendering of the one-dollar bill: "Washington again, on the Dollar, same poetic black print, dark/words, The United States of America, innumerable numbers...."[103] One of the numbers, "R956422481," instantly aroused this author's penchant for resolving historic obscurities, as did the series, "Ivy Baker Priest Series 1953F." Serial numbers beginning with the letter "R" were used only on notes of Series 1935A, the "R" standing for an internal control number. Normally, bills would have serial numbers prefixed and suffixed by letters A to L, similar to the letters used to represent any one of the twelve Federal Reserve Districts. The name Ivy Baker Priest indeed appeared on the paper currency, as she served as Treasurer of the United States between 1953 and 1961. Thus, her signature would also be on $1 Silver Certificates, though *not* on Series 1953F, which are inexistent.[104]

Altogether, it is unclear whether Ginsberg looked at an actual one-dollar bill when he wrote his poem or whether he composed the inscription from scratch notes or journals or simply made the details up. One thing is clear, though. He cannot have used a $1 Federal Reserve note, as notes of this type were only issued beginning with Series 1963.[105] These notes also bear on their backs the national motto, printed in prominent letters above the word "ONE." At least for now, there are no plans to redesign this note. Nor are there plans to discontinue printing and putting it into circulation. The $1 Federal Reserve note thus is not only the most familiar of all United States paper currency but is also *the* national money icon. Despite or even because of its special status, commentators have been making derisive remarks of the note. For David Standish, it "isn't just dull; it's fairly weird." G.B. Tate, a contemporary trompe l'oeil money artist, refuses to paint them. "They're too ugly," he says. "Even the faces of the presidents look distorted to me."

Jason Goodwin for his part seems offended by the absence on the current one-dollar bill of features invariably found on bills around the world — landmarks, splendid new dams, characteristic animals, or funky graphics. He also bemoans the fact that with its homespun classicist aesthetics the national money icon is no longer as strident as, say, the triumphalist bills of the 1880s and 1890s. Altogether, Goodwin finds the bill solidly dull-looking, with its tufts of laurel leaves, its scrolls and cobwebs, its table mirror portrait frame and the numeral 1 in each corner, all in stark contrast to the streamlined Art Deco artifacts and skyscrapers of the roaring twenties, the period preceding it. On the other hand, upon its introduction the new paper dollar "no longer had to toot and trumpet: America *was* the future." Thus, the currency could be "unabashedly American, reflecting the point where history and myth collide."[106]

Just as "unabashedly American" is the coinage, for which symbolic design was likewise abandoned in favor of real people. The shift was first visible with the Lincoln cent of

1909. This coin, which superseded the 1864 "copper" cent with the head of Liberty in an Indian bonnet, came into existence on the initiative of an enlightened Theodore Roosevelt seeking "moderation and seriousness of purpose" in the arts.[107] It was the first regular issue United States coin to portray an actual historic figure; next came the Washington quarter of 1932, the Jefferson nickel of 1938, and the Roosevelt dime of 1946.[108] In 1948 came the Franklin half-dollar, which was replaced in 1964 by a new coin paying homage to the martyred president, John F. Kennedy. Dwight Eisenhower appeared on the one-dollar coin in 1971, only to be replaced in 1979 by the much smaller Susan B. Anthony dollar that, as is well known, was simply a fiasco. The trend away from local places, people, and events towards events, persons, and places of national significance, has also been observed on commemorative coins from the 1920s. These coins have recognized, paid homage to, or celebrated General Lafayette, the Sesquicentennial of American Independence in 1926, Daniel Boone, the Old Spanish Trail, the Battle of Gettysburg, the Korean War, Olympic Games, the bicentennials of the United States Congress and of the Bill of Rights, the 250th anniversary of Washington's birth (in 1982), the 200th anniversary of his death (in 1999), and so on, including, most recently, the Bald Eagle.[109]

The nation's Presidents are being honored in their own right, in the order that they served, on the new $1 circulating coins. In compliance with the Presidential Coin Act of December 22, 2005, the U.S. Mint will mint and issue four presidential coins per year, beginning with Presidents Washington, Adams, Jefferson, and Madison in 2007. Each coin in the program will have a reverse design featuring a rendition of the Statue of Liberty. Edge-incused inscriptions will bear the year of minting or issuance, "*E Pluribus Unum,*" "In God We Trust," and the mintmark.[110] Presidential $1 coins are legal tender. Beyond that, they are expected to be "a great educational tool for citizens of all ages." Hence, the coins were introduced to the public with much fanfare. For one thing, the Mint embarked on a ten-city Presidential Coin education tour beginning in Chicago in January 2007 and ending in Charlotte, South Carolina, in early February. Historians were invited to give talks, and local residents were able to see the new coins up close and personally even before the first coin's official release. Take-home educational materials from the Mint are also made available. Businesses, consumer groups, media outlets, and schools receive special material, including brochures, a release schedule, informational take-ones, collector boards, bookmarks, program tent cards, a variety of posters, durable door/window clings, and a CD-ROM containing web-based tutorial and computer-based presentations for employee training. "Presidential $1 Coin e-Newsletters" are sent out regularly.[111]

Whenever a new Presidential coin is introduced, the Mint stages a ceremonial launch event, which includes a coin exchange and an official ceremony with the Mint's Director and other dignitaries (the George Washington $1 Coin event was held on February 15, 2007, in New York City's Grand Central Station). To ensure adequate supplies for commerce and collectors, the coins are shipped to banks and other financial institutions in rolls and bags. The question is, has the program paid off? According to information released by the Mint, by May 2007 nearly half a billion George Washington and John Adams $1 coins have been ordered for circulation. In addition, public awareness of the new coins has tripled from 15–20 percent in November 2006 when the designs were first unveiled to approximately 60 percent in March 2007. On the other hand, in a recent Harris Poll, 75 percent of the respondents claimed that they had not seen a presidential dollar coin in circulation, and only 13 percent said that they preferred it to the paper dollar. The poll also noted that the coins were least used in the Eastern United States.

The fate of the new Presidential coins goes to show that the project of constituting Americans is by no means as easy to manage as the elites envisage it. While it has always been a source of antagonism, this is so most notably today. For in our day and age, "the nation" clearly has ceased to be the single or even the dominant point of reference for constructing identities. Of course, the state still co-opts dissent, and there is still plenty of repression, but it is not nearly as total or totalizing as it was a hundred years ago. The results are often frantic and

Left: George Washington $1 Coin, obverse (United States Mint image) *Right:* George Washington $1 Coin, reverse (United States Mint image)

sometimes pitiful efforts by state apparatuses to endorse and enforce and, on occasion, advertise and promote through educational outreach, the national symbolic. Generally, however, new traditions never fill more than a small part of the space left by the secular decline of both old traditions and customs. This is probably "normal" in societies in which the past becomes increasingly less relevant as a model of precedent for most forms of human behavior. Especially the days in the private lives of most people are rarely touched by external compulsions of "the state."[112]

All this is to say that projects undertaken in the name of the nation should not be understood as one-way communications in which the American people passively accept meanings put into circulation by cultural elites. More often than not, these meanings are challenged, which only helps explain the elites' ongoing attempts towards "inventing" patriotic or nationalistic traditions, including those represented on the currency. However, there is never a simple "fit" between production and consumption, that is, between state and citizens. The following chapter will highlight a number of the difficulties inherent in the elites' attempts towards achieving such a close fit by combining cultural "hardware" (the paper bills themselves) with cultural "software" (the beliefs, attitudes, and values that are important in the project of nation-building).

FIVE

The Cultural Consumption
of the Paper Dollar

The cedi lay there on the seat. Among the coins it looked strange, and for a moment the conductor thought it was ridiculous that the paper should be more important than the shiny metal. In the weak light inside the bus he peered closely at the markings on the note. Then a vague but persistent odor forced itself on him and he rolled the cedi up and deliberately, deeply smelled it. [...] Fascinated, he breathed it slowly into his lungs. It was a most unexpected smell for something so new to have [...] Strange that a man could have so many cedis pass through his hands and yet not really know their smell. [...] After the note the conductor began smelling the coins, but they were a disappointment. Not so satisfying, the smell of metal coins.

— Ayi Kwei Armah, *The Beautiful Ones Are Not Yet Born* 3

Introduction

"Consumption," in the sense that it is used here, goes beyond a narrow understanding of it as the mere purchase of goods, extending it to include what people make or do with paper money once the bills leave the printing presses and bank or government offices. Throughout this chapter, practices of consumption will become recognizable as crucial elements in the process of meaning making, as usage changes or inflects the meaning of all objects in particular ways. Over time, in different periods or contexts, and in relation to new situations, new meanings or inflections will emerge. This is not unusual. The practice of withdrawing dollar bills from circulation in the economy, making them over into collectors' items, testifies to this; so do dollar bills that are turned into works of art, both in the still-life paintings of the *trompe-l'oeil* school of the late nineteenth century and in contemporary works of art. Another example concerns the little posters one used to see in stores throughout the United States, near the cash register, which jokingly read, "In God We Trust, All Others Pay Cash." There have also been misunderstandings, deliberate "misreadings," and even "subversive" or "iconoclastic" usages of the paper dollar. Good examples are the Continentals, which were used to wallpaper rooms with; equally iconoclastic is the practice of marking out the national motto on dollar bills, in protesting the use of it on the currency.

Appropriations of paper dollars by consumers relativize the power of producers, be they private banks or government institutions. However, the focus on consumption serves not just to extending the explanatory reach of a study of the paper dollar's cultural work, but also to bringing into the discussion some important theoretical issues. The first concerns a body of criticism that we will simply term the "production of consumption" perspective. The second concerns the concept of consumption as socio-cultural differentiation. The third and final one concerns a body of theoretical work commonly referred to as the "consumption as appropriation and resistance" perspective.

Paper Dollars and the Production of Consumption Perspective

A distinct criticism was made of the paper dollar as its acceptance grew. This criticism focused upon the dollar as both currency and religious object. Not in a real religion, of course, but in something resembling it, the kind of "religion" in which the dollar serves as an "object of worship," as Washington Irving put it. Critics regarded worship of the "almighty dollar" as potentially dangerous because it would undermine confidence through increasingly anonymous relations between individuals. In these relations, "everything has its price," Thoreau wrote. For Emerson, the price was "duplicity and falsehood." The painter Thomas Cole echoes these views in a didactic poem: "Each hill and every valley is become / An altar unto Mammon, and the gods / Of man's idolatry — its victims we." The poem, which dates from the 1830s, treats the future of America as fatally entangled with an expanding market economy made possible by the availability of abundant money in the form of paper notes issued by private banks, often in excess of the "real" money on deposit.[1]

There is an interesting parallel between Cole's poem and landscape paintings of the time, which typically depicted an Arcadian America beset by the storms of modernization. However, did Americans of the nineteenth century really confer the status of deity to pieces of paper? We may have an answer to this question by returning to the issue of money and value. Irving, Emerson, Thoreau, Cole, as well as a whole range of other artists and intellectuals were united in their suspicion not of money in general but of paper money. Being contemporaries, they could not fully comprehend that the way in which paper money was so widely accepted, despite its lack of any intrinsic value, was a phenomenon based on a deep level of mysterious faith. Later commentators such as Georg Simmel would describe the transformation of money into a token form, that is, from substance to function, as the "growing spiritualization of money."[2]

The importance of the "spiritualization of money" lies in "a significant relationship to the notion of God," Simmel contends.[3] We can trace instances of such a relationship to the earliest years of the American republic. When in 1791 Alexander Hamilton, working on a policy regarding debts, suggested that the federal government take responsibility for all public debts, including the debts of individual states, that policy became known, with biblical simplicity, as "assumption."[4] Another biblical term used in connection with money is "redemption," the buying back of a piece of paper money with gold, silver, goods, or services.[5] Redemption was referred to by the phrase "will pay to the bearer on demand" on United States notes before Series 1963. Thereafter, the "will pay to the bearer" clause was dropped from the obligation, and with it reference to redemption, the religious or at least spiritual connotations of which had seemingly outlived themselves.[6]

Dropping the redemption clause from the obligation was coincidental with putting on the currency the declaration, "In God We Trust." One wonders what the German critic Walter Benjamin would have made of the practice of giving the currency a divine imprimatur. In a 1921 fragment titled "Kapitalismus als Religion" ["Capitalism as Religion"] and unpublished in his lifetime, Benjamin suggested that a comparison be made between religious paintings ("the images of the saints of the various religions") and the ornaments on bank notes. Such a comparison, Benjamin suggested, would reveal the religious structure of capitalism, as well as the fact that capitalism, by colonizing religion, had itself become a religion. Already Max Weber had brought together capitalism and religion. He explained the spirit of capitalism as an ascetic form of Protestantism leading to a specific way of life that at the same time buttresses and sanctifies capitalist economy. With this argument Weber was contradicting Marx, who had rather thought that it was social being that determined consciousness. Benjamin rejected both Marx and Weber. He saw the connection between being and consciousness not as causal but rather as one of expressiveness. In addition, unlike Weber, he did not see capitalism as embedded in a religiously motivated life, thus not as an ethic, but as possessing an essentially religious structure. Benjamin, who had studied with Simmel in Berlin, argued that capitalism had emerged as religion's parasite, drawing on its resources until it became identical with it. Thus, capitalism appears as a religion without dogma, hence a religion that placed the cultic over the doctrinal. The logic of images on bank and government notes therefore bears only a structural similarity to the images of the saints of the various religions.[7]

Under capitalism, the originally religious emblems return as commodities: the ornamental design of banknotes serves to normalize capitalist exchange. That exchange is based on credit, the receiving of which creates indebtedness, or guilt, though under capitalism, there is no release from either debt or guilt.[8] Since neither can be atoned or expiated for, the best we can do is to hang on, mitigating the chaos and meaninglessness in the modern world through cult and ritual. This is the reason why capitalism in its classical and allegorical costume via bank and government notes has been said to contribute towards civilizing, in the realm of culture, the excesses of industrial capitalism. Consequently, capitalism could not only claim but also was acclaimed as progress. Benjamin would have disagreed. He had experienced both the erosion of political power and economic and fiscal crash, none of which contributed towards sustaining faith in capitalism.[9]

At the end of the 1920s, a period characterized both by rampant inflation and by philosophical attention to the relation between monetary values ("*Geld*") and intellectual validity ("*Geltung*"), Benjamin came back to the research agenda he had sketched in "Capitalism as Religion." The gist of this later work, which was originally published in German as "Einbahnstrasse" ("One Way Street") in 1928, is that the form of paper money conveys not only economic but also social and cultural values. Once again, Benjamin is observant of the religious dimension fostered by the various iconographies. Words such as "solemn," "cupids" and "goddesses," and "hell" clearly spell this out. Yet unlike in the earlier fragment, the tone in "Einbahnstrasse" is satirical, and the mood is full of pessimism with regard to the future, as if in anticipation of the "Great Crash" of October 1929. Any analysis of bank notes, Benjamin concludes, should be driven by "satirical force."[10]

There is likewise a tremendous satirical force in the depiction of a church full of people with a large dollar sign behind the altar. The picture formed the centerfold in *Puck* magazine of May 15, 1907. A contemporary echo of the nexus between capitalism and religion can be found in Mark C. Taylor's book *Altarity*. Taylor describes capitalism in terms of an "ontotheological political economy," in that capitalism is guided by a "fundamentalist belief—belief in the fundaments named identity and unity." Thus, Taylor claims, "The

THE ALMIGHTIER.

God in whom ontotheology trusts is ONE." There are many references to ONE-ness on the national currency. Already the motto "*E pluribus unum*," "From Many, One," testifies to it. The motto appears in many sites, including the Great Seal, appropriately depicted on the back of the current one-dollar note. Taylor is at great pains to point out that the word "ONE" appears at the center of the bill. (In fact, the word appears five more times, four times in each corner, written over the numeral "1," and once spelled out at the bottom, in the phrase "One Dollar.") Also connected to ONE-ness is the motto, "In God We Trust." As Taylor concludes, "[t]he God in whom we (but who is this 'we,' this 'magisterial *wir*'?) trust" is "*the God named ONE.*"[11] Drawing out Taylor's deconstructivist approach a bit further, we might ask why monotheism is at its most glaring on the smallest denomination, the one-dollar note. That note is not likely to circulate among the rich and affluent. Is it that those who possess the least are the ones who are most in need of protection?

Like, for instance, women, whose wages historically have been a very different kind of payment from a "man's wage," not set by their efficiency or productivity alone but also by custom or tradition, which set the parameters of the income women supposedly needed. As the ideal of a "family wage" (income earned by the man sufficiently large to support his wife and children) spread, women's wages were defined as supplementary income at the same time as women were charged with transforming their husbands' wages into domestic money. Although this turned women into the household's purchasing agents and budget experts, *his* money became *hers* only as his gift, not as her earned share of the income. Tellingly, *her* money even had a special vocabulary that set it apart from ordinary cash — allowance, pin money, egg money, butter money, spending money, pocket money, or dole. Women, Viviana Zelizer explains, were thus "caught in a strange predicament of being cashless money managers, expected to spend properly but denied control over money." Not even a wife's right to support was legally considered "a right to any definite thing or to any definite amount. [...] Whether the wife will get much or little is not a matter of her legal right but is a matter for the husband to decide."[12]

Paper Dollars and Social Difference

Different sorts of people are situated differently in relation to their practices of consumption. Consumption thus is at the same time a material and a symbolic activity. Following the French sociologist Pierre Bourdieu, we can say that our capacity to consume involves both our social position materially (for instance, in terms of the financial resources at our disposal) and our social dispositions and taken-for-granted assumptions. Bourdieu calls the latter our "cultural capital," that is, the norms of conduct we learn through our upbringing and education. Symbolic consumption means, then, to bring to bear our symbolic capital on a cultural object in terms of its appropriateness for us as certain sorts of people.[13]

No doubt for Brian Burrell's fictive businessman to have his identity confirmed through the dollar bills in his wallet requires a particular set of dispositions and preferences, taste and lifestyle, which may in turn be mapped onto a particular social class, solid, mid–American, loyal and patriotic but nonetheless haunted by the very real possibility of social decline.

Opposite: The Almightier, **from** *Puck* **magazine (May 15, 1907) (Library of Congress, Prints and Photographs Division, LC-USZ62-96301)**

Quite a different picture emerges from the talk of rebellious young people resentful of what their parents told them. What the dollar means to the new generation, a twenty-three year old man told Studs Terkel in the late 1960s,

> is blood, sweat and tears ... what you had to do to make a buck. [...] When a group of young people burnt money at the stock exchange and threw the bills down from the balcony, it caused pandemonium. There was a scramble for the dollar bills on the floor of the exchange. They were trying to say something about the value of money. A Vietnamese person can be burned with napalm. Animals are slaughtered. But a dollar is sacred. A dollar is not to be burned. In fact, it's a federal crime. This worship of the dollar is inherently an alienated idea. The people who killed themselves in 1929 were victims of it.[14]

Using money as a marker of social difference also plays a role in the custom to present as change only carefully polished coins, appropriately on a silver tray. Lewis Lapham observed such a practice in the Pacific Union Club in San Francisco. The club is a for-men-only club. Men traditionally have stood for the public sphere, for competition and self-interest; by contrast, women have stood for morality, religion, the arts, and social relationships. Men, Eva Boesenberg contends, therefore used to allay their bad feelings by making generous donations for charitable and cultural purposes, thus cleansing their names and their wealth from the odor of dubious business practices.[15] Rich men in particular are suspected of thinking of money in terms of the power its possession implies. Consequently, they have been lampooned by comically suggesting that they light their cigars or stoke their fires with paper bills. The gag, which may have been vaudevillian in origin, has been repeated from the Marx Brothers to Looney Toons cartoons to *The Simpsons*. There may even be a remote echo of this in the idea that one blow one's nose into a bill. A paper products company recently put on the market tissues that have images of the $100 bill printed on them.[16] The possibility that consumers stick their noses into Benjamin Franklin's face, as well as all the other examples suggest that it is not very useful to maintain that cultural representations are merely "reflections" of economic developments. Rather, people give meaning to cultural representations by projecting onto them wishes and emotions of their own. We can illustrate this point by further exploring some of the practices involving the two-dollar bill.[17]

Two-dollar notes turn up occasionally, but merchants and consumers do not commonly use them. Cash-register drawers often do not have a space for them, so they must go in another location, an annoyance for everyone involved. The Treasury Department, in compliance with their customers' preferences, announced on August 10, 1966, that no further $2 United States notes would be printed. Their successors, the Federal Reserve notes of the Series 1976 (the "Bicentennial" issue), also were not printed for almost ten years, that is, until the Series 1996 and 2003 notes. In addition, even of these two series were respectively printed only some 153 million and 121 million items, that is, about one percent of all notes produced.[18] How do we account for such a small number of two-dollar notes put into circulation? The Bureau of Engraving and Printing prints notes according to demand. In itself, the low demand for two-dollar bills may be linked to the peculiar reputation that the two-dollar note has. For one thing, the note is suggestive of twins, which may not be so bad. However, the "2" or "deuce" is also the lowest card in a deck. Getting it meant bad luck in gambling (hence the chorus line in a folk song recorded in Missouri, "I lost all my money but a two dollar bill").[19]

The two-dollar bill may also have acquired some of its lowly reputation from betting (two dollars used to be the basic bet in horseracing), or else from being used in voter payoffs in 1880, during a notoriously corrupt pre–Presidential campaign in Ohio and Indiana. The vote price was two dollars, and anyone who cashed a two-dollar bill at the time was branded a traitor, whether or not they received the bill to buy a vote.[20] The jinx may likewise have grown from people knowing that the term "deuce" also denotes the devil. This tradition is apparently still held on to "by some. To counteract the 'hex,' these people tear a corner off the deuces they meet. For some reason, that's supposed to ward off the evil."[21] The two-dollar note is even referred to as "whore note." Since it used to be the proper tender for houses of prostitution, it came to signify a measure of impropriety, a stigma that lasted long after the price for "a bit of action" was out of date.[22]

It is impossible to determine when exactly the two-dollar note began to acquire its stigma. One clue is price. Two dollars, it is said, was a good price for a bit of action — "back before inflation made prices soar."[23] Yet when is "back"? Certainly not as far back as the seventeenth century, when a large silver coin emerged among the pirates of the West Indies. The coin was worth about two dollars today, but at the time it was equal to thirteen *reales* in Spanish currency. All of the bad luck and superstition attached to the number 13 blanketed the new two-dollar note issued by the Continental Congress in 1775. The second issue of deuces came in 1862. Yet already the bill was unpopular. Its unpopularity is even a minor theme in the first of Horatio Alger's Ragged Dick novels, published in 1867. In the third chapter of the novel, Dick is in trouble, as his mentor has sent him into a store to get a two-dollar bill on the Merchants' Bank of Boston changed. Cashiers were always leery of the two-dollar bill, fearing they would give it out in change as a one-dollar bill. However, Dick is in trouble for a different reason: he is suspected of passing a counterfeit bill.[24]

More recently, the two-dollar bill has come to feature prominently in Stuart Woods's novel *Two-Dollar Bill*. In this 2005 novel the hero, Stone Barrington, a detective turned attorney, untangles the doings of a Texan criminal named Billy Bob Barnstormer, whose calling card is a two-dollar bill. (By way of another intertextual relation, a dead prostitute turns up in Barrington's spare bedroom, where his client has been staying.) One wonders what kind of two-dollar bill Barnstormer is using on his calling card. One possibility would be a Series of 1928 Legal Tender note, which was the first note of its kind with a portrait of Jefferson on the face and a view of his stately Monticello mansion on the back.[25]

The 1928 series was the only two-dollar note issued between 1929 (when the United States replaced its large size currency with small notes) and 1966. In 1976, an attempt was made to revive the two-dollar note as a Federal Reserve note, amid fanfare and excitement. Called the "Bicentennial" note, it featured a new back, showing an adaptation of Trumbull's *The Signing of the Declaration of Independence*. It was kept in use both for the Series 1996 and for the current Series 2003 notes. The "Bicentennial" note was hardly a smashing success. Its introduction was intended, in conjunction with the Susan B. Anthony one-dollar coin, to accompany the phasing out of the one-dollar note. However, the Anthonys were not popular, and the public seemed to maintain their mixed feelings about the two-dollar note. The one-dollar note thus continues in its accustomed role as the national money icon, whereas the deuce or two-dollar denomination enjoys a greater popularity as a collector's item — certain notes of the Series 2003 for instance sell for $100.[26]

People also like to tell funny stories about two-dollar bills, like the one about a man stopping at a Taco Bell for a quick bite to eat. In the man's billfold are a $50 bill and a $2 bill. This is all the cash he has on him. He thinks that with a $2 bill he can get something to eat and not have to worry about people getting mad at him. However, when the cashier

$2, Legal Tender (United States) note, Series 1928G, face, portrait of Thomas Jefferson (American Numismatic Association Money Museum)

$2, Legal Tender (United States) note, Series 1928G, back, vignette of Monticello (American Numismatic Association, Money Museum)

sees the $2 bill, he looks at it in a peculiar way and goes to talk to his manager, who appears never to have seen one and thus believes it is a fake bill. So the manager gets security:

SECURITY: "Mike here tells me you have some fake bills you're trying to use."
ME: "Uh, no."
SECURITY: "Lemme see 'em."
ME: "Why?"
SECURITY: "Do you want me to get the cops in here?"

At this point I was ready to say, "SURE, PLEASE," but I wanted to eat, so I said

ME: "I'm just trying to buy a burrito and pay for it with this $2 bill."

I put the bill up near his face, and he flinches like I was taking a swing at him. He takes the bill, turns it over a few times in his hands, and says

SECURITY: "Mike, what's wrong with this bill?"

MANAGER: "It's fake."
SECURITY: "It doesn't look fake to me."
MANAGER: "But it's a **\$2** bill."
SECURITY: "Yeah?"
MANAGER: "Well, there's no such thing, is there?"

The security guard and I both looked at him like he was an idiot, and it dawned on the guy that he had no clue.

My burrito was free and he threw in a small drink and those cinnamon things, too. Makes me want to get a whole stack of \$2 bills just to see what happens when I try to buy stuff.[27]

Consumption leaves untouched neither the people engaged in it, nor the objects involved, nor the sphere of production. Meanings may be attached to (or coded into) cultural objects in the process of their original production, but they are never automatically grafted onto the mental universes of those to whom they are addressed. This is strikingly obvious already from certain colonial paper money usage patterns. Goldstein and Lasser, in a recent essay, point out that "because paper money was money, it was valuable, and because it was valuable, torn currency notes were repaired. Such repairs commonly were made with pins, glue, paper tape, sealing wax, newspaper, old letters, and sometimes needle and thread." Resourceful menders even used fragments of other notes to keep them in circulation.[28] Practices of this kind not only demonstrate that during the colonial era paper money was valued and used extensively on a day-to-day basis. In addition, they are a reminder that historically the term "consumption" was not associated with the satisfaction of needs and wants; on the contrary, the root meaning of the word "consume" was to eat up, to waste, to dissipate, and even to decay. Consumptive bodies, for example, are bodies wasting away through illness. Religious imagery has preserved the notion of the fires of hell consuming the bodies of the damned.[29]

Of course, dollar bills are not conventional consumer goods: normally, they are not so much consumed as temporarily held before they are relinquished in the course of economic exchange. This particular practice can be illustrated by looking at the different kinds of money people are constantly creating. There is a remarkable variety of ways in which people "identify, classify, organize, use, segregate, manufacture, design, store, and even decorate monies as they cope with their multiple social relations." People distinguish lottery winnings from ordinary paychecks, as well as from an inheritance. A thousand or "grand" won in the stock market is not the same as \$1,000 stolen from a bank, or \$1,000 borrowed from a friend. A wage earner's first paycheck is not the exact equivalent of the fiftieth or even the second. A distinction is also made between an "honest dollar" and "dirty money," made by reference to the money's origin, which in the latter case is ethically dubious. Hence, there is the ubiquitous metaphor of "laundering" money. Tellingly also, a gang recruit, when asked by his social worker why he would donate to his church the twenty-five cents his mother gave him but not the money he got from the gang's robberies, answered in the following way: "Oh no, that is bad money; that is not honest money." Only honest money was to be offered to God.[30]

The term generally used for the creation of different kinds of money is "earmarking." As Viviana Zelizer explains, it means the creation of distinct kinds of moneys by attaching to existing currencies a variety of social relations. Thus, despite the anonymity of cash, not all dollars are equal or interchangeable, as they routinely acquire different meanings and separate uses. When Ishmael and Queequeg are starting their "hearts' honeymoon" early into Melville's *Moby-Dick*, the ceremony includes dividing into equal portions "some thirty dollars in silver"— not paper. By the same token, the owners of Captain Ahab's fated ship, mostly worthy Nantucket Quakers, were all "bent on profitable cruises, the profit to be counted in dollars from the mint"— not from any of the paper mills.[31] To a different world altogether belongs the "tin-can accounting" typical of working-class women, who were keeping apart moneys for separate expenses in tin cans— one for the house, another for food, for going out, and the like. People also keep "cash stashes"— generally one in the billfold of each adult, children's allowances, a "petty cash" fund in, say, a teapot, a dish of change for the parking meter, and so on. Likewise to "earmarking" belong attempts to "disguise" the money so that as a gift it would be different from a commercial transaction. (The practice would have seemed preposterous to Simmel, for whom a sum of money had an uncompromising "objectivity.")

One way to differentiate gift money is to use only special kinds of money such as gold or silver coins or brand-new dollar bills.[32] Another way to differentiate gift money is to gift-wrap it. Gift-wrapping legal tender, Zelizer suggests, is "one of the most dramatic ways in which people distinguished gift money." In the old days, dollar bills could be found decorating a belt-buckle, or being encased within a picture frame; at times they were even skillfully transformed into an artwork: an anecdote from the December, 1909, issue of *The Ladies' Home Journal* tells of a $10 note having been changed into ten one-dollar notes and inserted into a couple of posters. "One picture showed five sad dollar bills not knowing where to go while the second poster depicted a happy ending: 'five little dollars speeding joyfully' towards [the recipient's] purse. A 'dollar ode' completed the gift." Gifts of money were also an important part of immigrants' gift giving, from the Christmas dollars shipped each December to their families back home to money gifts sent to relatives for Easter, weddings, or other joyful events. Giving money as a gift still goes on. A study done by American Express in 1990 said that over $54 billion are being spent by Americans annually on money gifts, including cash, personal checks, and gift certificates. Another study says that after clothing and toys, money is, with food and beverages, the third most common gift item.[33]

All these distinctions are forms of consumption through which people create their own distinctions within a standardized currency, bringing dollar bills into meaning through a wide variety of signifying practices. These practices directly affect people's social lives. People not only think or feel differently about their various monies, but they spend them, save them, or give them away for different purposes and to different people. Earmarking money thus serves to make sense of people's individual and collective lives by personalizing purportedly neutral objects like dollar bills. Earmarked monies thus are not curious residuals of a primitive life in which, as Simmel put it, money still retained "sacred dignity" or the "quality of an exceptional value," but are a central feature of advanced capitalist economies. As a cultural practice, earmarking clearly shows that the supposedly defenseless consumers are not so defenseless after all: they are creative participants in the creation of modern culture rather than the alienated victims of a government-sponsored monetary system.[34]

Earmarking also shows that people care about what kind of money is involved in their transactions, and whose money it is. Nor are these distinctions erratic, romantic, or isolated exceptions to a dominant rational monetary system. On the contrary, social differentiation is pervasive, as not just individuals but also organizations and even the government distinguish among forms of legal tender and other monies. The greenbacks, for example, at first were not receivable for duties on imports, or for interest on bonds and notes. At the same time gold, though designated largely for foreign transactions, also was accepted for certain domestic payments, such as custom duties. Likewise of interest is the issue of managing one's money. For new immigrants in particular, it was not simply a matter of adopting a different currency; these new Americans had to learn the modern rational approach to money management. They were warned not to carry money in their pockets or leave it at home. Other sections offered guidelines on how to deal with savings banks and on "safe" ways to send money abroad or within the United States. Money management was likewise of concern to charitable organizations. For instance, *Charities and the Commons* in 1910 reported of immigrants that "carry greenbacks in their boots and seldom part company with their boots even in the hours of sleep." Others supposedly kept their savings in "bedticks, holes in the wall, or down the cellar," and even "in the gob in the mines," while thousands, noted the journal, "trust the store keeper or a private banker with their spare cash." Immigrants confirmed that many of them, wary of banks, "hid their money in their socks and buried it behind the plaster of their walls." It was expected (or hoped) that they would respond more favorably to postal savings banks, a popular institution in European countries.[35]

Consumption as Appropriation and Resistance

When immigrants, wary of banks, hid their money in socks or buried it behind the plaster of walls, they engaged in practices of difference that challenged and subverted the dominant dollar culture, which already was one deployed by the state, the "gigantic." The immigrants' practices clearly jarred with the symphonic effects of an official culture oblivious to local and regional, and ethnic or racial distinctions, subjecting people to the conceptual paradigm of the state. In the following, we will be discussing practices that involve re-appropriations of dollar bills through their translation into art objects. These "iconological vacillations between art as money and money as art," as Marc Shell calls them, likewise challenge and subvert the dominant culture.[36]

The observation that banknote engraving was "the only true American contribution to the arts" was doubtless justifiable, though it should be extended to include *trompe l'oeil* paintings. These paintings, a few European works notwithstanding, became "a predominant and widespread art form only in America."[37] Bruce Chambers in an exhibition catalog writes, "from 1877 through the first decades of the twentieth century more than 20 painters addressed themselves to this theme, some to the exclusion of all else."[38] Trompe l'oeil (trumping, or fooling the eye) paper money paintings are in the tradition of still life works. Some of the most famous arrangements of life-like monetary tokens are by John Haberle. His *One Dollar Bill* represents a single note, the $1 Silver Certificate of 1886 carrying a portrait of Martha Washington, life-size, seemingly attached to a board parallel to the picture. Another one, *Can You Break a Five?* (1888), depicts a five-dollar bill with a newspaper clipping, presumably by an art critic, which reads, "'Imitation' ... is one of those clever pieces of artistic mechanism showing an old greenback and other objects." His *Perfect Counterfeit*, which alludes to one of the worst social and economic problems of the time, counterfeiting, was refused a showing in Philadelphia in the aftermath of the Secret Service's fuss over a display of trompe l'oeil money paintings by another artist.[39]

Nicholas Brooks and John F. Peto likewise delighted in painting dollar bills or constructing elaborate collages. Other examples of trompe l'oeil money artworks include Ferdinand Danton, Jr.'s *Time Is Money* (1894), which pokes fun at Franklin's wisdom through the image of a bundle of dollar bills balanced against an alarm clock.[40] Victor Dubreuil's *Barrels of Money* (1893) looked so authentic that viewers were tempted to touch the barrels filled with dollar bills in order to participate in the displayed wealth. Few viewers were ready to confront the moral problem raised by the painting, that of the laying up of earthly treasures in a Christian society. There is likewise a measure of seriousness in Dubreuil's *Don't Make a Move* (ca. 1900), which shows a man with one eye closed pointing a gun at the viewer. A woman bank robber grabs bills from the money drawer. The painting has been said to recall the late nineteenth-century robber barons who, backed by bank tellers and guns, routinely extorted money from the people.[41]

The popularity of trompe l'oeil money paintings has been explained as a response to American materialism and worship of the dollar during the Gilded Age. The subjects, Edward Nygren summarizes, "were repeatedly discussed and often reviled in books, articles, novels, poems, songs, and caricatures by Europeans and Americans alike."[42] When painters turned to money as a subject, they left no verbal commentaries on the theme. Thus, we must deduce their attitudes from the visual evidence found in the pictures. In the case of Haberle's *The Changes of Time* (1888), there clearly is an allusion to the transience of time, as it treats the viewer to a procession of presidents via a selection of bills from colonial times to the $5 Silver Certificate of 1886. Together with other objects, such as a broken magnifying glass and a damaged old door, these objects evoke the passage as well as the ravages of time. Their placement also comments on American society, in particular on money, which is protected by or is at the core of the presidency. Yet money is also tainted. Thus, the picture alludes to the fate of the Continentals, which through mismanagement and corruption in a short time became worthless. At the top of the matrix of bills is the bill featuring a portrait of President Ulysses S. Grant, which speaks loudly of the financial scandals that riddled Grant's administration. Thus, what Haberle seems to be saying is that "types of money, like presidents, change, but money, like the presidency, endures. But he also perceives money as being at the center of the American political system, capable of being corrupted."[43]

On occasion, viewers were actually trumped into taking the imitation for the real thing. It is no surprise, therefore, that authorities were greatly concerned about what they considered a transgression of the boundary between official and illicit paper money. Generally such boundaries become more and more important the more centralized a state becomes. Artists from William Harnett, who began painting still lifes of Treasury notes in 1877, to J.S.G. Boggs, who became famous for persuading merchants to accept his personalized renditions of legal tender, would have their works impounded. Congress even passed a law in 1909 prohibiting all nonofficial copies of currency except those made by the United States Treasury.[44] Arists were never intimidated for long, though. Among more recent trompe l'oeil money artists is Otis Kaye, whose later works—like *Ten Dollar Bill* (1950)—have been described as "life size meticulous reproductions of specific bills which, if they had not been signed and dated by the artist, might easily be mistaken for counterfeit notes."[45]

Artists who play upon the distinction between real and ideal by reproducing dollar bills are not, of course, per se counterfeiters. Since the authorities often prosecute them, many trompe l'oeil money artists take to creating pieces that do not present or represent existent bills but instead "typify" or "idealize" them. Well-known examples are Roy Lichtenstein's 1956 painting *Ten Dollar Bill*, which occupies an entire canvas, and Robert Dowd's

Van Gogh Dollar (1965). More recent is *One Dollar*, by The Art Guys, a 22 × 30 inch computer vector drawing using graphite on paper.[46] Andy Warhol's screen prints *One Dollar Bills* likewise belong here. The prints, which are also known as *Printed Dollar Bills*, came about when in 1962 Warhol claimed to have run out of ideas and decided to ask a friend what he should paint next. His friend said she knew just what he should do, but it would cost him $50 for the idea. As soon as the ink was dry on the check, she held up her end of the bargain by asking Warhol, "What is it that you love more than anything else?—Money!"[47]

Each of Warhol's *Printed Dollar Bills* consists of 24 × 8 identical dollar notes, the multiplicity of which transforms the code of exchange value into a visual sign. Almost twenty years later, in 1981, Warhol returned to the idea with a variation on the theme of money. He began screening dollar signs on canvases in three sizes: 10" × 8", 20" × 16", and 90" × 70". A small *Dollar Sign* now sells for approximately $25,000, though the auction record was achieved in 1990, when one brought $46,750. *Dollar Sign* paintings are important, firstly because they personify the Warhol philosophy, "being good in business is the most fascinating kind of art,"[48] and secondly because they in pure form express an artistic point of view: dollar notes, the symbols of modern consumer culture, are empty signs that only refer to themselves. The artistic strategy makes them correspond to the new level of abstraction money has reached because of its electronic ubiquity, which stripped it of any materiality it possessed. Money, Warhol's paintings seem to suggest, exists only as a metaphysical order, the only exception being the poor, who are still and in all likelihood will continue to be collecting money in its concrete form of coins and notes in their paper cups.

Artistic (re-)appropriations of the national money icon unleash a tremendous creative potential in reinterpreting a seemingly banal everyday item through its translation into an art object.[49] Additionally, they make us aware that consumption is not passive but is active, involving practices that reveal the multiple meanings that can be attached to dollar bills. In Arman's (Armand Fernandez's) *Venu$* (1970)—dollar bills embedded in clear plastic in the form of a woman's torso—money is the apparent content, though it is significantly ambiguous whether it is the visible money or the less visible woman that is the artwork.[50] In 1972, Edward Kienholz composed *Their Brand X*, which juxtaposes nine dollar bills in a variety of denominations with four of his own notes. By calling the Kienholz notes the "better brand Y," the artist shows that unlike genuine dollar bills his notes increase in value over time. Artists like Ray Johnson and Robert Watts also turned to the theme of value. They would either integrate real dollar bills into their collages, or print realistically drawn replicas that were conceived to be given away free in large quantities in order to "devalue money and art at the same time." The two men were related to the art movement "Fluxus," an art exchange network that started in New York in the 1960s. In 1994, artists in Texas started a new project called "Fluxus Bucks," greenback look-alike bills that ostensibly are backed by "The Sticker Dude Institute." Upon request, any amount is given to artists who are "tired of worrying about money."[51]

Altogether, iconological vacillations between art as money and money as art are thriving. For instance, in the fall of 2006, an exhibition titled "Currency: Art as Money/Money as Art" was on display at The Mary Brogan Museum of Art and Science in Tallahassee, Florida. The exhibition presented an overview of the world of currency and value through the eyes of many contemporary artists, including David Greg Harth.[52] Early in 2009, in Brooklyn, NY, the BRIC Rotunda Gallery's exhibition "A New Deal, Art and Currency," highlighted relationships between American presidents and the economy, while observing how these relationships affect art-making. Artists included Mel Chin's Fundred Dollar Bill Project, Peter Simensky, Fine Art Adoption Network, David Greg Harth, Mark Wagner, Jesús Jiménez, Jon Kessler, Jonathan Herder, Anais Daly, and Anissa Mack.[53] Still other artworks play upon the erasure of money's materiality in the age of electronic money. A good example is *Laser Art You Can (Almost) Spend*, a holograph of a genuine $10,000 bill, series 1934-A, listed in the mail-order catalog of the trendy Sharper Image store. The bill carries a portrait of Salmon P. Chase, who as Secretary of the Treasury under Lincoln oversaw the printing of the nation's first greenbacks. Both the holograph and the electronic money it evokes point to the separation of the original link between the material substance that pieces of money were made of (the *electrum* in the case of coins) and the inscription stamped into or printed on them (the *intellectum*).[54]

Erasure of a different kind plays a role in the case of *Monopoly*, an artwork done in 1984 by David Bradley, an Ojibwa or Chippewa Indian. In 1995, it became part of *Indian Humor*, an exhibition of contemporary American Indian arts organized by American Indian Contemporary Arts (AICA) of San Francisco, and was shown at ten other venues around the country. *Monopoly* invites the viewer to confront and reinterpret the realities of bank and government notes as agencies of social influence and control: they enforce ethnic and class distinctions, endorse established institutions and authorities, and elide other historical events and persons. The artwork self-consciously plays on the national money icon (the one-dollar bill) both in order to depict the sale of Indian Territories and to conjure up an alternative history.[55] Other instances of producing meaning in acts of consumption involve the visual alteration of currency. These can take the form of creating fake denominations for playing practical jokes, of altering the images into hard-core porn, or of individualized statements scrawled onto bills. Some bills are more overtly political, such as those inscribed with the words "gay money" or a pink triangle, apparently as efforts to dramatize gay economic power.[56] Still other bills carry political slogans, such as a cartoon speech balloon coming from George Washington's mouth saying "I Grew Hemp!" Or else, they carry gospel messages around the back, or they may take up current issues, such as illegal immigration, by depicting, on the back of the "$5 Dólares Border Bill," a size thirteen boot at the backsides of America's "snoozing politicians."[57]

Also popular are rubber stamps with political slogans that can be imprinted in ink directly onto a bill. When France refused to join the United States in the coalition it was trying to build against Iraq, many American politicians were irate. Some tried to get people to boycott France, for instance by refusing to buy French goods. At least one "patriot" stamped dollar bills with the slogan "FRANCE NO GOOD / FRENCH GO HOME / U.S.A. #1."[58] Beginning in 1998, New York artist David Greg Harth stamped the words "I AM AMERICA" on a one-dollar bill. That started a large project in which the artist usually introduces a new message about once a year. The messages, which are stamped on various denominations in red or black ink, are political or social based. After the events of 9/11, Harth, who lives twenty blocks from the Twin Towers, put into circulation over a million one-dollar bills stamped with phrases like "I AM NOT AFRAID" or "I AM NOT TERRORIZED."[59]

Leaving marks on bills has been related to the graffiti tagging movement of the 1980s. The practice has also been related to the "Kilroy Was Here" markings, which were ubiquitous during World War II, as well as to the hobo markings on freight trains during the Great Depression.[60] In actual fact, the idea that dollar bills are texts to be read goes back much further. As early as 1834, William Leggett, a staunch supporter of President Jackson's hard

David Greg Harth, "I AM NOT TERRORIZED," from Currency Works, ongoing multi-media work (© 2009 David Greg Harth, courtesy of the artist)

money policies, suggested that a "cheap ... and most effectual method of disseminating the principles of those opposed to incorporated rag-money factories would be for them to write upon the back of every banknote which should come into their possession, some short sentence expressive of their sentiments. ... 'No Monopolies!' ... 'Jackson and Hard Money!' 'Gold before Rags!'" In proposing that paper dollars be turned into political leaflets, Leggett recognized that these texts offered new possibilities of public communication.[61] Paper bills, though they were often derided as rag money, derived special power and appeal from the fact that they could address a broad and impersonal readership anonymously. So did the mock shinplasters parodying the fractional currency that had come into circulation as a result of the shortage of hard money that accompanied the limited-currency policy Leggett endorsed.

One such mock shinplaster, of fifty cents denomination, is depicted in chapter One. The caricature has President Jackson riding a pig headlong towards a precipice; his congressional ally, Missouri Senator Thomas Hart Benton, on an ass, follows him. Both men are in pursuit of the "Gold Humbug" butterfly, symbolizing their efforts to restrict the ratio of paper money in circulation to gold and silver supplies. As President Jackson reaches for the butterfly, he cries "By the eternal!! I'll have it, Benton!" While Benton shouts encouragement, Van Buren, riding a fox, cunningly deviates from the two men's disastrous course and follows a downward path towards the bank — the Second Bank of the United States, against which Jackson led his famous "war." From below the precipice, Nicholas Biddle, the Bank's president, sights Van Buren. The note is endorsed by the publisher, Henry R. Robinson, who promises "to pay Thomas H. Benton, or bearer, Fifty Cents, in Counterfeit Caricatures at my store." It is dated May 10, 1837, the date of the emergency suspension of specie payments by New York banks. By that time, genuine as well as mock bills already were part of a whole network of written and printed words proliferating across their spatiality — like street signs, handbills, trade cards, sandwich-board advertisements, parade banners, and daily newspapers. Both Leggett's ironic awareness of paper dollars as handbills and the proliferation of mock shinplasters are good reminders that money never was simply an economic issue; it was also always a cultural issue, linking unrelated people and objects in networks of circulation and exchange, and thus a powerful symbol of the way of life that came with modernization and modernity.

Marking out the national motto, "In God We Trust," is a classic, though rarely has it been done as originally and intelligently as in an artwork by David Greg Harth.[62] Clearly, the "texts" on all these altered —"defaced"?[63]— notes belong to a discourse running counter to the official, grand discourse of the state in which the Founding Fathers and other public figures are properly honored. Other examples of insurgent practices include "Fnording" notes, which means writing the word "FNORD" over the eye-in-the-pyramid symbol on the back of the one-dollar bill. To do so supposedly disrupts the Illuminati's ability of receiving the power generated by people thinking about and using money.[64] Whereas "Fnording" owes its logic to the Voodoo practice of sticking pins in a doll to hurt by some kind of "magic" the person the doll is linked to, the so-called "Deception Dollars" were a more down-to-earth phenomenon. These bills formed part of a movement protesting the Bush administration's policies in the aftermath of the events of 9/11, in particular the "U.S. government's attacks upon Afghanistan, the Bill of Rights, the Constitution, and Iraq."

The first issue of Deception Dollars was given away at an anti-war march in San Francisco in October 2002. Additional issues soon followed. The bills became a veritable "consciousness raiser" for people who had been "bombarded with mainstream and government propaganda and want to know the truth." Deception dollars did not just expose President Bush as an "International Terrorist"; they also served as portals to information on 9/11, for instance by listing a number of sites, with each site providing links to other sites. The high denominations of some of the bills—for example, "One Billion Deception Dollars"—obviously served to highlight the magnitude of the "BIG LIE" dished up by the Bush administration.[65] Paradoxically, using the national money icon in this way nevertheless shows a pristine commitment to American ideals, ideals that the dissenters cherish even as they reject the prevailing policies of their day. This use is part of a ritual of consensus that works as a particularly American strategy of containment. By reducing every struggle to another ratification of the American dream, identity politics ultimately affirms the national culture.

Other appropriations of the national money icon reveal a desire to get a sense of security, comfort, and legacy. Supporters of President George W. Bush may have drawn all this from the "Federal Millennium Notes." Privately issued in 2000 as fantasy notes, they are also known as "Bush Notes" because of the oversize portrait of the 43rd president on the

David Greg Harth, "REMOVE," from Currency Works, ongoing multi-media work (© 2009 David Greg Harth, courtesy of the artist)

face.[66] That president also appeared on the so-called "2001 Note," which was put on the market in the aftermath of 9/11. The note's back shows, in lieu of the two sides of the Great Seal, pictures of the World Trade Center and the Pentagon. The arms of the New York Fire Department and of the New York Police Department also appear on the note, together with a number of slogans, such as "Time marches on ... but we will never forget" and, on the note's face, "You can run, but you can't hide."

Earlier examples of appropriating the national money icon for security, comfort, and legacy are the "Liberty Banknotes." Produced in 1986 by the Statue of Liberty-Ellis Island Foundation on the one-hundredth anniversary of this all-American icon, the notes are advertised as "a personal memento to be cherished in the homes of patriotic American families for generations to come."[67] The "Federal Inaugural Notes" that were put on the market by American Art Classics, Inc., for President Barack Obama's inauguration in January 2009 doubtless were also intended as personal mementoes to be cherished. A similar function, though in a more subdued form, pertains to "souvenir" notes, which are often genuine notes featuring a string of signatures, location, and/or a time. Replica notes of selected currency are also made into popular "souvenir cards," which may be engraved and printed by the Bureau of Engraving and Printing, though some are privately issued.

Also into the category of security, comfort, and legacy belong the "short snorters," pieces of paper money that bear the signatures, good wishes, and sometimes the hometowns of officers, enlisted personnel and others connected with a war effort. On occasion, bills are taped together to accommodate a string of signatures. The tradition of signing and swapping dollar bills and other notes appears to have started among pilots, crew and passengers in the early days of trans-oceanic air travel, but spread widely among American military personnel during World War II. The U.S. Series 1935A $1 Blue Seal Silver Certificate was the most common bill in circulation then and became the note of choice for short snorters, though other bills were also popular, as was foreign currency acquired during duty in various theaters of operation. The term itself originated from "short snort," which was a slang expression for less than a full shot of liquor, or what was considered to be just about enough for responsible airmen about to fly their craft. The connection to drinking stuck. A wounded soldier going home would collect an autographed dollar bill from each of his friends. "When you get home, pal," they would say, "have a snort on me."[68]

It is perfectly legal to put one's own mark on a dollar bill, as long as it does not intentionally render the bill unfit to be reissued. Legality is made use of through the practice of money tracking. A website called Wheresgeorge.com invites players to purchase a small rubber stamp and use it on their dollar bills. The stamp allows people to track a bill's journey by its serial number on the web. The game was started in 1998 and has become hugely popular. At present, over 100 million bills are being tracked and located, to a total value of over $560 million. Most of the bills are of the $1 denomination, 83 million of them, or 72.56 percent of all bills. Californians seem to be addicted to the game the most: by March 2007, California players had entered 9,650,278 bills, though the top-scoring place by ZIP code is Wattsburg, PA, with some 626,972 bills entered. The top-scoring individual user reportedly entered more than 124,000 bills. The game is competitive, the point being to get the most "hits" from the most interesting places. (To date, the bill with the most "hits" has been registered thirteen times.) Understandably, people try to cheat. In order to prevent this, the game's creator continually updates the validation process for the bills that are entered into the system, weeding out serial numbers that are obviously false or bills entered repeatedly by someone trying to claim a higher hit ratio.

Money and dollar bills have been all-important in film. Three hundred or so of the films produced by Hollywood after 1915 bear the word "money" in their titles; and hundreds of the films produced after 1910 have sported the word "dollar"—from *The Almighty Dollar* (1910) to *The Last of the Two Dollar Bills* (1970).[69] A number of films are also titled *In God We Trust*, from the earliest one in 1913 to Jason Reitman's celebrated one of 2000. In 2005, episode twenty of the TV series *The West Wing*, then in its sixth season, was likewise titled *In God We Trust*. As regards the cinematography, money shots traditionally include scenes such as "poker games, bank robberies, payoffs, ransoms and oldtime gangsters lighting up stogies with $100 bills. Today, money shots of drug buys, lap dances, and dollar bills stuffed in G-strings or rolled to snort coke have proliferated." There are also innumerable shots of fists full of cash, of bill wads, stuffed suitcases, or carpet or duffle bags—all for feeding our cinematic imagination, where cash transactions, though becoming obsolete in real life, live on in fetishized form.[70]

Filmmakers did not at first use genuine notes in their productions.[71] Instead, they would use what is called "prop money," that is, bills (and coins) that somehow look like genuine currency. Over the years, the film industry has produced an immense wealth of imitation greenbacks, which have also become popular with collectors.[72] A relation can be made out even between the type of motion picture money and genre. For Western films, the prop notes often suggest "Mexico," or more specifically "Pancho Villa," a leader of the

Canyon Raiders (Monogram, 1951), film still (courtesy of Fred Reed)

Mexican revolution and provisional governor of the state of Chihuahua in 1913 and 1914, whose notoriety attracted journalists, photographers, and filmmakers alike. Hence, we frequently see provisional state notes from Chihuahua, usually "Dos Caritas" notes, so called because of the two small portraits on their faces. Notes of this kind were used for instance in the 1951 film *Canyon Raiders*. "Dos Caritas" notes are also found in films of other genres, as the film industry did not print its own money but would rent it from specialized companies nicknamed "prop houses," and thus would have to make do with whatever was on the market.

To portray United States currency more realistically in film, prop notes gradually evolved to single portrait-style. At first, the preferred color was orange, which made the notes appear somewhat like Gold Certificates; more recently, prop money has come to more closely resemble Federal Reserve notes. This would create more movie realism at the same time as it would bring film companies and prop providers under closer government scrutiny, as stray notes occasionally wind up in merchants' tills. In order to avoid this risk, prop masters would see to it that the notes were inscribed with "For Motion Picture Use Only" or "MOTION PICTURE MONEY." In other instances, the notes were made to bear the film company's name so that they could be more easily traced back to their place of origin — a strange case of the working of the logic of spatiality spelled out by Emily Gilbert.[73]

Another trend in the motion picture industry is to rent bills from currency dealers. This is often a godsend, especially for meticulous filmmakers like Martin Scorsese, who employed a great quantity of historically accurate real United States coins and paper money when filming *Gangs of New York* (2002), which is set in the 1846–1864 period. As for the future, it can be expected that increasingly motion picture companies will be opting for real currency rather than symbolic money. Not only is this now legal, but also in light of skyrocketing production costs the expense of using genuine bills for dressing a scene is becoming a rather negligible quantity. Special unique notes have been and will be produced for fantasy and science fiction movies, from *Blade Runner* to *Total Recall* to *Coming to America*, with Eddy Murphy as the Prince from Zamunda. Also worth noting are bills using portraits of actors or celebrity. As Fred Reed found, "Celebrity Cash" is available for "just about any contemporary or vintage actor or celebrity from Katie Holmes to Marilyn Monroe to Martha Stewart."[74]

Also a part of the world of entertainment are "Disney Dollars," which may be used as legal tender, at par with United States Dollars, though only at Disneyland, DisneyWorld, and other company locations, including Disney stores. Thus, these dollars belong to the world of corporate scrip or tokens, a form of private currency that in the past used to be issued by stores, businesses, churches, and other organizations. The first Disney bills came in one and five dollar denominations from 1987 to 1989, and in 1990 the company added the ten-dollar bill to the list. The $1 Disney Dollar bears the image of Mickey Mouse where one would be looking for Washington's portrait, while Scrooge McDuck signs as Treasurer. Goofy appears on the $5 bill. Minnie Mouse, who was featured on the original $10 bill, gave way to Donald in 2003. The backs of the 2003 series are all about Disney theme park castles: Sleeping Beauty Castle from Disneyland Resort ($1), Cinderella Castle from Walt Disney World Resort ($5), and Le Chateau de la Belle au Bois Dormant from Disneyland Paris ($10).[75]

Disney Dollars are usually printed on paper, with a number of anti-counterfeiting features such as micro printing, so they can be safely redeemed for goods and services. Some will never be redeemed, but will be kept as souvenirs, forgotten, or simply thrown away.

Some Disney Dollars are even made of wafer. In their case, the stereotypical mom saying, "Get that thing out of your mouth! You don't know where it's been!" clearly does not apply, as wafer dollars are specifically created to be eaten. Note that the word "wafer" is synonymous to the word "host," the bread consecrated in the Christian Eucharist and regarded as the body of Christ sacrificially offered to the faithful at communion services. The Eucharist wafer — usually manufactured like a coin — suggests the representation of the spirit (the ideal) and matter, or spirit together with matter, which in another context could verge on idolatry. In the context of the Disney Dollar wafers, only capitalism and religion converge. There is likewise at least a faint echo of the Eucharist in chocolate bar wraps that are styled as dollar bills and thus are a distant reminder that, as Bernard Laum wrote in the 1920s, one origin of money was shared food.[76] In our case, what is intended for eating is of course not the wrap bearing the image — the $20 bill featuring Andrew Jackson — but the sweet content.

Definitely not for eating are the "Dream-Dollars," which are the official currency of Nadiria, a fantasy world thought up by artist Stephen Barnwell that purports to be the lost colony of Antarctica. Dream-Dollars are free, but purely fictive, though they have their own history, and they feature many peculiarities. One of them is that there are four variations or editions of each note of a specific value — spring, summer, autumn, and winter. Another is that the notes come in unusual denominations, with values of 1, 4, 7, 13, 28, 52, 91, and 365 dollars. The "natural" numbers system serves to introduce a different form of thinking and is even said to have an influence over the colonists' subconscious and their dreams.[77] "Linden Dollars" ("L$") are the official currency of *Second World*, an Internet-based virtual world that opened in 2003 and that by the end of January 2007 allegedly claimed more than three million registered accounts worldwide.[78] Linden Dollars constitute a fully dematerialized form of money, marking the final stage in the historic development of modern money from specie to paper money to electronic money. By contrast, million-dollar bills are collectibles, meaning that they are still very material. They are not real United States currency, though, not real money. A bill of this kind therefore is not worth $1,000,000 in United States Dollars; one cannot "cash" it, "convert" it or "sell" it for

$20 gift pack, original size 1.6 × 5.6 in.

$1,000,000 in United States Dollars. One such Million Dollar Bill, dated 1997, shows an American eagle on the face and a picture of the Fort Knox Gold Depository on the back, a nostalgic reminder of the time when there was still enough gold at Fort Knox to back the country's currency.[79]

The producers claim that their million-dollar bills are printed from engraved steel plates on real currency grade paper with a unique watermark. This should give the notes the "feel of real money." In addition, safety features such as micro printing, a fluorescent seal, and what is called "Invisible Printing," are included. The back of each note is printed with a special high security "invisible" ink. If the note is placed under an ultraviolet or black light, the words "A SYMBOL OF THE AMERICAN DREAM" can be clearly seen repeated across the note. Thus, each bill is an "excellent item for promotions, gifts or simply having fun." At present, the company prices the bills at $9.50 (€ 7.13) apiece in "uncirculated" (UNC) condition.[80] Somewhat pricier are the Million Dollar Bills created by the North American Bank Note Company in 1988. In that year, the I.A.M., the International Association of Millionaires, commissioned 825,000 of these bills to be used as certificates of wealth. The bills somehow resemble the $100,000 Gold Certificates of 1934/1935, which carried a portrait of Woodrow Wilson. On the I.A.M. bills, however, an image of the Statue of Liberty appears on the face, while on the back there is the denomination in number and in wording. Advertised online as "The Original Authentic I.A.M. Million Dollar Bills," they now sell at $75.00 apiece (up from $12.50 per in 1988).

Also on the market is a Million-Dollar Bill featuring the Statue of Liberty on the face and a picture of the United States Capitol on the back.[81] A portrait of former President Ronald Reagan graces yet another Million-Dollar Bill. Advertised as "political funny money" by the company producing it, the bill is overwritten "The Grateful States of America," in recognition of "America's most beloved president."[82] People can make different statements with personalized business cards, such as the custom million-dollar bill offered by Million-Bill.com, which suggests that its bearer (whose portrait is on the bill) has made it with KPMG.[83] Businesses often have advertising handbills printed, sometimes in the form of currency look-alikes. Or else, they issue gift certificates, which may likewise resemble genuine currency. As do bills that belong to play money or educational money. All these bills, funny money, personalized money, and collectibles alike, consciously mimic the national money icon, building on the widespread recognition of it as a sign.[84]

Turning paper dollars into objects of personal adornment and display involves re-appropriations of and, sometimes, even resistance to the currency (and through it, to the authorities issuing it). In each instance, people make statements about their identity in relation to the conventions of mainstream or official (state-sanctioned) culture. Through the symbolic work of "consuming" paper dollars, then, commodified objects are translated from an "alienable" (because linked to capitalist production and the government) to an "inalienable" condition; from being apparent symbols of estrangement (alienation at work; from the political process) to being objects that symbolize identity and "belongingness" (as part of the culture of a particular group). Like artistic appropriations, these forms of consumption are not passive processes but active ones. People style identities for themselves through practices of consumption that overturn, transgress, or at least bracket (as in the case of Monopoly-like board games play money) established social divisions and that resist easy classification by providing a temporary relief from the monopoly of the federal government over the currency.

Popular culture also has made ample use of the national motto. In 1988, the Christian glam metal band Stryper released an album bearing it as the title. In 1981, the hard-core punk band Dead Kennedys released an album titled *In God We Trust, Inc.*, containing all-out attacks on organized religion ("Religious Vomit"), President Reagan ("Bleed for Me"), and rightwing extremism ("Nazi Punks Fuck Off"). Finally, in 1993 rapper Brand Nubian released an album titled *In God We Trust*, which for the most part is a rallying cry for Louis Farrakhan's Nation of Islam. Not everyone seems to have taken the national motto quite so seriously, though. Such as, for instance, the people who produced or put up the little posters one used to see in mom and pop stores, diners, gas stations, and many other establishments throughout the United States, near the cash register. The posters had "In God We Trust, All Others Pay Cash" written on them.[85]

Although the posters, which obviously relate to President Eisenhower's patriotic gesture of 1957, are somewhat less often seen today, they are a good illustration of the fact that icons circulate among and are interpreted by socially differentiated groups of users. In the case of the cash desk posters, the users proclaim that they are not able to place trust in people they do not know. The unspoken idea behind the posters seems to be better to be safe than sorry. This says a lot about prevailing views of human nature and about where we should be placing our trust. It is no surprise, therefore, that the website maintained by the Michigan Bar Association is likewise graced by a poster-like sign with the national motto, advising members on the proper action in the case of a client's inability to pay before work starts. Even less subtle is a publicity poster produced by Universal Studios to promote the film *Scarface* (1983). The poster, which uses the face of the current one-dollar bill as a template, features a portrait of Al Pacino as the fictional drug lord and lead character Tony Montana; it carries "SCARFACE" as a denomination and, in an intertextual relation to the national motto, is inscribed with the question "WHO DO I TRUST?" and the answer "I TRUST ME."[86]

Each of the artifacts discussed in this section makes use of an icon's main characteristic — its wide recognition as a sign. Only wide recognition makes possible the inversion of established hierarchies in the various representations, when low becomes high, and high becomes low. The inversion is only temporary, though, and it does not altogether dissolve the "contractual relationship" of Americans with the state. Hence, there is a good deal of ambivalence: paper dollars serve as signs of value and identity and, contrariwise, as signs of the failure to create value and identity.

There is a good deal of ambivalence in popular renderings of a well-known cartoon figure, Scrooge McDuck, or rather, "$crooge," as the "S" is usually realized as a dollar sign, hence "$." Donald Duck's wealthy uncle came into being when in 1947 comic-book cartoonist Carl Barks (a former story man for Disney cartoons) needed a miserly old relative for a story, "Christmas on Bear Mountain." In this tale, Scrooge serves as a mere prop, a simple caricature of his namesake from Dickens's *A Christmas Carol*, Ebenezer Scrooge. Barks would later claim that he originally intended to use Scrooge only once, but eventually was able to draw more from him. Obviously, Scrooge, who is supposed to have made his fortune between 1890 and 1920, has certain similarities to the robber barons and industrialists of that era. Thus, he proudly asserts, "I made it by being tougher than the toughies and smarter than the smarties!" Yet he is also allowed to say of himself, "*And I made it square!*"[87] Scrooge McDuck is the noble capitalist of the Cold War era who by luck and by pluck has risen from obscure and humble origins in the Old World. This is not a very original idea. In this regard, the Scrooge stories are very much like the Horatio Alger stories of the late nineteenth century — or like *Acres of Diamond*, the famous inspirational lecture of

Russell Cromwell, of the same era. They all suggest that the escape from suffering and poverty lies in "the individual plugging away, searching for a break, and walking away a millionaire."[88]

Scrooge McDuck is usually depicted, not with paper dollars but with gold coins. (He also searches for gold on several occasions throughout his long career.) "Buckaroo," a known alias for Scrooge, thus is a somewhat unhappy choice of name in that, through its allusion to "buck," it evokes paper money rather than gold. Taking into account the hero's predilection for gold, the Scrooge McDuck stories foreground the sensual experience of money, which is so much stronger and more direct with coins. Tellingly, Scrooge's hobbies include diving into his money like a dolphin, burrowing through it like a gopher, and throwing coins in the air to feel them fall upon his skull. Scrooge's fixation on coins, which verges on fetishization, evokes a long tradition. Around 110 BCE, the Roman historian Suetonius portrayed his Caius Caligula as being seized "with a mania for feeling the touch of money [so that he would] pour out huge piles of gold pieces in some open place, walk over them barefooted, and wallow in them for a long time with his whole body."[89]

George Eliot's Silas Marner is a bit more restrained, though he too at night "closed his shutters, and made fast his doors, and drew forth his gold." Silas would then spread his gold out "in heaps and bathe his hands in them"; then he would count the coins and set them up "in regular piles, feeling their rounded outline between his thumb and fingers," thinking of the many more that were still to come through the labor of others "as if they had been unborn children."[90] One also should not forget Frank Norris's Trina who, when McTeague is gone, would play with her money "by the hour, piling it, and repiling it, or gathering it all into one heap." Trina would "bury her face in it, delighted at the smell of it and the feel of the smooth, cool metal on her cheek. She even put the smaller gold pieces in her mouth, and jingled them there. She loved her money with an intensity that she could hardly express. She would plunge her small fingers into the pile with little murmurs of affection, her long, narrow eyes half closed and shining, her breath coming in long sighs."[91]

The "lust of counting" that we observe in all these fictional and not-quite-fictional characters, their lust of "seeing numbers mount up, derives largely from treasure and is most comprehensible there," Elias Canetti writes in *Crowds and Power*. Other forms of counting or, rather accounting, are much less concentrated. This is why the figure of the owner secretly counting his or her treasure is so deeply engraved in people's minds. No less deeply engraved, Canetti continues,

> is their hope of discovering treasure for themselves, treasure that has been so well hidden that it lies forgotten in its hiding-place and no longer belongs to anyone. Disciplined armies have been corroded and overcome by their greed for treasure, and many victories turned to defeat. The transformation, even before battle, of an army into a band of treasure-seekers is described by Plutarch in his life of Pompey.[92]

Some treasures are collected quite openly, as a kind of "voluntary tax," as Canetti puts it, "and in the understanding that they will fall into the hands of one person, or of a few."[93] The greed that unites people on such occasions—as during a lottery—clearly was the driving force in popular comedies of the 1930s such as *Gold Diggers*, a Hollywood extravaganza featuring Ginger Rogers that portrays ordinary people suddenly coming into money.[94] At the time, this Hollywood preoccupation—people looking for money—spoke of economic anxieties, which it channeled not into new values, but into traditional ones. Thus, people were not after paper money so much as they were after specie, gold and silver, or diamonds. Even Dorothy's slippers in the film are not ordinary, no longer silver, as in the original novel, but still precious, ruby. Traditional values die hard, no matter what the government is doing.

In the 1930s, the government was certainly doing many things, but one action in particular directly relates to obsession with specie. In 1933, the year *Gold Diggers* was produced, President Roosevelt signed the Gold Reserve Act, which stipulated that paper money no longer was redeemable in gold. The fact that the currency in circulation all of a sudden was purely symbolic must have had far-reaching psychological consequences. One was the undermining of trust. Seen in this light, the later claim by leaders of the movie industry that it had been they, rather than the Roosevelt administration, who had staved off revolution, because by producing comedies they had worked hard to make people happy, makes perfect sense. Gold, specie, was after all considered the real thing, the natural money, though ironically, representations thereof "provided some outlet for some of the frustrations of the 1930s by turning them into farce, comedies about money and the effort to get it."[95]

Bringing together politics and the entertainment industry serves to counter the seductive power of attempts to "romanticize" the purportedly "subversive" nature of consumption. It is certainly true that users are made "similar to" what they are in processes that some critics have connoted pleasurably.[96] However, the "pleasures of consumption" thesis only works in certain instances—such as in comic imagery, on cash desk posters, chocolate bar wraps, etc. In addition, both the "pleasures of consumption" and the "subcultural" approach to consumption are prone to disconnecting consumption entirely from the forces and relations of production. If applied too closely to the usages of paper dollars, there is always the danger of neglecting questions of the relative power between producers and consumers. Furthermore, there is the danger of eliding the differences that are reflected in consumption—differences of class, age, gender, race and ethnicity, political leanings, even of place or geography.

Practices of consumption cut across given social divisions, creating new social identities and differences in the process. A good example is "American Change." The poem, which Ginsberg might have written in response to New York critic and social analyst John Jay Chapman's *cri du coeur* of 1895—"Why doesn't someone write a poem on money? Nobody does anything but abuse it. There's hardly a good word for money to be found in literature"—is quite literally all about the currency, though the imagery comes into view, not literally but figuratively. Thus, in a rare ekphrastic encounter we meet "Washington again, on the Dollar, same poetic black print, dark / words [...] surrounded by green spiderwebs designed by T-Men / to prevent foul counterfeit."[97] The poem's lines are highly concentrated, with an astonishing exactness of focus, though as has been noted, the facts are not always quite right. In this, as well as in its incantatory tone, "American Change" anticipates Ginsberg's later poems such as "The Change," which are often made from scratch notes of what he saw through the window on bus, plane, train, or boat trips.

The epigraph, "*S.S. United States*, July 1958," suggests that the poem was written during Ginsberg's return to New York from an extended trip to Europe. (Ginsberg had met Ezra Pound in Italy, and he may have taken inspiration for the poem from Pound's attacks on money-mad materialism.) "American Change" retains the long, surging lines reminiscent of the poetry of Walt Whitman, which Ginsberg had already used in "Howl," "A Supermarket in California," and "America." In choosing to write about the Almighty Dollar, however, Ginsberg found the perfect object for his favorite technique, which links the transcendent with the materially mundane. In this, the poem goes beyond a mere denunciation of the pieties of the Eisenhower era. To the extent that the national money icon is brought to the mind's eye, the rhythm of the money experience is open to discovery — the rhythm of money, "looked on, after a long time far from home in mid / Atlantic on a summer day," of money providing "memory in my aging hand," and of money becoming a reminder for instance of the Statue of Liberty ("I ride enfolded in money to you").[98]

Preferred Readings

Any social order, if it is to last, depends on some form of consensus, made possible through concessions by the ruling classes and cemented by intellectual and moral elites. Thus to assume that consumption practices are inherently democratic and even implicitly "subversive" not only entails a failure to recognize the particular "geometry of power" in which the paper dollar has come to be triangulated; also it is to imbue consumption with a romantic glow of creativity. In theory, everything is of course possible. In practice, however, one particular attribute has governed the consumption of the paper dollar for the past century and a half — nationalism or statism. Brian Burrell's story about the American businessman stranded abroad is a fiction but it is tied to its creator's imagination by a sense of national belongingness. This is evident from the good man's habit of flipping through his wallet in search of a one-dollar note in order to have his identity confirmed. It is also evident from the author's lament that the manifest ignorance, on the part of most Americans, of the "story" the one-dollar note has to tell is quite a "sad aspect of the American sense of civics."[99]

Burrell's lesson on civics begins with the story of the Great Seal of the United States of America. Work on it (and on the mottoes) had begun as early as 1774, when Thomas Jefferson realized the importance of creating symbols to represent the new order of the ages. On July 4, 1776, right after the signing of the Declaration, Congress likewise felt that a seal would somehow legitimize the historic endeavor of breaking away from England. A committee of three distinguished men was appointed — Franklin, John Adams, and Jefferson. Since the three men did not get anywhere near an acceptable design,[100] a call went out to Pierre Eugene du Simitière, a Swiss-born artist with considerable knowledge of heraldic devices. Du Simitière, Burrell suggests, contributed the motto "*E pluribus unum*," from many, one. Simitière also contributed the all-seeing eye of Providence, described by Burrell as both a quite common artistic motif and a Masonic symbol. Still, Congress did not find acceptable any of the suggestions. Another committee went to work, now with a young Philadelphia lawyer named William Barton, a skillful draughtsman and with a passing knowledge of heraldry. From his attempts survived the unfinished pyramid which in Burrell's words suggests "a solid foundation with work yet to be done."[101]

Burrell devotes a great deal of space to the Great Seal's three mottoes and to how they have been used and, as well, abused during the course of time. He suggests that "*E pluribus unum*" is the most familiar motto by far, having been used not only on the face of the seal, which in its final version was adopted on June 20, 1782, but also on the national currency, on commemorative coins, the presidential seal, and other ceremonial emblems. Originally, Burrell says, the motto connoted the joining of thirteen separate colonies into a single nation, whence the term "federation motto." Yet the literal translation also conveys the —

much more modern—concept of many peoples joined as one nation. As regards the two additional mottoes on the reverse of the Great Seal, Burrell claims that they are only "vaguely familiar to most Americans, and not very well understood." He therefore explains that "*Annuit coeptis*" translates as "He favors our undertaking," whereas "*Novus ordo seclorum*" means "A new order of the ages." However, when Burrell adds that "A new order of the ages" has "*recently* been construed to mean 'A new world order,'" this alters our perception of national icons in some basic ways. In particular, it makes us aware that readings of them are far from universal or timeless but always determined by their specific historic contexts.[102]

Burrell views national belongingness with a measure of emotional distance. Thus, he quite matter-of-factly tells us that the reverse of the Great Seal has been printed on the back of the one-dollar note only since 1935. Because of this decision ("one of those quirks of fate"), the three mottoes "found their way into every wallet, purse, and pocket in America" and are now "distributed more widely in this country than the Bible." The colloquial tone is upheld in Burrell's saying that exactly how this happened and why "is not entirely clear, which opens the door to all manner of conspiracy theorists who see apocalyptic doom in the words 'new world order,' if not in the New Deal itself." By bringing together words and phrases like "conspiracy theorists," "apocalyptic doom," and "New Deal," Burrell positions himself at a distance, from his main source, a government document, as well as from the lunatic fringe and from opponents to the New Deal and whatever it stood or has come to stand for.[103]

$1 note, detail: The Great Seal of the United States, obverse

Although Burrell concedes that Roosevelt "definitely interpreted [the reverse of the Great Seal] as a Masonic symbol," he is careful to point out that the President was never too close with the Masons. The Masons, Burrell tells us, were at the height of their power in the early twentieth century, yet their ritualism declined and their activities became more and more degraded, mostly taking the form of drinking and womanizing. Roosevelt, we are told, "understood his brothers well enough to make a point of being out of town when they held their annual convention and parade in Washington." The image emerging of Roosevelt's relation to the Masons is one of ambivalence. As a politician and political leader, Roosevelt "knew better" than to become associated with them. Yet, lodge members constituted a significant proportion of the

$1 note, detail: The Great Seal of the United States, reverse

political and social elite in America, so making a good impression on them was good politically. Given this situation, Roosevelt must have been only too glad when the Great Seal came on his desk as part of a proposal to change the one-dollar note.[104]

The story continues with the heraldics of the Great Seal. In this, Burrell faithfully follows his source, Patterson and Dougall's *The Eagle and the Shield*. He tells us, for example, that in contrast to what is often thought "*E pluribus Unum*" is not the national motto. It may have been around for a very long time, and it also seems to be falling easily off the tongues of Americans, but it is not. The national motto, Burrell emphasizes, "lies elsewhere on the dollar bill — not the one that Franklin Roosevelt designed in 1935, but a much newer one." This was the $1 Silver Certificate of the 1935G Series in 1957, issued two years after Congress decided on an official national motto; it was followed in 1963 by the $1 Federal Reserve note. The motto in question is of course "*In God We Trust*," which is not only the most recent American motto but also "by far the most controversial." There is, Burrell claims, "some truth" to the frequently heard complaint that the motto owes its place to the efforts of "a religious fanatic who pressured the secretary of the treasury during a time of civil war." In addition, Burrell concedes that there is "something to" the civil libertarians' claim that a reference to God on United States currency "violates the separation of church and state."[105]

Civil libertarians have not been the only ones unwilling to quietly tolerate state-sponsored forms of worship. Challenges towards legislating God into public life have come from a variety of corners. Burrell's reading of the national money icon may be patriotic, but it is not nationalistic, least of all jingoistic. Equally balanced, if not distanced, is his reading of various court decisions, for instance when he says that the motto could only be defended "at the expense of its meaning." That is to say, every time a court defends the motto, it does so by claiming that it has lost any specifically religious significance, or else that it does not promote any particular belief. Burrell is aware of the implications of such rulings. By protecting the motto in this way, the courts ultimately acknowledge that it is "*central to the patriotic fervor that zealously guards national symbols.*" None of this is characteristic of Burrell's discourse. This is evident from his saying that, "The God 'we trust' is the one whose all-seeing eye looms over the unfinished pyramid on the back of the dollar bill." Of course, by saying "we trust," Burrell identifies himself as an American, though he puts "we trust" under inverted commas. What perhaps most clearly identifies Burrells' subject position as a concerned but not zealously patriotic citizen is the concluding sentence: "Tempting as it might be to write off the motto as so much bunk, it is here to stay."[106]

To write off the national motto as so much bunk is definitely not on the agenda of the people for whom "In God We Trust" is indeed a sacred symbol, along with the Declaration of Independence, the American flag, or the Statue of Liberty. These people's responses to the national money icon are indeed unequivocally nationalistic. Their existence in contemporary America and, by extension, of nationalistic practices in the consumption of the national money icon, is evident from various web documents that can be found in a variety of versions on private or officially instituted websites, including those of American schools. The title of one such document is "The Dollar Bill." The document boldly declares that, "what is on the back of that dollar

In God We Trust, $1 note, detail

bill is *something we should all know*." The first thing we should all know is that on one side of the Great Seal there is the famous image of the pyramid with the all-seeing eye at the top and the year 1776 written in Roman numerals at the base. In addition, we should all know that the pyramid has thirteen steps, representing the thirteen original colonies; and that it does not have a peak but is so to speak uncapped, meaning that in 1776 the building of the United States was not yet finished. This is how the document's author remembers and interprets the picture of the uncapped pyramid: "This country was just beginning. *We* had not begun to explore the West or decided what we could do for Western Civilization."[107]

The subtitle of the document in question, "Proud to be an American — a dying tradition," is of particular interest for our discussion, as is the lament that "no one knows what the symbols [on the $1 bill] mean." The words are indicative of the nationalist context within which the author interprets and remembers the national money icon. Readings of the American eagle on the reverse of the Great Seal bring this home even more forcefully. There is no particular reason to say that the American eagle is in "every National Cemetery in the United States" and thus also on the "Parade of Flags Walkway at the Bushnell, Florida National Cemetery." Or else, that the national bird is "the centerpiece of most hero's [sic] monuments" and, slightly modified, is part of the seal of the President of the United States, "always visible whenever he speaks." Furthermore, why are we asked to remember that the American eagle "is a symbol for victory," and was "selected as a symbol [...] for two reasons: first, he is *not afraid of a storm*; he is strong and he is smart enough to soar above it. Secondly, he wears no material crown. *We had just broken from the King of England*."[108]

Also important in the document's meaning-construction and remembering is the theme of unity. "At the top of the shield," we learn, "you have a white bar [the sign of the United States Congress] signifying congress, a unifying factor. We were coming together as one nation." Moreover, this text continues, "the shield is unsupported. *This country can now stand on its own*." As regards the words written on the ribbon in the eagle's beak, they are rendered in this way: "'*E Pluribus Unum*,' meaning, one nation from many people." Historically, this is nonsense: originally, the phrase referred to the union of thirteen colonies into states: this is the unity represented by the thirteen stars in the constellation. "*E pluribus Unum*" thus originally echoed the often uneasy relations between the thirteen original states and the federal government. "The Dollar Bill" instead notices the picture that shows the stars surrounded by what appear to be clouds. According to its author, they are the "clouds of misunderstanding [as they are] rolling away. Again, *we were coming together as one*."

In "The Dollar Bill," the relationship between the one and the many is construed as one of individual and society, possibly also of the integration (or assimilation) of immigrants into America, and thus as a reformulation of the melting pot metaphor, which goes back to Crèvecoeur's Farmer James. The function of such a construction is, again like Crèvecoeur's, to transcend social contradictions. This means that the discourse of "*Unum*" stands for unity and homogeneity when in fact the predominant social norms are and always have been rather individualistic. The contradiction is only a seeming one, and can be explained in terms of confusion between likeness and identity, or sameness. Americans know perfectly well that the national monetary icon is *not* identical with the nation or the nation's history. Only the ideological use of iconicity makes a claim to identity or sameness. More generally, we can say that the rhetorical force of the iconic correspondences in question resides in their being perceived as somehow natural.[109]

The rhetorical strategy of making things appear natural or regular is evident also from the use of numeral magic for supporting the idea that the United States is somehow exceptional. "They say," we learn from "The Dollar Bill," that "the number 13 is an unlucky number and this is almost a worldwide belief. You will usually never see a room numbered 13, or any hotels or motels with a 13th floor." Symbols of the United States are said to be different, though, as is America itself. We only need to "think about this:

13 original colonies, 13 signers of the Declaration of Independence, 13 stripes on our flag, 13 steps on the Pyramid, 13 letters in the Latin above [the pyramid, i.e., in the phrase *annuit coeptis*], 13 letters in '*E Pluribus Unum*,' 13 stars above the Eagle, 13 plumes of feathers on each span of the eagle's wing, 13 bars on the shield, 13 leaves on the olive branch, 13 fruits, and if you look closely, 13 arrows. Interestingly, also, the 13th Amendment provided a new birth of freedom for many Americans.[110]

The use of numeral magic is a good illustration of the symbolic potency of the one-dollar bill. It continues to be an important factor in readings of the eagle on the Great Seal. (It should also be noted that the document in question personifies the eagle by using the masculine possessive pronoun "his," a noticeable departure from the bird's original construction as feminine.) The author of "The Dollar Bill" construes the pictorial detail of the eagle holding an olive branch and arrows in the following way: "This country wants peace, but *we will never be afraid to fight to preserve peace*." Clearly, these words recall the theme of the United States as an example to the rest of the world, a "Citty on a Hille" as it were, and with a special mission. In "The Dollar Bill," the theme is expressed in the following way: "The Eagle also wants to face the olive branch, but *in time of war*, his gaze turns toward the arrows."

The question is, in time of what war? Since the temporal reference is so vague, we can only guess. Are we to recall the historical events of the War of Independence? Alternatively, of the War of 1812? Maybe the Civil War? Or else events of the more recent past? World War II maybe? We might also be referred to the Cold War of the 1950s, which was the immediate context of various strategies of cultural continuity, such as the acceptance of the national motto or the addition of the phrase "under God" to the Pledge of Allegiance. As an even more recent example, the First Gulf War seems to suggest itself. That possibility seems plausible in light of the time reference in the copyright note, which reads "1996–2000 Mary Alice McLarty." However, since "The Dollar Bill" was still online in February 2002, its meaning is subject to at least one more revitalization. To the contemporary reader, the phrase "*in time of war*" may well refer to "America's new war," that is, to the "war" against terrorism. There is no way to decide conclusively which war is meant, nor do I believe are we supposed to.

We can decide more conclusively on the political ideology that buttresses a text like "The Dollar Bill." "Why didn't we know this? [Meaning the bill's symbolic dimension.] Your children don't know this and their history teachers don't know this. Too many veterans have given up too much to ever let the meaning fade. Many veterans remember coming home to an America that didn't care. Too many veterans never came home at all. Tell everyone what is at the back of the one dollar bill and what it stands for, because nobody else will." Language of this kind speaks of the ideology of the political Right who believes that Vietnam was lost because the young and the Left had betrayed the country through resisting what to them mistakenly seemed an unjust cause.[111]

It would be presumptuous to ascribe similar ideological leanings to Kenston High School of Chagrin Falls, Ohio, though the school's website displays "The Dollar Bill" in almost identical form. Possibly, this reveals that national myths are mostly revitalized in times of crisis, when the national culture seems under attack. The cultural continuity that such documents define may be imagined; yet at least it is defined as offering some certainty in a climate of change and uncertainty. Altogether, then, the consumption of the paper dollar does not follow a pre-written script. It is predominantly an active process. Dollar bills are translated from a mere medium of exchange into objects with meaningful connotations, contingent upon the position they occupy within the cultural life of particular individuals and groups. Consumption therefore is a form of "production" in its own right, though given the uneven and differentiated nature of dollar bill use it is not a good idea to entirely divorce consumption from production. Instead, it is necessary to bear in mind the complex geometry of power that it is subject to and that gives shape to the relationship between production and consumption. In the final chapter, we will examine questions of power geometry in detail by exploring the ways in which the consumption of the paper dollar has thrown up some interesting questions about the regulation of cultural life.

SIX

Cultural Regulation

Paper Dollars and the
Conduct of Life

> Money! A special piece of paper, decorated in somber colors, which everyone agreed was worth something — and she believed it, everyone believed it — until you took a pile of that paper to a bank, a respectable, traditional, highly confidential Swiss bank and asked: "Could I buy back a few hours of my life?" "No, madam, we don't sell, we only buy."
>
> — Paulo Coelho, *Eleven Minutes* 240

Introduction

Those who wish to govern and regulate the conduct of others always seek to structure and shape the meanings of things. They do so by implementing a variety of policies or "regulations," which serve to reproduce a particular pattern and order so that things will appear "regular" or "natural." This applies as well to the currency, which can serve as a symbol of government power, at the same time as it can serve as a reminder of the limits to that power. Until the Civil War, on American currency would be deployed images and techniques that would reassure as well as inspire — from vignettes suggesting fiscal trustworthiness to the judicious choice of a bank's name. Today's monetary texts are the only medium of exchange authorized by the state. Consequently, people will recognize themselves and each other in precisely the terms specified by the state or, rather, by the dominant ideology. This process, though symbolic, is one of repression. Not surprisingly, therefore, regulations are often fiercely contested.[1]

Contestations over the regulation of currency include struggles over meanings and interpretations, as in debates over the differences between paper money and specie. Paper money, unlike specie, cannot be put away in reserve as a real value. Trust or confidence therefore make up the difference between the piece of paper with specific marks and images on it that enables its bearer to command a measure of food, drink, clothing, and other goods, and a piece of the same size torn from a newspaper or magazine that is fit only to light a fire. As long as that difference was not fully established, paper dollars would offend people's sense of a social order, endangering the established classifications. Gold and silver were considered to have intrinsic value; consequently, they were considered "natural" money. The paper dollar only had extrinsic value; at best, it would *represent* value. As a medium of exchange it would take elements associated with specie, allowing it to leave its normal position within the social order and to enter a domain where it was materially and symbolically out of place, the ghost of money, the shadow of a shade, to paraphrase Hawthorne. The paper dollar's breaking with the logic of intrinsic (or "natural") as opposed to extrinsic (or "unnatural") values would often create a kind of moral panic. Common reactions were attempts to exclude or reject this form of money.

In the period following the Civil War, the greenbacks were rejected for being "purely symbolic" money. The term means that the money's value is not grounded in the value of the precious metal represented by it but merely upon a general forbearance and acceptance of the issuing institution on the part of buyers and sellers. This was also the case with subsidiary small coins, introduced in the nineteenth century. More importantly, it was the case with the Treasury (United States) notes, whose value from the beginning was grounded solely in people's acceptance of and faith in the Union government. In a more general sense, purely symbolic money is fungible only as long as there is trust in its ability to be passed to someone else in a seemingly endless but highly unstable chain of credit. Specialized institutions therefore concerned themselves with the value of paper dollars, such as the Treasury Department or, later, the Federal Reserve System. These bodies would adopt a variety of measures to regulate the usage of the bills and thus to assuage people's anxieties.

Among these measures were promises of negotiability, such as the pay the bearer on demand and the legal tender clauses, which began to be printed on notes issued by these institutions. Other measures involved efforts towards curbing counterfeiting. Even more important, perhaps, were measures that would limit the supply of paper money in order to retain its value.[2] More recently, there have been defenses, on the parts of both the Department of the Treasury and the Department of Justice, against challenges to the use of the national motto on the currency. Still other measures include efforts towards educating the public about monetary matters, as well as towards "marketing" new fiscal products such as the new Sacagawea dollar coin. In addition, it leads us on to plans to introduce a new $500 note as a measure to fight against "jumbo" euro notes. That measure connects paper dollars to the rise of credit and debit cards, and other forms of cyber cash or electronic money, which point to the radical dematerialization as well as the denationalization of money.

Paper vs. Coinage, or, Printing Currency, Creating Confidence

The paper money form prompted considerable debate and gave rise to much anxiety already during the colonial period. The circulation of paper bills depended on what seemed to contemporaries an almost magical belief that the notes constituted wealth, that paper, though considered worthless, could pass as gold. Thus from early on paper money was recognized as a signal of value that presumed on the trust of others in a highly unstable community of debtors and creditors. Still, the costs of fighting all those little wars—against the French, or the Indians, or both together—made the printing of paper money a necessity, and the question of faith in it a matter of principle: "What," Cotton Mather asked, and one can almost hear the preacher's voice, "is the word Paper a scandal to them? Is a Bond or Bill-of-Exchange for £1000, other than paper? And yet is it not as valuable as so much Silver or Gold, supposing the security of Payment is sufficient? Now what is the security of your Paper-money less than the Credit of the whole Country?"[3]

If paper money in America began as a means towards achieving an alchemical effect, at the same time as it symbolized the limits of economic and political authority, in the early days at least acceptance of the bills needed a bit of encouragement. The reason is that most of the pro-paper voices were those of debtors and speculators, while other groups often suffered considerably from paper currency, such as creditors, larger farmers, and the wholesalers and merchants who had trading links with England and needed "sound" money for their imports. Their views are expressed in a number of pamphlets that were very bitter about soldiers and widows having to buy things they did not need in order to get rid of the depreciating paper bills at a discount. What was to be done? In Massachusetts, for instance, a five percent premium was granted to those who were willing to use paper bills for tax payments. This practice was followed by South Carolina in 1703 and by New Hampshire and other colonies in 1710 and 1712, respectively. Concerns would prevail, though.

Even Benjamin Franklin, though in 1729 he had argued for *The Necessity of a Paper-Currency*, in his *Autobiography* ruefully conceded that there were "Limits beyond which the Quantity [of paper money] may be hurtful."[4] If a Franklin can be in doubt, it is no surprise that the rich generally opposed any addition to the volume of money in circulation. Distrustful of the idea of a "general" prosperity, these people were ranged against all ventures into paper money. Typically, Governor Thomas Hutchinson of Massachusetts saw supporters of paper money as an "ignorant majority [...] unrestrained by a superior class."[5] The same stance was taken by Crèvecoeur, who in the guise of the ingenuous Farmer James wondered about the strangeness of people who "can live upon what they call bank notes, without working, they think that all the world do the same."[6] Behind such words is the suspicion that a paper currency would become the cause of social upheaval, a suspicion that was connected to the aspirations that wealth founded on paper entailed. What both Crèvecoeur and Hutchinson and others dreaded was a new type of personality arising from people whose wealth was no longer based on property or specie, and thus would be incompatible with earlier social and moral values and with tradition.

The fears that the proliferation of paper money would be a threat to social stability nevertheless were those of a distinct minority who had taken their views largely from the classicist English tradition that considered paper money scandalous. The majority of Americans appears to have loyally followed Adam Smith, who in his *Enquiry into the Nature and Causes of the Wealth of Nations* had declared, "The trade of Scotland has more than quadrupled since the first erection of two publick banks at Edinburgh."[7] In America, too, great quantities of bills were constantly being created, revolutionizing money as well as life. Around 1800, coins comprised most of the currency. By 1811, about half of the available coin was in bank deposits, as backing for the paper currency. A great deal was hoarded by individuals, while substantial amounts, gold coins in particular, were exported, for overseas purchases and to be sold there for profit — hence the contemporary colloquialism of the American eagle taking wings and flying away. The following print, which probably dates from 1808, takes on the practice of selling specie coins for a profit. It caricatures Philadelphia merchant and financier Stephen Girard, here called "Stephen Graspall, Banker and Shaver," as saying: "I declare I have not seen such a thing [as a dollar coin] since I sold the last I had in my vault at 18 per cent premium." Behind him hangs his signboard, advertising "Paper Wholesale and Retail. No foreign bank notes taken on deposit except such as are about 5 per cent above par."

In order to make coins reappear in circulation, many states passed laws prohibiting banks from issuing bills with denominations under five dollars. The Maryland legislature

The Ghost of a Dollar, print, c.1808 (Library of Congress, Prints and Photographs Division, LC-USZ61-908)

even imposed a penalty of five dollars on "any person who shall pass such notes of banks not chartered by this state." The desired effect — to "get rid of an amazing quantity of filthy rags," to use the words of a contemporary observer[8] — was never achieved. People just had to rely more and more on paper money. Note issues were reported as high as $100 million in face value as early as 1815. Their real value, however, had slumped in most cases, though most people continued to accept the notes at a lower value. Some people, however, did so only with a grudge, and in 1833 a critic called paper money a "curse" and, in his capacity as financial advisor to President Jackson, wrote a long treatise on the "ruinous effects" that commercial banking had on landowners, farmers, traders, and on all the industrious classes of the American commonwealth.[9] Three years later Ralph Waldo Emerson observed that, "a paper currency is employed, when there is no bullion in the vaults." Therefore such practices were symptomatic of "the corruption of man," of "duplicity and falsehood," and of "rotten diction." Emerson's view would have been a familiar one with his contemporaries, with other "Locofocos," as supporters of Jackson's hard money politics were commonly known, as well as, strangely, with the English Tories.[10]

For cultural critics like Emerson, paper money evoked the dangers of big cities and the treacherous instability of urban societies where confidence men and swindlers thrived. Cultural critics and middle-class reformers had yet to wait for a time when, as New York merchant William Dodge proudly noted, "we never think of looking at bank-bills."[11] That time arrived with the relative stability of the postbellum period, though one of the first contemporaries to recognize the importance of a common economic language had been Alexander Hamilton, whose belief in a large national debt was based on the conviction that in this way the government's creditors would be tied to the new government. Critics of Hamilton's plan — largely anti–Federalists who would later become Jeffersonian Republicans — argued that it would only benefit speculators. It is easy to see why Emerson, good Jeffersonian that he was, would have felt bad about this. Yet Emerson's anxieties were leading into a profound quandary. Not trusting the central state to ensure that the paper dollars retain their reliable value, he would be just as unhappy with notes from private banks. The alternative, to do entirely without paper money, of course meant living in the past.

There were no banks in America before the Revolution. If people wanted to borrow money, they got it from other individuals. Brokers would also step in, as readers of Washington Irving's tale "The Devil and Tom Walker" will recall. Not all lenders would make a pact with the devil, though, but rates for borrowers generally were extortionate at two to four percent — per month.[12] Nevertheless, immediately after the Revolution, individual states (most notably Pennsylvania, Massachusetts, and New York) began to incorporate banks. Their precedent was soon followed by states that had no local branch of the Bank of the United States, and that would charter both private commercial banks and state banks. These banks not only loaned money and engaged in various financial services (they would finance the state of New York for building the Erie Canal, completed in 1825), but also emitted notes to be used as currency. The notes were backed by specie and other securities deposited in the bank.[13] Of course the notes were only as good as the amount of "bullion in the vaults," to use Emerson's words, or at least of a portion of it. As Adam Smith had calculated in his *Wealth of Nations* of 1776, a bank might safely loan about five times as much cash as it actually possessed in specie. Thus as banks proliferated, their old critics appear to have been quietly maneuvered out of politics.

The issuance of paper money under the scheme of free banking encouraged the spread of agriculture and industry, making possible the payment of wages in factories and workshops. In this regard at least, it fulfilled its function as symbolic money.[14] James Stewart in 1767 had described it in *An Inquiry into the Principles of Political Economy* as "no more than a species of what is called credit [and which is] principally useful to encourage consumption and to increase the demand for the produce of industry."[15] This scheme worked, though not without disruptions. In January 1842, a number of Cincinnati banks, "not in fair repute perhaps," were assaulted, "and their books, papers, notes and fixtures were destroyed and thrown into the streets." The "most alarming such situation in American banking history" occurred when in March 1834 the Bank of Maryland failed, after years of operating at a deficit and after its notes had become unacceptable to many in the financial community. Creditors and note holders began to riot and mobs raged out of control in the city of Baltimore for almost a week, destroying houses and personal property of the former bank owners.

Incidents of this kind lend additional weight to a point made by Richard Doty, that "the private note was the victim of its own success."[16] Although at first the procurement of a banking charter appears to have been a matter of having the proper political connections, the number of note-issuing banks increased dramatically—from a few dozens by 1810 to hundreds by 1830, to thousands by 1850. At the same time, there were new freedoms of design. The great days of the private bank note thus were marked both by a multiplicity of excellent designs and by an increasing risk from the forger. That risk increased almost exponentially in light of widespread illiteracy, unfamiliarity with printing of any type, and the fact that genuine notes were often issued for fraudulent purposes. Especially vulnerable to counterfeiting were the South, the Southwest, and the West, which were more short of specie and correspondingly more dependent on paper money than the rest of the country. Consequently, many sound-looking bank notes were, to borrow an expression Marx used in *Capital*, quite literally "worthless tokens." Accepting these notes was risky, and might easily lead to bankruptcy, a fate that lies at the core for instance of Edgar Allan Poe's immensely popular tale "The Gold-Bug."

The tale, which first appeared in 1843 in Philadelphia's *Dollar Newspaper*, begins with an account of the bankruptcy of a Mr. William Legrand, his forswearing of all business practices, and his subsequent voluntary exile on a remote island off the coast of South Carolina. There he engages in a quest of "entomological specimens," that is, of beetles. A golden-colored Scarabaeus beetle sets him off on a wild treasure hunt. Incredibly, the hunt is successful, and Legrand is finally rewarded with the "real" thing, gold: he unearths an "oblong chest of wood" that contains, in coin, "rather more than four hundred and fifty thousand dollars [in] gold." Additionally, the hunt yields hundreds of objects, also in gold and exceeding "three hundred and fifty pounds avoirdupois." Yet not only are both the amount itself and its estimated value of "a million and a half of dollars" verging on the miraculous. The story in particular foregrounds (and implicates the reader in) the incredible ingenuity and resourcefulness that human greed—lust for gold or, again following Marx, worship of the "Lord of commodities"—is capable of spawning.[17]

Poe does not tell us whether the treasure will allow Mr. Legrand to live happily ever after. Instead, he leads us into several contexts at once. First there is, for instance in Legrand's bug for gold, which appears to drive him almost to madness, an echo of traditional dislikes of money, such as Aristotle's verdict that its pursuit was unnatural, or its association, in Christendom, with avarice.[18] Not surprisingly there is, secondly, the connection with death and violence. In the pit, there are also two skeletons, presumably of two associates killed by the legendary Captain Kidd when the treasure was buried. Thirdly and finally there is, via the Scarabaeus beetle, the "gold-bug" of the title, the association with dung, which is not necessarily of any intrinsic value — like paper money that is not backed by precious metal, or like the "ideal" cryptographic drawing that the treasure-hunting protagonist cashes in for "real" gold, so much of it that he could easily pay all his dues to the United States government, which under the Independent Treasury Act of 1846 should be paid in specie.[19]

Had the happy Legrand really used his treasure for the purpose of paying his dues, surely the act would have raised some eyebrows. For, the treasure was all "gold of antique date and of great variety," while there was "no American money." Taken together, the references in the story to, on one hand, the cryptographic map Legrand finds as well as the "scrap" on which he makes a "rough drawing" for the narrator and, on the other hand, to gold seem to suggest that treasure is precious metal and American money is paper money. On the basis of such evidence it is safe to say that Poe's tale engages in contemporary debates over what was to constitute America's money.[20] Indeed, the tale abounds with words and phrases that suggest the world of paper or paper money. Already the "dirty foolscap" upon which Legrand makes his pen drawing points beyond its literal meaning of a cap worn by fools or jesters to a watermark for paper and, additionally, to writing- or printing-paper. The piece of paper in question bears a watermark that, because he "perceive[s]" it, leads Legrand to the buried treasure, while the incredulous narrator and, by extension, the reader, are quite literally left wearing a fool's cap. Tellingly also, Legrand, after examining the drawing, "took from his pocket a wallet, placed the paper carefully in it, and deposited both in a writing-desk, which he locked."[21]

Another detail of the paper's surface appears as a "signature," while the "death's head at the corner diagonally opposite, had, in the same manner, the air of a stamp, or seal." It is these details — the authenticating marks on paper — that lead Legrand to the buried treasure, that is, to "real" money. Yet Legrand finds the buried treasure only because he trusts these marks, while the narrator, to the annoyance of Legrand, is full of suspicions. Thus, the narrator cannot see that there is something in the paper after all; as a result, he remains under the spell of the gold bug, which he mistakenly believes to be the "index" to the treasure. This lack of trust, which also infects the narrator's relation to Legrand, about whose "sanity" he begins to harbor "suspicions," constitutes a breach of the friendship "contracted," as the narrator begins the tale by saying, between Legrand and himself. For, right at his first visit to Legrand, the narrator, rather than trusting Legrand and accepting his drawing or representation of the bug, demands a substantiation: "I must wait until I see the beetle itself." As Kevin McLaughlin puts it, "distrust here amounts to the unwillingness to accept a representation, perhaps a promise, and the insistence that something more substantial be delivered. *In financial terms, this is the insistence on gold, hence the appropriateness of the gold bug in the scene.*"[22] What Poe in his advocacy of paper over gold seems to suggest, then, is that in economic exchange Americans must have trust.

Poe's tale, which the *Public Ledger* in Philadelphia would call a "capital story," appeared at the end of a protracted period of financial and economic crisis. In that period, which had begun with the panic of 1837 as the aftermath of Jackson's war on the Second Bank of the United States, both the question what backs the value of gold and the authenticity of paper bills from the private (state-chartered) bank was of great concern to people. The absence of federal paper money only worsened the situation.[23] Whoever was wealthy yesterday could be poor today, and vice versa, as Hawthorne knew only too well.[24] It became everyone's vital interest to make monetary transactions as quickly as possible, to avoid long-term transactions, and to learn to take up economic opportunities instantly. "Never Keep a Paper Dollar in Your Pocket Till Tomorrow," read the inscription on a token issued by an observer of the difficulties with paper money in 1857.[25] What was there to do? Specie payment was impossible, since most of the coins in circulation had become so worn, clipped, and generally underweight from extended use that the banks would accept them only by weight, which was less than their face value. Any number of fraudulent banks was issuing paper money.

To alleviate the crisis, most states began to regulate banking, especially by introducing stricter reserve requirements. Louisiana state legislators initiated what is considered the most far-ranging action to regulate banking. Indeed, the Louisiana Bank Act of 1842 was the first law passed in the United States that required banks to keep a gold or silver reserve against notes and deposits.[26] The law also prohibited the practice, so popular with "wild-cat" banks, of issuing notes and then buying them up at a discount. Banks were also not allowed to pay out any but their own notes over their counters. Depositors were accorded protection. Banks that defaulted on the bonds they had guaranteed were taken over by the state and liquidated. Last but not least, banks were placed under the supervision of a Board of Currency from which bank directors or their commercial partners were excluded, as were exchange brokers. These measures certainly made banking safer, especially since they were copied by other states and by the federal government (as well as, for good measure, by the Bank of England).

Distrust of paper money remained, though, and was often well founded, especially in the 1850s, which saw new banks springing up everywhere. "Speculation in bank bills was rife," Q. David Bowers observes, and it was "aided by tricks and espionage, such as publishing false reports that a truly sound bank had failed, and buying up its notes in distant places for deep discounts."[27] Perhaps the most unusual caper is reported from a bank in Salem, New Jersey, which paid out notes that to the casual viewer looked as if they had been issued in Philadelphia, Pennsylvania. The intention was to ship the notes to Illinois. There, as well as in other distant places, Philadelphia bills were apt to be highly valued, while few people would have heard of Salem, New Jersey. Only with a magnifying glass is Salem visible in the bank title on the note's face.[28]

People and paper dollars were indeed hard to trust. Anyone trying to create a new town would try to drive up real estate values on land they owned. People would sell sections of land they knew were worthless. Others paid for goods in counterfeit bills. Still others sold useless patent medicine, watered-down whiskey, phony lottery tickets, stolen horses and cattle. As the frontier widened and the cities and towns spread, people would move far and move often, and not only in the West either. No matter how responsibly most of the private banks managed the flow of paper money, the general experience was one of a growing intensity in economic life or a quickening of its pace that also spread to other areas of social life. In short, the general experience was one of alienation. In American literature, that experience found a heroically sinister expression in Poe, a tragically romantic one in Hawthorne's *The House of the Seven Gables*, and a nihilistically comic one in Melville, whose novel *The Confidence-Man* appropriately is set on a Mississippi riverboat called *Fidèle*.

Melville's novel of 1856 — that "most thoroughly American story," as a contemporary reviewer remarked — traditionally has been read as an allegory on the devil boarding the riverboat for the purpose of luring the trustful to their spiritual death. Later criticism has turned on the confidence man's role in exposing the philosophical confusions of his victims. From another perspective, it has been recalled that this largely unpopular novel was suggested by the exploits, in 1849, of a shyster by the name of William Thompson, whose appeals for "confidence" gave a philosophical twist to the wiles of the swindler at the same time as they provide the link with paper money. As all kinds of paper money, genuine notes, ghost notes, counterfeit ghost notes, and phantom notes, are peddled about the ship, the reader learns one rule for telling the cheat: watch out for the man who walks away with the dollar bills. Yet with the introduction, in one of the novel's final scenes, of an old man poring over a counterfeit detector, the security of this sign system is put into question as well. As the old man notices, searching for authenticating signs on the dollar bills in his possession, "there's so many marks of all sorts to go by, it makes it kind of uncertain."[29]

The moral and epistemological dilemmas posed by the confidence man motivate and underwrite the novel's deepest desire — a desire for certainty grounded in a reliable authority. For the writer of fiction, the problem was insurmountable. There was no authority outside of fiction that the reader could trust. In the world of money, at least a measure of certainty had been provided by the promise of specie-backed money, though that promise was often merely illusory. Beginning with the Civil War, that promise was superseded by one that rested on a far more abstract and transcendent notion: the credit of the nation. The "monopoly" the federal government then acquired on the making and circulation of *all* money within the United States meant that paper, as well as coin, issues thereafter rested on that government's power. Consequently, the currency underwent a transformation from a commercial convenience into something more grandiose, a symbol of the nation itself. At first, this meant little more than a confidence that the federal government would be able to pay its bills. But with the war effort represented as a struggle for the preservation of the union, these obligations assumed a deeper significance. The greenbacks in particular came to represent the United States: they were issued "by the nation, for the nation, in order to pay for the preservation of the nation."[30]

The value of the greenbacks, because it rested solely on the future credit of the nation, depended on the outcome of the war that had prompted their issue in the first place. Indeed, this was something like a pyramid scheme, and merchants at first were often skeptical of the new, unfamiliar notes and in many instances refused to accept them. Some railroad companies and even various banks in New York City did the same. Government employees, Union soldiers, defense contractors, and others who only had such bills to spend were particularly hard hit. The situation was settled when the Treasury Department directed the various federal depositories to redeem the notes in gold, if requested.[31] Another problem arose when the greenbacks began depreciating to about a third of their face value, a development that is said to have introduced to the language the term "inflation," now in common usage.[32]

Greenbacks were not again accepted at face value until fourteen years after the Civil War. The forced recognition of their purely symbolic nature thus required the suspension of disbelief. Congress, it was said, could turn paper into gold by an "Act of Congress," that is, through magic. As a result, all paper money came to be associated with spiritualness, even ghostliness. Tellingly, one of Thomas Nast's cartoons depicted a precious coin casting on the wall a shadow inscribed with the word "GREENBACKS." The cartoon, which is captioned "A Shadow is Not a Substance," first appeared in 1876 in *Robinson Crusoe's Money*, a gold standard fable by economist David Wells. The book is symptomatic of the widespread conviction, shared likewise by the novelist Frank Norris in *McTeague*, that paper could be no more money than "a shadow could be the substance, or the picture of a horse a horse."[33] To think, as the Greenbackers did, that paper money could supplement or even replace specie was to succumb to what Wells, echoing sentiments from before the Civil War, called a "mere fiction of speech and bad use of language."[34] Issuing greenbacks thus was likened to a congressional confidence game by which Americans were conned, by a devilish suspension of disbelief, into accepting the notes.

Given the spiritual, even ghostly aura that surrounded the acceptance of paper for the real thing, the greenbacks had to be made more palatable by other means. Jay Cooke, a reformer and political ally of Senator John Sherman, who had led the nationalization of the currency during the Civil War, for instance extolled the greater security of the new notes. "It is impossible to alter [them] from a lower denomination to a higher, and there is not now one dangerous counterfeit where under the old system there were a hundred." More to the point, Cooke noted, it was impossible for the new notes "to become worthless, or even to depreciate in value, so long as the Government shall exist and continue to fulfill its pledges."[35] Both Cooke and Sherman stood for an economic policy that would represent paper dollars as elements of a genuinely *national* currency. Such a currency would foster a kind of collective faith in the nation and the state that issued it.[36]

Because of the dependence of the new, token currency on forms of trust, it is easy to see how their circulation could encourage identification with the nation. Like it or not, people were forced to recognize that the value of their money was now dependent on the trustworthiness of their national state and of their fellow citizens. This dependence, in turn, helped to foster a greater sense of belonging to, as well as a greater faith in, the national community, something that the "cosmopolitanism" fostered by specie forms of money clearly could not achieve. The significant role played by the "imagined" value of token or fiduciary money in encouraging recognition of one's membership in the nation is highlighted by the reverence with which the political economist William Graham Sumner later spoke of the rise of a national banking system. "Its first great feature," he wrote in his *History of Banking in the United States* published in 1896, "was that it was national and federal ... a thing which in the days of misery under the local bank system people had sighed for again and again as an unattainable hope." Sumner then went on to extol the system's many virtues— its uniformity, stability, and the fact that it operated under what he termed "federal control." With the currency thus entwined with faith in the nation itself, confidence in it had been restored.[37]

Monetary Debates and Practices

The forced recognition of the purely symbolic nature of paper money, together with a suspicion towards money that was printed on otherwise worthless pieces of paper, gave rise to vigorous monetary debates. The debates at first arose in Britain, which was the pioneer in state-issued paper money. Daniel Defoe, considering John Law's scheme of a bank that would issue paper money backed by lands owned by the state, in the 1720s called paper money a "chimera"— that is, "an unreal creature of the imagination, a mere wild fancy; an unfounded conception."[38] The 1720s in Britain were a period of monetary scandal and increasing influence of a new moneyed, mercantile class that was taking over power from the established, landed one. Hence, Alexander Pope in his "Epistle to Lord Bathurst" in 1733 satirized paper money as the root of all kinds of social evils and its devastating effect on personality: "Blest paper-credit! Last and best supply! / That lends corruption lighter wings to fly!"[39]

The debates fueled by the supposed unreality of wealth based on paper money (meaning that nothing is owned except worthless paper) did not escape the colonists across the Atlantic. In 1727, Ebenezer Cooke, a poet from colonial Maryland, took up the subject in his *Sot-Weed Redivivius*. The poem marks an important departure from the English tradition of satirizing paper money as incompatible with the supposed securities of land and precious metal. Slyly advertising his poem as "Waste Paper" (meaning not only "trash" but also "accounting book") and "Home-Spun Weeds," Cooke goes on to urge the colonial authorities to abandon its use of the traditional tobacco currency ("Indian Weed ... secure in bags") in favor of "Paper made of Rags."[40] Cooke never received the attention he deserved, though another colonist, John Wise did. Wise, a native of Roxbury, Massachusetts, who became a Congregationalist divine and political leader, wrote in support of a land bank the year after Law's scheme collapsed. Convinced that such a bank's paper bills would stimulate economic growth, Wise boasted that "we [...] can turn other matter into silver and gold by the power of thought as soon as any other people."[41]

In the writings of American colonists such as Cooke or Wise paper money becomes associated with a theory of value that resists the traditional identification of value with substance. The economic exchange based on that theory meant that soon all American colonies embraced paper money to solve their monetary and economic problems, though none came closer in influence to Benjamin Franklin, who almost single-handedly set the agenda for the discussion of the problematics (and advantages) of paper money. Franklin clearly saw that the value of paper (the material substance on which monetary engravings are printed) had nothing to do with the notes' value as money. Instead, their value depended on their being respectively backed by land, by gold or silver, by loans, or by actual or potential government power and commitment. Not everyone would accept the liberal thought that, because the value of money derived from extrinsic forces, a paper surrogate could do the job just as well. For instance, James Madison in the *Federalist Papers* of 1787 called the current "rage for paper money" an "improper or wicked project," whose effects on the "necessary confidence between man and man, on the necessary confidence in public councils, on the industry and morals of the people, and on the character of republican government" was simply "pestilential."[42]

Appearances were everything, and Madison's words aptly convey the apprehension towards a medium of exchange whose symbolic nature stood out so plainly and, even more importantly, whose value could not be guaranteed. Therefore, the government as a last resort turned to measures of suasion, linking trust in the paper currency with the new idea of civic virtue. Independence had barely been declared when the Continental Congress took the following resolution. "[A]ny person who shall hereafter be so lost to all virtue and regard for his country, as to refuse to receive said bills in payment [...] shall be deemed, published and treated as an enemy in this country and precluded from all trade or intercourse with the inhabitants of these Colonies."[43] The phraseology is telling, for embedded in it is the tension between a willingness to accept the new paper currency and the demand that it be accepted. This tension constituted an anxiety of power that eventually redefined civic virtue from its dependence on property and independence from power to its interdependence between citizens themselves, and between citizens and the government—through paper money, the public credit of the nation.

The American Revolution was actively supported by less than half of the people, yet the downfall of the Continentals affected the vast majority. There were ruinous losses, for rich and poor alike, as debts contracted for good money were paid off with almost valueless currency. Speculators of course profited by the situation. In patriot-controlled territories, prominent political leaders were sometimes suspected of profiteering and of fraudulent dealings in handling the monies or supplies. Sometimes riots resulted, as in Philadelphia in 1779, while the Continental Congress was in session. After the Continental issues had been stopped, the states began to print paper money of their own, also in large amounts and depreciating rapidly, sometimes more badly than the Continentals did. This practice was prohibited in 1789, when the Constitution of the United States was adopted and the balance of authority shifted from the states to the national government.

Under the Constitution, the states could make "silver and gold a legal tender in the payments of debts," but only the national government would have the authority to "coin Money, regulate the Value thereof, and of foreign Coin" (Art.I, Sec.8, §5). The Constitution's wording clearly reflects the framers' idea of making the United States a hard-money country, that is, a country whose currency consisted mainly of gold and silver, as impressive as the new nation and the new government. This government also would have had a King rather than a President if the "Anglomen" faction around Gouverneur Morris had had its way. Nevertheless, even Thomas Jefferson and the Republicans, though accused by the Federalists of speaking "all French," thought that the money of a free republic should be gold and silver. For Jefferson in particular only land and gold constituted "real" property. As for paper money, to most of the delegates it implied a promise that might be broken. While there was initially a clause in the Constitution that permitted the federal government to issue paper money, it was quickly eliminated. As a delegate from Delaware said, granting the government the right to issue paper money would be "as alarming as the mark of the Beast in Revelations." It would be better, another delegate urged, to "reject the whole plan than retain the three words 'and emit bills.'"[44]

The rhetoric of the constitutional debates is deceptively similar to the English neoclassical tradition of satirizing paper money as incompatible with the supposed securities of land and precious metal. Writers from Pope to Burke and beyond had argued that if property is the foundation of personality, the "unreal" wealth provided by a paper economy was bound to make personality unreal and words meaningless. Such moral arguments may not have been unfamiliar to the Americans, though overall, records of the convention rather bear testimony to more pragmatic reasons, in particular to the delegates' fears that if government held power to issue paper money, it simply could not be trusted to avoid inflation. (As we will see presently, similar arguments were used against the introduction of federal paper money during and after the Civil War.) When the delegates had finally thrashed out their Constitution, the document implicitly denied the federal government the right to issue paper money, at the same time as it explicitly denied the individual states the same prerogative. Effective of 1789, therefore, neither the states nor the federal government were authorized to issue paper money.[45]

Although the federal government was legally bound to stay out of the paper money business, it would return to it during abnormal times, such as the War of 1812, when the need to finance the conflict occasioned the issue of Treasury notes. Seeking that recourse had its price, though. The volume of paper money before long went out of all proportion to specie reserves; inflation was rampant, as were credit expansion and property and land speculation in the West. The Treasury notes fell to an ever-wider discount to specie, and reserves became exhausted. Thus was ushered in the panic of 1819. While Washington Irving responded to the "ungodly" financial practices he observed with a tale, "The Devil and Tom Walker," the government, like a burned child, called in the Treasury notes and, in

1836, effectively shut down the Second Bank of the United States. As a result, there was not enough currency of any kind, and Congress again authorized issues of Treasury notes in 1837 and 1838, against objections that they were bills of credit and that Congress did not have authority to create such forms of money. Thus, the Demand notes of 1861 and, beginning in 1862, the United States notes really were the first paper money under the Constitution.

Issuing the Demand notes was an unaccustomed task for the government, as the constitutional right of the United States government to circulate paper money had not yet been resolved. "It would eventually be decided that indeed it had that authority," Richard Doty notes, "but while legislators and jurists debated, there was a war demanding payment."[46] The angle the Union government took was that it may not have a right to *print* paper money, but it certainly had a right to *borrow* money. With a borrowing program authorized by Congress in July 1861, a portion of that money was turned into federal paper money, the Demand notes. The bills promised payment in specie "on demand," hence their name. By contrast, the United States notes (the "greenbacks") were not backed by specie and therefore people had to accept them upon trust, which is why they represent a type of money that is called "*fiduciary*" money. The term comes from the Latin word *fidere*, to trust or to have faith in, though some commentators have said that such money is acceptable as money simply because the government says so (hence the term *fiat* money). While the greenbacks were not redeemable in anything, they were exchangeable for Union bonds paying six percent, redeemable in five years. That was not much, considering the way the war was going, but it was as much as the Union government felt comfortable offering.

Public discontent and debate were bound to stay for as long as the monetary standard was not fully established. Defining American currency thus became one of the most explosive political and social issues of the time, as different social segments and classes wanted to use different kinds of money not only to solve their particular economic problems but also to settle the role of democratic government in the capitalist market. In pursuing these interests, each tried to impose their preferred version of money on all others. For instance, in 1876 the Republican Party platform included the following plank in favor of a fully convertible currency: "Commercial prosperity, public morals, and the national credit demand that the promise [to redeem the United States notes in coin] be fulfilled by a continuous and steady progress to specie payment." In 1880, the Democratic Party pledged itself to "honest money — the strict maintainance [sic!] of gold and silver, and paper convertible into coin on demand."[47]

It is no surprise that *Money* magazine, established in 1897 and "specially designed to simplify the present currency question in the United States," noted that voters were being "suddenly called upon to digest arguments and technical essays which would puzzle any man who had not previously investigated the subject." Only in the United States, one historian pointed out, did "the argument about the form and function of money [become] public."[48] By the turn of the century the controversy waned, following the defeat of the Silverites in the 1896 election and the passing of the Gold Standard Act of 1900, which established the gold dollar as the standard unit of value. When Congress in 1933 formally declared all United States coins and currencies as equal legal tender, this was merely an afterthought to the standardization of the currency that had been achieved within some four decades.

In the post–Civil War era, issuing paper money had been an easy means to increase the money supply, which in turn would lead to low interest rates and a rise in prices; debtors and the less moneyed in general gained, whereas creditors and the rich suffered. The conflict between those who wanted an inflated currency, or "soft" money, and those who wanted a deflated currency, or "hard" money based on the gold standard, thus came to be a sectional struggle between farmers of the West and South, joined by workers in the big cities, and the powerful industrial and financial interests in the North and East. However, as with the introduction of paper money in England, there were further social and cultural implications to the debate, especially the conflicting conceptions of the role of democratic government in the capitalist market. For instance, the remark that it was possible to turn paper into gold by an Act of Congress clearly was directed against the Greenbackers' position, derived mainly from Edward Kellogg, that the government conferred value on any kind of money.[49]

"All that is necessary for a government to do to create money," declared a "soft money" Congressman in 1874, "is to stamp upon what it would change into money 'its image and superscription,' and it will be money."[50] The "gold-bugs," by contrast, would rather be dead. For them, money was effectual only when it symbolized "real" money, that is, when it was convertible into gold, the uncontested general equivalent of all products and thus "the only true measure of value," as Treasury Secretary Hugh McCulloch insisted in 1865. Truthfulness, the Secretary added, came from God and nature: "I myself have no more doubt that [gold and silver] were prepared by the Almighty for this purpose, than I have that iron and coal were prepared for the purposes for which they are being used."[51] Only nature, not government or society, could create value and identity. Moreover, specie-based currencies had been tried; their historical importance was proof of the superiority of gold. Last but not least, a freely convertible currency could be taken as a sign of "the possession of that first of Christian values, upright and downright honesty."[52] Hence, a return to the gold standard would be necessary for the return of the United States to the ranks of civilized Christian nations.

If the Protestant churches almost always took the bullionist line, the search for intrinsic value — for a gold that always stays valuable — was also on the agenda of those in search of racial purity and stable social differences. Indeed, not only did debates emerge with respect to the paper money form, and not only did paper give rise to much anxiety among those who were or believed themselves to be in danger of losing money; paper also brought about the breakdown of former distinctions between high and low culture, between social elites and the common people. Formerly, the latter had used mainly other forms of money, like wampum, buckskin, nails, or (mostly foreign) coinage and, as well, low-denomination tokens or copper and bronze coins, which were often privately issued, and not easily convertible into the kinds of money used by the wealthier. During the colonial era, a variety of paper currency had acquired the symbolic significance of being the domain of the commoners. In the early nineteenth century, the idea that a paper currency would strengthen a sense of community from bottom up came back with renewed force. In contrast to specie, the *Morning Post* wrote in September 1810, paper "offers the Government a most indestructible support because it makes the daily bread of every individual depend substantially on the safety of government, whereas money which can be hoarded separates the individual from the public safety."[53]

In texts of this kind, paper becomes the very image of potential, an idea that is well known in the tradition of Western philosophy. Aristotle had used the trope of the writing tablet in *De Anima*; it became explicit again in John Locke's suggestion to imagine the human mind to be, "as we say, white paper, void of all characters, without any ideas."[54] The identification of paper with potential is also part of economic exchange, manifesting itself in the association of paper money with a theory of value that is in opposition to the traditional link between value and substance, specie for instance. The greenbacks of the post–Civil War era recognized and, at least in part, fulfilled the potential of paper. A plentiful supply of these notes led to lower interest rates and aided debtors; thus, a majority of those who favored this "soft" money were radical Republicans, for whom the greenbacks were symbols of more egalitarian social and economic conditions.

There was a problem, though, as greenbacks were thought to facilitate the political, social, and financial success also of ex-slaves. Put another way, the greenbacks not only represented equality, but also were themselves seen as a means by which equality might be achieved. While Greenbackers were more likely to be egalitarians who believed that racial characteristics were socially constructed, hence mutable, many Southerners (as well as disaffiliated Northerners) likened paper money to what they saw as specious bills of rights. The introduction of a paper currency that was merely symbolic thus triggered old anxieties about social class and tradition. Michael O'Malley's work remains controversial, though his summary of the arguments is salient: "Diluting the money supply diluted the nation's blood, and elevating the freedman depreciated the value of whiteness." Given such reasoning, many people demanded that paper currency be pegged to "authentic specie" (coin or precious metal) that had real value — like the scientific objectivity they saw in "species" or races.[55]

Supporters of a "hard" currency willingly overlooked the vicissitudes of the gold price in a market economy and took refuge in notions of genuine or "intrinsic" value, the kind of value, O'Malley found, "supposedly located in specie, oil paintings, wood paneling, and old family gentility."[56] For Greenbackers, such ideas only proved that bullionists were living in the past. The future, they argued, belonged to the people who would control the monetary system through a democratically elected government.[57] A government of the people, by the people, and for the people would grant full legal tender status also to unredeemable paper money. In doing so, it would enhance its exchangeability, which the Greenbackers saw as the basis for confidence and trust. Anyone would accept a paper dollar in payment if he or she knew it could be used later to buy whatever he or she wanted. Given that the industrial revolution led to more and more people being incorporated into the monetary economy, the idea that true money represented what it could purchase, not the specie it could be converted into, was economically sensible.

Equally sensible was another argument, that the greenbacks would protect poor and illiterate people from the consequences of their greater monetary "illiteracy." These people would be cheated less easily in that they would be able to tell "good" notes from "bad" ones, something they would not be able to do in a context in which many different issues of paper money existed. Indeed, during the era of the private note, a great number of poor and illiterate people even had ended up in prison because they unwittingly passed a counterfeit received from someone else. "I can't read," complained one accidental passer, adding that he could recognize "a one and a two dollar but no other bill." An ever-growing proportion of those arrested were immigrants. "I have only been in the country 18 months and begin to speak English within the last three months," one French man charged with passing counterfeits said. "I know nothing about the Bank Bills in this country."[58] Most banks proved deaf to such complaints. Though banks lost some money by mistakenly redeeming bad bills, tellers caught most of the counterfeits. Thus, the desired uniformity and, with it, the "vertical integration" of money in society, was not to be for another half century.[59]

For Greenbackers, rejecting a specie-based currency was a way not only to amend the unequal distribution of wealth *within* the United States but also to improve the country's position in the *world* economy. Under the gold standard, Greenbackers suggested, the bankers and financiers who controlled the gold also controlled the money supply for the entire nation. Consequently, gold came to be considered "unpatriotic" because it was thought to serve only an alien class living under the belief that money capital has no allegiance to any country. A truly patriotic fiscal policy, economic nationalists like E.H. Heywood or John G. Drew argued, therefore would be governed by the idea that money was a thing of or belonging to the nation, not of or belonging to the world, whose debtor the United States at the time was.[60] Henry Carey also was among those who advocated an inconvertible national currency. Such a currency, he announced, would discourage international trade and remove any external constraint on the creation of domestic money to promote the economic growth of the American nation. Whatever the merits of the rhetorical battle, the "gold-bugs" won the political war. Specie convertibility was resumed in 1879 when, in the aftermath of the economic crisis of 1873–74, a Republican-dominated Congress adopted the gold standard.

Following the adoption of the gold standard, the gold dollar was becoming something more than a circulating coin; it was becoming a symbol of the United States' imperial ambitions.[61] However, gold did not fulfill the grandiose expectations vested in it by the powerful. The problem with a currency based on gold is that it is limited by the amount of gold in the world. The amount fluctuates with each new discovery and each new development in technology. At times, newly found gold floods the market unexpectedly. At other times, it comes in very slowly, though the economy may desperately need an influx of fresh money. In the late nineteenth century, the demand for gold increased dramatically because a large number of nations worldwide accepted gold as the monetary standard. Consequently, the gold price rose; at the same time, product prices fell. The political discontent following from this, as well as the fluctuations of the value of gold on the international market ultimately led to the abandonment of the gold standard in 1933. In the same year, the paper dollar was devalued in order to attract more money from abroad.

The place of silver in the monetary system constituted another controversy that dominated the financial scene for decades. A crucial factor had been a 4-to-3 decision of the Supreme Court in 1870, which ruled that the Acts authorizing the Legal Tender issues (the greenbacks) were unconstitutional. Perhaps the most exhilarating aspect of this decision is that Chief Justice Salmon P. Chase, who had been Secretary of the Treasury when the first greenbacks were issued, including the one-dollar note bearing his portrait, delivered it. As Friedman and Schwartz wryly observe, "Not only did [Chase] disqualify himself, but in his capacity as Chief Justice convicted himself of having been responsible for an unconstitutional action in his capacity as Secretary of the Treasury."[62] The issue did not go away with the greenback cases, which were reconsidered and the greenbacks declared constitutional in 1871. (Chase stuck to his views of two years earlier and submitted a minority vote.) The divisiveness of the greenbacks' constitutionality is reflected in the organization in 1875 of the Greenback Party, which captured a variety of third parties in different states under various titles. Fortunes of the party were at a high point in the elections of 1878, when as the Greenback-Labor Party it won about ten percent of the votes and fourteen seats in Congress. The ticket the party ran on included a government monopoly of paper currency, and the unlimited coinage of silver, which, like printing more issues of legal tender notes, would expand the money supply, always the preferred choice for the less privileged, who would blame a slump in product prices on the reduction of the supply of greenbacks.

The Greenbackers even had their own song, which illustrates the sentimental feelings aroused in monetary struggles:

> Thou, greenback, 'tis of thee,
> Fair money of the free,
> Of thee we sing.
> And through all coming time
> Great bards in every clime
> Will sing with joyful rhyme,
> Gold is not king.
> Then smash old Shylock's bonds,
> With all his gold coupons,
> The banks and rings.
> Monopolies must fail,
> Rich paupers work in jail,
> The right will then prevail,
> Not money kings.

The song, in Arthur Nussbaum's opinion, is "noteworthy far beyond the greenback episode."[63] The Greenback-Labor Party's political success led to a compromise that in 1878 froze the circulation of greenbacks at the then current amount of $346,681,016. The compromise halted the trend towards growth-inhibiting hard money, at the same time as it put a limit on inflationary easy credit. On hindsight, however, it really made no difference whether dollars were gold, silver, paper, or bank credits. In practice, dollars at the time were generally credits. The country was already moving on to the use of checks, and by the end of the century, four out of five dollars existed only on bank ledgers. Many people would see it in that way, yet their arguments went down against those from the pro-silver factions, who were seeking to repeal the Coinage Act of 1873, which had demonetized silver.

The Act contained a list of all the coins the United States Mint could produce as legal tender—cents, nickels, dimes, eagles, and so on, but it made no mention of the standard silver dollar. To discontinue the coinage of the silver dollar was only sensible since for the last several decades the market price of silver had been higher than the mint price. (Silver producers, able to get more for their product on the open market, had simply stopped shipping silver to the Mint. As a result, the silver dollar had not been in circulation since 1836 and was an unknown coin to most Americans.) Nevertheless, when the price of silver began to fall because of overproduction and a decreased demand, American silver producers discovered that they could not bring silver to the mints even if they wished to do so. Their original support for demonetized silver instantly melted into air. They called the Act of 1873 a crime, letting it be known that the provision for dropping the standard silver dollar had been secretly introduced into the Act as the result of a conspiracy. The conspiracy allegedly involved Eastern bankers and legislators, and their friends and allies, the British or "Anglomen," as they were called in the works of E. J. Farmer, Sarah E. V. Emery, or William "Coin" Harvey.

Congress had carefully considered the coinage bill, and there had been open debate for months before its passage. Nevertheless, from the events a mythic conspiracy theory was concocted—silver had been betrayed, and those who wanted to create tighter credit as opposed to an inflationary or soft currency that would have benefited mortgage holders and debtors had duped the common people. None of the arguments was sensible, though as late as 1896 the Democratic Party platform denounced the gold standard as a British policy that would have in its wake the "financial servitude" of other nations. Such a policy, the Democrats concluded, was "not only un–American but anti–American, and it can be fastened on the United States only by the stifling of that spirit and love of liberty which proclaimed our political independence in 1776 and won it in the war of the Revolution."[64] Even as discriminating an observer as Henry Adams in 1893 would come to the support of free silver. "To him," he remembers in *The Education of Henry Adams*, "the interest was political; he thought it probably his last chance of standing up for his eighteenth-century principles, strict construction, limited powers, George Washington, John Adams, and the rest. He had, in a half-hearted way, struggled all his life against State Street, banks, capitalism altogether, as he knew it in old England or new England, and he was fated to make his last resistance behind the silver standard."[65]

By the time Adams was at work on the *Education*, the political party originally supported by the Silverites, the Greenback Party, had long been defunct, brought down by the abysmal results in the elections of 1884. By 1892, a new party had silver on its platform — the People's (or Populist) Party of the United States, an agrarian party formed out of a number of already existing alliances. Thanks to this party, silver once again became an issue in Congress, which in 1894 passed a bill providing for the coinage of silver. President Grover Cleveland, a Democrat, vetoed the bill. He did, however, agree to John Pierpont Morgan's offer to bail out the government by purchasing federal bonds with $100 million in gold. The deal rescued the Treasury, whose gold reserves had dwindled to about a tenth of what the government needed to ensure liquidity, yet it won neither the President nor the financier any friends. Instead, it catapulted into the presidential campaign William Jennings Bryan. At the Democratic national convention in Chicago in July 1896, Bryan declared the silver question the paramount issue, famously saying in his speech, "You shall not press down on the brow of labor this crown of thorns, you shall not crucify mankind on a cross of gold." The speech reflected the popular feeling about gold. However, the Republican William McKinley won the elections.[66] Americans had taken their choice of the two "bills."

A cartoon created in 1900 shows McKinley and Bryan on one-dollar bills, respectively worth "one dollar in gold" and "53 cents only—free silver." Finley Peter Dunne's sketches on the Irish saloonkeeper Mr. Dooley also satirized the Silverites. The sketches were first published in the *Chicago Journal* and then collected in many volumes, beginning with *Mr. Dooley in Peace and War* in 1899. William Jennings Bryan became immortalized as the Cowardly Lion in L. Frank Baum's children's classic *The Wizard of Oz*. Baum's all–American fairy-tale, known to everyone thanks to the 1939 musical with Judy Garland, appeared in 1900, the year President McKinley saw to the passing of the Gold Standard Act. This act, in a bid to the hard-money faction, declared the gold dollar to be the monetary standard of the country. The passing of the Act was uncontested largely because of the accompanying rise in prices, which was itself the result of a prodigious increase in the international supply of gold, bringing the price of gold down. Although the "money issue" thereafter retreated from the center of political controversy, the entire episode has been understood as an example of how important what people think about money can sometimes be.[67]

Right: Morgan Dollar, obverse ***Left:*** Morgan Dollar, reverse

"Take your choice of the two bills!" (Political cartoon, 1900) (Library of Congress, Prints and Photographs Division, LC-USZ62-66516)

While the controversy about the monetary standard withered away, the attention of
the financial and political world shifted to the banking structure. There was widespread
dissatisfaction, bank failures, runs on banks, and fear of other catastrophes. Consequently,
there were several banking crises, most notably in 1893, when the banks once again suspended the convertibility of deposits into currency. Another crisis, in 1907, only repeated
earlier episodes. In the absence of a central bank, smaller banks would rely on larger banks
for credit whenever depositors demanded larger sums of cash. In the summer of 1907, several large brokerage firms and corporations went bankrupt. Stock prices fell, and owners
withdrew large sums of cash to cover their losses. A recession was imminent, but resolved
by J.P. Morgan's investment bank. The crisis rallied the federal government into action. In
1908, Congress stepped in, calling for the establishment of a National Monetary Commission, which would work on the idea of establishing a central bank. The Commission's
reports laid the foundation for the adoption in Congress of the Federal Reserve Act, signed
into law by President Woodrow Wilson on December 23, 1913.[68]

The creation of the Fed was a watershed, an event of fundamental significance in the
monetary field. Before, money had consisted of gold, National Bank notes, silver and minor
coins, and "an assemblage of assorted relics of earlier monetary periods"—greenbacks, silver dollars, silver certificates, and Treasury notes of 1890. Once central banking had become
a government monopoly, the mainstay of money were Federal Reserve notes, which were
to be used as hand-to-hand currency or as vault cash for banks (deposits to the credit of
banks were equivalent to Federal Reserve notes). Federal Reserve notes are issued in denominations of $1, $2, $5, $10, $20, $50, and $100. It appears the American people tend to use
the $20, the $5, and the $1 predominantly. The $100 in a U.S. House of Representatives
hearing has been said to be "a phenomenon offshore primarily," meaning that it is mostly
used outside of the United States for long-term household savings.[69] All other larger denominations—from $500 to $10,000 — have not been printed since 1945 because of fears of German counterfeiting and have not been issued since July 14, 1969, as use of them had declined
sharply (the notes had a function in exchanges between banks and in large cash transactions) and was no longer warranting the added cost of production and custody of new supplies.

More recently, it has been suggested that a new $500 bill might be appropriate. As
the chairman of a congressional subcommittee stated on October 8, 1998, the euro "aspires
to replace the U.S. dollar as the currency in which petroleum is priced and ultimately it
aspires to challenge the dollar as the preferred world reserve currency."[70] Since the grand
total of United States currency held abroad is estimated at about $250 billion, any substan-
tial move to the euro would be felt in dollars and cents: the Treasury books substantial
yearly earnings—called "seigniorage"—from interest savings and from currency. Prefer-
ence for the euro, the representative of the Federal Reserve said in his testimony, might be
likely in areas where large cash transactions take place. If these transactions are made in
$100 bills (as in real estate transactions in the republics of the former Soviet Union), they
take an awful lot of time, whereas they would take considerably less time if they were done
in €500 notes. Also to be taken into consideration are the costs for the shipment and stor-
age of bills. Moreover, there is inflation, as a 1995 $500 bill was worth only about $111 in
1967 dollars.

These arguments could have tipped the balance in favor of reissuing $500 notes. How-
ever, it was also noted in the hearing that many of the gains would accrue, "not only to
legitimate users of bank notes, but also to money launderers, tax evaders and a variety of

other law breakers who use currency in their criminal activity." Criminals are generally deterred by the law enforcement community from placing illicit proceeds directly into the financial system at home; consequently, they often seek to hide the money and transport it for placement outside of the country and then launder it back in. As the representative of the Treasury Department said in his testimony, "the weight of currency is a practical deterrence. [...] So high denomination notes would make it easier for criminals to transport and hide cash, make the money laundering process cheaper and more likely to evade detection, and as a result, the net cost of committing many crimes could decline as with the Government's ability to punish and deter such crimes. In addition [...] it may lead to a larger underground economy to avoid taxes."[71]

As the pros and cons of once again distributing higher-value notes were being debated, the chair of the subcommittee, a bit ludicrously perhaps, made two suggestions. The first suggestion was that little weights be attached to all the existing paper money for the criminals. The second was to eliminate all paper currency whatsoever, using instead dollar coins—"and see how the criminals like hauling that around for their drugs." In contrast to the honorable chair, law enforcement agencies would rather see the elimination of any money that can be used anonymously. If cash could be entirely replaced, drug warriors have suggested, the drug trade would not survive. People could not put drug purchases on their credit cards. Nevertheless, in 1998 no legislation concerning the re-issuing of $500 bills was prepared, though if the Treasury were to decide to go ahead, the Bureau of Engraving and Printing could supply the notes in a year to eighteen months, state-of-the-art security features included.[72]

Endorsing and Enforcing a Single Currency

All attempts to maintain or establish the obedience, loyalty, and cooperation of the members of the state as a fiscal community, as well as its own legitimacy in their eyes, are accompanied by measures of domination and control. Such measures include the taxing out of existence of other currencies, the suppression of the private issue of tokens, paper notes, coins by stores, businesses, churches, and other organizations, and the stamping out of personalization of money by individuals. Economic historians therefore refer to the process of endorsing and enforcing a single, homogeneous national currency as the "standardization" or "territorialization" of money.

Already the early colonial bills caused problems. Because of their size — about 4 inches wide and 5¼ inches high — they were too large to be put conveniently into a purse or pocket without folding. People would therefore fold them in half in each direction and then unfold them when spending them. Of course, this created creases and splitting along the folds, but people found it convenient when a bill split apart to use a half or a quarter section as change rather than paste or sew the parts together. Some people tore the bills deliberately to make change. This was not quite what the issuers had intended. Thus, colonial authorities for instance in Massachusetts set up a special committee to investigate the sectioning of bills. Connecticut in May 1726 even prohibited the use of sectional bills, but people simply responded by circulating sections on large bills. As of 1735, each quadrant on a note's back was made to read "Quarter of"—as in "Quarter of 2 shillings" or similar appropriate language for other denominations. On later issues, the calculation of the quadrant's value was printed on each of the four quadrants on the back, thus: "Quarter 2s. & 6d. / Seven-pence-half-penny."[73]

The Continental currency created its own problems. Although the notes were backed by the "Resolution of the Congress," Congress had no authority to enforce their acceptance. In the end, the individual states made them legal tender, setting penalties for anyone refusing to accept them. Such refusal would result in forfeiture of the debt owed or in the person being branded "an enemy of the country."[74] There is a noticeable irony in threatening to brand someone an enemy of the country for refusing to accept the Continentals: the Continental Congress itself had pledged to redeem the currency in Spanish milled dollars, that is, in foreign coins. The fact did not escape Gouverneur Morris, the Deputy Superintendent of Finance, who hoped that Congress would standardize the currency so that "the same names of money will mean the same things in the several parts of the United States." After arduous deliberations and a number of — sometimes quite bizarre — suggestions, Congress in May 1785 reported favorably on the dollar as a unit of account and agreed that, "All accomptants must prefer Decimals." On July 6 Congress resolved that the money unit of the United States would be one dollar and that coins "shall increase in a decimal ratio." Additionally, the weight of fine silver in the dollar was fixed and the ratio of silver to nonprecious metal set at 11 to 1.[75]

Legislators also complied with Hamilton's ideas of creating a national mint, as well as with his proposal to establish a national bank of sorts. A single currency, emitted through a national mint, would function both as an indispensable lubricant to these measures and as a gauge of economic progress. This was not to be, though, as the combined result of the unresolved issue of a paper currency, the lack of mintable gold or silver, and the reluctance, on the part of individual states, to recognize the dollar as the new unit of account. One consequence was that foreign coins, mostly of Mexican and Spanish-American origin, continued to be in use for a considerable time to come. They comprised about forty percent of all coins as late as 1830, according to a Senate committee report of that year. So badly were these coins needed that Congress repeatedly had to pass laws to maintain their status as legal tender. People tolerated them in almost any condition, worn, clipped, or underweight, and the prices of many goods and services showed how much the people relied on them. Prices might be quoted in dollars and cents, but the fractional amounts represented the Spanish coins still in use. As Earl Massey found, it was still common in the 1840s to see prices quoted at 6¼, 12½, 37½, and 6½ cents, amounts that could be readily paid in Spanish coins.[76]

While a guide to the coinage of the United States published in the 1840s reproduced images of 750 different kinds of coins to help people sort out the currency, by the 1850s, the situation had changed dramatically. This was due largely to California gold and the establishment of new mints as well as to the greater productivity of the parent mint in Philadelphia. For the first time in their history, Americans were getting enough precious metal. Now they could seriously turn their attention to foreign coins, repealing their status as legal tender in 1857.[77] That was in February. By the summer of the same year, rumors concerning unsound bank loans began to spread. In September, the *S.S. Central America* sank in a hurricane off the coast of South Carolina — with tons of California gold on board, intended as securities for the banks in the east.[78]

There was worse to come. The end of the Crimean War meant that European farmers were again able to produce their own wheat; wheat farmers in the American west were left sitting on their harvests. In the east, shares fell, bank liabilities rose, specie payment was suspended, coins were hoarded, though no new notes were printed and issued. Karl Marx, then working as the London correspondent for the New York *Tribune*, was delighted. The

"American crash," he pondered, meant that the end of capitalism was near.[79] Other people simply longed for the good times of long ago. Thus, there is a certain symbolism in the fact that in 1858 Horace Greeley's *Whig Almanac* was still priced at 12½ cents a copy, the amount of a Spanish *real*.[80] Moreover, throughout the Gilded Age, a number of merchants' tokens would bear the same denomination. In the words of Richard Doty, "a portion of Americans were still thinking in Spanish-American monetary terms, decades after their government had passed a law to wean them from such thoughts."[81] Old habits die slowly.

The prohibition against using foreign coins was introduced at a time when Americans felt confident that their currency was finally on the way to that plentiful, national coinage that Hamilton had dreamed about, but that had eluded him and his successors for almost a century. The currency may have been on the way, but the goal of reducing the nation's dependence on paper was never reached. The panic of 1857 has been mentioned. It was overcome in due time, discounted as a "natural" progression in a long-term economic cycle. Yet as soon as the first shots had been fired at Fort Sumter, American coinage began to disappear, both in the North and in the South, turning Americans back to the unappreciated paper dollar. (That development followed a deeply ironic path. 1857 had also been the year in which the green ink was invented that would earn the new notes their lasting nickname, "greenbacks.") This time, however, acceptance of the new paper currency was made mandatory. This was a momentous decision. It not only put an end to the business of note issuing by private banks but also completely upset another time-honored expedient, the production of private monies.

Through the Civil War, stores, businesses, and other organizations were privately issuing tokens, paper notes, trade cards, or coins, often as substitute currency, promising payment in specie in exchange for paper notes. There were even instances of "church money," such as the Albany church pennies of 1790, the fourpence notes issued in 1792 by a church in Schenectady, New York, or the notes issued by the Kirtland Safety Society in the late 1830s.[82] Also in the 1830s, merchants' copper cents would serve as both commercial advertising and small change. Other businesses would manufacture their own low-value currency—called "scrip"—because they simply could not carry on business without change. Still other businesses—most notably railroad companies—would issue paper money to create the capital to see their projects to conclusion. There were also tokens bearing patriotic emblems or political slogans, thus combining economic exchange with timely debates, often satirizing Andrew Jackson's policies. Even gold coins were privately issued, especially in the South, beginning in the early 1830s, and in the West, between 1849 and 1860.

European commentators, used to considering the sovereign's or state's prerogative over the currency to be self-evident, have been astounded by these private ventures with the currency, deeming them expressions of such quintessential American qualities as individualism and a love of freedom.[83] Another interpretation might focus more on material changes, beginning with the growth of the population from about 4 million in 1789 to 23 million in 1850 to 31 million in 1860. Significant changes were taking place also in other areas. Although by mid-century Americans were still primarily engaged in agriculture, the country was rapidly becoming urbanized. Manufacturing, industry, and finance were flourishing, and railroads were being built at a feverish pace, in response to and making possible the relocation of large parts of the population from the Atlantic seaboard to the South and West. Because of these changes, more and more people came to rely on monetary transactions. These transactions were often heavily disrupted by the sudden disappearance of silver coins from circulation, which happened every time there was a change in the price of silver. The presence of foreign coins caused further transaction costs by encouraging the use of multiple standards. Until the early 1860s, neither the federal government nor state governments were capable of doing much about these "inconveniences," to use Helleiner's term.[84] Consequently, private coinage and currency issue was tolerated or ignored.

In 1864, state forbearance ended and the federal government stepped in to make the private production of monies illegal. The postage currency law of the same year criminalized the so-called "shinplasters," declaring that no "private corporation, banking association, firm, or individual" could issue or circulate any "note, check, memorandum, token, or other obligation, for a less sum than one dollar, intended to circulate as money." To meet the demand for fractional currency or small change, the government produced new low denomination bronze coins and declared them legal tender. Postage stamps too were converted into money. Legal restrictions against private monies were stepped up in 1867. "Flash notes" (advertisements rigged up to look like dollar bills) were ruled illegal, at the beginning of the 1880s, when toy stores like Macy's had to surrender all their toy money. Even more forceful were the restrictions of 1909, which included a broad prohibition not only against the private issue of currency "in the resemblance of coins of the United States," but also against currency "of original design." Violators were threatened with a fine of no more than three thousand dollars, imprisonment for no more than five years, or both.[85]

John Sherman, Senator from Ohio, in his plea for the adoption of a national currency asserted that Congress had "the power to borrow money, which involves the power to emit bills of credit." These powers, he emphasized, "are *exclusive*. No state has the power to interfere with this exclusive power in Congress to regulate the national currency [or] provide a substitute for the national coin." To support his position, Sherman cited original intent. "It was the intention of the framers of the Constitution," he pontificated, "to destroy absolutely all paper money, except that issued by the United States."[86] Sherman's national bank bill was passed in Congress and was signed into law on February 25, 1863. Thanks to the Senator's efforts, the federal government now had a complete monopoly over the making of money. The only thing that remained was to protect the money supply from counterfeiters. The challenge fell to the Secret Service, whose work greatly contributed to the currency's taking on an ever more sacrosanct quality. Indeed, in 1886, Andrew Drummond, who was then head of the Service, solemnly proclaimed, "The securities and coins of all countries should be held sacred, that people, especially manufacturers, should not seek to transform them into curiosities."[87]

If the Secret Service prosecuted anyone who trifled with the symbolic value of the currency, the courts would be obliging. In 1889, an Indiana court ruled that the United States government "should unyieldingly maintain the right to protect the money which it makes the standard of value throughout the country." The ruling provides another good illustration of how seriously the endorsement and enforcement of a single, homogeneous national currency was taken. Even new immigrants were promptly instructed that in America, "the right to *coin money* belongs to Congress alone." Thus, the United States Department of Labor's *Federal Textbook on Citizenship Training* of 1926 warned that when people "manufacture metal or paper money, they must pay a heavy fine and are sent to prison for a number of years." The federal government in 1909 had moved as well against the personalization of money by individuals; it forbade the common practice of inscribing coins with sentimental messages, calling it "mutilation." Thereafter, the popular "love token" gifts became an illegal currency. Broadened definitions of counterfeiting and mutilation also led to pursuing the popular late nineteenth-century trompe l'oeil paintings of dollar bills.[88]

A major step in the enforcement of a single, homogeneous currency had been the affirmation of the constitutionality of the "death tax" by the United States Supreme Court in 1869. When the National Bank notes were introduced as a uniform national currency, the private commercial banks had to pay an issuing tax, at first of two percent, later of a prohibitive ten percent. They had few choices left: they could convert to national banks or else go out of business. At least one bank went to court, challenging the constitutionality of the tax — and lost the case. Salmon P. Chase, who was now Chief Justice, wrote the opinion in *Veazie Bank v. Fenno.* Its gist is that the tax indeed was a proper way of regulating money as the federal government had to possess greater power in the monetary field than did the State governments. Chase, whose vision of an "exclusive *national* currency" had led to the passing of the National Bank Acts, must have known that by undoing the typically commercial banks as banks of issue he was deliberately breaking the old common-law tradition with its emphasis on the supremacy of local power. He therefore shrewdly emphasized the power of Congress "to secure a sound and uniform currency for the country" and "to restrain by suitable enactments the circulation as money of any notes not issued under its own authority."[89]

The degree of standardization and monopolization in the physical form of legal tender that the central state achieved in less than half a century was truly momentous. Complete homogeneity of the currency could not be reached, though, as other notes such as Treasury Notes and Gold and Silver Certificates continued to be in circulation. Private power also prevailed, with private banks changing the medium, from notes to checks and deposits, thus continuing to create money. Other disruptions of monetary uniformity occurred when individuals actively created all sorts of monetary distinctions. An interesting example are merchants' tokens, which in compliance with the law were no longer exchangeable for specie or paper but instead promised payment in a specific article (a five-cent cigar, for instance), or "in trade," which meant that customers might use the tokens as they pleased for the amount indicated on the pieces.[90] Even Congress resisted when the government's efforts to make the dollar an affair of state went too far. The proposal to restore on United States gold coins the inscription "In God We Trust," which had been removed by presidential order, provoked an intense debate. Although a few Congressmen applauded President Theodore Roosevelt's decision to remove the motto, on the grounds that "our coin ... is a medium of secular, not sacred, transactions," their more successful opponents argued eloquently in favor of the ritual marker, insisting that while "the removal of it did not depreciate its monetary value ... it depreciated its sentimental value."[91]

A much more complete standardization and monopolization came with the redesign and the reduction in size of all United States notes in 1929. The change has been seen as coincidental with the October 1929 stock market crash, thus as truly "emblematic of the fall."[92] This is a point on hindsight, as the beginning of the reduced size notes can be traced to a committee recommendation under Treasury Secretary Franklin MacVeagh. The recommendations were not realized at the time. World War I and MacVeagh's leaving office only one week after accepting them prevented the adoption of the idea. Nevertheless, in August 1925, another committee, appointed by Secretary Andrew W. Mellon, once again began to study the whole question of "currency design, printing operations, issuance, and related interests associated with replacing the large size currency with smaller notes."[93] In May of 1927, Secretary Mellon accepted the committee's recommendations and directed the Bureau of Engraving and Printing to translate the plan into reality, beginning with the Legal Tender notes, series 1928. The measure of cutting the size of all dollar notes was adopted in order to save paper and ink and thus to cut down on the cost of production. The change, which must have delighted thrifty Mr. Hoover, indeed saved the Treasury millions of dollars, though it did nothing to stave off the Great Depression.[94]

The Great Depression would leave an indelible trace on the currency. It would do so in two ways. Following Richard Doty, it would "create a last flowering of localism, of individualized money of various types," at the same time as the seeds were planted "for a greater monetary centralization and conformity than ever before seen."[95] As regards the localism, the government would allow banks that had remained solvent to have their own currency printed up by the United States Mint. More pronounced instances of localism were all kinds of makeshift money — or "Depression scrip," to use the name collectors most commonly apply to it. Some of this emergency money lingered on through the mid–1930s, though most of it was gone by the time President Roosevelt stepped in to provide an adequate supply of currency. Also under Roosevelt, most types of paper money were being curtailed, including the venerable National Bank notes as well as Silver Certificates and Legal Tender issues. In addition, all United States currency was made redeemable "in lawful money" rather than spelling out precisely what sort of coin might be received for each note.

All these measures speak of the claim, conveyed by Roosevelt in a letter to Congress in 1934, to "the inherent right of Government to issue currency and to be the sole custodian and owner of the base or reserve of precious metals underlying that currency."[96] The measures also strengthened the Federal Reserve notes, and beginning in the mid–1930s, they would "reign supreme," to borrow Richard Doty's words. America's money would "lose much of its individuality" because of all this and, with the disappearance of emergency scrip issues as better times returned, it would also lose "much of its localism." On the other hand, "the celebration of the local, the nonstandard element of American life" would live on in altered form — in the commemorative coin as well as in new forms of scrip money used by local groups in a variety of states across the entire nation.[97]

Overall, cutting the size of all dollar notes may have been a measure to save paper, but it was at the same time indicative of the expansion of the daily use of paper dollars by the public. For instance, use of Federal Reserve notes rose from a mere seven percent in early 1917 to thirty-eight percent in November 1918. The notes continued to be hugely successful. By 1920, sixty percent of high-powered money consisted of Federal Reserve notes and deposits. Circulation of Federal Reserve notes increased dramatically when in 1945 Congress reduced gold reserves against Federal Reserve notes and deposits from forty to twenty-five percent. It increased further when in 1965 gold securities against deposits were eliminated, and again in 1968, when Congress took the ultimate step in eliminating all gold cover against the notes themselves. Henceforth, government bonds and commercial paper, and nothing else would support Federal Reserve notes.[98]

By the early 1980s, Federal Reserve notes constituted over ninety-nine percent of the total paper currency in circulation. The rest was made up by United States notes, which are now being printed only in the $100 denomination, as well as by small amounts of several discontinued classes of currency notes still outstanding, most of which now are "in the possession of collectors."[99] Also in the possession of collectors may be any notes larger than $100. With the development of other financial instruments, and now electronic transfers, there is not generally felt to be any need for larger notes. (Also important in this regard are law enforcement considerations.) Instead, the government is adopting other measures towards maintaining the currency's stability and reliability in the contemporary world and, in particular, its competitive edge against more ethereal forms of money such as checks, and telephone debit and credit cards, or "smart cards," as they are often called.

The shift from paper—cash and checks—to electronic forms of money began in the late 1950s with the introduction of plastic charge cards. By the 1970s, the "credit card revolution," to borrow an expression used by the late Hal Rothman, a historian, was in full swing. "Within a few years, anyone with halfway decent credit and the prospect of paying back at least part of what they borrowed received offers of credit cards with limits that sometimes exceeded their annual income. With credit, people could truly attain the be-all and end-all of post–1960s culture: they could have whatever they wanted now and pay for it later, if at all."[100] Although credit or debit cards may have an arbitrary charge or call limit (as in the case of telephone cards), it is nevertheless the user who, as Richard Doty argues, "choose[s] how much of its value to employ and where it will be employed." Credit and debit cards thus represent an entirely new concept, an economic unit whose value is fixed in part by the user rather than by the issuing institution. Consequently, these new forms give users "far greater flexibility than orthodox, 'official' types of money. As they are privately-produced and -distributed, they are not subject to the standardization seen on coinage and currency."[101] It has even been suggested that the new concept erodes the state's control over the currency since the cards are neither regulated nor backed by the federal government (they also do not generally have any national symbols on them).[102]

Credit and debit cards appear to make money "less anonymous, more personalized," as the cards may be used to store on small microchips all kinds of information, from personal credit information to medical information, about their holders.[103] Personalizing money is a form of earmarking. Checks too may be said to constitute a form of earmarking, as in transactions by check each party is identified by a proper name: the banker, the bearer, and the beneficiary. However, checks are one step behind in the historic order of forms of monetary usage and are no match to the new electronic (and internationalized) currencies. Given the increasing importance of credit and debit cards, "the scope of earmarking may increase and techniques for earmarking may vary, but differentiation persists."[104] Credit and debit cards are types of money that can bear any design desired by the user, and that come from a great variety of issuers, as every bank from coast to coast is issuing them. Just to be clear: it *does* matter which card one possesses, or flashes to a salesperson. The cards therefore "combine availability with distinction and attractiveness," that is, they possess "most of the elements of collector appeal" and are, moreover, proof of the fact that "the exceptional, the unusual, and the local have by no means disappeared from America's media of exchange."[105]

All kinds of "exceptional and unusual" forms of money have been generated by the Internet, from online shopping and eBay™ to DigiCash, CyberCash, Beanz, and Flooz.[106] These forms of money, together with electronic money transfers, direct bank deposits, computerized shoe shopping, or automated telephone purchases involve little or no personal contact between payer and payee. As the sociologist James Coleman points out, "In a cashless society where most people pay by credit cards, interpersonal ties and trust in specific others become irrelevant as sellers no longer depend on buyers but on an impersonal, central, electronic clearinghouse of debts."[107] Thus as long as personal contact between payer and payee remains a social value, the paper dollar will remain, like the English language. This may be comforting to many Americans, especially to those reluctant to speak or learn a foreign idiom. With all of that said, we will now move on to the triangulation involving the paper dollar, the public, and the private.

Paper Dollars, Public and Private

In a paper money economy, negotiating the difference between the public and the private is crucial. Ordinarily, iconography and portraiture are means by which an image can be "turned into a thing, which can then be 'possessed' privately."[108] The verbal and visual images on a national currency, however, identify citizens as subjects, at the same time as citizens recognize themselves and each other in the terms specified by the state. A hierarchy of values that symbolically prioritizes one over the other thus is attached to the differences between public and private. Prioritization of the public domain and the related marginalization of the private domain are important for understanding the history of and debates surrounding the role and impact of paper money. For one thing, the relative importance of these two spheres bracketed the fierce contests involving local, regional, and private currencies, as opposed to the currency issued by the national government. For another, credit and debit cards offer more choice and freedom for the individual, while seemingly making irrelevant interpersonal ties and trust in specific others, including the state. Equally important are counterfeits, which invert known priorities by assuming the public production of paper money into the private domain and reintroducing the products back into the public sphere. Last but not least, there is the case of art. Paintings or other artistic representations of dollar bills likewise assume the public production of paper money into the private domain and reintroduce the product into the public sphere.

Both artistic representations and counterfeits play upon and upset the distance between monetary substance and sign, between the real and the ideal. However, unlike with counterfeits, the status of artworks as non-legal tender is marked, for instance by using oil on canvas and framing the painting, or else by printing only one side of a bill and in sizes notably different from the original notes. None of this was any help to Pittsburgh-based artist J.S.G. Boggs, whose plight began in 1984 when, penniless, he drew a dollar bill on a napkin, gave it to a waitress in payment for a 90-cent coffee and a doughnut and even collected the change. Later Boggs began to document monetary exchange relations. He would put each of his hand-drawn bills into circulation, with a minimum number of five people, whose fingerprints, receipts, and change he would use to document the transactions, then frame the documents and put them on display. All these transactions, Boggs claimed, documented the performance of value.[109]

Boggs's artwork is provocative in that it foregrounds the codes and conventions that regulate the circulation of paper money in modern societies. The symbolic quality of the paper money form, Boggs is suggesting, leads to a paradox. While the value attached to paper money is baseless, and needs to be renegotiated every time a transaction takes place, the economy and the government issuing it demand our continual trust in its worth. Boggs always made it clear that the bills he produced were artworks, not currency. Not only are they printed just on one side, leaving the back free for the fingerprints he needs to document the transactions his bills go through. It is also difficult to see how a one-dollar note issued by "The United States of Florida" and worth "One FUN Dollar" could have been produced by the Bureau of Engraving and Printing. ("FUN" is an acronym for Florida United Numismatists, which is reminiscent of the fact that Boggs printed and "spent" 900 one-dollar Boggs bills that he "paid" to the organizer of a coin collectors' convention of that name.)[110]

Whereas the status of Boggs's bills as non-legal tender is clearly marked, this is not the case with counterfeits. The purpose of the latter is to intentionally deceive other people. This makes counterfeiting illegal and punishable by law. Cultural theorists describe counterfeiting as the assumption of a public prerogative (the production of currency by the state or any other authority) into the private domain (where a person or persons produce likenesses of the currency), and subsequently reintroducing the products into the public domain (by circulating counterfeit bills or coin). This process inverts the established pattern of the public domain as the originator of currency. Counterfeits are always somehow out of place, at least symbolically, located in the wrong context. They offend both consumers (who wish to rely on redemption and/or acceptance) and producers (as only certain bodies are authorized to issue notes or mint coin). A counterfeit bill (or coin) constitutes a borderline signifier that disguises the difference between true and false. It dislodges and corrupts the certainties of established classifications.

Although modern theoreticians have established the fictitiousness of such classifications, it is nevertheless true that any classificatory system is an ordering that in itself requires the rejection of "inappropriate elements."[111] If an order or systematic pattern is to be maintained, we must reject or exclude that which would challenge the pattern and its constitution. In the years following the Civil War, the greenbacks, as fiat money, challenged the pattern that would accept as "natural money" only gold or silver. Paper thus was rejected as inappropriate. The metaphor of worthless material ("rag money") expressed the point that it did not fit the established symbolic ordering and thus had to be eliminated. Counterfeits are likewise rejected as inappropriate. They clearly represent a danger to the established classifications of public and private domains. This is where the term "illegal tender" stems from.

In modern western societies at least, the separation into the two spheres or domains of public and private constitutes "one of the foremost material and symbolic decisions framing the organization of social life."[112] The public is commonly represented as the formal institutions of the state, with the rule of law and the world of work and the economy; by contrast, the private is associated with the personal, the emotional, and the domestic. (The division is also gendered, in that the public world of power and influence is associated with the masculine, while the private sphere of domestic life is associated with the feminine.) Not surprisingly, therefore, because of their transgression of established boundaries, counterfeits always create something of a moral panic when they appear. (They also unfailingly titillate the popular imagination as, most recently, through the Academy Award winning film by Stefan Ruzowitzky, *The Counterfeiters*.)

Counterfeits — and moral panics — have been the bane of America's monetary history from its colonial beginnings. America may have been the first country in the world where paper money was widely used, though this was "scarcely an unmixed blessing." From the beginning, more notes were issued than the colonial authorities had the ability or the intention of redeeming. In addition, there was the problem of numbers. Between 1690, when Massachusetts issued the first bills of credit, and 1789, when George Washington was inaugurated as the first President of the United States, more than 100,000 different bills in many denominations were issued to meet a wide range of financial needs. Finally, under the rather primitive technological conditions (printing was done either from an engraved copper plate or by using an ordinary printing press), early paper money was easy to counterfeit or fake. Indeed in the early years of America's paper money, "virtually *any* crooked country printer could make a plausible counterfeit of any typeset note — and a good many did so."[113]

Capture of counterfeiters and passers was difficult because bills of one colony or state were often passed in neighboring colonies and states. Moreover, punishments meted out to offenders apparently were not enough of a deterrent. Colonial authorities took to intimidation, as in the case of a bill issued by Pennsylvania in 1773, on the back of which was the reminder, "To Counterfeit is DEATH"— directly below a woodcut scene of a truly pastoral landscape, the very incarnation of Jefferson's vision of an agrarian America.

Despite threats of capital punishment and vocal protests, colonial officials tended to look the other way. Only half a dozen executions of counterfeiters are known for the entire colonial era.[114] Another, perhaps more effective strategy was to employ the best artists that could be found — mostly silversmiths, including the renowned Paul Revere — to engrave the copper plates. Other measures included the use of special paper, indentures (cutting a wavy line between a numbered note and its stub kept in a book at the site of issuance, thus making redemption safer), border cuts, different type fonts, even the use of Greek and Hebrew letters and zodiacal symbols— and Benjamin Franklin's gift, the nature print.[115] Still, counterfeiting did not go away. Soiled, torn, patched, and sewn bills made detection of counterfeits a daunting task. As did the fact that counterfeit bills or plates were often produced in Europe. During the War of Independence the British, who knew that the Continental Congress lacked adequate specie to back its paper money, produced counterfeit Continental paper dollars to such an extent that entire issues had to be called in. From the perspective of the British, of course, producing Continentals was not really counterfeiting at all: the Revolutionary currency itself was seen as "unlawful" so that they would consider it quite "lawful" to counterfeit the "counterfeit" Continentals. For the British, a ruinous attack on the Revolutionary currency thus was a matter of returning the colonists to their allegiance. In retaliation, the Revolutionaries, who did not take well to the ruin of their circulating medium, began to produce counterfeit British money — which adds an interesting facet to the division into public versus private.[116]

Following independence, the situation hardly improved. If early nineteenth-century reports can be trusted, up to fifty percent of the paper in circulation was fraudulent or, to use the idiom of the time, "bogus." Illicit entrepreneurs across the border in Canada ran workshops producing enormous numbers of counterfeits. Thanks to their efforts, many of the early notes

15s, Pennsylvania, 1773, back: "To Counterfeit is DEATH" (American Numismatic Association Money Museum)

(especially those of the Second Bank of the United States, which circulated at par throughout the country) are known today only from counterfeits.[117] In other instances, an exchange broker would purchase large numbers of notes of a bank that had become worthless through bankruptcy, usually at two to three percent of the notes' nominal value. The broker would then sell the notes to a counterfeiter, who in turn altered them to a bank with a similar look elsewhere. Roughly this summarizes the history of an altered note from the Blackstone Canal Bank, Providence [sic], Rhode Island. This note, which originally had been produced by The New England Bank Note Company in the 1830s, was altered from the Stillwater Canal Bank of Maine. While the word "Blackstone" is beautifully lettered, it is spaced too closely to "Canal." Also noteworthy is the misspelling of "Providence." In addition, "Rhode Island" was drawn in (vertically, on the right of the vignette) after "Maine" had been removed.

Early in the nineteenth century, there had been hope when Jacob Perkins invented a method of using steel for engraving plates. Perkins's notes had little aesthetic appeal, and they may look downright homely to modern viewers. Still, great hopes were invested in them, and use of the Perkins system even became mandatory in Massachusetts in 1809. However, in 1818 Hezekiah Niles predicted that the United States was on its way to becoming "a nation of counterfeiters." Niles, who had made himself a name with the *Weekly Register*, then the most important financial publication, was horrified at the proliferation of fraudulent paper money. "Counterfeiters and false bank notes are so common," he wrote in the July 4, 1818, issue, "that forgery seems to have lost its criminality in the minds of many."[118] By the early 1850s, banks had had enough, as the Perkins notes no longer constituted a challenge to the counterfeiter. "A successful counterfeit of a general plate," an 1852 report acknowledged, "may easily be applied to a great number of banks."[119] Altogether, the nineteenth-century American bank note has been described as "one of the most widely counterfeited of all fiscal documents, and its forgery [...] a permanent problem for issuers, printers, and the public alike."[120] The problem was indeed real, general, and it might one day become fatal. Reports of forgeries being confiscated and destroyed abounded. Only expert knowledge would enable contemporaries to tell a genuine note from a fraudulent one.[121]

The shift from private money to public paper brought about by the fiscal demands of the Civil War also had a profound effect on the perceptions of counterfeiting. Pre–Civil War

$5, Altered Note, Blackstone Canal Bank, Providence [sic], RI, 1840 (courtesy of Mark. D. Tomasko)

paper currency was a commercial convenience; after, it became something more grandiose, a symbol of the nation itself. Because of this shift, forgery no longer was merely an unavoidable evil and a nuisance but an intolerable affront. Beginning in 1865, therefore, counterfeiters who were caught were brought to trial by the United States Secret Service, the body specially established in order to control counterfeiting and to generally protect the currency — and, later, the president. Both the dollar and the president were seen as representing the sovereign majesty of the United States. Thus the establishment of the Secret Service or, as it was euphemistically called in the 1860s, the "National Detective Police Force," was really a symptom of the city of Washington's — the center's — rising influence in all walks of American life.[122]

In 1864, Congress had ruled the private production of monies illegal, and the Secret Service enforced the law. Gone were the days when responsibility for counterfeit detection had been with bank clerks and the people at large. Respectable businessmen were astonished to find themselves suddenly ordered by federal law enforcement officers to surrender their advertising copy, dies, and plates for producing dollar bill look-alikes they were using as advertisements, or face arrest. A year later, the Secret Service made a sweep of Western counterfeiters and secured two hundred convictions. When the capable administrator Hiram Whitley took over the Service, a number of reforms were introduced, such as standardized procedures for arresting suspects, seizing evidence, receiving reimbursement for expenses, and circulating correspondence. In addition, Whitley issued badges to agents, giving them the imprimatur of federal authority. In 1882, the year the Service finally received statutory recognition by the Congress, a "rogue's gallery" was set up in the Treasury Department's Washington, DC, headquarters. Visitors could peruse more than 2,000 photographs of some of the most notorious counterfeiters. Deemed "one of the most interesting places for sight seers in Washington," it was said to entertain guests for more than an hour.[123]

Altogether, by the early 1900s counterfeiting no longer was the common danger that it had used to be. Methods for detecting counterfeits had been improved, far more than counterfeiting methods. Moreover, the courts were more severe in the punishment of counterfeiters, under the insistence of the federal government.[124] According to one government survey conducted in 1911, counterfeits constituted a mere thousandth of one percent of the total paper currency in circulation, a dramatic decrease from earlier times.[125] Before long, inscriptions on bank and government notes threatening counterfeiters with severe punishment — the so-called "counterfeit clauses" — disappeared. Introduced in the 1860s, they were last seen on the Legal Tender issues of the 1917 series and were never even used on Federal Reserve notes.

Writing in the 1950s, Arthur Nussbaum interprets the disappearance of the counterfeit clauses as a "gratifying omen."[126] Were this scholar to publish his history of the dollar in a new edition, he might want

$100, Legal Tender note, 1869, back, detail (counterfeit clause) (American Numismatic Association Money Museum)

to reconsider. To be sure, the dual meanings of "making money"—circulating currency and accumulating wealth—had drifted apart for good. If a profit was to be made, it was no longer in the circulation of bank notes but in the purchase of stocks and other financial operations. However, the machinations of speculators like Jay Gould and others would take the capitalist confidence in new and startling directions, putting to shame the more modest feats of earlier generations of counterfeiters.[127] Nor has counterfeiting disappeared entirely. A friend of this author remembered seeing a Public Broadcasting documentary on American money in which it was noted that the United States was "pissing off European nations by refusing to change its currency." The problem was that the bills had been around so long that they were easy targets for counterfeiters. As this friend recalled, the American response was to the effect that, "'This is the dollar,' as if one had been asked to change the teachings of Jesus because of religious counterfeits."[128] The documentary was broadcast some time in the 1980s.

As for now, "this is the dollar" no longer is the predominant attitude, least of all with the Bureau of Engraving and Printing. Beginning in the 1990s, the paper currency has been enhanced with about a dozen new features to bust counterfeits, including chemical markers, holograms, micro-printing, an embedded polymer strip, and the use of more colors, to upset photocopy machines. Current estimates put the rate of counterfeit $50 notes in circulation worldwide at less than one note for every 25,000 genuine notes in circulation. Law enforcement has remained aggressive. In 2003, the Secret Service made 469 seizures of digital equipment involved in currency counterfeiting, such as personal computers, and made more than 3,640 arrests in the United States for currency counterfeiting activities. The conviction rate for counterfeiting prosecutions is about 99 percent.[129]

If counterfeiting has not died out, this is because counterfeiters are increasingly turning to digital methods. In 1995, less than one percent of counterfeit notes detected in the United States were digitally produced. Since then, digital equipment has become more readily available to the public, and the amount of digitally produced counterfeit notes has risen to about forty percent. A pattern that has been detected only recently is that counterfeiters bleach the ink off $5 notes, and then print counterfeit $100 notes on the paper, deceiving the public because of similarities between the placement of the security features on the $5 and $100 notes. While these counterfeit attempts pose no significant economic problem today, officials say a redesign of the $5 will help ensure such problems do not develop in the future.[130] Overall, what Treasury Secretary John W. Snow said on April 26, 2004, the day the $50 note was officially unveiled in Fort Worth, Texas, is characteristic of current monetary policies: "U.S. currency is a worldwide symbol of security and integrity. These new designs help us keep it that way, by protecting against counterfeiting and making it easier for people to confirm the authenticity of their hard-earned money."[131]

In Defense of the National Money Icon

Today, responsibility for defending and protecting the currency rests with the Department of the Treasury, the Bureau of Engraving and Printing, and the Secret Service. Michael P. Merritt of the Secret Service summarizes this responsibility in the following way: "Aggressive law enforcement, an effective design, and public education are all essential components of our concerted anti-counterfeiting efforts."[132] Still, note design is not simply concerned with creating functionally apposite (counterfeit-proof), intelligible ("American"), and stylistically pleasing bills but is also concerned with recruiting a target group of patriotic Americans. The latter becomes patently obvious from the debate and controversy in the wake of Theodore Roosevelt's decision to remove the inscription "In God We Trust" from coins or else when beginning in 2005 the U.S. Mint "negligently" shifted the motto to the edge of the new Presidential Dollar coins. The hullabaloo was considerable in each instance, yet it was a ripple when we compare it to what happens when use of the motto on the currency comes to be challenged in court.

Challenges to the national motto have happened many times over the years it has been in official use, that is, since July 1955. One particularly notorious case was not even originally related to the motto. In June 1962, the United States Supreme Court upheld a challenge to school prayer by the famed atheist Madalyn Murray O'Hare. The decision, Brian Burrell remarks, "sent many people into a panic," among them the director of the Bureau of Engraving and Printing, who feared that "In God We Trust" might be the next to fall, even before it was fully implemented. To avoid the expense of redesigning plates and introducing new bills all over again, the director ordered that the printing process be speeded up, and that the plates for every denomination be redesigned to incorporate the motto. Burrell's commentary is telling: "[T]he loss of school prayer was quietly compensated for with the inclusion of God in another area of public life."[133] As regards the future, any "In God We Trust" lawsuit is certain to meet with the declared intention, on the part both of the Department of the Treasury and of the Department of Justice, to "actively defend against challenges to the use of the national motto."[134]

All strategies in defense of the national money icon serve two purposes. The first is to suppress transformations, reshapings, disfigurements, revaluations, reconfigurations, or renewals of form and content. The second is to guarantee the retrieval in always-identical ways of its formulation and performance. The various attempts, on the part of government agencies and/or institutions or individuals allied to them, towards regulating (structuring, shaping) the conduct of social life in relation to the national money icon thus further emphasize the overall importance of the currency towards constructing and reinforcing an American national identity. A key element in that identity is that the United States is "not a heathen nation." The message is evident also from various opinion polls of the recent past. In 1998, a Harris poll found that 66 percent even of non–Christian Americans believed in miracles and 47 percent of them believed in the Virgin Birth; the figures for all Americans were 86 percent and 83 percent respectively. While in 1998 some 73 percent of Americans believed there is a Devil, according to a 2000 *Newsweek* poll 79 percent of American respondents also accepted the idea that miracles described in the Bible actually took place. According to the same source, 40 percent of all Americans (and 71 percent of Evangelical Protestants) believe that the world will end in a battle at Armageddon between Jesus and the Antichrist.[135]

The image emerging from these polls is that America really is a credulous and religious society. In contrast to Europe, where since the mid–1950s churches have been abandoned, in the United States there has been virtually no decline in churchgoing (and synagogue attendance). As Tony Judt remarked, an "American president who conducts Bible study in the White House and begins cabinet sessions with a prayer may seem a curious anachronism to his European allies, but he is in tune with his constituents." That president surely was in tune also with the Treasury Department, or rather, the Treasury Department was in tune with its president. From the Department's website we learn, *inter alia*, that "[s]ymbolically, the [Great Seal of the United States] reflects the beliefs and values that the Founding Fathers attached to the new nation and wished to pass on to their descendants."[136]

Clearly, what is presented as "Money Facts" suggests timelessness, as if the one-dollar note on which the Great Seal has come to be fixated had been in circulation from the beginning of the American republic. Everyone knows that this is not the case. However, we can describe the role of the Treasury Department in terms of a "gatekeeper," shaping and even constructing America's stories or, rather, mythologies from the nation's past. The story about the Great Seal serves as a kind of creation myth of the national money icon, much as the Declaration of Independence serves as the creation myth of the nation itself. As regards the web pages, they function as a kind of hall of fame. Although unlike the Rotunda in the National Archives Building the website is merely a virtual hall of fame, it is nevertheless the site of interrelation and overlap of the production and consumption of the national money icon. With "Money Facts," consumers are "sold" on timelessness and the hallowed tradition of the nation's most precious symbols.

A survey about new website features that the Bureau of Engraving and Printing sent out to subscribers to its email list in October 2008 shows just how carefully the Treasury is planning its promotional and marketing activities and just how much eagerness, aptitude, and even dedication to "the cult" there is on the part of those responsible for launching the national money icon. The survey, which was conducted by PBS, is one of the longest and most complex undertakings of its kind this author has seen. Its apparent purpose was to gauge the efficacy of Internet efforts towards educating people about the redesigned United States currency.[137] Another government agency maintains a special website for children. Called "Brain Food," the site offers what are called "Cool Facts," including facts about the national currency.[138] As in the case of "Money Facts," the rhetorical strategies in the website for children are designed to "naturalize" the national currency so that its reproduction becomes automatic. The Treasury also launched a strategy aimed at appealing to various social segments and thus including displays at numismatic conventions and the sale of sheets and souvenirs. Federal Reserve Board Governor Mark W. Olson called this strategy "educational outreach."[139]

Educational outreaches are not merely a matter of institutions such as the Bureau of Engraving and Printing, the Federal Reserve, or the Secret Service, but are also on the agenda of "ideological" state apparatuses or their representatives, such as teachers and educators. A good example of such an outreach is "training currency," make-believe dollar notes that in the late nineteenth century were widely used by business schools and textbooks.[140] A contemporary example is a book by Barbara Johnston Adams titled *The Go-around Dollar*. The book, which is listed under juvenile literature, provides plenty of information about dollar bills, skillfully woven into a story of a single dollar bill changing hands as it is passed from one person to another, until the bill ends up in a picture frame as the first dollar earned by a new store.

Although *The Go-around Dollar* is designed for children, its target audience is adults, or more precisely, parents who will read the book to their children. This is an important point as children generally have their consumption mediated by their parents. Supposing that the parents are patriotic citizens, reading the book to their children can be expected to elicit the same or a similar response on their part. At the very least, the children will have a measure of exposure to where current dollars bills originate (the Bureau of Engraving and Printing), how and where they are put into circulation (the Federal Reserve Banks, which send them to commercial banks), and what pictures and other pieces of information are on them (a portrait of George Washington, the Great Seal). They will also learn that dollar bills are legal tender for all debts, private and public, that counterfeiters sometimes make fake bills, that a special ink is used on genuine ones, that the Treasury Department will replace most damaged bills, and that occasionally people will keep a bill because it has a special meaning for them. In all, the effect of *The Go-around Dollar* is to build "brand loyalty," to use a term that is common in the language of advertising and marketing.

People ordering online their personal copies of *The Go-around Dollar* would be directed to a list titled "Good Books to Teach Children about Money." The list, which appears to have been put together by a teacher, comprised some twenty-five titles, including one concentrating on the meaning of the art and symbols on the paper currency, another one providing a mini-history of economics, and one musing on the idea of making a million.[141] Also on that list would have been *The Buck Book*, which opens to children the wide field of money folding (adults can do Origami or Hawaiian-style folds with their dollar bills). All these books (there are many more) are good examples of social practices with which paper dollars have become associated. In a more general sense, they connect to traditional concerns with children's money. As Viviana Zelizer notes, a child's allowance, popular from the 1870s, was defined primarily as educational money. Closely supervised by parents, the money allocated to children was to teach them proper social and moral, as well as consumer skills. From 1885, school savings banks too assumed the guardianship of children's monies. Penny Provident Fund stations joined these "banks" in 1894. By 1906, Penny Provident had opened 227 stations, and collected over $50,000,000 in deposits from almost 90,000 depositors. Many of these "banks" were opened in public schools, where according to Penny Provident "every classroom" was to be turned into a savings bank, with "every teacher a bank president, every girl and boy and every mother and father a depositor with a bank account." It was hoped that the monetary alchemy of the savings system would also work with the children, redirecting their "candy pennies" or cigarette cash into money for books, clothes, or other "useful" purposes.[142]

God is not merely connected to patriotic fervor but also has been made a principal in financial education. For instance, a 2001 book titled *In God We Trust* is described as a "Christian kids guide to saving and spending" and marketed as an "entertaining way to help your child learn the basics of God's plan for money—how to earn, give, spend, and save the money God provides."[143] The book's author receives praise for being one of the primary trailblazers and leaders in Christian financial teaching, the purpose of which is to provide direction and confidence in building a financial portfolio that will provide for the family and help readers to honor God. Nor is monetary management exclusively a matter for children. Young adults too are to be drawn into the world of Christian finance, as per a 2001 book by Bob Santos that likewise bears in its title the phrase "In God We Trust." Advertised as a resource for college students and other young adults, the book purports to be "both biblical and practical. It will help you find financial freedom and learn to plan how to use your money wisely."[144]

These few examples of educational outreach show that the symbolic process by which the national currency positions individuals as patriotic citizens is not a "natural" one but stems from the intellectual labor of cultural elites. These elites know very well that for any sign to stay popular, it must be constantly recalled. With the increasing distance from George Washington's lifetime, for instance, both his name and his portrait need to be reintroduced to each new generation of Americans. Already the mere mentioning of (or naming after) Washington intensifies his popularity as the Founding Father of the Republic, but semiotically this is far less effective than a pictorial representation. With the current one-dollar bill in particular, both the name-symbol and the visual symbol are secured in the collective memory. The same is true of the inscription "In God We Trust," which has replaced the obligation to pay "on demand." The change as it were notarizes the completion of the monetary cycle, at which point the paper currency is backed by nothing more — and nothing less — than confidence in the nation state.[145]

It is tempting to see, now that all paper dollars are mere signs of value, the phrase "In God We Trust" as a kind of spell, intended to alleviate the public's anxieties.[146] This is not so far off, for the more uncertain the future is, the more will people imagine differences that resist negotiation because of their "intrinsic" character. In November 2005, a FOX News/Opinion Dynamics poll found that 95 percent of registered voters nationwide wanted the motto "In God We Trust" to remain on U.S. currency and coins.[147] Possibly, these people indeed trust that God has empowered the state to fulfill the promises and obligations articulated on the currency, in particular the paying back of debts. In addition, they may trust that God will continue to provide money. There is even a certain justification in saying that the motto engages the people managing the currency, as they are the ones who will be held accountable for the fiscal disaster threatening to hit the nation. Now that the banking crash of 2008 has, in Alan Greenspan's apt words, turned into a "once-in-a-century credit tsunami," and is threatening to undermine even the fundamental belief in capitalism's power to heal itself, the meaning of the canonical phrase has taken an altogether new turn. People now may trust that God, too, "finally takes on the entire burden of guilt," as Walter Benjamin foresaw it in 1921.[148] In each case, the currency is quite literally "faith-based," with the trust in question blending secular monetary and divine categories. In this, the phrase "In God We Trust" is not only symptomatic of the fact that the great confidence game of capitalism is alive and well; it also echoes the Christian tradition that saw God both as the Father and as chief accountant.[149]

The importance of Protestant Christianity for Americans' self-identification as well as for the country's political institutions and ethos is well known. Today's currency continues to bear the stamp of its religious origin, though neither gold nor any other commodity imposes discipline on politicians. This puts a great burden on them to validate faith in the currency. "Reckless U.S. fiscal policy," a commentator wrote in May 2007, "is undermining the dollar's position even as the currency's role as a global money is expanding."[150] With the current account deficit of $521 billion running at an incredible 6.6 percent of GDP (the gross domestic product — the market value of goods and services produced), and with an out-of-control national debt (which as of February 5, 2009, was spiraling upward of $10.6 trillion — way above 60 percent of GDP, and visible to everyone on the National Debt Clock), a tide of red ink threatens to engulf the nation, bankrupt its future and undermine the faith foreigners have placed in the dollar.[151] In light of this scenario, the appearance of God's name on the national currency takes on a new meaning, from establishing the United States as a Christian nation visibly different from the atheist Soviet Union to a cry for help — if not a gesture of mourning. As Jean-Joseph Goux remarked, "The inconvertible signifier that circulates today, that floats, that always postpones its 'realization,' guarantees the monetary function in the realm of pure symbolicity, but only by mourning the loss of the unlocatable (or floating) standard and the uncertain reserve value, secured by nothing."[152]

The loss of the standard is quite literally painted, or rather gilded over, by all the insignia of the state's officialdom with which United States coins and notes have become embellished. A beginning was made in 1909, when the government abandoned the Indian-head penny in favor of the Lincoln penny. Thereafter, each coin in turn was changed to bear the image of a politician. The first portraits were those of the Founding Fathers, but gradually, images that are more contemporary began to appear. Paper bills that had carried scenes from the nation's history or allegorical images similar to those on the coins likewise switched to portraits of politicians. Their "hard images" were to give "soft currency" a good name by magically transforming worthless pieces of paper into priceless tokens. During the Middle Ages, essentially this function was performed by the communion wafer, which often took the form of a stamped coin. The wafers constituted something like *fiat* money backed by the priest, whose words—"*crede ut edes, et edes*" ("Believe that you eat the flesh of Christ in the wafer, and you do eat it")—magically transformed worthless bread into the priceless body of Christ. Now that religion, art, and economics have been folded into one another in such a way that each "shadows" the other, the politicians' "hard images" stand in for the fathers who have become absent in modern society.

The one-dollar bill in particular is so ceremoniously laden, its "emblematic proliferation" (the term is Goux's) upholding the function of the sign. As Goux writes,

> The State (and its Treasury), God (and our faith in him), the Father (founder), the dead and sacralized Language (Latin): all these powerful, central signifiers converge, combine, and intensify each other so as to provide the one-dollar note with its force. It is the State in all of its foundational stability that guarantees the value of the bill, under the authority of the Treasury. By design [...] the American bill, through the almost Roman austerity that characterizes its engraving, remains strongly marked by the emblems of civil religion: that is, by the imaginary realm of guaranteed value and fixed standards. The value of the bill still refers to a certain depth, a certain verticality. Somewhere, a treasure is present, a reserve, a fund, upon which this bill is staked. There exists an underlying, protected value, which the State holds, preserves, and guarantees by its institution, and which this bill represents.[153]

The treasure represented by the one-dollar note, its protected value, is of course gold, the "Lord of commodities," to repeat Marx's phrase. In the word "Lord" the two realms of Christian doctrine come together, the secular one of economic exchange (in which the dollar is a monetary token), and the divine one of the exchange of gifts (in which the dollar is an infinitely large and archaic gift, which obligates the recipient to give back something, or at least to be grateful). In earlier Christian thinking, the gift figured as the Holy Grail, the container of Christ's blood. It was a gift of boundless wealth, pictorialized in grail-like cornucopias, which appeared in allegorical depictions of commerce in seventeenth-century paintings.[154] Cornucopias also were popular images on nineteenth-century bank notes. The illustration on this page represents a female figure with a staff tipped by a liberty cap and a cornucopia from the tip of which flows a seemingly endless stream of precious coins.

The two realms—the secular one of economic exchange and the divine one of the exchange of gifts—are held to be mutually exclusive. Therefore, the object that appears as both money and gift is granted a privileged status. This status is provided by the manifestation of money as an ideal *and* a real thing, an instance

$5, Citizens' Bank of New Orleans, c. 1860, detail: allegorical depiction of commerce (Louisiana Division/City Archives, New Orleans Public Library.)

of value impressed into a material thing. The pagan gods and goddesses appearing on bills issued by private banks highlighted this. These figures were not unproblematic, as they also deflected from the Christian One, who might have considered greed as sinful. On the other hand, they restored the ancient practice of touching the deity. Every time someone held a piece of paper money in their hands, they would touch the deity, in hope that its power would be transferred, and encourage people to proceed on. In Catholic countries at least, the practice of touching the deity lived on in the practice of touching the saints. Protestants have always been wary of this practice. Americans in particular have preserved the taboo against graven images in that only the name of the deity appears on paper money. Yet people always choose the gods that are socially needed. Since the pagan gods and goddesses are no longer seen as capable of blessing and protecting the currency of a Christian nation, the Christian One comes in.

In its purest form, the symbolic value of the current one-dollar bill rests on the tension between the visual image of the secular Lord, George Washington, whose claim is to a superior status, and the verbal image of the Lord God, whose claim is likewise to a superior status. Washington's status has the imprimatur of history and myth; God's is represented by the phrase "*annuit coeptis,*" the mark of approval of what the nation's founders had undertaken. Thus, the gift was bestowed by God's grace or, in the diction of the Founders, through God's providence. Both visual and verbal images therefore re-connect Americans to the belief of the early Protestant settlers that piety and economic success were sure signs of salvation in the hereafter. Both, it would seem, were a matter of faith, and required moral limits. Today, such limits are no longer allowed to get in the way of success, though politicians keep repeating that "trust" is essential to free enterprise. Theoretically this makes sense, as investors should not play in the stock market if they cannot trust corporate executives to do right. There is, however, no guarantee that this will happen. All we have is a promise in which we must believe. We must have faith in those taking our money. We must believe that corporate executives will do what they have promised. That is why God is so important to free enterprise.[155]

If the entreaty to unquestioned belief is given weight and depth through God's name, the name's appearance on the currency is also limiting: the quasi-religious practices associated with paper dollars are valid only for those who possess them. Until recently, this used to be the rich. Now that money is becoming ever more ethereal, those in possession of dollar bills increasingly are the less affluent. As those who possess the least are the ones who are most in need of protection, they will likely also be the ones to protect the national motto, aside from those for whom patriotism sells. Thus, the motto both foregrounds and conceals the social construction of the currency, that is, the fact that people attribute worth to a medium whose material is essentially irrelevant to its monetary function. Therefore, no matter how the Supreme Court will decide in the next motto elimination suit, in the paper dollar's cultural work the early days of the new republic will live on. They will live on specifically in the religious language used in the founding documents, such as the phrase "Nature and Nature's God" in the Declaration, or else the words of a committee report to the Continental Congress, which in November 1777 recommended to the states a national day of Thanksgiving on the grounds of "the indispensable duty of all men to adore the superintending providence of Almighty God; to acknowledge with gratitude their obligation to him for benefits received ... but also to smile upon us in the prosecution of a just and necessary war, for the defence [sic] and establishment of our unalienable rights and liberties."[156] The need appears no less so today, and America's money bears evidence of this.

Conclusion

ROSSE: "That now
Sweno, the Norway's King, craves composition;
Nor would we deign him burial of his men
Till he disbursed at Saint Colme's Inch
Ten thousand dollars to our general use."
— William Shakespeare, *Macbeth*, 1. 2. 67–71

This book owes its origin to the question of what we learn about American culture by just looking at dollar bills. Dollar bills give us insights into the shared meanings and social practices — the distinctive ways of making sense and doing things — which are the very basis of American culture. Already during the colonial era — *before* dollar bills even existed — paper money for a variety of reasons became bound up with issues of political sovereignty. Thus, as soon as the first paper dollars were put into circulation, they evolved into veritable metaphors of the evolving American state of mind during the revolutionary era, which was clearly centered on independence from England. The fiscal disaster engulfing the Continentals had dramatic consequences on the development of paper money in the new nation. Thereafter, paper dollars came from a variety of origins and, additionally, had to somehow appeal to multiple constituencies. These facts also bore on design, with a rather abstract symbolism becoming typical of banknote design in the early nineteenth century. Following the Civil War, a more distinctively American imagery came into play, relating to politics and history and foregrounding the integrity of the Union. This phase played itself out in a society the economic and social structures of which differed profoundly from those which had existed earlier. As a result, the motives of the people who promoted and "invented" the new bills, together with the manner in which contemporaries interpreted and understood them, also changed profoundly. While both were still centered on republican loyalties, they were increasingly directed towards the strengthening of a central state authority that, like the Treasury Department, had on its agenda the education of (an increasing number of new) citizens about their country.

A new phase in the development of currency iconography was reached with the period of international competition. In this period can be located the origin of an iconography that many commentators erroneously assume goes back to the time of the Founding Fathers. Once the iconography invented in the nineteenth century was swept away, along with the policies whose image they were designed to enhance, currency iconography achieved a unique continuity. Thus, the look of the entire currency stayed more or less the same until the 1980s, when the government began to redesign the entire currency — the $1 and $2 notes excepted. We can expect these two notes to prevail, providing at least a semblance of stability in periods of domestic change, and of continuity and comfort in times of international crisis and decline.

National currencies depend on being accepted by a large number of people and therefore have to win the consent also of the marginalized and the subordinated. Thus, national currencies must be capable both of symbolizing a community based on a political territory and of transcending social contradictions. Paradoxically, nationalist sentiments seem strongest today where there have been the most decisive shifts in cultural values. In the United Kingdom for instance, successive Conservative administrations privileged the private over the public in all realms of social life. In particular, they took the provision of goods and services away from state bureaucracies, transferring them to private markets and, in general, encouraged the development of acquisitive and entrepreneurial forms of individual conduct among the populace at large. The shift in values did not extend to the currency, though. In that realm, the state bureaucracy prevailed, together with the symbolic baggage deployed to make sure that citizens will recognize themselves and each other in precisely the terms specified by the dominant order.

It is thus no contradiction that Margaret Thatcher, one of the leading figures in the neo-liberal counterrevolution against Keynesian orthodoxy, presented herself as a staunch nationalist when she defended her desire to maintain an independent currency. Similarly, Mr. Heathcote-Amory, a British politician vehemently opposed to the European Union's common currency project, in May 1994 expressed his concern that the introduction of the euro would "dilute" national identity. The archbishop of Canterbury too has been quoted as saying, "I want the Queen's head on the bank notes."[1] There have been many other "badges of national identity," especially during the "Keep the Pound" campaign, in which imperial or martial images were evoked as Britain was "under attack" from the Continent in the form of the euro. On a 1999 campaign postcard, for example, Britannia is depicted on the white cliff of Dover, with her back to the wall ready to take on the enemy from Continental Europe.[2]

The French too rose to the challenge the euro posed to the idea that every nation-state must have its own territorially homogeneous and exclusive currency. In a book titled *La Monnaie souveraine*, economists and social scientists attempted to find answers to the question why abandoning the franc and replacing it by the euro so dramatically stirred up people's emotions. The general hypothesis is telling. What allegedly caused so much restiveness was not the transfer of economic power so much as it was the question of national identity. For, the euro as a form of supra-national currency was about to circulate in a space of markets that is completely detached from the idea of a community of common social values.[3] This brings us back full circle to the French scholar Bruno Théret, who criticized the euro's designers for grossly neglecting the lived experience and social fantasies of a dominant majority within Europe's societies, coming up instead with "sad symbols" on a currency "without soul or culture." For modern currencies to be accepted and considered legitimate, they must be able to both symbolize a community based on a political territory and transcend social contradictions — as is provided by the United States' national currency, which Théret cites as a model.

Théret offers two explanations for the "symbolic deficit" in the postmodern aesthetics of the euro notes. The first is that symbolic, psychological, or political dimensions were entirely outside the horizon of the social scientists responsible for the design of the euro.

The second is that the economists on the project had been exclusively interested in the exchange value of the euro, and thus had a profound distrust of political or symbolic dimensions, which for them were only archaisms or expressions of special interests. However, does the euro really contribute nothing towards a culturally constructed sense of inclusion? To most people, the bridges and arches, windows and gateways that appear on the various denominations of euro notes seem to suggest little more than a kind of coming together, which would make the euro a bank draft drawn on some kind of remote future. Maybe that was the intention of the designers. Yet upon closer inspection, the monuments on the notes — Romanesque gateways, Roman aqueducts, Victorian iron and glass windows, or modern bridges — are not timeless so much as they are rooted in a time *before* the modern nation-state. They may also be rooted *after* it, which would make them post-national as it were. At any rate, the notes had to say "*Europe*," all of it, and there could not be anything too particular, or anything that might offend the nationalistic feelings of any participating country.

All the Eurocrats could agree on as being quintessentially European — without offending anyone — were generic architectural details.[4] Still, in 1995 the European Commission felt that, "for some people, the change [to the new euro notes] will feel almost like a change of identity."[5] On the other hand, the people who were responsible for *not* selecting any of the old national symbols for the new currency may have been emboldened by the fact that activist monetary management (the kind of management Roosevelt was pursuing in the 1930s) had become less popular at the time. This is true both of "the people" and of liberal policy-makers, who just loved to see the management of money taken away from governments. When we view the monetary policies pursued by institutions such as the European Central Bank or the Deutsche Bundesbank, the political costs of giving up national currencies indeed seem to have diminished. As a species, national currencies thus may quietly disappear, like the dodo or the passenger pigeon and other animal species. What the introduction of the euro as a supra-national form of currency suggests, then, is the probable dissolution that long-standing economic and fiscal national borders are presently facing.

The monetary practices connected with the global market likewise are typical of late modernity or postmodernity. For Jean-Joseph Goux, they are even evidence of the dematerialization of money to the point where all we ever get is an "indefinite play of referrals which forever postpones the possibility of an actual value."[6] The move from modern to late modern therefore must be seen as highly dramatic in terms of our understanding of money for, as Goux had argued in an earlier essay, all economies, whether barter or monetary, create symbolic value in that "it is always through replacement that values are created."[7] Yet the process of abstraction and acceleration, brought into the world by the circulation of real money, has struck back at money itself. Now that money is linked to a medium such as the internet, it has become a chimera. No more than a messenger from the order of values, it has become pale and invisible, like the messengers in religions. "Real" money, meaning coins and bank or government notes, remains as a concept, like "the real" itself, if only liminally. However, once the community of faithful loses their faith (trust) in the invisible god of values, the system that has accrued around that god implodes.

Gold, paper, or plastic give rise to philosophical speculation, at the same time as they remind us of the close connection between culture and media, that is, between the meanings and practices that form the basis of culture and the technological means — the media — by which a great deal of culture is produced, circulated, and consumed. Each of these media has a particular set of practices associated with it — a way of using them, a set of knowledges or "know-how," called a "social technology."[8] Although each technology both sustains culture and produces or reproduces it, capitalism as a system moves on very rapidly, leaving only residual cultures stuck with their failures and worked-out areas, such as national cultures, together with the idea of the nation-state. Regardless, for a great many Americans the nation still is important, and their feelings of patriotism run high. This is evident from polls and studies done by a variety of institutions and individual scholars over the past twenty years.

For instance, in 1985 about 87 percent of a sample of United States citizens said that they were "very proud" to be American.[9] In 1998, a telephone survey of 1,004 adults again probed people about their feelings of loyalty and patriotism toward America. Asked to rate their feelings on a scale of 1–10, 78 percent of Americans gave them at least a seven, with an overall average of 7.8.[10] To the European observer, such rates are simply astounding. Only 21 percent of Germans said that they were proud to be German, while 58 percent of British people said they were proud to be British, and, surprisingly, 61 percent of Austrians said the same about being Austrian. The high percentage of Austrians expressing a feeling of national pride warrants a closer look. Tellingly, almost all the Austrians polled (97 percent) said that they were proud of the country's mountains, forests, and lakes; only a mere 25 percent said that they were in any way proud of the political system. This figure puts Austrians back in line with the Germans, which is not really a surprise. Both peoples have traditionally defined their nations in terms of culture, not in terms of a political system.[11]

The indifference so many Austrians appear to feel towards their political system has been explained by the reduction of the nation, following World War I, to a mere fragment of its imperial, Austro-Hungarian greatness. Because of this sea change, there have been numerous attempts towards building a national identity on the "*heimat*" and, concomitantly, on narratives of vigorous and morally commendable characters stemming from the native soil.[12] The rhetoric of a sanitized and optimistic nativism is also reflected in the national anthem, which begins with a celebration of "great mountains and rivers" and other features of the landscape, before it goes on to acknowledge the country's "great sons." Tellingly, "great sons" does not include political figures, past or present. In this regard, the anthem is quite similar to the old Austrian currency, the schilling, which likewise spoke of the country's "great mountains and rivers" and of its "great sons"—and, to be fair, also of a few of its daughters—but did not honor any statesmen, deceased or alive. In fact, like on the modern United States currency, none of the men or women depicted on schilling notes ever was a living person.[13]

Yet the days of the schilling, which began with the demise of the imperial kronen in 1925, are gone, leaving the mental universe of Austrians exposed to the euro as a single, supra-national currency. Like it or not, eventually the euro *will* contribute towards the development of single, supra-national forms of identity. For people who remember the catastrophic inflation of the post–World War I years, this may not be such a bad thing. Those who have no personal memories of the time may return to the picture used in the preface to this book of a Berlin woman who, realizing that fuel costs money, is starting the morning fire with marks not worth the paper they are printed on. Such experiences, which doubtless impacted on the collective psyche, have found a distant echo in the emphasis put on the euro's capacity to alter the mental universe of users. "People do not become instantly accustomed to a new money. In at least one respect, adjusting to it is somewhat like learning a language—it takes time and practice before it is possible to think in the new currency."[14]

The idea of "thinking in a (new) currency" has put its mark also on the present book, whose author recently unearthed a postcard sent to his grandfather from Sidman, PA. in 1912. The postcard shows one of the grandfather's brothers, together with another distant relative. The sender, who had left the old country a few years previously, is asking to understand that once again he would have to postpone his visit for, as he proudly announces, he was making a hundred dollars a month — about twenty times the amount people in his community of origin would live on at the time. Seen in this light, the five dollars he on occa-

Postcard from Sidman, PA, 1912, detail

sion sent his mother would have been a princely sum.[15] Altogether, then, the present book owes its existence to an impulse to show that social phenomena customarily framed in economic terms may be deepened through considering their wider cultural ramifications. Economists are not generally much interested in symbolic or imaginary aspects of money. For them, the thought that money exists only as long as people agree that it does often seems shameful. Thus, economists appear to prefer looking at money as more like a quantifiable entity, fungible, neutral, and colorless.

Nevertheless, money has always had two functions, a primary one as (legal) tender, located in the realm of society and the economy, and a secondary one as a cultural medium, located in the domain of the symbolic. Currencies thus may be linked not just to the goals of economic efficiency but also to various non-economic goals, of which the constitution of a whole range of identities—individual, social, local, regional, and national—is one. Currencies are agents of culture, nationalism, and, increasingly, post-nationalism, even if many politicians do not seem to be prepared to see it that way. Post-nationalism is seemingly incompatible with national sovereignty, if by that is meant freedom from all foreign entanglements. Small wonder, then, that few Americans seem willing to embrace a borderless world, let alone to relinquish some national sovereignty to international authorities for the benefit of all.

Yet to see national sovereignty as diametrically opposed to a post-national or global world is to ignore the status quo. Of course, the United States is unique, as only in America can anyone still use currency issued over 150 years ago. Yet the United States is already inextricably integrated into a complex web of agencies and networks—from formal ones like the World Trade Organization and the World Court, to more informal ones, like the United States Committee on International Judicial Relations or the International Postal Union. These agencies and networks, Anne-Marie Slaughter demonstrates in her new book, *A New World Order*, inform, oversee, regulate, and in actual practice shape much of what is going on in America no less than in the rest of the world. The fallacy, as Slaughter points out, is to assume that all this either signals or necessitates the end of national sovereignty and the coming of a supra-national, global system of government. States exist, and, as the only imaginable form of legitimate political organization and government for the near future, they are not likely to go away.

Americans, whether they are politicians or ordinary citizens, may relax. Rules affecting the almighty dollar will continue to be imposed top-down, but by the United States government (if at all) and not by any form of world government. The real question is whether the national government will stay put in excesses of uplift and a commitment to the realm of the symbolic or whether it will once again recognize the need for the security and resources that only governments can provide. The latter includes social stability and the relative ideological quiescence that once characterized the administrations of Franklin Delano Roosevelt and, later, Lyndon B. Johnson and that made possible the prosperity in the world of our parents and grandparents.[16] Put differently, even markets, whether national or global, require norms, habits, and sentiments external to themselves to ensure coherence and stability. The material symbolicity of paper dollars provides just that. In all likelihood, then, dollar bills will continue to exist, albeit along other, newer money forms, much in the same way that coinage has endured since before the seventh century BCE. Thus, dollar bills will remain especially resonant American icons, and the semantic universes that are placed on them will, for all their fantasy and allegory, remain the universes Americans inhabit daily.

Chapter Notes

Preface

1. Jonathan Duchac, "The Perfect Storm: The Global Financial Crisis of 2008," Talk given to Amerika Haus Vienna, October 30, 2008. The term "high rollers" belongs to Charles R. Morris. Also of interest is Baily et al.

2. Cassidy (14). Even more dangerous could be a flight from the dollar in the global economy, which, in providing a ready market for U.S. exports and in providing cash by buying U.S. government bonds, has helped to prevent an even sharper downturn. A flight from the dollar, if it should happen, in all likelihood would end the "symbiotic relationship between the U.S., which was happy to consume more than it produced, and China and other Asian exporters, which were happy to produce more than they consumed" (Soros 18). In this connection, one should also consider how the dollar has been performing against the euro. The euro has even surpassed the once Almighty Dollar in terms of the combined value of notes in circulation. In December 2006, it stood at €610 billion, equivalent at the time to $802 billion, compared with approximately $700 billion in United States currency. Thus, the euro is now the world's most popular form of cash. (Financial Management Service of the U.S. Treasury, "U.S. Currency and Coin"; and see Acton 66)

3. On October 24, 2008, Greenspan conceded to the *Chicago Tribune* that the crisis had developed into a "once-in-a-century credit tsunami." (*www.chicagotribune.com*, October 24, 2008, accessed 12/01/08)

4. Reforming the weaknesses of the system, Krugman wrote in November 2008, can wait. First, policymakers need to do "two things: get credit flowing again and prop up spending" ("What to Do" 8). In order to achieve the first goal, Krugman is convinced that the $700 billion the U.S. government proposed to use for recapitalization is too small, relative to GDP. Similarly, the fiscal stimulus the administration should provide for "jump-starting" the economy would have to be in excess of 4 percent of GDP. And, he adds, it should come, not as tax rebates, but in the form of public spending. This would have the advantage that the money would actually be spent; in addition, it would create something of value, such as "bridges that don't fall down" (ibid.).

5. Currency holdings by the American public (that is, not including holdings by banks, nor deposits) rose from $94 million in 1830 to $585 million in 1867 to $29 billion in the 1960s (Friedman and Schwartz 4–5). Other figures are even more astounding, such as the grand total of dollars in circulation, which in 2004 was set at $7 trillion. Although more than ninety percent of these dollars exist electronically or as numbers in ledgers, around $700 billion's worth, in denominations from $1 to $10,000, is printed, on 22 billion paper bills or notes, of which almost a third are held outside the United States (see USBEP, "International Training and Education"). The most recent figures, published in September 2006 by the Financial Management Service of the U.S. Treasury, put the amount of currency in circulation at just over $760 billion (U.S. Treasury, "U.S. Currency and Coin").

6. Generally on the power of objects to awaken and inform scholarship, see Turkle. On the nexus between the acceptance and legitimacy of currencies and their symbolic power, see Théret.

7. On this point, see Jules David Prown (1). For a radicalization of "understanding" to include intervention, see Grossberg et al. (*Cultural Studies*).

8. Prown has observed, *inter alia*, that "poetry, because more abstract, is considered loftier than prose, chess than wrestling, or the practice of law than collecting garbage. In the world of scholarship the more abstract subjects—mathematics, philosophy, literature—are more highly regarded than concrete and practice subjects such as engineering. [...] Higher value has been attached to works of art than to utilitarian craft objects since the Renaissance when a distinction was made between the arts, which require intellectual activity, and the crafts, which require greater physical exertion and mechanical ingenuity" (2).

9. On the "anti-idealist conception of consciousness" as relating consciousness to human productiveness, to practical activity, see R. Johnson (280–81).

10. Friedberg and Friedberg (*Paper Money* 5).

11. Mihm ("The Almighty Dollar at Home and Abroad" 3).

12. One of the first critics to warn against being "left alone with America" has been Amy Kaplan. A particularly harsh dismissal of the "linear narrative" of nationhood has come from Saldívar.

13. E. P. Thompson, as cited in Sardar and van Loon (33).

14. Helleiner ("National Currencies" 1419). For the thesis that state policy determines the development of finance, not vice versa, see Niall Ferguson.

Introduction

1. From a different perspective, this point has been brought forth by Jules David Prown (3). It might be paraphrased as follows: Literacy in America is and has never been universal, and the people who write literature or keep diaries are a relative minority. Objects—which evidently include monetary tokens—are used by a much broader cross section of the population and are therefore

potentially a more wide-ranging, perhaps even more representative source of information than written words.

2. Faul (21).

3. Anthropologists like Jack Weatherford call this focus on money in American culture the "cash configuration" (8–11). Importantly, Adrian Furnham and Michael Argyle have argued that there is a gendered difference in the significance of money, with women thinking of money "in terms of the things into which it can be converted, while men think of it in terms of the power its possession implies" (40).

4. Cited in McGinley (249).

5. Newman (*Early Paper Money* 13).

6. Doty (*America's Money* 11).

7. Mihm (*Nation of Counterfeiters* 12).

8. Thomas Churchyard, as cited in McLaughlin ("Just Fooling" 41).

9. Alexander Del Mar (*History of Money in America* 96), as cited ibid. (46).

10. Helleiner, "Territorial Currencies" (310n.1). Helleiner's is a much broader definition than "national" currency, the term that monetary historians use the most widely. A "national" currency is not "territorial" unless and until 1) there are no other currencies—whether foreign or privately issued domestic—in the land, and 2) the currency is homogeneous in quality—not varying, for instance, in value in different regions. Economists following the Nobel laureate Robert Mundell have described regions sharing a single currency as "optimum currency areas" (OCA's), claiming that a single currency would maximize economic efficiency.

11. See Taylor (*Confidence Games* 326).

12. "[...] le ciment des sociétés, les plus archaïques comme les plus contemporaines" (Aglietta and Orléan, *La Monnaie souveraine* 9). Alexander Hamilton knew this well. In April 1781 he declared that issuing paper currencies would "constitute a wholesome, solid and beneficial government credit" in the form of the national debt. This debt, through financing all kinds of grand projects such as territorial expansion and wars, would be "a powerfull cement of our union," capable of reconfiguring the relationship between citizens and the national government (Wright and Cowen 16).

13. Today, national currencies have become so indelibly associated with national identity that they are often considered as a "natural" monetary phenomenon. However, there is no intrinsic reason why monetary responsibility should be the exclusive domain of the nation-state. Indeed, before the advent of national currencies money was organized in quite different ways; now that nation-states are weakening, it is again undergoing radical transformations.

14. As Stuart Hall expresses the point, we should look at culture as "*both* the meanings and values which arise amongst distinctive social groups and classes [...] *and* [...] the lived traditions and practices through which those 'understandings' are expressed and in which they are embodied" ("Cultural Studies" 199).

15. Terminology is somewhat confusing. As Arthur Nussbaum explains, "In the technical terminology of American legislation, bank notes as well as other paper money, such as the later U.S. Notes, National Bank Notes, and Federal Reserve Notes, are called 'currency' (a term meaning simply circulation in early legislation), whereas the term 'money' is generally reserved for coins. This is a residue of the common-law tradition, which considered bank notes simply as commercial instruments. The old terminology, however, has not been sustained in more recent legislation and, in conformity with the economic

and legal literature of our day, we shall speak of 'paper money' and, on the other hand, include coins in the term 'currency'" (52). For a 1740 pamphlet published by Hugh Vance in Boston, which uses the term "currency" in the sense of anything "passing current in the market as money," see Eagleton and Williams (188).

16. Thus, terms like "United States paper money" or "United States currency" would rather limit the period. "United States" currency or paper money began with an Act of Congress of July 17, 1861, authorizing the issuance of Demand notes.

17. André Blum (*On the Origin of Paper* 26–27), Johannes Trithemius (*In Praise of Scribes* 62–63), both cited in McLaughlin ("Just Fooling" 39).

18. Gilbert (59). Focusing on the symbolic character of money originates with Marx. In his early writings, he had described money as "only a symbol whose material is irrelevant" (*Grundrisse* 226). Later, Marx distinguished the money form from "any palpable form: it is, therefore, a purely ideal or mental form" (*Capital* 3: 86). The practice reappears with Marc Shell, who characterizes coins as being "both symbol (as inscription or type) and commodity (as metallic ingot)," whereas paper money, like subsidiary small coins, is "virtually all symbolic" (*Money, Language, and Thought* 19).

19. Cited in K. Jackson, ed. (414). Aglietta and Orléan expressed the idea in a more densely theoretical way, describing currencies in terms of "une expression de la société comme totalité [y un] operateur de l'appartenance sociale" (*La Monnaie souveraine* 10).

20. Kevin Jackson (xiv).

21. Buchan (19).

22. Friedberg and Friedberg (*Paper Money* 5).

23. Heritage Auction Galleries, online. Similarly, Bowers and Sundman list the "Grand Watermelon" note as their number one, the "Holy Grail" of collectors (20–21).

24. Doty (*America's Money* 223).

25. Du Gay et al. (3).

Chapter One

1. Cited in Friedberg and Friedberg (*Guide Book* 104).

2. Foucault (175–76).

3. Althusser (146).

4. The name of the bank is found on the rim of the small circle to the left of the portrait. The letter is in the center of the circle. For a list of all twelve Federal Reserve Banks, together with the twenty-four branches, see O'Donnell (23–24). The "FW" in the lower right corner indicates that the note was printed at the Western Facility in Fort Worth, Texas. By 2006, a total of 294,400,000 one-dollar notes had been printed at this facility (Friedberg and Friedberg, *Guide Book* 83).

5. Prior to 1974, the series date indicated the year in which the face design of the note was approved, with a capital letter following indicating that a minor change (for instance, a change in the signature on the face) was authorized (O'Donnell 21).

6. For a full definition of "Legal Tender," see Public Law 89–91 (the Coinage Act of July 23, 1965): "All coins and currencies of the United States (including Federal Reserve Notes and circulating notes of Federal Reserve banks and national banking associations), regardless of when coined or issued, shall be legal tender for all debts, public and private, public charges, taxes, duties, and dues." This means that U.S. paper dollars (and coins) are good not only for their exchange value in the circulation

of commodities but, first and foremost, for the paying back of two kinds of debts. The former is incurred in commercial transactions, the latter in transactions between the government and the citizens, that is, in transactions involving taxes and interest incurred on government bonds. The "legal tender" quality of money is discussed in full in Hurst (40–45).

7. Press release by the Treasurer of the U.S., December 13, 1969. By June 2006, the number of one-dollar notes in circulation was at 8.7 billion, according to the Financial Management Service of the U.S. Treasury ("U.S. Currency and Coin"). As regards the number of notes printed, about ninety-five percent of the notes printed each year are used to replace notes already in circulation. Figures for the series 1999 are 10,326,400,000, that is, over 10 billion; figures for the 2003A series are 749,120,000 (Oakes and Schwartz 89–91); in the fiscal year 2005, a total of 3,475,200,000 one-dollar notes were printed (USBEP, "Annual Production Figures").

8. USBEP ("Cool Facts about Money"). According to another estimate, paper currency is lost or destroyed at the rate of $1 per year for each $1,000 (Friedman and Schwartz 443). The emphasis here should be on *totally* lost or destroyed. As O'Donnell explains (26), if clearly one half of the original note remains, it will be still exchanged at its face value. Even fragments of notes are not necessarily a total write-off, for they too will be exchanged at their face value if the Treasurer of the U.S. is satisfied that the missing portions have been destroyed.

9. Figures collated from U.S. House of Representatives ("Jumbo Euro Notes"). For the cost of the war in Iraq, see Stiglitz and Bilmes.

10. Doty (*America's Money* 198).

11. USBEP ("Selection of Portraits and Designs," online). In actual fact, other public figures were also included. "This decision," the text continues, "was somewhat altered by the Secretary of the Treasury to include Alexander Hamilton, who was the first Secretary of the Treasury; Salmon P. Chase, who was Secretary of the Treasury during the Civil War and is credited with promoting our National Banking System; and Benjamin Franklin, who was one of the signers of the Declaration of Independence. All three of these statesmen were well known to the American public."

12. Goux ("Cash, Check, or Charge?" 115–16).

13. Ashley, a banjo player and folk singer, recorded the song in 1933, at the height of the Great Depression, when many people feared that the dollar's devaluation in relation to gold spelt a return to the days of "worthless tokens." "Greenback Dollar" was also featured on Harry Smith's *Anthology of American Folk Music*.

14. Cited in O'Malley (383).

15. Clearly in the worthy lawmaker's opinion, the notes' value came from cooperative work and sacrifice. However, O'Malley notes, "By lowering interest rates and aiding debtors, by stimulating the economy, greenbacks supposedly helped create the same egalitarian economic conditions they symbolized. Just as each citizen required political representation, each citizen required a physical representation of his value" (383).

16. Cited in Mihm (*Nation of Counterfeiters* 315).

17. USBEP ("The New Color of Money").

18. Burrell (181).

19. Generally on the "alphabet" for national subjectivity, see Berlant.

20. Hall (*Representation* 5).

21. Nussbaum (10).

22. The term "milled" (as in "Spanish Milled Dollars") means that the edge is marked with a series of tiny ridges and grooves. Corrugating the edges through a milling procedure was a measure adopted in order to curtail the "clipping" of coins by cutting or boring into their edges. It was first applied in France during the seventeenth century, and later adopted by Spain and the American colonies (Nussbaum 24–26).

23. The uncertainty as to the origin of the dollar sign was pointed out in the fourth edition of *Webster's Unabridged Dictionary* in 1859. In 1865 a monetary treatise by Wilber and Eastman was published, which pointed out the then existing controversy. For more than a century thereafter, theories and explanations abounded. Some fourteen of them, plus additional findings are listed in Newman ("Dollar $ign").

24. Newman ("Dollar $ign" 3–5).

25. Ibid. (7, 22–28). Here as elsewhere Newman draws on the seminal work done between 1912 and 1929 by Florian Cajori, a professor of mathematics.

26. Newman ("Dollar $ign" 36).

27. Tocqueville (42, 238, 514).

28. Irving (23, 27, my emphasis).

29. Emerson ("American Scholar" 1499, 1500).

30. Thoreau (2, 3).

31. Brooks (84). Reference to Eugene Debs is to Bellah et al. (260).

32. Dickens (*Martin Chuzzlewit* 277).

33. Chief among those changes must have been the abolition of slavery, which in *American Notes* is described as a "most hideous blot and foul disgrace" (24).

34. Spengler (*Hour of Decision* 163).

35. To colloquially refer to the Austrian schilling as the "Alpendollar" (or the "Alpine dollar") may strike one as quaint. If anything, the schilling should have been called the "Alpine mark," which it really was, because of numerous policies, in the past, of tying it to the deutschmark. Yet such was the actual power and reputation of the United States that the name of its currency was adopted, in colloquial parlance, for Austria's native currency. Generally on the effects of U.S. cultural hegemony on Austria, see Wagnleitner. For an account of the Bretton Woods conference and its aftermath, see Frankel.

36. References in this and the following two paragraphs are to Goodwin (8, 56, 119–20), and Lighter (1: 343). Thank-yous for valuable leads also go to Murray Forman and Roger W. Hecht.

37. Lemon (43).

38. There is a noticeable shift in hiphop iconography over the years as rap artists, for example, were in the mid–1980s pictured with wads of $20 bills but ten years later the images depicted cash stacked in $100 denominations. It reflected a growth of hiphop in the industry but also suggests other more complex issues as to how material wealth, success, and achievement are semiotically conveyed over time.

39. The word "bogus" appears to reach as far back as 1797 (Barnhart and Metcalf 17). For the word's nineteenth-century usage, there is no better example than the parody of a five-dollar bill of 1824 on which the proprietors of the Mechanics' Bank in the City of New York promise *not* to pay the bearer — a small detail that might escape the notice of a careless reader, which was of course intentional (Henkin 150–51).

40. The practices of some of these "shovers" or "passers," many of whom were female, are vividly retold in Mihm (*Nation of Counterfeiters*, chapter 5). For more detailed stories, see O'Donnell (14), Barr (747), and Bowers (*Obsolete Paper Money* 499).

41. The word "cash" meaning coin or specie is derived from the French word *casse* (modern French *caisse*).

There is also an Indian word *karsha*, meaning "copper coin" (Eagleton and Williams 141).

42. An essay published by E. H. Heywood in 1874 ties the phrase "cold hard cash" to the agenda of the Silverites.

43. Bryson (25).

44. This is the reason why some notes show pin holes when they are held to the light, which today is often puzzling to collectors, while for contemporaries it was a sign that a note was genuine: it implied that the bank itself had authenticated it, as see Bowers ("Introduction" 41), and Philpott ("Pin Holes").

45. Zelizer (18, 208–9).

46. *The Numismatist*, 101: (April 1988) 615–16, and 101:6 (June 1988) 991.

47. Eagleton and Williams (153–55). These imitation dollar bills are usually in the form of notes printed in the name of the Bank of Hell.

48. Cited in Bowers ("Introduction" 43). The currency-laundering machine, which was operated by only two "washer women" and could process up to 5,000 notes per hour, was discontinued in 1918 (Kranister 303).

Chapter Two

1. Nussbaum (15). John Kenneth Galbraith makes a similar point: "If the history of commercial banking belongs to the Italians and of central banking to the British," that of paper money issued by a government belongs indubitably to the Americans" (*Money* 45). Act of December 10, 1690, as cited in Nettels (254). It is not clear, Donald Kagin notes (549), but references are made in various colonial documents to the use of some sort of paper money prior to 1652. In 1656, a bank began issuing forms of credit under a royal permission, but was soon forced to close. In 1686, the Massachusetts Council approved of a bank that would issue bills of credit. A rolling press was purchased, but the scheme was abandoned two years later and the bills were never issued. Thus, it was really the exigencies of the frontier war that led to the western world's first emission of paper money in 1690.

2. Friedberg and Friedberg (*Paper Money* 6); Nussbaum (viii).

3. Del Mar (*History of Money in America* 80).

4. Doty (*America's Money* 47).

5. Galbraith (*Money* 59).

6. On the legality of the Continentals, see Hurst (5–6). For a detailed schedule of their depreciation, see Bowers (*Obsolete Paper Money* 20).

7. Bullock (32, 43, and 69).

8. Nussbaum (61). Breck and Phillips, Jr., are discussed in McLaughlin ("Just Fooling" 45).

9. In 1837, the U.S. Supreme Court had affirmed the constitutionality of the Bank of Kentucky and, by extension, of all state-chartered banks. Henceforth under a typical state law, any group of citizens could apply for a bank charter. This charter would be given if securities, or evidence of such securities, could be furnished to state officials. A great variety of securities were deemed acceptable, though they usually included government bonds and state bonds. See Bowers (*Obsolete Paper Money* 241, 245–46); Hurst (137–45); and Hammond (*Banks and Politics* 563–71).

10. James Madison, *Records of the Federal Convention of 1787* (2: 309), as cited in Hurst (15). Secretary of the Treasury Alexander Hamilton was of a different opinion, admonishing that in its own actions Congress should observe the spirit of the Constitution's ban on bills of credit.

These forms of money, he thought, "are of a nature so liable to abuse and [...] so certain of being abused that the wisdom of the government will be shown in never trusting itself with the use of so seducing and dangerous an expedient." Hamilton, *Works* (3: 388), as cited in Hurst (135).

11. Doty (*America's Money* 141).

12. David Wells, the Special Commissioner of Revenue, in 1869 estimated the costs incurred directly by the Union government as $4,171 million, with directly incurred costs for the Confederacy of $2,700 million. A remaining sum of $2,323 million, not divided between North and South, included such items as pensions, state and local government debts, and losses to shipping and industry, making a total war cost of $9,194 million, as cited in Glyn Davies (487). Generally on banks and politics in the Civil War, see Hammond (*Sovereignty and an Empty Purse*).

13. Galbraith (*Money* 95). I have also drawn in this paragraph on Mihm (*Nation of Counterfeiters* 319–21, and 328–30). For an in-depth study of the South's monetary and fiscal programs, see Lerner.

14. The very first note to have a green back was the $500 interest-bearing Treasury note authorized by the Act of December 23, 1857. These notes were not intended as general currency, even though they did at times pass from hand to hand (Hessler, "First Dollar Note" 1106).

15. Nussbaum (101). "Lawful money" has been a technical term since the colonial era, when authorities placed foreign coins at a particular exchange rate to English specie. The specie so rated was declared "lawful money," a term that stuck even though its premises have long disappeared (ibid. 11–12).

16. Massey (156). The boldness is particularly striking when considering the issue of the constitutionality of these notes. When Supreme Court Justice Roger B. Taney died in 1864, there were two principal concerns among Unionists. The first was finding a replacement who would support the Emancipation Proclamation; the second was sustaining the ability of the government to issue paper money. As Congressman George Boutwell wrote in his diary, "we want a man who will sustain the Legal Tender Act and the Proclamation of Emancipation." That man was Salmon P. Chase, an outspoken abolitionist and a man who had concluded, in 1862, "that the legal tender clause is a necessity" and that he supported it "earnestly," as cited in Ganz ("Reconsidering" 442). It turned out Chase did not.

17. State bills (notes from private commercial banks) also traded at a discount in terms of gold and silver, though when given a choice, most people preferred to own greenbacks or, after 1863, other federal paper money such as National Bank notes. For some well-authenticated tables illustrating the fluctuating value of the greenbacks through 1865, see Krooss (2: 280–81).

18. For a more detailed story, see Brands (138–58).

19. On the issue of strengthening the link between the state and domestic society by maximizing public revenues, see Helleiner ("Territorial Currencies" 324–26).

20. Massey (212).

21. Nussbaum (159–60).

22. Cited in Friedman and Schwartz (*Monetary History* 189). The issue of activist monetary policy as a means to strengthen the link between the state and society is discussed in greater detail in Helleiner ("Territorial Currencies" 326–28). For a position that strongly opposes or at least doubts the effectiveness of monetary policy, see Galbraith (*Money* 305–8).

23. Friedman and Schwartz (*Monetary History* 213).

The Federal Reserve's lack of power had stemmed at least in part from the fact that a large proportion of the nation's banks was simply beyond its control: by the early 1930s, fewer than 1,000 state banks were national banks, out of a total of some 16,000.

24. Doty (*America's Money* 202).

25. Nussbaum (210). Numismatic aspects relating to World War II are treated at length in Schwan and Boling.

26. O'Donnell (21).

27. Cited in Goodwin (54). For a reading of Hawthorne's anxieties about ownership in *The House of the Seven Gables* of 1851, see Michaels (85–112). In addition to the sources cited, I have also drawn in this section on Wright and Cowen; Brands; and Redlich.

28. Cited in Krooss (1:11).

29. Ibid. (1: 56). What Franklin did not say was that the development of paper money alongside credit took place in an inherently unstable signifying structure. The principal reason was that the main investment outlet was not land so much as land *speculation*. This, John Kleeberg found, "meant high indebtedness, meager cash flow, and frequent financial catastrophes" (ix). Harvests in particular were a problem, as they "always put unusual strains on the financial system, often leading to collapse: this is why stock market crashes occur in October" (ibid.).

30. Generally on the currency in the American colonies, see Nettels, and Brock. On the crisis of authority in colonial America, see Fliegelman.

31. Brigham gives historical information, printing costs and the like, and has many illustrations of Revere's works. Generally, see Esther Forbes's Pulitzer-prize winning biography.

32. Nussbaum (vii).

33. Cited in Brands (39). Hamilton's distrust of paper money is obvious: a public debt also would remove the temptation to turn on the government printing presses for paper. As regards Hamilton's estimate of the Revolutionary War, it amounted to over $135 million, in specie (Krooss 1: 93). For these and other original documents relating to Hamilton, see Syrett et al.

34. Cited in Goodwin (103); and see Wood ("Hamilton" 132). The term "fiscal-military state" refers to the state's ability to mobilize wealth and to wage war, primarily by means of centralized tax collection and the funding of the national debt, together with a central bank and a market in public securities such as government bonds.

35. Doty (*America's Money* 71, my emphasis).

36. Ball (24)

37. Goodwin (167). For Biddle's life, see Govan.

38. Goodwin (171).

39. Jackson (203–4). Jackson had used quite similar words in his Bank Veto Message of July 10, 1832, which is reprinted in Krooss (2: 21–37). For exciting narratives of the Bank War, see Remini, and Brands (72–95). The hostility to "rag money" that Jackson instilled in Western farmers held firm until the 1870s, despite the brunt of the credit squeeze they felt then. On this and other instances of social groups holding positions counter to what their economic interests would suggest, see Unger.

40. All cited in Goodwin (189, 199).

41. These institutions were officially called "deposite [sic] banks," but were popularly referred to as "pet banks" for their loyalty to the Jackson administration. The amount to be deposited in the bank of each state was based on the number of Electoral College votes of that particular state (Bowers, *Obsolete Paper Money* 154). Reference to Tocqueville is to *Democracy in America* (268).

42. All cited in Goodwin (203, 202). Generally on Jacksonian democracy, see Schlesinger Jr. (*The Age of Jackson*).

43. For texts of the National Bank Acts, see Krooss (2: 297–327). On the process itself, see Niven (*The Samuel P. Chase Papers*). For an analysis of the shift in monetary policy, see Mihm (*Nation of Counterfeiters* 309–19).

44. Standish (130).

45. Friedman and Schwartz (*Monetary History* 149).

46. Ibid. (150–51).

47. Ibid. (412).

48. Cited ibid. (413n172, my emphasis).

49. Cited ibid. (414).

50. Ibid. (416, 417).

51. Cited ibid. (385).

52. Ibid. (418, 420, my emphasis).

53. Schlesinger Jr. (*The Age of Roosevelt* 253).

54. Cited in Schlesinger, Jr. ("History" 14). For Roosevelt's inaugural address, see Lott (279).

55. For a different reading both of the Depression era and the Roosevelt administration, see Galbraith (*Money* 168–82, and chapters fourteen to fifteen). For a critical but fair summary of Friedman's economic thought, see Krugman ("Friedman"). For a full-length exposition of Friedman's life and ideas, see Ebenstein.

56. Cited in Terkel (251). The contemporary was Raymond Moley, one of Roosevelt's original Brain Trust.

57. Friedman and Schwartz (*Monetary History* 463). Today, gold bullion and coin may again be collected and saved by anyone, as all restrictions from the 1933 Act were lifted as of December 31, 1974.

58. Ibid. (492). Legal historian James Hurst likewise views the allocation of control over money a crucial issue in American history (133–51, 176–81, 199–211).

59. Doty (*America's Money* 27–28); and see Jones (132–33). On the circulation of Portuguese, Spanish, French, and other foreign coins, see Solomon. Reference to John Winthrop's journal is to an entry dated September 22, 1642 (75).

60. Cited in Garson (32, my emphasis).

61. The unit of account, Wright and Cowen explain, is a "measure of value; it answers the question 'what is the value of that?' just as inches answer 'what is the length of that?' or grams answer 'what is the weight of that?'" (32). By contrast, the medium of exchange is whatever people agree to exchange, be it silver, paper, deerskin, cowrie shells, or golden eggs, it does not really matter much. What does matter is to have a reliable, stable method for defining or measuring value. Such a method allows people to compare, and hence exchange, unlike things. "How many chickens is a cow worth? A horse? A farm? A bond? Without a common measure, without a unit of account, answering such questions is nearly impossible [and] all trade is barter" (ibid.). In short, then, the act of 1792 declaring that one had to give $19.39 in exchange for a troy ounce of gold and a correspondingly lesser amount for silver, established a measuring rod for the means of payment (or medium of exchange) Congress had created in 1785. Thereafter, money would be measured in the same units, the U.S. dollar, that would be used to trade or exchange. For a more technical discussion of the crucial distinction between the unit of account and the medium of exchange, see Michener and Wright.

62. Nussbaum (53).

63. See Wright and Cohen (16). The phrase "wicked states" belongs to Calvin Johnson.

64. United States Constitution (Art. I, Sec. 8, §5). Clearly the phrase "to coin" shows the hand of hard-money man Alexander Hamilton, who already during

the War of Independence had articulated his firm conviction that finance was critical and that therefore Congress must have control of "coining money, establishing banks [...] appropriating funds and doing whatever else relates to the operation of finance." Hamilton, as cited in Brands (25).

65. For the congressional plan, see Krooss (1: 140–44); for the act of charter, see ibid. (181–88).

66. Cited in Krooss (1: 189). The decision in Congress was a narrow one, though: the bill providing for a renewal of the charter was defeated by a single vote in the House of Representatives; in the Senate it was lost by a tie (Scroggs 14–15).

67. While it was true that foreigners owned a majority, at one time about 72 percent, of the Bank's shares, the related claim that foreign stockholders might take control of the bank and consequently of the entire United States was, as Wright and Cowen note, "preposterous, as only citizens could vote for, or serve as, directors of the Bank" (109). Given the outcome of the debate, playing on xenophobia was a most opportune strategy for opponents to the Bank.

68. Cited in Krooss (1: 215).

69. However, these Republicans—Madison, Calhoun, Gallatin, Stephen Girard, and Dallas—only loved banks "as long as they were under their control." Wright and Cowen (160).

70. Walter B. Smith (37–43).

71. Thomas Hart Benton, *Thirty Years' View* (New York: D. Appleton, 1864) 443, as cited in Mihm ("The Almighty Dollar at Home and Abroad" 11).

72. Jackson's "Specie Circular" of 1836 is reprinted in Krooss (2: 117–18). On the role of the land speculator in western development, see Paul Wallace Gates.

73. Cited in Mihm ("The Almighty Dollar at Home and Abroad" 9).

74. Nussbaum (49–52, 64–65, 71–74), and Bowers (*Obsolete Paper Money* 141). For a thorough discussion of the First and Second Banks, see Redlich (chapter six). For more detailed analyses of the nation's two early central banks, see respectively Holdsworth and Dewey; Cowen; and W. B. Smith.

75. Now that governments across the world are trying frantically to restore confidence following the collapse of investment banks and other private enterprises, Irving's moral fable of financial hubris once again can serve as a pretext to the drama unfolding before our eyes.

76. "The word *panic* as it pertained to money entered the language [during the crisis of 1819]," John Kenneth Galbraith claims. "Later, in eager search for milder, less alarming terms reference to *crisis, depression,* and now, of course, *growth adjustment,* came successively to denote the economic aftermath." Galbraith (*A Short History of Financial Euphoria* 45–46)

77. The amount of specie in circulation was $48 million in 1813 and $28 million in 1836; also in 1836 there were some $45 million in specie in banks (Treasury Reports cited in Krooss 1: 266; 2: 130). Friedman and Schwartz provide slightly different figures (*Monetary Statistics* 214–59). The classic sources for the number of commercial banks are Fenstermaker, and Hammond (*Banks and Politics*). For more information about banking in the antebellum era, see Bodenhorn.

78. For a table correlating banking, the growth of the money supply and the growth of the population for the period 1830–1860, see Glyn Davies (484).

79. For a detailed description in terms of the note's history, function, identity, and cultural work, see Tschachler ("Louisiana DIX Notes and the Dixieland Myth").

80. Doty (*Pictures* 10, 7). There were other colloquialisms for worthless bills and dubious banks, such as "wildcats," "red dog," "blue pup," "owl creek," "coon box," "stump-tail," and "Cairo swindling shop"—nearly all of which were used by Senator Thomas Hart Benton, a hard money man and staunch ally of Andrew Jackson, in a speech to the United States Senate on January 13, 1842, as cited in Bowers (*Obsolete Paper Money* 14). On the many origins of the term "wildcat," see Mihm (*Nation of Counterfeiters* 186).

81. Nussbaum (89–90), and Bowers (*Obsolete Paper Money* 215–16). State banking laws for Georgia, New York, and Louisiana are reprinted in Krooss (2: 202–27).

82. The research is cited in Weatherford (272). For other more detached accounts of free banking, see Redlich, chapter seven, and Rockoff (66–68). For the observation about private banks as the "cause of social evil," see Nussbaum (67). Cooke's complaint is cited in Brands (123). For a truly exaggerated summary of the early period in the era of free banking, see Hepburn (89–90). For a thorough discussion of the conflict over the control of money and banking, see Hurst (154–59, 167–86, 207–11).

83. W. L. Ormsby, as cited in Bowers (*Obsolete Paper Money* 285). Thus, a view of the Niagara Falls would form a part of the design to designate an institution in that part of the country; similarly, the Bunker Hill Monument might be used for banks in Boston.

84. In 1859, there were listed some 9,916 different genuine notes *and* some 5,400 different kinds of counterfeit notes in circulation. For a detailed treatment of counterfeiting in antebellum America, see Bowers (*Obsolete Paper Money,* chapter nine, 157–76), and Mihm (*Nation of Counterfeiters* 209–304). The expression "bearing a common impression" belongs to Samuel P. Chase, as cited in Mihm (ibid. 312).

85. Doty (*America's Money* 164). For Cooke' campaign efforts in behalf of Chase's national banking bill, see Brands (125–28).

86. Cited in Bowers (*Obsolete Paper Money* 440).

87. "By making the greenback a 'legal tender' for public and private debts, the Union in effect made the acceptance of paper currency mandatory in all contracts and transactions in which money changed hands if those obligations were to be enforceable in court" (Bensel 162).

88. Doty (*America's Money* 166).

89. An important legal basis for this transformation was the 14th Amendment to the Constitution of 1868. This amendment regulated the relations between the federal government and individual states. Specifically, it declared any debts or obligations in aid of insurrection or rebellion against the United States to be illegal and void. The amendment thus spelt the end of monetary sovereignty for the former CSA—a clear index to the fact that money is not merely a medium of exchange or a means for the paying back of debts but also an instrument of dominance and control.

90. Walter Bagehot, founding editor of London's *Economist* magazine first used the term "monetary language" in 1869 (Helleiner, "National Currencies" 1415).

91. All cited in Steel (58).

92. Cited ibid. (59).

93. The Report from the Pujo Commission is reprinted in Krooss (3: 181–233).

94. Nussbaum (161). For a number of draft bills, first prints, reports, and senate provisions leading up to the Federal Reserve Act, see Krooss (3: 234–413); for the final Act, which was passed on December 23, 1913, see ibid. (4: 1–35).

95. Federal Reserve Board, *The F.R.S.: Its Purposes and Functions*, 1963 edition, cited in Krooss (4: 412).

96. For a summary account of the history of the Federal Reserve, see Galbraith (*Money*, chapter 10); Meltzer's history of the Federal Reserve is monumental. The term "regional federalism" is Hursts's (207–11).

97. National Bank notes also ceased to be issued in 1935. They are still redeemable by the Treasury Department at their face amount, but may have added value in the numismatic market, where according to Doty they stand "as one of the few remaining monuments of monetary localism in the increasingly national, conformist atmosphere of the late nineteenth and early twentieth centuries" (*America's Money* 165). References to Roosevelt's 1933 inaugural address are to Lott (278, 279).

98. The Great Seal's obverse (face), which shows the American eagle holding the United States coat of arms, had already appeared, *inter alia*, on the back of the $50 National Bank note of the Second Charter period, and on the backs of two Gold Certificates. One was the $20 of the Series of 1905 and later (the "Technicolor" note). The other was the $1,000 of the Series of 1907 and later. The two Gold Certificates were produced and put into circulation through 1922.

99. References in this paragraph are to Burrell (186).

100. Ibid. (184, 186).

101. Ibid. (188, 189); and Hessler ("Precursors" 10).

102. Bowers and Sundman (50).

103. Zelizer (107–8).

104. There was considerable confusion, as the series 1935 notes without the motto were also being printed at the same time. This fact caused much dismay among the Christian Right, who petitioned Congress to discontinue these "godless" notes. So, as of September 15, 1961, a series 1935G was printed with the motto. Models were made also for other denominations, though they were never printed, since the Bureau of Engraving and Printing finally discarded its old flatbed presses. The new sheet fed rotary presses from 1963 were used to print $1 Federal Reserve notes bearing the motto on their backs, printed in prominent letters above the word ONE. All other denominations likewise bear the motto beginning with the Series of 1963 (Burrell 191).

105. Carruthers and Babb (1557).

106. Cited in Helleiner ("National Currencies" 1421).

107. See Tocqueville (68).

108. See USBEP ("Money Facts"). There were also more practical considerations, which concerned the identification of each picture with a bill of a certain denomination. If the public learned to know its money by the pictures on it, this would make it much harder for the crooks who, the reasoning was, would find that they "cannot change a '1' to a '100' and hope to pass the bill. The tell-tale portrait will stand in the way." "Our Paper Money to Be Smaller," *New York Times* (June 5, 1927).

109. See Lundstrom.

110. United States General Accounting Office ("Financial Impact of Issuing the New $1 Coin"), and "New Dollar Coin" (36).

111. Vending machine companies, video arcade owners, and the soft drink industry funded the Coin Coalition. They all had an interest in eliminating maintenance costs associated with dollar bill validators. The National Bulk Vendors Association also supported the Coalition, and copper miners and other interest groups likewise backed the Coin Coalition on this issue. (Wikipedia, "Coin Coalition"; and Lundstrom)

112. Wikipedia ("Save the Greenback").

113. In 2007, the U.S. House of Representatives voted to give a new look to the Sacagawea dollar in hopes of renewing interest in and eliminating the surplus of this coin (H.R. 2358). Thus, as of 2009 the Sacagawea reverses will honor Native American tribes through a variety of design themes honoring Native American achievements.

114. Cited in Goodwin (394); and see Gibbs (1–2).

115. Standish (142).

116. USBEP ("The New Color of Money").

117. Although the appearance of the new notes is the same as the ones of the Series 1996, there are differences. For one thing, the notes are the first small-size notes to be printed with background color (they have peach, green, and blue tints). The color-shifting ink now shows a greater color change than did that used on the Series 1996 notes, changing from green to a bright copper color instead of to black. For the $50, the polymer security strip embedded in the paper has been widened slightly, to make the flag design and "USA 50" on it larger and easier to see when the note is held to the light (USBEP, "The New Color of Money"). It yet remains to be seen whether Hamilton will be replaced by Ronald Reagan, which is at least the intention of a faction in Congress, the same one that proposed replacing Franklin Delano Roosevelt's portrait on the dime with one of Reagan.

118. There is more reason for hope for the blind and visually impaired people that the government follows a 2006 court order to change the bills so that it would be easier to determine the denominations. Although at first the government balked at the expected costs for improving bills for the visually impaired, on May 20, 2008, a federal appeals court in Washington upheld the 2006 ruling. It now remains to be seen whether the government will appeal to the full court or seek quick review by the Supreme Court (Andrews; and *The Numismatist*, July 2008, 39).

119. USBEP ("The Western Currency Facility"). The WCF is the only location other than the Bureau's Washington, DC, facility that prints the nation's currency. It prints 55 percent of all U.S. paper currency.

120. USBEP ("New Money Information").

121. USBEP ("The Redesigned $10 Note").

122. Lemon (50).

123. USBEP ("The New Color of Money").

124. Newman (*Early Paper Money* 9–10); O'Donnell (17).

125. Hessler (*The Engraver's Line* 132–33).

126. Doty (*America's Money* 95). For an account of Perkins's innovations, see a. Mihm (*Nation of Counterfeiters* 263–69).

127. *Bankers' Magazine and Statistical Register* 10 (1861) 723, as cited in Mihm (*Nation of Counterfeiters* 303).

128. Friedberg and Friedberg (*Paper Money* 75).

129. Doty (*America's Money* 97). For an illustration of a geometric lathe as it was used in the 1880s, see Bowers and Sundman (67).

130. Bowers ("Introduction" 35, 52), and Doty (*America's Money* 98). For colorful illustrations of such bills as printed by the ABNCo, as well as an article about the tint from a contemporary magazine, see Bowers (*Obsolete Paper Money* 321, 329, and 330).

131. Cited in Goodwin (68).

132. Bowers ("Introduction" 12). To worry about the value of signatures was appropriate in an era when handwriting was an index of character. Thus, see Thornton (73–107).

133. Bowers ("Introduction" 12).

Chapter Three

1. Cited in Bowers (*Obsolete Paper Money* 425).
2. Gene Hessler recounts that some designers operated a drawing school or taught painting. Others made maps or sold books and prints; one advertised that he would ornament guns and pistols; another one that his engraving included "Shop Bills; Bills of Exchange; Bills of Lading; Maps; Portraits and other things too tedious to mention" — like mending a saucepan and removing and replacing a crest (*Engraver's Line* 3). As regards Franklin, he proudly tells us in his autobiography that the printing of notes was "a very profitable jobb [sic!] and a great help to me" (827). Generally on the early history of design in the United States, see Dunlap.
3. In the nineteenth century, the best artists would earn from $2,000 to $4,000 per year, as see Gilbert (66), Hessler (*Engraver's Line* 3, 108, 180, 290–92), Newman (*Early Paper Money* 20–21), and Bowers (*Obsolete Paper Money* 424).
4. Cited in Hessler (*Engraver's Line* 2).
5. Ibid. (2, 248, 251).
6. Newman (*Early Paper Money* 20).
7. Hessler (*Engraver's Line* 71–75).
8. See Chapter 4 for an illustration.
9. Ibid. (280–85).
10. For an illustration of the note, see Gender, Race, and the Paper Dollar, in this chapter.
11. The earlier Demand notes had been contracted out entirely, to companies such as ABNCo, which were also printing bills for the Confederacy at about the same time (Doty, *America's Money* 161).
12. USBEP ("Bureau History").
13. Bowers (*Obsolete Paper Money* 406).
14. Hessler ("First Dollar Note" 1106).
15. Hessler ("Unofficial Commemorative Notes" 657).
16. Proof notes are samples that are not intended for circulation; they are produced only for internal examination by the management and staff. These people would compare the proposed note to other notes issued by their own institution (and, on occasion, by competitors) and decide which design elements would produce the desired effect, whatever that may be. These internal deliberations are rarely documented, let alone publicly reported. Thus, rationale for selection most often dies with the passing of internal staff and management.
17. O'Donnell (18).
18. Ibid. (20).
19. Friedberg and Friedberg (*Paper Money* 148).
20. The law specifies that, "No portrait shall be placed upon any of the bonds, securities, notes, fractional or postal currency of the United States while the original of such portrait is living" (31 U.S.C. 413, as cited in O'Donnell 20).
21. Bolin (77–80).
22. Cited in USBEP ("The New Color of Money").
23. "'People's capitalism' is a myth," Edward Wolff writes. "The inequality generated by the wealth and income gaps is exacerbated by the fact that during the boom of the last eight years, corporate profitability has been rising" (1). It is thus no surprise that this inequality is often compensated for by a variety of strategies towards getting rich quick, such as large-prize television game shows, big-jackpot state lotteries and compensation lawsuits (Warshauer, online). The vogue of such shows seems to have started with *The $64,000 Question* in the mid–1950s, following a Supreme Court ruling of 1954 that exempted jackpot quizzes from charges of gambling.

By 1957, the year the national motto was put on the currency, five of the top ten TV programs were quiz shows, each with dramatically upped stakes (Halliwell 156–57). Generally on antitheses of the Protestant work ethic, see Lears.
24. Franklin's dream has even been surpassed by the creation, also under the Coin Act of 2005, of the First Spouse $10 Gold Coins as the pure gold collectible counterparts of the circulating Presidential $1 coins (United States Mint, "The First Spouse Gold Coin Program"). For Franklin's dream, see chapter 4, note 16.
25. Nora (7). Also useful is Raphael Samuel's term "theatre of memory," which specifically describes public or civic representations of memory.
26. Gilbert (69). For images of the "You Can Trust Me" class of notes, see Doty (*Pictures* 148–58).
27. Cited in Henkin (159). Ormsby's philosophy involved a limited number of panoramic or scenic illustrations from American history that were designed in such a way that each note would be "one thing, one design, one picture, with the necessary lettering interwoven, one — inseparable — and unalterable" (Mihm, *Nation of Counterfeiters* 296).
28. Henkin (160).
29. Cited in Bowers (*Obsolete Paper Money* 253).
30. Brands 98; and see Miller. Reference to the "machine in the garden" is to Leo Marx.
31. Doty (*Pictures* 160).
32. Thus, chimneys spewing smoke (as on notes from Massachusetts or Ohio) likewise symbolized the better life promised by Progress. A particularly striking example in the coinage is Christian Gobrecht's medal for an industrial exhibition in 1826 (Vermeule 39). The medal, which was commissioned by the New England Society for Promotion of Manufactures and Mechanic Arts, shows a bust of Archimedes on the obverse, and three vignettes on the reverse. The inscription states, "Genius, Intelligence, and Industry Triumph." In addition, Gobrecht enshrined the names of a range of scientists from antiquity to modern America, Archimedes, Galileo, Newton, Franklin, Watt, and Fulton.
33. Although the exact number of images appearing on notes between 1790 and 1865 is not known, it must amount to tens of thousands. Thus, American paper money from that era offers "a pictorial richness never approached, let alone exceeded, before or after" (Doty, *Pictures* 10).
34. Ibid. (98, 113–15).
35. Goodwin (158). For a reproduction of the 1815 image, see Doty (*Pictures* 99).
36. Cited in Goodwin (152).
37. Ibid. (151).
38. Standish (126).
39. Cited in Bowers (*Obsolete Paper Money* 425).
40. Cited in Hessler (*Engraver's Line* 93).
41. Cited in Goodwin (150).
42. Doty (*America's Money* 223).
43. Gilbert (68).
44. Benjamin ("One Way Street" 87).
45. The development from aureole to aura to gilt frame to portrait frame on paper bills thus corresponds to the larger historical movement in which religion first gives way to art, which then is displaced by economics. Mark Taylor has described this movement in terms of a dialectic without synthesis (*Confidence Games* 25–26).
46. Benjamin ("The Work of Art" 222).
47. Ibid.
48. Shell (*Art and Money* 155).
49. Nicholson (15).

50. Veblen (37).
51. Nygren (140–41).
52. Doty (*America's Money* 169).
53. Cited in Robert A. Ferguson (156, 158).
54. Hewitt ("Soft Images" 156).
55. McGinley (26). Susan B. Anthony has also received recognition through a local monument. A statue of this notable woman exists in the Capitol building in Washington, DC, though as John R. Gillis notes, it is only "in an obscure corner of the lower floor" (23, n.35).
56. Doty ("Surviving Images" 122).
57. Cited in Robert A. Ferguson (160).
58. Swanson (138, ill. 4); and Doty (*Pictures* 74). Maria Crittenden likewise was the wife of a governor, John J. Crittenden, of Kentucky, who later served as attorney general under President Millard Fillmore. Her portrait appeared on $5 notes issued in the 1850s by the Farmers Bank of Kentucky, Frankfort, as well as by the Rockingham Bank, Portsmouth, New Hampshire, as see Bowers (*Obsolete Paper Money* 458).
59. Doty (*Pictures* 77–78).
60. Fred Reed recently has trotted out the names of altogether seventeen, possibly even eighteen, actual women who appeared on U.S. paper money ("Paper Dolls" 50).
61. Doty (*Pictures* 67).
62. Ibid. (75, 82).
63. Ibid. (82, 85).
64. Friedberg and Friedberg (*Guide Book* 106).
65. Doty (*Pictures* 37).
66. Standish (107). Critics in the nineteenth century were much less diplomatic. "Nothing can be more rude than the Massachusetts notes issued in 1690, the first American paper money," a writer for *Harper's New Monthly Magazine* pronounced in 1862, as cited in Bowers (*Obsolete Paper Money* 241).
67. Parry (14). For the "Standing Indian," see Bowers and Sundman (24); for the "Indian on the colony Seal," see Newman (*Early Paper Money* 180). The "Wildman" was the Bigfoot or Sasquatch figure of medieval Europe. As Bernheimer explains, "wild men" were a link between "civilized" humans and the spirits of natural woodlands. In Anglo-Saxon, the figure was called *wudéwása*, meaning "man-of-the-wood" as well as "savage." Geoffrey of Monmouth, in his twelfth-century *Life of Merlin*, describes how a mourning Merlin, after a battle, became a "Man of the Woods [...] discovered by none, forgetful of himself and of his own, lurking like a wild thing [...] living an animal life" (Geoffrey of Monmouth, web document). "Wildman" figures were popular among engravers from early on, including Albrecht Dürer, and they survived to appear as heraldic figures well into the sixteenth century and beyond. (The Grand Arms of Prussia of 1873 bears two "Wildman" figures supporting the coat-of-arms.) Thereafter, the memory of "genuine" wildmen appears to have become indistinct, and the figures began to play a role in accounts of newly discovered "savages" in the New World, as see Colin. Hence the connection to the Massachusetts issues. For a history of the Bigfoot legend's social and cultural context, see Buhs.
68. Doty ("Surviving Images" 119).
69. Wood ("Apology" 51).
70. Doty ("Surviving Images" 126).
71. Bowers (*Obsolete Paper Money* 275).
72. Doty (*Pictures* 50).
73. Cited in Kotte (564).
74. Bakeless (71).
75. To draw out the cultural differences between Europe and the United States served as the declared rhetorical strategy in George H. Colton's *Tecumseh. A Poem* (New York: Putnam, 1842), though his contemporaries were not convinced. Ralph Waldo Emerson, who reviewed the poem in *The Dial* of July 1842, felt that the "wild beauty" of the "noble aboriginal names" would have been better served by "a foreign metre." Edgar Allan Poe also reviewed it, for *Godey's Lady's Book*, in 1846, describing it as "insufferably tedious." Nevertheless, the poem in actuality was written to celebrate the achievements of William Henry Harrison, as see Keiser (34–37).
76. Doty (*Pictures* 37, 53–54).
77. Hessler ("American Indian" 77).
78. Doty ("Surviving Images" 113, 112); Clain-Stefanelli (42).
79. Doty ("Surviving Images" 128, 121–23).
80. Clain-Stefanelli (25).
81. Doty (*Pictures* 45–46).
82. Ibid. (53–54, 48).
83. McGinley (261).
84. Fleming ("The American Images" 65–81). Regarding paper money, the trend of using women to symbolize national sovereignty was started by the Bank of England, which on its foundation in 1694 decorated its first notes with a figure of Britannia. This female figure, which from the Roman period had stood for the islands off the northwestern coast of Europe, *Britanniae*, had appeared on Roman coins already during the reign of Hadrian, 76–138 CE. Needless to say, Britannia became a standard feature on Britain's coinage (Hewitt, *Beauty and the Banknote* 5; and Brothers).
85. One is the $10 United States (Legal Tender) note, Series 1869, which shows Pocahontas being presented to the English royal court; another one is the $20 National Bank note for the back of which Charles Burt's engraving of Chapman's mural *Baptism of Pocahontas* was chosen as illustration.
86. Clain-Stefanelli (42–43).
87. Several publications have incorrectly identified the portrait as "Onepapa," as see Jackson. The Bureau of American Ethnology, Smithsonian Institution, attributes this to a typographical error, on the original photograph, for "Oncpapa," the tribe of Sioux to which Running Antelope belonged.
88. Fleming and Luskey (181).
89. Deloria (65).
90. Parry (xiii).
91. Cited in Waldstreicher (302). On the natural history of skin color, see Wheeler.
92. Waldstreicher (303, 304).
93. Cited ibid. (307).
94. Doty ("Surviving Images" 130).
95. Doty (*Pictures* 56–60).
96. Ibid. (60). Tellingly, all pronouns in the Constitution of 1789 referring to gender were in the masculine — with one exception: if a person was in service, "he or she shall not be discharged" if he or she escapes into another state, but shall be returned to the "owner."
97. Several Confederate States notes issued in 1861 bore a vignette of the "Sweet Potato Dinner," from an 1836 painting by John Blake White. The painting, which was very popular in the South and was the subject of a Currier & Ives print, depicts a famous incident from the Revolutionary War. British General Banastre Tarleton had relentlessly pursued Brigadier General Francis Marion, the "Swamp Fox" of South Carolina. Under a flag of truce, Marion invited Tarleton to dinner, the meal consisting simply of sweet potatoes, a staple of the local economy and reflective of the hard times Marion had gone through. It is said that years later Tarleton commented

that men who could live without the comforts of life could never be subdued. The image on the note shows the two generals standing before the dinner table, while a slave is kneeling behind. (Bowers, *Obsolete Paper Money* 447)

98. A $5 note printed by ABNCo during the early days of secession (before the Confederacy was cut off from experienced printers from the North) portrays a black slave picking cotton, opposite whom, under the supervision of a white manager, other slaves mill raw cotton. Above these vignettes, allegories of Industry and Agriculture sit together on a cotton bale, as if blessing the scenes of forced labor shown below. "The clever juxtaposition of classical icons and idyllic scenes of modern involuntary servitude," Harold Holzer suggests, "serves notice that the government bases its economy on slaves, and that history and heritage validate the system" (online).

99. Doty (*Pictures* 62–65). Northern banks increasingly were using imagery of their own, putting on their notes scenes that were suggestive of the North's industrial superiority. The message was clear: "how could the South expect to make good on its bid for independence?" (ibid. 108)

100. Doty (*America's Money* 115).

101. Doty ("Surviving Images" 125). A few years ago, John W. Jones began to reproduce images of slavery on Confederate and Southern States notes in acrylic on canvas paintings. To view the artworks, as well as to read essays by, *inter alia*, Richard Doty, go to *www.colorsofmoney.com*.

102. The four African American men whose signatures appeared on the currency were Blanche K. Bruce, Judson W. Lyons, William T. Vernon and James C. Napier. These men served as Registrars of the Treasury. Until the series 1923 currency, the two signatures on almost all currency (except on fractional currency and Demand notes) were of the Treasurer and the Registrar. During this period, four of the seventeen registrars were African American. The fifth African American whose signature appeared on the currency was Azie Taylor Morton, 36th Treasurer the United States, September 12, 1977, to January 20, 1981. (USBEP, "Money Facts: African Americans")

103. Vermeule (53).

104. Cited in Kuhl (154). It is more accurate to describe the portraits on the 1859 penny and on the 1907 Eagle as the female heads of Liberty wearing an Indian headdress. Although the two heads are not identical and although they are separated from one another by about a half-century, they enhance rather than diminish the coins' nationalistic character, as the depictions include iconographic attributes taken from Liberty and America. For illustrations of the two coins, see Yeoman (110 and 255, respectively). For detailed descriptions and aesthetic analyses, see Vermeule (53–55, 114–15, and 121–24). On the partnership that Saint-Gaudens forged with Roosevelt to reinvigorate America's numismatic art, see Moran.

105. In 2001, Fraser's design reappeared on a one-dollar commemorative coin struck to benefit the Smithsonian Museum of the American Indian. The popularity of this coin played a role in the next triumph of American retro design, the hugely successful Buffalo $50 gold bullion coin of 2006 (Vermeule 230, 232–33).

106. As of 2009, the Sacagawea reverses will honor Native American tribes through design themes such as the creation of the Cherokee written language, the Iroquois Confederacy, the Olympian Jim Thorpe, even the Pueblo Revolt. The basis for the new reverses is the Native American $1 Coin Act of September 20, 2007. Interestingly, the first coin in the series will have a more down-to-earth theme, as the Citizens Coinage Advisory Committee in June 2008 put a design featuring a Native American woman planting maize in first place. (*www.usmint.gov/mint-programs*)

107. Doty (*America's Money* 224).

108. Du Gay et al. (62).

Chapter Four

1. Helleiner ("National Currencies" 1418).

2. Hobsbawm ("Mass-Producing Traditions" 281).

3. Zelinsky (154, 153, 246, my emphasis). As stated in the introductory chapter, Michael Billig subsumes the images on coins and currency under "banal nationalism." These images are ubiquitous, and people use the objects on which they appear without thinking every day. Thus, Billig distinguishes between "banal nationalism" and "hot nationalism," which involves practices like active flag waving and political mobilization. On the persistence of the latter, both in the United States and in Australia, see Lynette Spillman.

4. Ibid. (152). Also useful is Garson's summary: "The pictorial images and the promises of negotiability conveyed on coins, banknotes and other financial instruments were repetitively encountered on a daily basis. They were visual reminders of the connection between finance, stability, and national authority" (22).

5. Newman (*Early Paper Money* 167, 14); and see his "Earliest Money" (2181–87).

6. Goodwin (33).

7. Doty (*America's Money* 51).

8. Newman (*Early Paper Money* 170); Kraljevich Jr. ("Freedom of Expression" 74–75).

9. Cited in Goodwin (61).

10. Cited in Irvin (web document).

11. Ibid. For a complete list of mottoes and emblematic legends, see Newman (*Early Paper Money* 484–87).

12. Ibid. (15). The currency of the states was faring even worse: in the spring of 1781, Virginia was issuing two-thousand-dollar bills. They were worth a couple of dollars in "hard" money (Shafer and Bruce 24).

13. Madison (1018). For Shays's Rebellion, see Leonard L. Richards.

14. Thomas Jefferson, *Report on Copper Coinage* (New York: Francis Childs and John Swaine, 1790), as cited in Mihm ("The Almighty Dollar at Home and Abroad" 7).

15. Vermeule (12). Reference to the Confederatio copper is to Doty (*America's Money* 63).

16. Benjamin Franklin, in a letter to John Jay of 1785, wrote that America should place images of her honored great on the money, as the ancients had done. "[By] this means the honour was extended through their own and neighboring nations ... and the numbers struck gave such security to this kind of monument against perishing and being forgotten, that some of them exist to this day." (Cited in Bowers and Sundman 63)

17. Notes issued in 1800 by the Washington Bank of Westerly, Rhode Island, were the first paper bills to carry a vignette of George Washington.

18. Waldstreicher (119).

19. See Mudd (30–32).

20. Standish (123).

21. George Washington ("Farewell Address," online).

22. Goodwin (98).

23. Tocqueville (251).

24. Zelinsky (4).

25. Crunden (x, my emphasis). The gap between local activity and nationalist ideology was itself the result of the political constellation during the early republic, with the Federalists getting their nationalism and the legitimating of their quest for order in the Constitution, and the Jeffersonians gaining high ground in popular politics. For more on this theme, see Waldstreicher (173–201).

26. Crunden (xi).

27. Hedges (108).

28. Cited in Blanke (137).

29. The story is of course more complex, as see James Oakes; Foner; and Gates Jr.

30. Cited in McMurtry ("Separate and Unequal" 21).

31. Levin (32).

32. Hedges (109).

33. Cited in Wright and Cowen (24).

34. Emerson ("American Scholar" 1510).

35. Cited in Lewis (5).

36. On the symbolic conquest of the West, see Tschachler ("'I send you 19 small flaggs'" and "'Sacred Emblems of Attachment'"). For accounts of Western communities boasting both of their American heritage and their Western virtues, as well as using Lewis and Clark as their John Smith, see Waldstreicher (288–89).

37. Cited in McMurtry (*Sacagawea's Nickname* 90).

38. Ferguson (167).

39. This fact certainly contributed to the two men's contemporary evaluation, by Albert Furtwangler, as "emissaries of peculiar American ideals of freedom among the great powers contending for empire along the Pacific" and, furthermore, as part of a long tradition of "westering idealism" that began with the Puritans and continued through the proponents of the "Great Society" in the 1960s (10). On the issue of place names, see Gasque.

40. Generally in this connection, see Bodnar.

41. Waldstreicher (187).

42. Cited ibid. (186).

43. Cited in Blanke (237).

44. Cited in Wood (*Revolutionary Characters* 158).

45. For images of notes cited in this and the following paragraphs, see Doty (*Pictures*).

46. Doty (*America's Money* 100).

47. Doty (*Pictures* 51–52).

48. Nolt (31).

49. Doty (*America's Money* 111).

50. Doty (*Pictures* 33).

51. Ibid. (189).

52. "Bond after bond, bill after bill," Harold Holzer found, "suggests a preoccupation with reminding noteholders, investors, debtors, and ordinary citizens alike, that slavery, one of the most important elements of Southern economy, would continue to exist in perpetuity, protected by law and sanctioned by tradition, and all but divinely ordained in iconography" (online). Even more telling is the inclusion, on a $10 note produced for the Central Bank of Alabama by a group of Northern printmakers hired by the Confederacy, of the iconic Gilbert Stuart portrait of George Washington. Clearly, the portrait served as "a reminder that the greatest of all American presidents to date had been a Southern slaveholder, and, by implication, a supporter of the Confederacy and the perpetuation of the slave system" (ibid.).

53. Doty (*Pictures* 197).

54. Cited in Kotte (558).

55. *The Landing of the Pilgrims* was also used for the new National currency (in an engraving by Charles Burt), and was subsequently re-entered on other notes.

56. Cited in Kotte (561).

57. The "Father of his Country" theme is also clear from Rembrandt Peale's 1824 painted portrait of Washington, which is emblazoned with the Latin title *Patriae Pater*. The painting (the so-called "Porthole Portrait") now graces the office of the Vice President in the Capitol in Washington, DC. It can be viewed online at *www.senate.gov*.

58. Cited in Kotte (563).

59. Cited ibid. (564).

60. Cited ibid. (566, my emphasis).

61. Trumbull's painting can be viewed online at the Yale University Art Gallery, New Haven, CT.

62. The paintings had been expressive of domestic policy already at the time of their origin, from the late 1830s to the 1850s. This was the time of major westward expansion under the doctrine of "manifest destiny," and the indigenous people who stood in the way were forced to either submit or assimilate. If they did not comply, they were eliminated. While Powell, Weir, and Chapman were busy fulfilling their commissions for the Rotunda, United States troops were fighting the Seminole Indians of Florida as well as "relocating" the Cherokee nation in a journey modern history books refer to as the "Trail of Tears." For this and more information, see The Capitol Project at the University of Virginia, online.

63. Zelinsky (219).

64. Cited in Mihm (*Nation of Counterfeiters* 333).

65. Helleiner ("Territorial Currencies" 323).

66. Hewitt (*Beauty and the Banknote* 11).

67. John Sherman was Senator from Ohio. He had replaced Salmon P. Chase when he departed for the Treasury Department. His words are cited in Helleiner ("National Currencies" 1411).

68. Mihm (*Nation of Counterfeiters* 305). On Lincoln's role in the project of economic nationalism, see Boritt.

69. Two five-hundred dollar bills from Lowell, Massachusetts neatly suggest the transition. The note from the Appleton Bank dates from around 1860. It says "Appleton Bank, Lowell, State of Massachusetts." At right is an eagle, but at left is an image of a dog, a popular symbol of trustworthiness. The note's counterpart from the Appleton *National* Bank dates from 1865. It no longer says "Massachusetts," but "United States," and its two vignettes clearly depict scenes of national import. At left is a standing female figure with a sword, appropriately titled "Civilization" by the Treasury Department. (Friedberg and Friedberg refer to the vignette as "The Spirit of the Navy" [*Paper Money* 85].) In the foreground is a cannon, a battleship is to the left, and an armed camp in the distance to the right. On the right side of the note is a vignette of a ship, the *Sirius*, arriving in New York harbor. The event had made the national news about a generation earlier, as the *Sirius* was one of two ships that had made the first Atlantic crossing entirely under steam power in April 1838. (Bowers and Sundman 22)

70. For illustrations of the engraving plate Burt created as well as the steel cylinder roller die, see Reed ("Portrait" 47).

71. Friedberg and Friedberg (*Paper Money* 77).

72. Cited in Bowers (*Obsolete Paper Money* 406). Clark had advocated the use of panoramic scenes already during the planning stage for the Legal Tender Notes. Such scenes did not come to pass on these notes, but Clark continued to persist, including the idea in the letter to Chase (Records of the Bureau of Engraving and Printing).

73. American history books of the nineteenth century commonly represented Burgoyne as the one British

general from the War of Independence who was the most responsible for plundering and looting, massacres, unspeakable cruelties, and destruction — and for stirring up the native tribes against the Americans (Kotte 564–65).

74. See Helleiner ("National Currencies" 1412–14).

75. Mihm (*Nation of Counterfeiters* 339). The Confederacy, by contrast, at this time printed two-dollar notes bearing an allegory of the South slaying the Union (Newman, *Paper Money* 78, 243–44).

76. Standish (139).

77. O'Leary (220).

78. Cited in Helleiner ("National Currencies" 1416).

79. Anderson (6, 7).

80. Hobsbawm ("Mass-Producing Traditions" 264).

81. Ibid. (279).

82. Ibid. (280, my emphasis).

83. Doty (*America's Money* 169).

84. On a different level, the bison also may have stood in as an echo of the sacrificial economies of ancient Greece and Rome in which money was frequently associated with cattle and bulls. For example, the Greek god Dionysus was traditionally represented as a bull. In Rome the Mithraic cult centered on the sacrifice of the bull. In Latin the word *pecunia*, which is the root of the English *pecuniary*, stems from *pecus*, meaning cattle. (Taylor, *Confidence Games* 66)

85. Standish (140–41).

86. Bowers ("Introduction" 31). The "Battleship Note" made reappearance on a Bureau of Engraving and Printing souvenir card issued for the 1988 American Numismatic Association convention in Cincinnati, OH ("Numismatic Narratives"). In Bowers and Sundman's roster of "100 greatest American currency notes," it is ranked 22. The related "Green Eagle" bill, surprisingly, did not make the cut, though the $500 Gold Certificate of the series 1882, which bears an identical image, did (51, 78).

87. References in this paragraph are to Cannadine (172). For a comprehensive cultural history of Washington, DC's monuments, statues, and memorials, see Goode.

88. Between 1871 and 1910, a total of thirty-five commemorative statues were erected in Washington, DC. By contrast, the total for the period 1801–1870 is a mere three. The number again declined after the peak decade of 1901–10 (Cannadine 164).

89. Cannadine (129). Everything has its price, though. As Cannadine wryly notes, one consequence of making powerful presidents (and monarchs) more grand, and therefore more public, was an increase in the number of assassinations during this period. Presidents Garfield and McKinley were assassinated respectively in 1881 and 1901; Alexander II of Russia in 1881; President Carnot of France in 1894; Prime Minister Canovas of Spain, in 1897; Empress Elisabeth and Archduke Ferdinand of Austria respectively in 1898 and 1914; King Umberto of Italy in 1900, to cite but a few. And when attempts were made to enlarge the White House, the main concern was that its cramped quarters were inadequate for receptions, which resulted in "a consequent loss of that order and dignity which should characterise them" (ibid. 130).

90. Doty (*America's Money* 197).

91. The coinage too paid tribute to the sentiment of the time. On the quarter dollar of 1916, Liberty is presented as the Athena of the Parthenon, with her head and arms conveying a strong sideways motion, and the shield emblazoned with the stars and stripes, in the heraldic form of the Great Seal. Clearly this Liberty, a commentator observed, was "intended to express the awakening of the country to the need of preparedness [for battle]" (cited in Vermeule 132–33).

92. Adams (466).

93. Surprisingly, U.S. coin design followed a different trajectory. Beginning with Saint-Gaudens and Bela Lyon Pratt in 1907, the U.S. Mint would entrust coin design to leading sculptors of the age. The result has been coins displaying an astounding variety of subject matter (Vermeule 5).

94. Goodwin (287–88.)

95. Doty (*America's Money* 217, 223).

96. Hessler ("Unofficial Commemorative Notes 656–58). There does not appear to be an explanation for the switch from Garfield to Jefferson. As Oakes and Schwartz explain, USBEP records generally do not explain why particular statesmen were chosen over others equally prominent and important (14).

97. Cited in O'Donnell (314).

98. Note that the series year is 1934, not 1935, for the series number then identified the year of the approval of the design. The design of the one-dollar note, which was done in part by Edward Mitchell Weeks from the Bureau of Engraving and Printing, was approved by President Roosevelt, and signed by Henry Morgenthau, Jr., who was then Secretary of the Treasury, and W.A. Julian, the Treasurer of the United States.

99. A companion project in the South — the Stone Mountain project that Gutzon Borglum began in northern Georgia — was halted in 1928 for lack of money (Vermeule 157–59).

100. Zelinsky (219).

101. Ibid. (219, 220).

102. O'Donnell (41–44).

103. Ginsberg (2114).

104. Ms. Priest's signature appeared on $1 Silver Certificates Series 1935F and 1957, the former without the national motto, the latter with it.

105. Other types of one-dollar bills, like the Legal Tender issues, are equally impossible as models for Ginsberg's poem, as they all bore obligations different from the one cited — "This Certificate is Legal Tender (tender!) for all / debts public and private."

106. Goodwin (287). Other references in this paragraph are to Standish (141), and Clark (35).

107. Reference to "moderation and seriousness of purpose" is to art historian Chandler Post, as quoted in Vermeule (102).

108. The Lincoln cent, which was created in 1909 by engraver-sculptor Victor David Brenner, received new back designs in 2009 to commemorate the 200th anniversary of Lincoln's birth. If the 1909-cent was the first regular issue United States coin to portray an actual historic figure, the first American coin to depict a President was the Lafayette Dollar of 1900, a one-dollar commemorative coin, which on its obverse bears a portrait of George Washington, together with one of Major General Lafayette.

109. Generally, commemorative coins are available only from collectors, though beginning with the Jackie Robinson silver dollar of 1997 they have been available directly from the United States Mint, at *www.usmint.gov*. For an overview of "commems," see Yeoman (264–322); on the 2008 Bald Eagle Commemorative Program, see Meyers.

110. Presidential Coin Act, December 22, 2005 (Public Law 109–145). As regards the motto "In God We Trust," many conservatives opposed placing the motto on the coin's edge, believing it was a step towards removing it altogether. In response to the criticism, Congress in late 2007 approved a bill that provides for moving the motto to a more prominent position on the obverse or

reverse. On December 26, 2007, President George W. Bush signed into law the Consolidated Appropriations Act, which gives the U.S. Mint until 2009 to put God back in plain view on the Presidential Dollar coins ("New Laws Impact 2009 Coins").

111. All references to the Presidential Coin Program in this and the following paragraph are to U.S. Mint, "The Presidential $1 Coin Program." The U.S. Mint offers free informational materials via *www.usmint.gov/$1coin*.

112. Zelinsky (220, 252). Similarly, in a broadly based empirical study historians Roy Rosenzweig and David Thelen have shown that identification with official stories such as the discourse of the nation is relatively small—at a mere twenty-two percent of Americans. For a majority of them, family histories seem more important than national history, or at least they would situate events of national importance within family histories or individual biographies. As Rosenzweig and Thelen conclude, "respondents rarely mentioned the triumphal national narrative favored by those who write textbooks or advocate history as a means of teaching patriotism and civics" (116).

Chapter Five

1. R. Hughes (146). Other references in this paragraph are to Thoreau (*Walden* 145), and Emerson ("Nature" 1480).

2. Simmel (198).

3. Ibid. (236). Elsewhere in *The Philosophy of Money*, Simmel writes that money "is the symbol in the empirical world of the inconceivable unity of being, out of which the world, in all its breadth, diversity, energy and reality, flows" (497).

4. The biblical meaning of "assumption," according to the *Oxford English Dictionary*, is the action of receiving up into heaven, especially of the Virgin Mary, with the body preserved from corruption. The specific ecclesiastical use was the earliest in English. The specific legal meaning of "assumption" in the sense of a promise or undertaking dates from 1590. Use of "assumption," in the sense of taking possession of or appropriation, dates from the mid-eighteenth century.

5. In this sense, "redemption" has been used in English since the mid-sixteenth century. Yet like in the case of "assumption," the specific ecclesiastical use of "redemption" dates back much earlier, to 1340. Then it meant deliverance from sin and its consequences by the atonement of Jesus Christ. The word "redemption" is also used in the Jewish "seder" ceremony during the feast of Passover, describing what God did for the Israelites when he freed them from slavery in Egypt.

6. Lest these connotations drop out of the cultural memory altogether, recall that the debt of Marlowe's Doctor Faustus inexorably comes with a date on which payment is due—thus on demand. What Faustus longs for is something Goethe's hero actually gets at the end of *Faust Part Two*: the due date on the Doctor's contract never arrives when heavenly angels take his soul away from Mephistopheles, assuming him into heaven while singing that "for him whose striving never ceases, we can provide redemption" (Goethe, *Faust Part Two* 147; and see Binswanger, and Atwood 166–69).

7. Bolz (194–99).

8. In the German language, "debt" and "guilt" converge in one word, "*Schuld*."

9. See Soosten (122).

10. Benjamin ("One Way Street 87).

11. Taylor (*Altarity* 256, 259).

12. Zelizer (42, 44).

13. Bourdieu (197).

14. Terkel (27).

15. Boesenberg (36–37). Another instance of cleansing may be seen in the practice of putting images of women on paper money, though the bills' "handsome appearance" usually was the result of much idealization. By idealizing women through classical allusions and allegory men would also evoke an era *before* paper money and credit became dominant, an era when their civic personalities were still grounded in real property. For an extended discussion of gendered differences in the significance of money, see Furnham and Argyle (24–48).

16. Products may be viewed online at *http://www.ppp.tv* <07/02/09>.

17. Another example concerns the cultural biography of a pre–Civil War ten-dollar note from the Citizens' Bank of Louisiana, which for many people especially in the South has come to mean "Dixieland" (Tschachler, "Louisiana DIX Notes and the 'Dixieland' Myth").

18. O'Donnell (15, 20).

19. For the Missouri folk song, see The Max Hunter Folk Song Collection. Outside of folklore and popular culture, the stakes in gambling were considerably higher. It is well known, for instance, that most of the $1000 bills still outstanding were issued to Brett Maverick in the 1880s for his high stakes poker games (U.S. House of Representatives, "Jumbo Euro Notes" 1).

20. Brinkman (1243–44).

21. Little Lost Star, at *www.everything2.com*; there is more on folk beliefs associated with the $2 note in Claudia de Lys. The association of the two-dollar bill with gambling is also a reminder that in colonial Canada playing cards were used as money.

22. Little Lost Star (online). These days, two-dollar bills are given as change at the Mouse's Ear Lounge, a strip club in Johnson City, TN (Wikipedia, "United States Two Dollar Bill").

23. Little Lost Star (online).

24. Alger (11–14). It was common practice among counterfeiters to employ children to pass their notes, as most shopkeepers were reluctant to have them arrested (Mihm, *Nation of Counterfeiters* 231–32).

25. In 1938, Thomas Jefferson was also placed on the nickel. Obviously, this was a political act through which President Franklin Roosevelt got back to the Republicans for relegating Jefferson to the little-used and highly unpopular two-dollar bill. In itself, the decision is ironic. If Jefferson stood for any one thing in particular, it was minimal government. This was something that Roosevelt and the New Deal clearly did not stand for. The irony is even more pronounced in the Jefferson Memorial, built at the height of Roosevelt's power—and likewise against all the logic of the New Deal. Aptly, the Memorial does not contain a word about the beauties of small government. (Wood, *Revolutionary Characters* 122)

26. Oakes and Schwartz (101); and see Wilson and Wilson (online). In the summer of 2008, the Bureau of Engraving and Printing offered Series 2003A $2 notes with a serial number beginning with "2008xxxxD" (issued in Richmond, VA) for $7.95 a piece; the notes were sold out within a month or so. Richard Jurek has amassed a collection of two-dollar bills that astronauts purportedly carried into space as mementos or (yes!) good luck charms, starting with a 1917 bill astronaut Gordon Cooper Jr. took along for the last flight of the Mercury program in 1963 (Jurek, online). An astronaut friend of mine has not been able to confirm this practice, though.

27. See Wocka, web document; for more stories, see Wikipedia ("United States Two Dollar Bill").

28. Goldstein and Lasser (46, 48). Other practices made use of snips from patriotic and loyalist publications, which appeared on the backs of bills issued just prior to or during the Revolutionary War. Goldstein and Lasser have found a 2s Patriot note from Connecticut, dated July 1, 1775, which was repaired with a pro–British poem cut from a newspaper. The poem praises British warships, calling them "Dreadful as Demons" and encouraging the British fleet "with your sails filled by storms of Vengeance, bear down to Battle" (ibid. 49). A repaired 20s Delaware note of February 28, 1746, provides another glimpse into the problem of keeping colonial paper money moving. The note is backed by a scrap from a German medical guide, thus telling of commercial interaction between the colony of Delaware and its German neighbors in northern Pennsylvania (ibid. 47).

29. On this point, see du Gay et al (87).

30. Zelizer (1, 3).

31. Melville, *Moby-Dick*, Chapters X (51, 50), and XL (162).

32. So widespread has the habit become that each Christmas, the demand for gold coins and crisp new bills creates additional work for the United States Mint as well as for the banks that distributed the money. Zelizer (107); Simmel (65).

33. Zelizer (105, 71–72, 115, 248).

34. The classic thinkers, Zelizer contends, absolutized market money and were not therefore able to make sense of a growing paradox: "As the physical forms and legal status of money became more standardized, the use of legal tender in many areas of life turned into a more delicate social process, making cultural and social differentiation increasingly elaborate." Ibid. (205).

35. Ibid. (119–20, 140–41).

36. Shell (*Art and Money* 58).

37. Ibid. (87).

38. Cited ibid. (169).

39. Ibid. (88).

40. Nygren (140–42).

41. Shell, *Art and Money* (92–94).

42. Nygren (130).

43. Ibid. (138). An illustration of Haberle's *The Changes of Time* can be viewed online at the Grand Rapids Art Museum.

44. As Marc Shell notes with amusement, also prohibited were copies of currency "in the form of cookies and hooked rugs" (*Art and Money* 103).

45. Shell, *Art and Money* (92–94).

46. Ibid. (103–5).

47. Polsky (online).

48. Warhol (92). For a discussion of Warhol in the wider context of a postmodern alliance between art and business, see Taylor (*Confidence Games* 31–38).

49. It appears people still respond to money paintings. The Trompe l'Oeil Society of Artists was formed in 2001 for the purpose of promoting and publicizing the genre (Clark, "Fool the Eye" 32).

50. Shell (*Art and Money* 108).

51. The Dude (online).

52. More information on the museum's website at http://www.thebrogan.org/.

53. The exhibition took its name from the social and economic reforms implemented by Franklin Delano Roosevelt in the 1930s. "For better or worse," the catalog explained, "each president affects the course and stability of the economy, and likewise, the changing economy affects the stability and reputation of each president. Artists in this exhibition play within the space of literal and imagined artifacts of currency and alternative methods of exchange to push social protest and reconsider material value" (http://www.briconline.org/rotunda).

54. Thus see Marc Shell's words, "The *matter* of electronic money does *not matter*" (*Art and Money* 108).

55. For a more detailed discussion of Bradley's artwork, see Tschachler ("From 'Wildman' to 'True Native American'" 9–10, 20–21). For a discussion of John W. Jones's reproductions of slave images on Confederate and Southern States notes, see chapter three.

56. Zelizer (224).

57. Slick Times, online. For the fake bill carrying a gospel message, see Wikipedia ("Fake Denominations of United States Currency").

58. *FoundMagazine* (online).

59. Harth's bills were on show, *inter alia*, at an art show honoring the victims of the September 11 terror attacks in St. Petersburg, Florida, in December 2001, and, in association with the Smithsonian Institution, at the Mary Brogan Museum of Art in Tallahassee, Florida, in the fall of 2006, as part of the exhibition "CURRENCY: Art as Money / Money as Art"; early in 2009, they were on show at the BRIC Rotunda Gallery in Brooklyn, NY, as part of the exhibition "A New Deal, Art and Currency" (Harth, online). To view more bills and read articles about Harth's art, for instance from *The New York Times* or the New Orleans *Times-Picayune*, see the artist's web site at *www.davidgregharth.com*; to read the article from the *St. Petersburg Times*, go to *http://www.sptimes.com/ News/122701/Weekend/Art_show_honors_terro.shtml*.

60. See MacCash (3).

61. Henkin (137).

62. For an illustration of a bill with the motto marked out in a conventional way, see Wikipedia, "In God We Trust."

63. Defacement of currency is a violation of Title 18, Section 333 of the United States Code. If it is done in such a way that the currency is made unfit for circulation it comes under the jurisdiction of the United States Secret Service (USBEP, "Defacement of Currency").

64. See ODD#III(a);pQ$:10Afm3155.p. (sic!), online. For extended treatments of the Illuminati conspiracy, see the books by Des Griffin.

65. Brouillet ("Unmasking the Big Deception," online).

66. "Bush Notes" (online).

67. Ron Wise's World Paper Money ("Liberty Dollars: Brochure Insert," online).

68. Marotta (1304). For the viewpoint of the collector, see McIlvaine. For personal reminiscences, including a fourteen-note short snorter, see Lasser and Goldstein. To view bills, including one that Eleanor Roosevelt carried on her trips during World War Two, go to Tom Sparks's website at *www.shortsnorter.org*. For a documentation of all kinds of currency that World War Two soldiers carried to spend or save as mementos, see Schwan and Boling.

69. An episode in the first season of the *Wonder Woman* series with Lynda Carter and Lyle Waggoner (1976) also bears the title *The Last of the Two Dollar Bills*. The plot centers on Wonder Woman thwarting the Nazis' plan to flood the United States with counterfeit two-dollar bills.

70. Reed (*Show Me the Money* 10).

71. There are exceptions, such as the film *A Piece of the Action* (1977), in which Sidney Poitier appears using "flash," legitimate hundred dollar bills on top of stacks of blank, cut paper (Reed, *Show Me the Money* 30).

72. Reed (*Show Me the Money* 1–3). This monumental work on its 800-some pages lists over 270 types of prop money, in about 1,800 varieties; the book has some 2,000 pictures and over 1,000 motion picture films detailed.

73. References in this paragraph are to Reed (*Show Me the Money* 24–52, 172–92).

74. Ibid. (159–60, 188, 37).

75. For images of "Disney Dollars," see Ron Wise's World Paper Money, online.

76. Generally on the origins of money in religion and cult, see Taylor (*Confidence Games* 57–68).

77. Barnwell (online).

78. Wikipedia "Second Life" (online). For the broader picture, see Malaby.

79. Banknotes.com (online).

80. Ibid.

81. Ron Wise ("Fantasy Notes," online).

82. Slick Times ("Political Funny Money," online).

83. KPMG is a global network of professional companies providing audit, tax, and advisory services, as see *www.kpmg.com.*

84. It is tempting to identify these bills as truly postmodern. As Mark Taylor argues, the signs that are important to postmodernists "are not original but are recycled; they are, in other words, signs of other signs. In the postmodern world [there is] no escape from recycling signs" (*Confidence Games* 173).

85. View images online at Tin Signs USA.

86. View an image online at 123posters.com.

87. Wikipedia ("Scrooge McDuck").

88. Brinkley (11).

89. Suetonius (1: 465).

90. Eliot (31).

91. Norris (499).

92. Canetti (397–98).

93. Ibid. (398).

94. The chorus line, dressed to sing the famous hit number "We're in the Money," is suitably wearing costumes decorated with Morgan Silver Dollars. For a scene still, see Eagleton and Williams (11).

95. Brinkley (13).

96. De Certeau (166).

97. Ginsberg (2114). "T-Men" are law-enforcement agents of the Treasury Department. Reference to Chapman is to K. Jackson, ed. (312). For discussions of "ekphrasis," see Mitchell (*Picture Theory* 151–81); Krieger; and Hefferman.

98. Ginsberg (2112, 2113). For discussions of "American Change," see Cargas (62–83), and Vendler (9–16). A more iconoclastic poem on the currency, specifically on the Buffalo nickel, is Howard Nemerov's "Money: an introductory lecture," as collected in *The Blue Swallows* (1967) and reproduced in K. Jackson, ed. (113–14).

99. Burrell (182).

100. Among the designs was one that showed Moses dividing the Red Sea and that had as its motto the words of Oliver Cromwell, "Rebellion to Tyrants Is Obedience to God."

101. Ibid. (343, 183). As regards the all-seeing eye, Burrell might have added that among the ancient Egyptians and in the Old Testament as well the all-seeing eye was usually focused on bad deeds rather than one good ones.

102. Ibid. (184, my emphasis).

103. Ibid. (184–85).

104. Ibid. (185, 186).

105. Ibid. (188).

106. Ibid. (193), my emphasis.

107. McLarty (online), my emphasis.

108. Ibid., my emphasis.

109. On this theoretical point, see Mannheim (192).

110. McLarty (online). The 13th Amendment of 1865 provided for the abolition of "slavery" and any other form of "involuntary servitude." The 2004 Disney movie *National Treasure* likewise contains numismatic references, as does the web site that promotes it. To locate 13 examples of the number 13 on the back of a dollar bill, click on the dollar bill icon under the "Games" heading.

111. Information provided on the website identifies McLarty as an Attorney at Law operating out of Dallas, Texas.

Chapter Six

1. See Althusser (168).

2. As John Kenneth Galbraith points out, it was "the fact of scarcity, not the fact of intrinsic worthlessness that was important. The problem of paper was that, in the absence of convertibility, there was nothing to restrict its supply. Thus it was vulnerable to the unlimited increase that would diminish or destroy its value" (*Money* 63).

3. Cited in Goodwin (43). On the conflation of categories—alchemy, economics, and political authority—see Mihm (*Nation of Counterfeiters*, chapter 2).

4. Cited in Krooss (1: 11).

5. Cited in G. Davies (465).

6. Crèvecoeur (48).

7. Cited in Wright and Cowen (27). For the English tradition that considered as "real" only wealth based on property or specie, see McLaughlin (*Paperwork*).

8. Cited in Bowers (*Obsolete Paper Money* 516).

9. Cited in Krooss (2: 38–42).

10. Emerson ("Nature" 1480). Andrew Jackson would have understood. In his farewell address of March 4, 1837, this President continued to rant about the evils inherent in a "paper system […] founded on public confidence, having of itself no intrinsic value [and thus merely encouraging a] wild spirit of speculation" (as cited in Remini 169). As regards the English Tories, the year 1837 also saw the publication of Thomas Carlyle's *The French Revolution*, a book that mocked as a sign of his own times what that author identifies as "the Age of Paper" in late-eighteenth-century France. Continuing the English Augustan tradition of superstition against paper money, Carlyle calls the period an age of "Bank-paper, wherewith you can still buy when there is no gold left" (31). Carlyle himself stands in a tradition of capital satirists of which Alexander Pope and Edmund Burke probably were the most prominent members. We will come back to Pope below. Here is an example of Burke: "All you have [in post–Revolutionary France] is a paper circulation, and a stock-jobbing constitution" (142). Burke's own ideal economy was one based on land. Thus he believes that "inheritance furnishes a sure principle of conservation" (119–20). For a commentary on Burke, see J.G.A. Pocock's introduction to *Reflections on the Revolution in France* (xxi–xxxiii).

11. Cited in Henkin (139).

12. Washington Irving's tale of 1824 is available online. For the historian's view, see Massey (113). Fritz Redlich, who also treats the land bank experiments in the 1680s as banks, provides a different reading (chapter one). For an in-depth analysis of the land bank system, see Thayer. For other attempts towards establishing banks in colonial Massachusetts, see Kagin.

13. Nussbaum (44–46).

14. Often that was true in theory only. William Leggett, a staunch Jacksonian, reported that it was "common practice" for employers to pay workers their wages in depreciated bills that had been purchased from exchange brokers expressly for cutting labor costs by reducing the real value of wages. (*Democratick Editorials* 83–84, as cited in Henkin 145).

15. Cited in Eagleton and Williams (177). Other references in this paragraph are to Bowers (*Obsolete Paper Money* 270, 35).

16. Doty (*America's Money* 97).

17. Poe ("The Gold-Bug" 578, 579, 580). Poe wrote "The Gold-Bug" in 1843, while he was still living in Philadelphia. It won him a cash prize and earned him a measure of fame. The story was widely reprinted and also appeared in *Tales* (New York: Wiley and Putnam, 1845). It also inspired Robert Louis Stevenson to write his own treasure-hunting novel, *Treasure Island*, in 1883 (Jeffrey Meyers 291). Reference to Marx is to *Critique* (141).

18. The Christian tradition is perhaps best exemplified by the following passage from the Bible: "For the love of money is the root of all evil: which while some coveted after, they have erred from the faith, and pierced themselves through with many sorrows" (1 Timothy 6). The passage, which in the Latin original reads as *Radix malorum est cupiditas*, is often misquoted as "*money* is the root of all evil," though this is rather to take the neutral instrument for the devil himself. The English divine Jeremy Taylor knew this pitfall well, summarizing, in *The Rule and Exercise of Holy Living* (1650), the apostle's words as "*Covetousness is idolatry*; that is, it is an admiring money for itself, not for its use; it relies upon money, and loves it more than it loves God and religion. And *it is the root of all evil*; it teaches men to be cruel and crafty, industrious and evil, full of care and malice [...] the father transmits it to the son [...] till a tyrant, or an oppressor, or a war, or change of government, or the usurer, or folly, or an expensive vice makes a hole in the bottom of the bag, and the wealth runs out like water, and flies away like a bird from the hand of a child" (in K. Jackson, ed., 280). As regards Aristotle, this philosopher in *Nicomachean Ethics* (1132b) distinguished between economic exchange based on barter — *oikonomía* (considered "natural") — and making money — *chrematistos* (considered "unnatural"), as see Gernalzick (145–47).

19. Hurst (80).

20. Poe ("The Gold-Bug" 579, 580). The issue of paper money versus gold money is at the core of essays both of Kevin McLaughlin ("Just Fooling") and Marc Shell (*Money, Language, and Thought* 5–23). H.R. Robinson expresses the link between the economic and aesthetic, and religious realms that drives Poe's narrative inadvertently in a caricature from 1837. The caricature is in the form of a joke note depicting Andrew Jackson's treasure hunt for the gold that "real" notes (the "gold humbug") are supposed to represent, as see Shell (ibid. 11–18). My reading of Poe's tale here builds on some of the implications of Shell's and McLaughlin's essays, so I would like here to acknowledge my debt, and express my gratitude, to these scholars.

21. References to Poe in this paragraph are to "The Gold-Bug" (581, 564).

22. McLaughlin ("Just Fooling" 54, my emphasis). References to Poe in this paragraph again are to "The Gold-Bug" (585, 595, 560, and 563).

23. Murray Bloom has referred to the entire period as "the Age of Counterfeit [...] in which the chief form of paper currency in the United States was notes issued by banks operating under charters from the states" (97). As regards federal paper money, Treasury notes had been issued in 1837 and 1838, but in 1844 the House Means and Ways Committee, which was then dominated by Whig partisans and thus extremely anti-federalist, declared that they were in effect bills of credit (money in the form of debt) and that Congress, in issuing them, had overstepped its powers (Hurst 136–37). Reference to "The Gold-Bug" as a "capital story" is to Thomas and Jackson (419).

24. The cultural anxieties that stemmed from these monetary uncertainties have, from the start, their place in *The House of the Seven Gables*. As Walter Benn Michaels has shown, perhaps the central point in the novel is "the implicit comparison between the impoverished capitalist and the dispossessed aristocrat. The capitalist who loses everything loses everything, whereas the nobleman, losing everything material, retains his nobility, which has a 'spiritual existence.' This title cannot be bought or sold; unlike the land you have 'hewn out of the forest,' it cannot be stolen either. Aristocracy's claim to land is unimpaired by the inability to enforce that claim" (93). However, in "'this republican country'" there no longer was any aristocracy, Hawthorne wrote. Hence, loss of wealth constitutes a deeply felt "'tragedy'" (92).

25. Cited in Bowers (*Obsolete Paper Money* 471).

26. The security consisted of ⅓ in specie and ⅔ in short-term loans, as see Caldwell (11–12, 64–68, and 71–89), and Redlich (chapter twelve).

27. Bowers (*Obsolete Paper Money* 499).

28. Ibid. (455).

29. Melville, *The Confidence-Man* (31). For scholarship addressing the theme of confidence and authority in Melville, see Milder (440), David S. Reynolds (300–304), and Shell (*Art and Money* 103).

30. Mihm (*Nation of Counterfeiters* 319).

31. Bowers ("Introduction" 12).

32. The word inflation," J. Earl Massey explains, refers to "the rise in prices that occurs when the public has a great deal of money, but the supply of goods is short. At such times the value of paper money is often reduced" (158).

33. Cited in Shell (*Art and Money* 79).

34. Ibid. For the theoretical point that both fiction and money function in essentially the same way, through an act of faith, see Derrida (*Donner le temps* 126), and Gernalzick (157).

35. *The New York Times* (June 22, 1871), as cited in Mihm (*Nation of Counterfeiters* 362). For Sherman's statement that, "if anything should be national, it should be bank notes," see ibid. (364).

36. As Eric Helleiner summarizes the development, "The construction of national currencies in the nineteenth century involved the transformation of money from a metallic form into a 'token' form. Before the nineteenth century, most official money in circulation consisted of gold and silver coins whose metallic value was, at least in theory, close to their nominal value. During the nineteenth century, token forms of money — both token coins and notes — whose face value derived not from their metallic content but from a value assigned by the state, increasingly replaced these full-weight coins." ("National Currencies" 1427–28)

37. William Graham Sumner, *A History of Banking in the United States* (465), as cited in Mihm (*Nation of Counterfeiters* 361).

38. Cited in Shell (*Art and Money* 68).

39. Pope (144).

40. Cooke (*Sot-Weed Redivivius*), as cited in McLaugh-

lin ("Just Fooling" 47). For an account of the rather obscure Cooke, see Cohen; on the historical context of Cooke's poem in the debates in the Maryland Assembly at this time over paper money, see Behrens (9–12).

41. Cited in Mihm (*Nation of Counterfeiters* 30).

42. Madison (1018).

43. Cited in Galbraith (*Money* 59).

44. Cited in Hammond (*Banks and Politics* 92–93).

45. Art. I, sec. 10, § 1 says, "No State shall ... make any Thing but gold and silver Coin a Tender in Payment of Debts." Therefore, the question is, if the States cannot issue paper money, this must mean that the federal government can. This is not the case, as the Tenth Amendment — which James Madison had drafted, along with the rest of the Bill of Rights — says, "The powers not delegated to the United States by the Constitution, nor prohibited by it to the States, are reserved to the States respectively, or to the people." This means that the Constitution does not "delegate" the power to "make any Thing but gold and silver Coin a Tender in Payment of Debts" to the federal government. Therefore, government at *no level* has the power to make anything but gold and silver coin tender in payment of debts. For a discussion of these legal aspects, see Hurst (8–14). For a discussion of Hamilton's admonition that in its own actions Congress should observe the spirit of the Constitution's ban on bills of credit, see ibid. (135–36).

46. Doty (*America's Money* 161).

47. Cited in Krooss (3: 149).

48. Cited in Zelizer (14).

49. Carruthers and Babb (1566–78).

50. Cited in O'Malley (379). In 1800, the German philosopher Fichte had made a similar point in a book on political economy: "Der Staat kann zu Geld machen, schlechthin was er will" (47; for a discussion of Fichte within a genealogy of monetary forms, see Gernalzick 159–61).

51. Ibid. (378).

52. Cited in Carruthers and Babb (1570).

53. Cited in Barry (189). Other references in this paragraph are to Nussbaum (238).

54. Locke (49). The link between paper and potential as part of the history of modern aesthetic and economic exchange is explored in greater detail in McLaughlin ("Just Fooling" 41–43).

55. O'Malley (381, 386). Generally on the nexus of money, class, and political affiliation, see Sharkey.

56. O'Malley (376).

57. Tellingly, in 1880 the Greenback Party's platform proclaimed that "all money, whether metallic or paper, should be issued and its volume controlled by the Government, and not by or through banking corporations, and when so issued should be a full legal-tender for all debts, public and private" (Krooss 3: 150).

58. All cited in Mihm (*Nation of Counterfeiters* 233).

59. Gilbert and Helleiner (5–9).

60. Carruthers and Babb (1575–76).

61. See O'Malley, "Free Silver and the Constitution of Man" (web document).

62. Friedman and Schwartz (*Monetary History* 46).

63. Nussbaum (132).

64. Cited in Krooss (3: 152).

65. Henry Adams (335).

66. Friedman and Schwartz (*Monetary History* 116–18). Bryan's speech is quoted in Brands (184).

67. Friedman and Schwartz (*Monetary History* 126–29).

68. As one proponent of the legislation said before its becoming law, "What the country needs is not a make-shift legislative deformity [...] but a careful revision and wise reformation of the entire banking and currency system." Richard Timberlake, as cited in Mihm (*Nation of Counterfeiters* 372). Also useful for the origin of the Federal Reserve System is Livingston.

69. U.S. House of Representatives ("Jumbo Euro Notes" 4).

70. U.S. House of Representatives ("Jumbo Euro Notes" 1).

71. Ibid. (5, 6).

72. Ibid. (7).

73. Newman ("Printing Features" 63–64).

74. Cited in Massey (57).

75. Garson (29, 31).

76. Massey (127).

77. See Krooss (1: 233). For a history of foreign money in the United States through 1857, see David Martin. For a typical guide to coinage from the era, see John Thompson, *The Coin Chart Manual* (New York: W.W. Lee, 1849).

78. For a historic rendering of the incident, see Bowers (*A California Gold Rush History*), and Evans. Generally on the impact of the California gold rush on America, see Rohrbough.

79. The crisis of 1857 certainly destroyed the institutional basis of Herman Melville's career as a writer. In the spring of that year, his novel *The Confidence-Man* had been published. The publishers, Dix and Edwards, went bankrupt within a month. By September, so were its successor companies. The plates for *The Confidence-Man* were sold for scrap. Arac (766). For a documentary history of the panic of 1857, see Bowers (*Obsolete Paper Money* 334–39).

80. Massey (128).

81. Doty (*America's Money* 192).

82. Bowers (*Obsolete Paper Money* 237–40). Other references in this paragraph are to Nussbaum (84–86), Yeoman (373–74), and Doty (*America's Money* 121–33).

83. Nussbaum (86).

84. Helleiner ("Territorial Currencies" 318). Generally on the growth of the state in the early republic, see John, and Formisano.

85. Zelizer (15–16); Hurst (37).

86. *Appendix to the Congressional Globe*, 37th Congress, 3rd session, January 8, 1863, 47–50.

87. Cited in Mihm (*Nation of Counterfeiters* 367).

88. Zelizer (16).

89. 75 U.S. 533, 1869, 549, as cited in Nussbaum (112). For the full text of Chase's opinion, see Krooss (2: 341–50). For a discussion of the decision within the legal history of money in the U.S., see Hurst (69–72). Generally on the role of the Supreme Court in the monetary history of the United States, see Dunne. Chase's opinion was repeated by the Supreme Court of Indiana in November 1889, which said that the government "has a right to provide a currency for the whole nation, and to drive out all other circulating mediums by taxation or otherwise" (Zelizer 17).

90. Doty (*America's Money* 192).

91. Cited in Zelizer (17).

92. Standish (141).

93. Oakes and Schwartz (14).

94. Friedberg and Friedberg (*Paper Money* 158).

95. Doty (*America's Money* 198). In the following, see ibid. (199–201).

96. Cited in Krooss (4: 239).

97. Doty (*America's Money* 202).

98. Friedman and Schwartz (*Monetary History* 216–17, 190). For the respective Amendments to the Federal Reserve Act, see Krooss (4: 341–42, 366, and 413–14).

99. O'Donnell (15).

100. Rothman (26). Cards already account for the vast bulk of monetary transactions. According to the *Nilson Report*, in 1990, some twenty percent of monetary transactions in America were done in cash; by 1996, the number had dropped to eighteen percent, and was predicted to reach a mere twelve percent by 2005 (Fuchshuber). For more discussion on the effects of a cashless society on America, see Robert Samuelson (online), and Taylor (*Confidence Games* 160–61). From a historic standpoint, the proportion of cash transactions has been surprisingly stable over the past century or so. In 1899, John Jay Knox estimated that between ninety and ninety-two percent of the nation's business was carried on by means of checks and other means of credit. The remainder, the amount of currency in circulation, was estimated at $1,210,000,000 — about a tenth of the value of series 1999 one-dollar notes alone.

101. Doty (*America's Money* 228).

102. In economic jargon, governments always want to create money "exogenously," as opposed to money supplies produced elsewhere under market conditions, or "endogenously" as economists describe the process (G. Davies 650). A passionate advocate of money created under market conditions was Friedrich von Hayek, who also used the distinction in an earlier book (*Rules and Order* 36–37).

103. Zelizer (272). For a detailed history of credit cards from their fictional origin in Bellamy's *Looking Backward* to the premium prestige-level cards of the present, see Weatherford (225–32).

104. Zelizer (215).

105. Doty (*America's Money* 28).

106. See Louderback. In developing this account of cybermoney, I have also drawn on Taylor (*Confidence Games* 160–61).

107. Cited in Zelizer (206).

108. McGinley (248).

109. For the following, see Boggs ("Under Arrest"), Weschler (*Boggs*), and Münder (vii). The notion that in the economy all value is connected with performance originated with Simmel (*The Philosophy of Money* 169).

110. An image of a FUN Dollar can be viewed online at the Museum of Money and Financial Institutions.

111. Jacques Derrida has written about the impossibility of distinguishing the fictionality of counterfeits from genuine money (see *Donner le temps*; and Gernalzick 152–54). Economists, too, have argued that counterfeits, so long as they are accepted, have the same power as their legal counterparts. This point is particularly salient when applied to the situation in America, where the pressure of population and the absence of adequate money inevitably led to a rather more "creative" use of the chaotic currency. In the antebellum period in particular, it was quite common among businesspeople to remark that they "preferred a good counterfeit on a solid bank to any genuine bill upon a shyster institution" (Mihm, *Nation of Counterfeiters* 10). Counterfeiters, the logic went, did a public service by increasing the amount of money in circulation in a part of the country where the demand for money invariably was greater than the supply. Thus we can follow Glyn Davies in concluding that, "[l]egally the counterfeiter is always a malefactor, but economically speaking he may often be a public benefactor" (485).

112. Du Gay et al. (113); for the term "illegal tender," see D. R. Johnson.

113. Doty (*America's Money* 37, 38). The principal work on the colonies is Scott. For the inner workings of a network of counterfeiters from Canada, see Mihm (*Nation of Counterfeiters*, chapter 2).

114. Nussbaum (25); and Scott (70–92). The difference to practices of punishing offenders in England is striking. As one historian aptly put it, in the mother country the death penalty was consistently used as "monetary policy" (Wennerlind).

115. See Newman ("Unusual Printing Features").

116. The most frequently targeted notes were the "Sword in Hand" notes. The notes' powerful polemic may have been especially offensive to the British, who employed so-called "Tory Passers" to spend the counterfeits in New England. In April 1777 a New York paper even carried an announcement offering to "Persons going into other colonies […] any number of counterfeit Congress-Notes, for the Price of the Paper per Ream." The announcement also assured potential buyers that the notes were "so neatly and exactly executed that there is no Risque in getting them off, it being almost impossible to discover, that they are not genuine." George Washington was outraged, commenting on this "unparalleled piece" that, "no Artifices are left untried by the enemy to injure us" (Newman, *Early Paper Money* 25). For the fuller picture, see Newman ("British Counterfeiting") and Del Mar (112–15). For a detailed account of counterfeiting within the Revolutionary era propaganda warfare, see a. Bivens.

117. See Doty (*America's Money* 94), and Mihm (*Nation of Counterfeiters* 113–25).

118. Cited in Mihm (*Nation of Counterfeiters* 6).

119. Cited in Bowers (*Obsolete Paper Money* 174). Even Santa Claus, a symbol of goodness and cheer, appears to have been desecrated repeatedly by counterfeiters; Roger Durand cites about seven vignettes of Saint Nicholas on a number of 1850s' bogus notes, though the darker side to Nicholas — the colloquial expression "Old Nick," meaning the Devil, as well as the slang term "to nick," meaning "to steal" — appears to have escaped him ("Here comes Santa Claus" 77–78).

120. Doty (*America's Money* 97).

121. This evaluation seems to reflect rather more the anxieties of the financial establishment in the eastern states. For the nation at large, wildcat banks, unincorporated banks, and fraudulent, nonexistent banks may have been even more disturbing. (Mihm, *Nation of Counterfeiters* 159–60).

122. It was also a symptom of bureaucratic entrepreneurship, as the Secret Service was very much the creation of William Patrick Wood, a veteran of the Mexican-American War who eventually became superintendent of the Old Capitol Prison. Mihm (*Nation of Counterfeiters* 340–59), and David R. Johnson (176–77).

123. Oliver and Kelly (53). For a modern "rogue's gallery," spanning the years between the 1790s and 1860s and graced by admirable scholarship, see Mihm (*Nation of Counterfeiters*).

124. Nussbaum (202–203). Under Title 18, Chapter 25, Section 472 of the U.S. Criminal Code of statutes, it is also against federal law to possess counterfeit American money of currently circulating designs. Sections 474 and 487 prohibit possession of plates for printing paper money and of counterfeit dies or molds for making coins. USBEP, "Counterfeiting Laws" (web document).

125. *New York Times* (January 29, 1911) SM3, as cited in Mihm (*Nation of Counterfeiters* 373).

126. Nussbaum (203).

127. See Lears (151–55).

128. Kevin McNamara (University of Houston-Clear Lake), email message to this author (May 10, 2002).

129. USBEP ("The New Color of Money").
130. USBEP ("Redesign of the $5 Note").
131. Cited in USBEP ("Safer, Smarter, More Secure").
132. USBEP ("Redesign of the $5 Note).
133. Burrell (192).
134. USBEP ("In God We Trust").
135. PollingReport.com ("Religion," part 2). Reference to the "heathen nation" is to Burrell (193).
136. Judt (27); USBEP ("The Great Seal").
137. USBEP ("Survey").
138. Ginnie Mae (online).
139. USBEP ("The New Color of Money").
140. See Schingoethe and Schingoethe.
141. Edwards (online).
142. Zelizer (66–67).
143. See Burkett.
144. The publisher's name, B.A.S.I.C., is short for "Brothers and Sisters in Christ."
145. Historically, Marx wrote, gold-money became "sublimated into its own symbol first in the form of worn coin, then in the form of subsidiary metal currency, and finally in the form of a worthless token, paper, mere *sign of value*" (*Political Economy* 149, my emphasis). There is a stage beyond the one Marx deemed final, one that he could not foresee, in the form of credit cards and other forms of electronic money, which are entirely devoid of any monetary signs. On the "spectral" character of these relational moneys, see Taylor (*Confidence Games* 117).
146. These anxieties may be well founded, considering that the abandonment of the gold standard constitutes the economic equivalent of the death of God. "God functions in religious systems like gold functions in economic systems: God and gold are believed to be the firm foundations that provide a secure anchor for religious, moral, and economic values. When this foundation disappears, meaning and value become unmoored and once trustworthy symbols and signs float freely in turbulent currents that are constantly shifting" (Taylor, *Confidence Games* 6).
147. PollingReport.com ("Religion," online).
148. Benjamin ("Capitalism as Religion" 289). Alan Greenspan, as quoted in www.chicagotribune.com, October 24, 2008, accessed November 2, 2008.
149. Late-medieval thinkers, Marc Shell found, identified the relation of a sinner to God with that of a customer to a shopkeeper (a thought that is still found in John Bunyan). They also suggested that God is essentially a money-changing banker, sometimes understood as the creditor of life — or death: "We owe God a death," Shakespeare wrote in *2 Henry V* (3.2.229–30). Tellingly, "death" was then usually pronounced "debt" (*Art and Money* 176). For a more recent exploration of "debt" as a metaphor in Western religion and literature, see Atwood (45–49).
150. Steil (7).
151. In itself, the deficit is not nearly as bad as it may seem. The United States can run a chronic balance-of-payments deficit and never feel the effects. Dollars sent abroad immediately come back in the form of loans, generally as purchases of United States Treasury bonds. The real problem is the national debt, the money owed by any level of government, which is only fueled further by the fact that personal debts too are at an all-time high, as see Gerald Swanson (17). The inimitable Bill Bryson has thought up a most ingenious—and funny—way of il-

lustrating the concept of a trillion. On the assumption that one could initial one dollar bill each second, he calculates that one could make $1,000 every seventeen minutes, $1 million in about twelve days, $100 million in something over three years, and $1 billion in close to 32 years. It would take almost 32,000 years to count a trillion, and then one would be only one-eighth of the way through the pile of money representing the national debt (Bryson 66–67).
152. Goux ("Cash, Check, or Charge?" 115).
153. Ibid. (117).
154. For a reproduction of Johann Heiss's painting *The Allegory of Commerce* (ca. 1680), see Shell (*Art and Money* 59).
155. "Both religion and the market," Ronnie Lipschutz, a professor of politics at the University of California at Santa Cruz emphasizes, "are based on similar principles of unquestioned belief." Lipschutz (web document). The frantic bail-outs by governments the world over, in the hope that faith might be restored and thus stemmed off the worst consequences of the failure of investment banks and other worthy private enterprises, bear testimony to Lipschutz's words.
156. Cited in Ganz ("Motto" 42).

Conclusion

1. Cited in Helleiner ("National Currencies" 1409, 1413).
2. See Haskill et al. (190).
3. Aglietta and Orléan (*La monnaie souveraine* 31)
4. For an overview of the entire design competition, see European Central Bank, *Euro Banknote Design Exhibition*. To view individual designs online, go to the European Central Bank at www.ecb.int.
5. Cited in Helleiner ("National Currencies" 1409).
6. Goux ("Cash, Check, or Charge" 115–16).
7. Goux ("Numismatics" 9).
8. Du Gay et al. (23).
9. Wodak et al. (54–55).
10. Maritz AmeriPol®, "Proud to Be an American," at www.maritz.com. Despite a high degree of national pride, 56 percent of all respondents thought that Americans are less patriotic than they used to be, the result, it seems, of the fact that they are more vocal about their criticisms of the government because they are concerned and involved. "It's not unpatriotic to criticize your government — quite the opposite," a war veteran is quoted.
11. Wodak et al. (54–55).
12. See Rathkolb.
13. To view schilling notes, go to Shafer and Bruce (2: 108).
14. "Practical Arrangements for the Introduction of the Single Currency," *Green Book* published by the European Commission in 1995, as cited in Helleiner ("National Currencies" 1419).
15. When Johann did return a few years later, the First World War broke out and he was drafted into Austria's imperial army. Johann survived and went back to the United States, never to return to Europe again.
16. For these and other historical ruminations, see Schlesinger Jr. (*Cycles of American History*). For the promise that the Obama presidency harbors, see John R. Talbott.

Bibliography of Works Cited

Printed Sources

Acton, Johnny. *Minted: The Story of the World's Money.* London: Think Books, 2007.

Adams, Barbara Johnston. *The Go-around Dollar.* New York: Simon & Schuster, 1992.

Adams, Henry. *The Education of Henry Adams. An Autobiography* [1918]. Introd. D. W. Brogan. Boston: Houghton Mifflin, 1961.

Aglietta, Michel, and André Orléan, eds. *La Monnaie souveraine.* Paris: Odile Jacob, 1998.

_____. *Souveraineté, légitimité de la monnaie.* Paris: Association d'économie financière, 1995.

Alger, Horatio, Jr. *Ragged Dick: Or, Street Life in New York with the Boot Blacks.* Introduction by Michael Meyer. New York: Signet Classics, 2005.

Alter, Jonathan. *The Defining Moment: FDR's Hundred Days and the Triumph of Hope.* New York: Simon & Schuster, 2006.

Althusser, Louis. "Ideology and Ideological State Apparatuses (Notes towards an Investigation)." *Lenin and Philosophy, and Other Essays.* Trans. Ben Brewster. London: New Left Books, 1971. 127–86.

Anderson, Benedict. *Imagined Communities: Reflections on the Origin and Spread of Nationalism.* 1983; London: Verso Books, 1991.

Anderson, Burnett. "Anti-Counterfeiting Design Efforts Nearly Done." *Bank Note Reporter (BNR)* 19:2 (February 1991): 10–11.

Andrae, Thomas. *Carl Barks and the Disney Comic Books: Unmasking the Myth of Modernity.* Jackson: University Press of Mississippi, 2006.

Andrews, Edmund L. "U.S. Currency Discriminates Against Blind, Judge Rules." *The New York Times* (November 29, 2006): 29.

Arac, Jonathan. "Narrative Forms." *The Cambridge History of American Literature,* ed. Sacvan Bercovitch. Volume Two, *Prose Writings 1820–1865.* Cambridge, UK: Cambridge University Press, 1995. 605–777.

Ardant, G. "Financial Policy and Economic Infrastructure of Modern States and Nations." *The Formation of National States in Western Europe,* ed. C. Tilly. Princeton, NJ: Princeton University Press, 1975.

Armah, Ayi Kwei. *The Beautiful Ones Are Not Yet Born.* Oxford: Heinemann, 1969.

Ashley, Clarence. "Greenback Dollar." County Records, 2002.

Atwood, Margaret. *Payback: Debt and the Shadow Side of Wealth.* Toronto: Anansi, 2008.

Babb, Valerie Melissa. *Whiteness Visible: The Meaning of Whiteness in American Literature and Culture.* New York — London: New York University Press, 1998.

Baecker, Dirk, ed. *Kapitalismus als Religion.* Berlin: Kulturverlag Kadmos, 2003.

Baily, Martin Neil, Robert E. Litan, and Matthew S. Johnson. "The Origins of the Financial Crisis." Business & Public Policy at Brookings. Fixing Finance Series — Paper 3. Washington, DC: Brookings Institution, November 2008.

Bakeless, John. *The Journals of Lewis and Clark.* New York: Penguin, 2002.

Baker, Jennifer J. *Securing the Commonwealth: Debt, Speculation, and Writing in the Making of Early America.* 2005; Baltimore, MD: Johns Hopkins University Press, 2008.

Balkum, Mary. *The American Counterfeit: Authenticity and Identity in American Literature and Culture.* Tuscaloosa: University of Alabama Press, 2006.

Ball, Douglas. "The Influence of the Bank of England and the Scottish Banks on American Banking, 1781–1913." *The Banker's Art: Studies in Paper Money,* ed. Virginia Hewitt. London: British Museum Press, 1995. 20–27.

Banta, Martha. *Imaging American Women: Idea and Ideals in Cultural History.* New York: Columbia University Press, 1987.

Barnhart, David K., and Allan A. Metcalf. *America in So Many Words: Words That Have Shaped America.* Boston: Houghton Mifflin, 1997.

Barr, Ken. "Small-Size Notes." *The Numismatist* 104:5 (May 1991): 747–49.

Barry, Kevin. "Crediting Power: Romantic Aesthetics and Paper Money 1797–1825." *Questione Romantica: Rivista Interdisciplinare di Studi Romantici (QuR)* 3–4 (Spring 1997): 169–92.

Baudrillard, Jean. *Selected Writings.* Cambridge, UK: Polity Press, 1988.

Behrens, Kathryn L. *Paper Money in Maryland, 1727–1789*. Baltimore, MD: Johns Hopkins University Press, 1923.

Bellah, Robert. "Civil Religion in America." *Daedalus* 96 (1967): 1–21.

_____, et al. *Habits of the Heart: Individualism and Commitment in American Life*. Berkeley: University of California Press, 1985.

_____. *Habits of the Heart: Individualism and Commitment in American Life*. Updated edition with a new Preface. Berkeley: University of California Press, 2007.

Benjamin, Walter. "Capitalism as Religion." *Walter Benjamin: Selected Writings*, Volume 1, *1913–1926*, ed. Marcus Bullock and Michael W. Jennings. Trans. Rodney Livingstone. Cambridge, MA: The Belknap Press of Harvard University Press, 1996. 288–291.

_____. "One Way Street." *One Way Street and Other Writings*. London: Verso Press, 1978. 61–94.

_____. "The Work of Art in the Age of Mechanical Reproduction." *Illuminations*. London: Collins/Fontana Books, 1970. 220–27.

Bensel, Richard. *Yankee Leviathan: The Origins of Central State Authority in America, 1859–1877*. New York: Cambridge University Press, 1992.

Benton, Raymond Jr. "A Hermeneutic Approach to Economics: If Economics Is Not Science, and If It Is Not Merely Mathematics, Then What Could It Be?" *Economics as Discourse: An Analysis of the Language of Economics*, ed. Warren J. Samuels. Boston: Kluwer Academic, 1990. 65–89.

Berlant, Lauren. *The Anatomy of National Fantasy: Hawthorne, Utopia, and Everyday Life*. Chicago: University of Chicago Press, 1991.

Bernheimer, Richard. *Wild Men in the Middle Ages: A Study in Art, Sentiment and Demonology*. Cambridge, MA: Harvard University Press, 1957.

Billig, Michael. *Banal Nationalism*. London: Sage, 1995.

Binswanger, Hans Christoph. *Money and Magic: A Critique of the Modern Economy in the Light of Goethe's Faust*. Trans. J. E. Harrison. Chicago: University of Chicago Press, 1994.

Bivens, Steven M. "Paper Bullets," *The Numismatist* 101:8 (August 1988): 1382–90.

Blanke, Gustav H. "Amerika als Erlösernation: Die rhetorischen Ausformungen des amerikanischen Sendungsglaubens." *Sociologia Internationalis* 17 (1979): 235–54.

Blue, Frederick J. *Samuel P. Chase: A Life in Politics*. Kent, OH: Kent State University Press, 1987.

Bloom, Murray Teigh. *Money of Their Own: The Great Counterfeiters*. New York: Scribner's, 1957.

Blum, André. *On the Origin of Paper*. Trans. Harry Miller Lydenberg. New York: Bowker, 1934.

Bodenhorn, Howard. *A History of State Banking in Antebellum America*. New York: Cambridge University Press, 2000.

_____. *State Banking in Early America: A New Economic History*. New York: Oxford University Press, 2003.

Bodnar, John. "Public Memory in an American City: Commemoration in Cleveland." *Commemorations: The Politics of National Identity*, ed. John R. Gillis. Princeton, NJ: Princeton University Press, 1994. 74–89.

Boehm, Gottfried. *Wie Bilder Sinn erzeugen*. Köln: Berlin University Press, 2007.

Boesenberg, Eva. "Männlichkeit als Kapital: Geld und Kultur in der US-amerikanischen Kultur." *Geld und Geschlecht. Tabus, Paradoxien, Ideologien*, ed. Birgitta Wrede. Opladen: Leske + Budrich, 2003. 32–45.

Bogart, Ernest Ludlow. *Economic History of the American People*. New York: Longmans, Green, 1930.

Boggs, J.S.G. "Under Arrest." *Art and Antiques* (October 1987): 99–104, 126–27.

Boime, Albert. *The Unveiling of the National Icons: A Plea for Patriotic Iconoclasm in a Nationalist Era*. New York: Cambridge University Press, 1998.

Bolin, Benny. "Spencer M. Clark, Cornerstone of the Bureau of Engraving and Printing." *Paper Money* 27 (1988): 77–80.

Boritt, Gabor S. *Lincoln and the Economics of the American Dream*. Champaign: University of Illinois Press, 1994.

Bourdieu, Pierre. *Distinction: A Social Critique of the Judgment of Taste*. Trans. R. Nice. Cambridge, MA: Harvard University Press, 1984; London–New York: Routledge, 1986.

Bowers, Q. David. *The American Numismatic Association Centennial History*. Wolfeboro, NH: Bowers and Merena Galleries, 1991.

_____. *A California Gold Rush History: Featuring the Treasure from the S. S. Central America. A Source Book for the Gold Rush Historian and Numismatist*. Newport Beach: California Gold Marketing Group, 2002.

_____. "Introduction and Narrative." Arthur L. and Ira S. Friedberg, *A Guide Book of United States Paper Money: Complete Source for History, Grading, and Prices. Federal Currency Complete 1861 to Date*. Racine, WI: Whitman, 2005. 1–41.

_____. *Obsolete Paper Money Issued by Banks in the United States, 1782–1866*. Atlanta, GA: Whitman, 2006.

_____, and David M. Sundman. *100 Greatest American Currency Notes*. Atlanta, GA: Whitman, 2005.

Boyle, David. *Funny Money: In Search of Alternative Cash*. London: Flamingo, 2000.

Bradfield, Elston G. "Benjamin Franklin: A Numismatic Summary." *The Numismatist* 103:4 (April 1990): 530–35, 595–98.

Brand Nubian. *In God We Trust*. Electra Records 1993.

Brands, H.W. *The Money Men: Capitalism, Democracy, and the Hundred Years' War Over the American Dollar*. New York: Norton, 2006.

Breck, Samuel. *Historical Sketch of Continental Paper Money*. Philadelphia: John C. Clark, 1843.

Breckinridge, S. P. *Legal Tender*. Chicago: University of Chicago Press, 1903.

Breithaupt, Fritz. "Money as a Medium of Communication and Money as Identification." *New Orleans Review* 24 (Summer 1998): 23–29.

Brigham, Clarence S. *Paul Revere's Engravings.* New York: Atheneum, 1969.

Brinkley, Alan. *Culture and Politics in the Great Depression.* Waco, TX: Markham Press Fund/Baylor University Press, 1999.

Brinkman, Grover. "The Slow Demise of the $2 Bill." *The Numismatist* 103:8 (August 1990): 1242–44.

Brock, Leslie V. *The Currency of the American Colonies, 1700–1764: A Study in Colonial Finance and Imperial Relations.* New York: Arno Press, 1975.

Brooks, Van Wyck. "America's Coming-of-Age." *Van Wyck Brooks: The Early Years, 1908–1921,* ed. Claire Sprague. New York: Harper & Row, 1968; originally published as *America's Coming-of-Age.* New York: Huebsch, 1915.

Brothers, Eric. "Inspiration or Imitation?" *The Numismatist* 121:9 (September 2008): 52–53.

Brown, Dan. *Angels and Demons.* 2000; London: Corgi Books/Transworld, 2001.

Bruckmüller, Ernst. *Nation Österreich. Kulturelles Bewußtsein und gesellschaftlich-politische Prozesse.* Second edition Wien-Köln-Graz: Böhlau Verlag, 1996.

Bruner, Robert F., and Sean D. Carr. *The Panic of 1907: Lessons Learned from the Market's Perfect Storm.* New York: Wiley, 2007.

Bryson, Bill. *Notes from a Big Country.* London: Transworld/Swan Books, 1999.

Buchan, James. *Frozen Desire: The Meaning of Money.* New York: Welcome Rain, 2001.

Buhs, Joshua Blu. *Bigfoot: The Life and Times of a Legend.* Chicago: University of Chicago Press, 2009.

Burke, Edmund. *Reflections on the Revolution in France.* Introd. by J. G. A. Pocock. New York: Penguin, 1986.

Burke, Peter. *Eyewitnessing: The Uses of Images as Historical Evidence.* Picturing History Series. Ithaca, NY: Cornell University Press, 2001.

Burkett, Larry. *In God We Trust: A Christian Kids Guide to Saving and Spending.* Ill. Keiko Motoyama. Cincinnati, OH: Standard, 2001.

Burrell, Brian. *The Words We Live By: The Creeds, Mottoes, and Pledges That Have Shaped America.* New York: Free Press, 1997.

Burstein, Andrew. *Sentimental Democracy: The Evolution of America's Romantic Self-Image.* New York: Hill & Wang, 1999.

Cajori, Florian. *A History of Mathematical Notations.* Vol. 2. *Notations Mainly in Higher Mathematics.* Chicago: University of Chicago Press, 1929; La Salle, IL: Open Court Press, 1952.

Caldwell, Stephen A. *A Banking History of Louisiana.* Baton Rouge: Louisiana State University Press, 1935.

Calleo, David P., and Benjamin M. Rowland. *America and the World Political Economy.* Bloomington: Indiana University Press, 1973.

Canetti, Elias. *Crowds and Power.* Trans. Carol Stewart. 1960; New York: Farrar, Straus and Giroux, 1981.

Cannadine, David. "The Context, Performance and Meaning of Ritual: The British Monarchy and the 'Invention of Tradition,' c. 1820–1977." *The Invention of Tradition,* ed. Eric Hobsbawm and Terence Ranger. Cambridge, UK: Cambridge University Press, 1983. 101–164.

Cargas, Harry J. *Daniel Berrigan and Contemporary Protest Poetry.* New Haven, CT: College and University Press, 1972.

Carruthers, Bruce G., and Sarah Babb, "The Color of Money and the Nature of Value: Greenbacks and Gold in Postbellum America." *American Journal of Sociology* 101 (1996): 1556–1591.

Cashman, Sean Dennis. *America in the Gilded Age: From the Death of Lincoln to the Rise of Theodore Roosevelt.* New York: New York University Press, 1984.

Cassidy, John. "He Foresaw the End of an Era." *The New York Review of Books* LV: 16 (October 23, 2008): 10–16.

The Centennial History Staff. *History of the Bureau of Engraving and Printing, 1862–1962.* Washington, DC: U.S. Government Printing Office, 1964.

de Certeau, Michel. *The Practice of Everyday Life.* Trans. Steven F. Rendall. Berkeley: University of California Press, 1984; orig. *L'invention du quotidien: Arts de faire.*

Chambers, Bruce W., *Old Money: American Trompe l'Oeil Images of Currency.* Catalog for an exhibition of paintings at the Berry-Hill Galleries in New York City, November 11–17, 1988. Essay by Bruce W. Chambers. New York: Berry-Hill, 1988.

Chambers, Ian. *Urban Rhythms.* Basingstoke: Macmillan, 1985.

Chandler, Lester V. *American Monetary Policy, 1928–1941.* New York: Harper & Row, 1971.

Chernow, Ron. *Alexander Hamilton.* New York: Penguin, 2004.

Chirico, Robert F. "John Haberle and Trompe-L'Oeil." *Marsyas: Studies in the History of Art* 19 (1977/78): 37–45.

_____. "Language and Imagery in Late Nineteenth-Century Trompe l'Oeil." *Arts Magazine* 59:7 (March 1985): 99–117.

Cipoletti, Christopher. "Can We Still Afford Money?" [Congressional Hearing] *The Numismatist* 119:9 (September 2006): 84–85.

Citizens' Bank & Trust Company of Louisiana. *The History of Dixie.* New Orleans, no date.

Clain-Stefanelli, Elvira. "A Historian's View of the State Bank Note: A Mirror of Life in the Early Republic." *America's Currency, 1789–1866.* Coinage of the Americas Conference, Proceedings No.2, ed. William E. Metcalf. New York: American Numismatic Society, 1986. 25–50.

Clark, Cathy L. "Fool the Eye." *The Numismatist* 116:4 (April 2003): 31–35.

Coelho, Paolo. *Eleven Minutes.* London: HarperCollins, 2003.

Coffin, Courtney, L. "The *Notgeld* Experience — Funny Money or Tragic Money." *IBNS (International Bank Note Society) Journal* 23:3 (September 1984): 86–88.

Cohen, Benjamin J. *The Geography of Money*. Ithaca, NY: Cornell University Press, 1998.

Cohen, Edward H. *Ebenezer Cooke: The Sot-Weed Canon*. Athens: University of Georgia Press, 1975.

Coleman, James. *Foundations of Social Theory*. Cambridge, MA: Harvard University Press, 1990.

Colin, Susi. "The Wild Man and the Indian in Early 16th-Century Book Illustration." *Indians and Europe: An Interdisciplinary Collection of Essays*, ed. Christian F. Feest. Aachen: RaderVerlag, 1987. 5–36.

Collins, Christopher. *Homeland Mythology: Biblical Narratives in American Culture*. University Park, PA: Penn State University Press, 2007.

Cowen, David J. *The Origins and Economic Impact of the First Bank of the United States, 1791–1797*. New York: Garland, 2000.

Craig, Lois. *The Federal Presence: Architecture, Politics and Symbols in U.S. Government Buildings*. Cambridge, MA: MIT Press, 1978.

de Crèvecoeur, J. Hector St. John. "Sketches of Eighteenth-Century America." *Letters from an American Farmer* and *Sketches of Eighteenth-Century America*, ed. Albert E. Stone, Penguin Classics. Harmondsworth-New York: Penguin, 1986.

Criswell, Grover C., Jr. *Confederate and Southern State Currency: A Descriptive Listing, Including Rarity and Values*. 2nd edn. Citra, FL: Criswell's and Criswell's, 1976.

Crunden, Robert M. *A Brief History of American Culture*. Armonk, NY–London, UK: North Castle Books, 1996.

Cuhaj, George S., ed. *Standard Catalog of World Paper Money*. Vol. 3. *1961–Date*. 11th Edition. Iola, WI: KP Books, 2005.

Darnton, Robert. *George Washington's False Teeth: An Unconventional Guide to the Eighteenth Century*. New York: Norton, 2003.

Dauer, Joanne C., and Edward A. Dauer. *American History as Seen Through Currency*. Ft. Lauderdale, FL: Dauer, 2006.

Davidson, Philip. *Propaganda and the American Revolution, 1763–1783*. Chapel Hill: University of North Carolina Press, 1941.

Davies, Glyn. *A History of Money from Ancient Times to the Present Day*. Third edition. Cardiff, UK: University of Wales Press, 2002.

Davies, Wallace Evan. *Patriotism on Parade: The Story of Veterans and Hereditary Organizations in America, 1783–1900*. Cambridge, MA: Harvard University Press, 1955.

Dead Kennedys. *In God We Trust, Inc.* Möbius Music, 1981.

Dean, Charles A., and Don C. Kelly. "What the Deuce!" *Paper Money* 37 (1998): 193–94.

DeLeonardis, William Justin. "America's First Dollar." *The Numismatist* 100:10 (October 1987): 2118–20.

_____. "The Eagle Motif on Early American Coinage." *The Numismatist* 100:5 (May 1987): 1017–1019.

_____. "The Liberty Motif on Early American Coinage." *The Numismatist* 101:10 (October 1988): 1741–44.

Del Mar, Alexander. *The History of Money in America: From the Earliest Times to the Establishment of the Constitution*. New York: Cambridge Encyclopedia Company, 1899.

Deloria, Philip. *Indians in Unexpected Places*. Lawrence, KS: University Press of Kansas, 2004.

Derrida, Jacques. *De la grammatologie*. Paris: Minuit, 1967.

_____. *Donner le temps: 1. la fausse monnaie*. Paris: Galilée, 1991. *Given Time: 1. Counterfeit Money*. Trans. Peggy Kamuf. Chicago: University of Chicago Press, 1992.

Dickens, Charles. *American Notes, etc.* The Nonesuch Dickens, vol. 18. Bloomsbury: Nonesuch Press, 1938.

_____. *Martin Chuzzlewit*. The Nonesuch Dickens, vol. 8. Bloomsbury: Nonesuch Press, 1937.

Dillistin, William H. *Bank Note Reporters and Counterfeit Detectors, 1826–1866*. New York: American Numismatic Society, 1949.

DiMaggio, Paul J. "Culture and Economy." *The Handbook of Economic Sociology*, ed. Neil J. Smelser and Richard Swedberg. Princeton: Princeton University Press, 1994. 27–57.

Doty, Richard G. *America's Money — America's Story*. Iola, WI: Krause Publications, 1998.

_____. *Pictures from a Distant Country: Images on 19th-Century U.S. Currency*. Raleigh, NC: Boson Books, 2004.

_____. "Surviving Images, Forgotten People: Native Americans, Women, and African Americans on United States Obsolete Banknotes." *The Banker's Art: Studies in Paper Money*, ed. Virginia H. Hewitt. London: British Museum Press, 1995. 118–31.

_____, ed. *The Token: America's Other Money*. New York: American Numismatic Society, 1995.

Douglas, Mary. *Purity and Danger: An Analysis of Pollution and Taboo*. London: Routledge, 1966.

Du Gay, Paul, et al. *Doing Cultural Studies: The Story of the Sony Walkman*. 1997; London: Sage, 2000.

_____, ed. *Production of Culture/Cultures of Production*. London: Sage/Open University, 1997.

Dunlap, William. *History of the Rise and Progress of the Arts of Design in the United States*. New York: G. P. Scott, 1834.

Dunne, Gerald T. *Monetary Decisions of the Supreme Court*. New Brunswick, NJ: Rutgers University Press, 1960.

Durand, Roger H. "Here Comes Santa Claus, Here Comes Santa Claus, Right Down Counterfeit Lane." *The Numismatist* 121:12 (December 2008): 77–78.

_____. *Interesting Notes About History*. Rehoboth, MA: R. H. Durand, 1990.

_____. *Interesting Notes About Indians*. Rehoboth, MA: R. H. Durand, 1991.

Eagleton, Catherine, and Jonathan Williams. *Money: A History*. Second edition. London: The British Museum Press, 2007.

Ebenstein, Lanny. *Milton Friedman: A Biography*. New York: Palgrave-Macmillan, 2006.

Edelson, Howard L. *The American Numismatic Society, 1858–1958*. New York: ANS, 1958.

Edensor, Tim. *National Identity, Popular Culture and Everyday Life*. Oxford: Berg, 2002.

Ehrenreich, Barbara. *Fear of Falling: The Inner Life of the Middle Class*. New York: Pantheon Books, 1989.

Eliot, George. *Silas Marner. The Weaver of Raveloe*. 1861; Mineola, NY: Dover, 1996.

Ellis, Richard J. *To the Flag: The Unlikely History of the Pledge of Allegiance*. Lawrence: University Press of Kansas, 2005.

Emerson, Ralph Waldo. "The American Scholar." *The Heath Anthology of American Literature*, ed. Paul Lauter et al. Vol.1. Lexington, MA–Toronto: D.C. Heath, 1990. 1499–1511.

_____. "Nature." *The Heath Anthology of American Literature*, ed. Paul Lauter et al. Vol.1. Lexington, MA–Toronto: D.C. Heath, 1990. 1471–98.

_____. "Self-Reliance." *The Heath Anthology of American Literature*, ed. Paul Lauter et al. Vol.1. Lexington, MA–Toronto: D.C. Heath, 1990. 1511–1528.

European Central Bank. *Euro Banknote Design Exhibition*. Frankfurt am Main: European Central Bank, 2003.

European Commission. *Green Paper: On the Practical Arrangements for the Introduction of the Single Currency*. Brussels, 1995.

Evans, Robert D. "The S.S. Central America Treasure: Lessons from the Past." *The Numismatist* 121:4 (April 2008): 44–53.

Faul, Stephanie. *The Xenophobe's Guide to the Americans*. Horsham, UK: Ravelte Publications, 1997.

Feldman, Gerald D. *The Great Disorder: Politics, Economics, and Society in the German Inflation, 1914–1924*. New York: Oxford University Press, 1993.

Felt, Joseph B. *An Historical Account of Massachusetts Currency*. Boston, MA: Perkins and Marvin, 1839.

Fenstermaker, J. Van. *The Development of American Commercial Banking: 1782–1837*. Kent, OH: Kent State University Press, 1957.

Ferguson, Niall. *The Ascent of Money: A Financial History of the World*. New York: Penguin, 2008.

Ferguson, Robert A. *The American Enlightenment, 1750–1820*. Cambridge, MA: Harvard University Press, 1997.

Fichte, Johann G. *Der geschlossne Handelsstaat*. 1800; Leipzig: Meiner, 1943.

Finley, Robert. "Dialogues on the African Colony." *Memoirs of the Reverend Robert Finley, D.D.*, ed. Isaac V. Brown. New Brunswick, NJ, 1819. 313–45.

Fiske, John. *Reading the Popular*. London: Unwin Hyman, 1989.

_____. *Understanding Popular Culture*. London: Unwin Hyman, 1989.

Fitzpatrick, Robert, Dorothy Lichtenstein, and Leo Castelli. *Roy Lichtenstein*. Manchester, VT: Hudson Hills Press, 2001.

Fleming, E. McClung. "The American Images as Indian Princess, 1765–1783." *Winterthur Portfolio* 2 (1965): 65–81.

_____. "From Indian Princess to Greek Goddess: The American Image 1783–1815." *Winterthur Portfolio* 3 (1967): 37–66.

Fleming, Paula Richardson, and Judith Luskey. *The North American Indians in Early Photographs*. New York: Harper & Row, 1986.

Fliegelman, Jay. *Prodigals and Pilgrims: The American Revolution Against Patriarchal Authority, 1750–1800*. New York: Cambridge University Press, 1982.

Fluck, Winfried. "'Money Is God.' Materialism, Economic Individualism, and Expressive Individualism." *Negotiations of America's National Identity*, ed. Roland Hagenbüchle and Josef Raab. Tübingen: Stauffenberg Verlag, 2000. 431–46.

_____. "What is so bad about being rich? The representation of wealth in American culture." *Comparative American Studies* 1:1 (2003): 53–79.

Foner, Eric, ed. *Our Lincoln: New Perspectives on Lincoln and His World*. New York: W. W. Norton, 2008.

Forbes, Esther. *Paul Revere and the World He Lived In*. Boston: Houghton Mifflin, 1943.

Formisano, Ronald P. "State Development in the Early Republic: Substance and Structure, 1780–1840." *Contesting Democracy: Substance and Structure in American Political History, 1775–2000*, ed. Byron E. Shafer and Anthony J. Badger. Lawrence: University Press of Kansas, 2001. 7–35.

Forster, Kurt W. "Abbild und Gegenstand: Amerikanische Stilleben des späten 19. Jahrhunderts." *Bilder aus der Neuen Welt. Amerikanische Malerei des 18. und 19. Jahrhunderts*, ed. Thomas W. Gaethgens. München: Prestel-Verlag, 1988. 100–107.

Foucault, Michel. *The Order of Things: An Archaeology of the Human Sciences*. New York: Pantheon, 1970.

Fox, Richard Wightman, and T. J. Jackson Lears, eds. *The Culture of Consumption: Critical Essays in American History, 1880–1980*. New York: Pantheon, 1983.

Frankel, Jeffrey. "Dollar." *The New Palgrave Dictionary of Money and Finance*, ed. Peter Newman et al. London: Macmillan — New York: Stockton Press, 1991. 1: 696–701.

Frankenstein, Alfred. *After the Hunt: William Harnett and Other American Still-Life Painters, 1870–1900*. 1953; Berkeley: University of California Press, 1969.

Franklin, Benjamin. "Advice to a Young Tradesman." *The Heath Anthology of American Literature*, ed. Paul Lauter. Vol. 1. Lexington, MA–Toronto: D.C. Heath, 1990. 793–94.

_____. "From *The Autobiography*." *The Heath Anthology of American Literature*, ed. Paul Lauer. vol. 1. Lexington, MA–Toronto: D.C. Heath, 1990. 823–81.

_____. "From *Poor Richard's Almanacks*." *The Heath Anthology of American Literature*, ed. Paul Lauer. Vol. 1. Lexington, MA–Toronto: D.C. Heath, 1990. 780–83.

_____. "The Way to Wealth." *The Heath Anthology*

of American Literature, ed. Paul Lauer. Vol. 1. Lexington, MA–Toronto: D.C. Heath, 1990. 784–89.

Friedberg, Arthur L., and Ira L. Friedberg. Introduction and Narrative by Q. David Bowers. *A Guide Book of United States Paper Money: Complete Source for History, Grading, and Prices. Federal Currency Complete 1861 to Date.* Racine, WI: Whitman, 2005.

_____. *Paper Money of the United States. A Complete Illustrated Guide with Valuations.* Sixteenth Edition. Clifton, NJ: The Coin & Currency Institute, 2001.

Friedman, Milton, and Anna Jacobson Schwartz. *A Monetary History of the United States, 1867–1960.* Princeton, NJ: Princeton University Press, 1971, 1993.

_____. *Monetary Statistics of the United States: Estimates, Sources, Methods.* New York: National Bureau of Economic Research, 1970.

Fuld, George. "Early Washington Medals." *American Journal of Numismatics.* Second Series. 14 (2002): 105–63.

Furnham, Adrian, and Michael Argyle. *The Psychology of Money.* London–New York: Routledge, 1998.

Furtwangler, Albert. *Acts of Discovery: Visions of America in the Lewis and Clark Journals.* Urbana and Chicago: University of Illinois Press, 1993.

Gabriel, Gottfried. *Ästhetik und Rhetorik des Geldes.* Stuttgart-Bad Cannstatt: Frommann-Holzboog, 2002.

Gaddis, William. *JR.* New York: Knopf, 1976.

Galbraith, John Kenneth. *The Great Crash, 1929.* Boston: Houghton Mifflin, 1955.

_____. *Money: Whence It Came, Where It Went.* Boston: Houghton Mifflin, 1975.

_____. *A Short History of Financial Euphoria.* Knoxville, TN: Whittle Direct Books, 1990.

Ganz, David L. "The Motto Must Go: Yes or No?" *The Numismatist* 116:5 (May 2003): 39–42.

_____. "Reconsidering the Small-Sized Dollar Coin." *The Numismatist* 101:3 (March 1988): 441–49.

Garrett, Jeff, and Ron Guth. *100 Greatest U.S. Coins.* Second Edition. Atlanta, GA: Whitman, 2005.

Garson, Robert. "Counting Money: The United States Dollar and American Nationhood, 1781–1820." *Journal of American Studies* 35:1 (2001): 21–46.

Gasque, Thomas J. "Naming with Lewis and Clark: 2002 Presidential Address, December 28, 2002." *Names: A Journal of Onomastics* 51:1 (March 2003): 3–11.

Gates, Henry Louis, Jr., and Donald Yacovone, eds. *Lincoln on Race and Slavery.* Princeton, NJ: Princeton University Press, 2009.

Gates, Paul Wallace. "The Role of the Land Speculator in Western Development." *The Public Lands*, ed. Vernon Carstensen. Madison: University of Wisconsin Press, 1963. 349–74.

Gernalzick, Nadja. *Kredit und Kultur: Ökonomie- und Geldbegriff bei Jacques Derrida und in der amerikanischen Literaturtheorie der Postmoderne.* Amer-

ican Studies Monograph Series, vol. 80. Heidelberg: Winter, 2000.

Gibbs, William. "Recent Dollar designs face critical onslaught: creative process different for each new dollar design." *Coin World* 27, no. 1387. Sidney, OH, November 12, 1986. 1–3.

Gilbert, Emily. "'Ornamenting the Façade of Hell': Iconographies of 19th-Century Canadian Paper Money." *Environment and Planning D: Society and Space* 16 (1998): 57–80.

_____, and Eric Helleiner, eds. *Nation-States and Money: The Past, Present, and Future of National Currencies.* London–New York: Routledge, 1999.

Gillis, John R. "Memory and Identity: The History of a Relationship." *Commemorations: The Politics of National Identity*, ed. the same. Princeton, NJ: Princeton University Press, 1994. 3–24.

Ginsberg, Allen. "American Change." *Concise Anthology of American Literature.* Fourth Edition, ed. George McMichael. Fourth Edition. Upper Saddle River, NJ: Prentice Hall, 1988. 2112–14.

Glaser, Lynn. *Counterfeiting in America: The History of an American Way to Wealth.* New York: Clarkson N. Potter, 1968.

Goethe, Johann Wolfgang von. *Faust Part Two.* Trans. David Luke. Oxford: Oxford University Press, 1999.

Goetsch, Paul. "The Fourth of July in American Literature." *The Fourth of July: Political Oratory and Literary Reactions, 1776–1876*, ed. the same and Gerd Hurm. Tübingen: G. Narr Verlag, 1992. 33–55.

Goldmann, Lucien. *The Hidden God. A Study of Tragic Vision in the Pensées of Pascal and the Tragedies of Racine.* Trans. from the French by Philip Thody. London: Routledge & Kegan Paul/New York: Humanities Press, 1964.

Goldstein, Erik, and Joseph Lasser. "Worn, Torn, and Soiled. Old, tattered, and mended notes from America's colonial era are the real thing." *The Numismatist* 121:9 (September 2008): 44–49.

Goode, James M. *The Outdoor Sculpture of Washington, D.C.: A Comprehensive Historical Guide.* Washington, DC: Smithsonian Institution Press, 1974.

_____. *Washington Sculpture: A Cultural History of Outdoor Sculpture in the Nation's Capital.* Baltimore, MD: Johns Hopkins University Press, 2009.

Goodwin, Jason. *Greenback: The Almighty Dollar and the Invention of America.* New York: Henry Holt, 2003.

Gorton, Gary. "Reputation Formation in Early Bank Note Markets." *Journal of Political Economy* 104 (1996): 346–97.

Gouge, William M. *The Curse of Paper-Money and Banking; or a Short History of Banking in the United States of America with an account of its ruinous effects on landowners, farmers, traders, and on all the industrious classes of the community.* London: 1833; New York: Greenwood Press, 1968.

Goux, Jean-Joseph. "Cash, Check, or Charge?" Trans. John R. Barbaret. *The New Economic Crit-*

icism: Studies at the Intersection of Literature and Economics, ed. Martha Woodmansee and Mark Osteen. New York–London: Routledge, 1999. 114–27. Orig. published in French in *Communications* 50 (1989): 7–22.

_____. *The Coiners of Language*. Trans. Jennifer Curtiss Gage. Norman: University of Oklahoma Press, 1994; orig. *Les monnayeurs du langage*. Paris: Galilée, 1984.

_____. "Numismatics: An Essay in Theoretical Numismatics." *Symbolic Economies: After Marx and Freud*. Trans. Jennifer Curtiss Gage. Ithaca, NY: Cornell University Press, 1990. 9–63; orig. published in French in *Tel Quel* in 1968–1969, and republished in *Freud, Marx. Économie et symbolique*. Paris: Éditions du Seuil, 1973.

Govan, Thomas. *Nicholas Biddle: Nationalist and Public Banker, 1786–1884*. Chicago: University of Chicago Press, 1959.

de Gramont, Scipion. *Le Denier royal, traité curieux de l'or et de l'argent*. Paris, 1620.

Greenberg, Maurice R. "Money, Money Everywhere...." *The National Interest* 6:2 (July/August 2007): 17–19.

Gregory, Barbara J. "Numismatist in Action." *The Numismatist* 119:9 (September 2006): 107.

Greider, William. *Secrets of the Temple: How the Federal Reserve Runs the Country*. New York: Simon & Schuster, 1989.

Griffin, Des. *Descent Into Slavery?* 1980; Colton, OR: Emissary Publications, 1994.

_____. *The Missing Dimension in World Affairs*. South Pasadena, CA: Emissary Publications, 1981.

Griffiths, William H. *The Story of the American Bank Note Company*. New York: American Bank Note Company, 1959.

Grossberg, Lawrence. "Cultural Studies: What's in a Name? (One More Time) [1995]." *Bringing It All Back Home: Essays on Cultural Studies*. Durham, NC: Duke University Press, 1997. 245–71.

_____, Cary Nelson, and Paula Treichler, eds. *Cultural Studies*. New York: Routledge, 1992.

Hacker, Andrew. "Patriot Games." *The New York Review of Books* LI: 11 (June 24, 2004): 28–31.

Hall, Dennis R., and Susan Grove Hall, eds. *American Icons: An Encyclopedia of the People, Places, and Things That Have Shaped Our Culture*. 3 vols. Westport, CT: Greenwood Press, 2006.

Hall, Stuart. "Cultural Studies: Two Paradigms [1980]." Jessica Munns and Gita Rajan, eds., *A Cultural Studies Reader: History, Theory, Practice*. London–New York: Longman, 1995. 194–205.

_____. "The Question of Cultural Identity." *Modernity and Its Futures*, ed. Stuart Hall, David Held and Tony McGrew. Milton Keynes: Polity Press/ The Open University, 1992. 273–316.

_____, ed. *Representation: Cultural Representations and Signifying Practices*. London: Sage/The Open University, 1997.

Hall, Susan Grove, with Dennis Hall. "Mount Rushmore." *American Icons: An Encyclopedia of the People, Places, and Things That Have Shaped Our Cul-* *ture*, ed. Dennis R. Hall and Susan Grove Hall. Westport, CT: Greenwood Press, 2006. II: 493–500.

Halliwell, Martin. *American Culture in the 1950s*. Edinburgh: Edinburgh University Press, 2007.

Hammond, Bray. *Banks and Politics in America from the Revolution to the Civil War*. Second edition. 1957; Princeton, NJ: Princeton University Press, 1991.

_____. *Sovereignty and an Empty Purse: Banks and Politics in the Civil War*. Princeton, NJ: Princeton University Press, 1970.

Harris, Marvin. *Cultural Materialism: A Struggle for a Science of Culture*. New York: Random House, 1979.

Harris, W. C. *E Pluribus Unum: Nineteenth-Century Literature and the Constitutional Paradox*. Iowa City: University of Iowa Press, 2005.

Harvey, James. *Paper Money: The Money of Civilization. An Issue by the State, and a Legal Tender in Payment of Taxes*. London: Provost, 1877.

Haskill, Irene, David T. Graham, and Eleonore Kofman. *Human Geography of the UK: An Introduction*. London: Routledge, 2001.

Haxby, James A. *Standard Catalog of United States Obsolete Bank Notes, 1782–1866*. Four volumes. Iola, WI: Krause Publications, 1988.

Hayek, Friedrich von. *Denationalization of Money*. London: Institute of Economic Affairs, 1990.

_____. *Rules and Order*. Chicago: University of Chicago Press, 1973.

Hayes, Carlton J. H. *Nationalism: A Religion* (New York: Macmillan, 1960).

Heclo, Hugh. "Is America a Christian Nation?" *Political Science Quarterly* 122:1 (2007): 59–87.

Hedges, William L. "The Myth of the Republic and the Theory of American Literature." *Prospects* 4 (1979): 101–20.

Hefferman, James. "Ekphrasis and Representation." *New Literary History* 22:2 (Spring 1991): 297–316.

Heintze, James R. *The Fourth of July Encyclopedia*. Jefferson, NC: McFarland, 2007.

Helleiner, Eric. "Historicizing Territorial Currencies: Money and the Nation-State in North America." *Political Geography* 18 (1999): 309–39.

_____. *The Making of National Money: Territorial Currencies in Historical Perspective*. Ithaca, NY: Cornell University Press, 2003.

_____. "National Currencies and National Identities." *American Behavioral Scientist* 41:10 (1998): 1409–36.

Henkin, David. *City Reading: Written Words and Public Spaces in Antebellum New York*. New York: Columbia University Press, 1998.

Hertsgaard, Mark. *The Eagle's Shadow: Why America Fascinates and Infuriates the World*. New York: Farrar, Straus and Giroux, 2002.

Hess, Wolfgang, and Dietrich O. Klose. *Vom Taler zum Dollar 1486–1986*. Munich: Staatliche Münzensammlung München, 1986.

Hessler, Gene. "The American West. A Glimpse on U.S. Paper Money." *International Bank Note Society Journal* 21:4 (December 1982): 110–11.

_____. *The Engraver's Line: An Encyclopedia of Paper*

Money and Postage Stamp Art. Port Clinton, OH: BNR Press, 1993.

_____. "The Environment and the American Indian as Seen on Nineteenth-Century Bank Notes." *Paper Money* 23:2 (March-April 1984): 75–78.

_____. "The History and Development of 'America' as Symbolized by an American Indian Female." *America's Currency, 1789–1866.* Coinage of the Americas Conference, Proceedings No. 2, ed. William E. Metcalf. New York: American Numismatic Society, 1986. 81–88.

_____. *The International Engraver's Line: Paper Money and Postage Stamp Engravers and Their Work from the 1700s to the Euro.* Port Clinton, OH: BNR Press, 2005.

_____. "The National Motto's Currency Evolution." *Bank Note Reporter* 9:6 (Citra, FL, June 1981): 16.

_____. "Precursors of the Motto 'In God We Trust' on U.S. Paper Money and Design Background for Related Notes." *Paper Money* 17:1 (January-February, 1978): 10–14.

_____. "A Sneak Peak at the Edison Essay." *The Numismatist* 117:5 (May 2004): 66–67.

_____. "Symbolism on the U.S. Greenback." *International Bank Note Society Journal* 22:2 (July 1983): 53.

_____. *U.S. Essay, Proof, and Specimen Notes.* 2nd edition. Port Clinton, OH: BNR Press, 2004.

_____. "The United States' First Dollar Note." *The Numismatist* 105:8 (August 1992): 1106–1107.

_____. "Unofficial Commemorative Notes." *The Numismatist* 105:5 (May 1992): 656–58.

_____. "Women on U.S. Banknotes." *International Bank Note Society Journal* 18:3 (January 1980): 67–68, 85.

_____, and Carlson Chambliss. *The Comprehensive Catalog of U.S. Paper Money, 1812 to Present.* 7th edn. Port Clinton, OH: BNR Press, 2006.

Hewitt, Virginia H. *Beauty and the Banknote: Images of Women on Paper Money.* London: British Museum Press, 1994.

_____. "Soft Images, Hard Currency: the Portrayal of Women on Paper Money." *The Banker's Art: Studies in Paper Money,* ed. the same. London: British Museum Press, 1995. 156–65.

Heywood, E. H. *Hard Cash: an Essay to show that financial monopolies ... will be effectively prevented only through Free Money.* Princeton, MA: Co-operative, 1974.

Hickman, John, and Dean Oakes, *Standard Catalog of National Bank Notes.* Iola, WI: Krause Publications, 1982.

Higonnet, Patrice. *Attendant Cruelties: Nation and Nationalism in American History.* New York: Other Press, 2007.

Hobsbawm, Eric. "Introduction: Inventing Traditions." *The Invention of Tradition,* ed. Eric Hobsbawm and Terence Ranger. Cambridge, UK: Cambridge University Press, 1983. 1–14.

_____. "Mass-Producing Traditions: Europe, 1870–1914." *The Invention of Tradition,* ed. Eric Hobsbawm and Terence Ranger. Cambridge, UK: Cambridge University Press, 1983. 263–307.

_____. *Nations and Nationalism Since 1870: Programme, Myth, Reality.* Cambridge, UK: Cambridge University Press, 1990.

_____, and Terence Ranger, eds. *The Invention of Tradition.* Cambridge, UK: Cambridge University Press, 1983.

Hochbruck, Wolfgang. "Edward Everett's Union Rhetoric." *The Fourth of July: Political Oratory and Literary Reactions, 1776–1876,* ed. Paul Goetsch and Gerd Hurm. Tübingen: G. Narr Verlag, 1992. 113–20.

Hodges, Edward M. *Hodges' American Bank Note Safe-Guard.* New York, 1865; reprinted Anderson, SC: Pennell, 1977.

Holdsworth, John T., and Davis R. Dewey. *The First and Second Banks of the United States.* Washington, DC: National Monetary Commission, 1911.

Houck, Davis W. *FDR and Fear Itself: The First Inaugural Address.* College Station, TX: Texas A&M University Press, 2002.

_____. *Rhetoric as Currency: Hoover, Roosevelt, and the Great Depression.* College Station: Texas A&M University Press, 2001.

Houghton, John W. *Culture and Currency: Cultural Bias in Monetary Theory and Policy.* Boulder, CO: Westview Press, 1991.

Hughes, Brent H. "How Dixie Got Its Name." *Paper Money* 25 (1986): 123.

Hughes, Robert. *American Visions: The Epic History of Art in America.* New York: Knopf, 1997.

Huntington, Samuel P. *Who Are We? Challenges to America's National Identity.* New York: Simon & Schuster, 2004.

Huntoon, Peter. "73 Years of United States National Currency, 1863–1935." *ANA (American Numismatic Association) Journal* 1:1 (Spring 2006): 19–28.

Hurst, James Willard. *A Legal History of Money in the United States, 1794–1970.* 1973; Frederick, MD: Beard Books, 2001.

Hutchinson, Harry D. *Money, Banking, and the United States Economy.* Seventh edition. Englewood Cliffs, NJ: Prentice Hall, 1992.

Ingham, Geoffrey. *The Nature of Money.* Cambridge, UK: Polity Press, 2004.

Irons, Peter. *God on Trial: Dispatches from America's Religious Battlefields.* New York: Viking, 2007.

Irving, Washington. "The Creole Village." *Wolfert's Roost,* ed. Roberta Rosenberg. *The Complete Works of Washington Irving,* vol. 27. Boston: Twayne, 1979. 22–28.

_____. "The Devil and Tom Walker." *Tales of a Traveller. By Geoffrey Crayon, Gent,* ed. Judith Giblin Haig, with the cooperation of Brom Weber and David Wilson. *The Complete Works of Washington Irving,* vol. 10. Boston: Twayne, 1987. 217–27.

Jackson, Andrew. "The Power of the Moneyed Interests" (1837). *American Culture: An Anthology of Civilization Texts,* ed. Anders Breidlid et al. London–New York: Routledge, 1996. 203–4.

Jackson, Glenn E. "The 'Eagle of the Capitol': the Bureau of Engraving and Printing alters an American Banknote Co. Vignette." *Essay-Proof Journal* 32:4 (Jefferson, WI, Fall 1975): 160–62.

———. "Side Lights on the Five Dollar 'Onepapa' [sic!] Note Design." *Essay-Proof Journal* 33:3 (Summer 1976): 140–42.

Jackson, Kevin. "Introduction." *The Oxford Book of Money*, ed. the same. Oxford–New York: Oxford University Press, 1995. vii–xvi.

———, ed. *The Oxford Book of Money*. Oxford–New York: Oxford University Press, 1995.

John, Richard R. "Governmental Institutions as Agents of Change: Rethinking American Political Development in the Early Republic, 1787–1835." *Studies in American Political Development* 11 (1997): 347–80.

Johnson, Anne Akers. *The Buck Book: All Sorts of Things to Do with a Dollar Bill — Besides Spend It.* Palo Alto, CA: Klutz, 1993.

Johnson, Calvin H. *Righteous Anger at the Wicked States: The Meaning of the Founders' Constitution.* New York: Cambridge University Press, 2005.

Johnson, David R. *Illegal Tender: Counterfeiting and the Secret Service in Nineteenth-Century America.* Washington, DC: Smithsonian Institution Press, 1995.

Johnson, Richard. "The Story So Far: And Further Transformations?" *Introduction to Contemporary Cultural Studies*, ed. David Punter. London–New York: Longman, 1986. 277–313.

"Join Us in Celebrating Our 100th Year." *The Numismatist* 101:1 (January 1988): 9.

Jones, Alice Hanson. *Wealth of a Nation to Be.* New York: Columbia University Press, 1980.

Judt, Tony. "Anti-Americans Abroad." *The New York Review of Books* (May 1, 2003): 24–27.

Kagin, Donald. "The First Attempts at Paper Currency in America." *The Numismatist* 86:4 (April 1973): 543–52.

Kaminski, John P., and Jill Adair McCaughan, eds. *A Great and Good Man: George Washington in the Eyes of His Contemporaries.* Madison: University of Wisconsin Press, 1989.

Kaplan, Amy. "'Left Alone with America': The Absence of Empire in the Study of American Culture." *Cultures of United States Imperialism*, ed. Amy Kaplan and Donald E. Pease. Durham, NC: Duke University Press, 1993. 3–21.

Kay, Marvin. "The United States $2 Bill, Series 1976." *Canadian Numismatic Journal* 21:7 (Willowdale, Ontario, July-August 1976): 289–91.

Keiser, Albert. *The Indian in American Literature.* New York: Oxford University Press, 1933.

Kennedy, Caroline, ed. *A Patriot's Handbook: Songs, Poems, Stories and Speeches Celebrating the Land We Love.* New York: Hyperion Press, 2003.

Kennedy, David M. *Freedom from Fear: The American People in Depression and War, 1929–1945.* Oxford: Oxford University Press, 1999.

Kennedy, Susan Estabrook. *The Banking Crisis of 1933.* Lexington: University of Kentucky Press, 1973.

Kiewe, Amos. *FDR's First Fireside Chat: Public Confidence and the Banking Crisis.* College Station: Texas A & M University Press, 2007.

Kirkland, Frazaar. *Cyclopaedia of Commercial and Business Anecdotes.* 2 vols. New York: D. Appleton, 1864.

Kirshner, Jonathan. *Currency and Coercion: The Political Economy of International Monetary Power.* Princeton, NJ: Princeton University Press, 1997.

Kleeberg, John M. "Introduction." *Money of Pre-Federal America*, ed. John M. Kleeberg. Coinage of the Americas Conference Proceedings, Number 7. New York: American Numismatic Society, 1992. ix–xi.

Knox, John Jay. *History of Banking in the United States.* New York: Scribners's, 1899.

Koja, Stephan, ed. *America: The New World in 19th-Century Painting.* Österreichische Galerie Belvedere, 13 March — 20 June 1999. Munich et al.: Prestel, 1999.

Korver, R. Bruce "'Tis Death to Counterfeit." *The Numismatist* 103:6 (June 1990): 896–904, 996–1000, 1006–1007.

Kotte, Eugen. "USA. Konsens und Mission." *Mythen der Nationen. Ein europäisches Panorama*, ed. Monika Flacke. Berlin: Deutsches Historisches Museum, 1998. 557–75.

Kraljevich, John J., Jr. "Freedom of Expression." *The Numismatist* 121:4 (April 2008): 73–76.

Kramer, Jürgen. *British Cultural Studies.* München: Fink, 1997.

Kranister, Willibald. *Die Geldmacher international.* Wien: Verlag der österreichischen Staatsdruckerei/Edition S, 1989.

———. *The Moneymakers International.* Cambridge, UK: Black Bear Publications, 1989.

Krass, Stephan. "In God We Trust. Der Dollar als Botschaft" [The Dollar as Message]." *Merkur* 56:5 (May 2002): 444–51.

Krause, Chester L., and Robert F. Lemke. *The Standard Catalog of United States Paper Money.* 24th edition, ed. Joel T. Edler. Iola, WI: Krause Publications, 2005.

Kreis, Karl Markus. "'Indians' on Old Picture Postcards." *European Review of Native American Studies* 6:1 (1992): 39–48.

Krieger, Murray. *Ekphrasis: The Illusion of the Natural Sign.* Baltimore, MD: Johns Hopkins University Press, 1992.

Krooss, Herman E., ed. *Documentary History of Banking and Currency in the United States.* Introduction by Paul A. Samuelson. 4 vols. 1969; New York: Chelsea House, 1983.

Krugman, Paul R. *The Great Unraveling: Losing Our Way in the New Century.* New York: W. W. Norton, 2003.

———. "What to Do." *The New York Review of Books* LV: 20 (December 18, 2008): 8–10.

———. "Who Was Milton Freeman?" *The New York Review of Books* LIV: 2 (February 15, 2007): 27–30.

Kuhl, Jason F. "The Portrayal of Native Americans on U.S. Coinage." *The Numismatist* 114:2 (February 2001): 150–55.

Lacan, Jacques. *Écrits. A Selection*. Trans. Alan Sheridan. New York: Norton, 1977.

LaHaye, Tim, and Jerry B. Jenkins. *Left Behind: The Earth's Last Days*. Carol Stream, IL: Tyndale House, 1995.

Lapham, Lewis. *Money and Class in America: Notes and Observations on Our Civil Religion*. New York: Grove Press, 1988.

Lasser, Joseph R., with Erik Goldstein. "My Short Snorter." *The Numismatist* 122:5 (May 2009): 44–49.

Laum, Bernard. *Heiliges Geld. Eine historische Untersuchung über den sakralen Ursprung des Geldes*. Tübingen: Mohr, 1924.

Lause, Mark A. *The Civil War's Last Campaign: James B. Weaver, the Greenback-Labor Party and the Politics of Race and Section*. Lanham, MD: University Press of America, 2001.

Lears, T. Jackson. *Something for Nothing: Luck in America*. New York: Viking, 2003.

Lemay, J. A. Leo. *The Life of Benjamin Franklin*. 3 Volumes. Philadelphia: University of Pennsylvania Press, 2005–2008.

Lemon, Alaina. "Your Eyes Are Green Like Dollars: Counterfeit Cash, National Substance, and Currency Apartheid in 1990s Russia." *Cultural Anthropology* 13/1 (1998): 22–55.

Lerner, Eugene M. "The Monetary and Fiscal Programs of the Confederate Government, 1861–1865." *Journal of Political Economy* 62 (1954): 507–25.

Levin, Harry. *The Power of Blackness*. Columbus: Ohio University Press, 1980.

Lewis, Michael. "Leave Home Without It: The Absurdity of the American Express Card." *Money Culture*. New York: Penguin Books, 1992. 11–20.

Lewis, R.W.B. *American Adam: Innocence, Tragedy, and Tradition in the Nineteenth Century*. Chicago–London: University of Chicago Press, 1955.

Lighter, J. E., ed. *Historical Dictionary of American Slang*. Vol. 1. *A–G*. New York: Random House, 1994.

Livingston, James. *Origins of the Federal Reserve System: Money, Class, and Corporate Capitalism, 1890–1913*. Ithaca, NY: Cornell University Press, 1986.

Livingstone, Marco. *Pop Art: A Continuing History*. London: Thames & Hudson, 2000.

Locke, John. *An Essay Concerning Human Understanding*. London: Elibron Classics/Adamant Media, 2006.

Locker, David J. "Native American Images on U.S. Coins, Part 1." *Numismatist* 119:8 (August 2006): 52–61.

_____. "Native American Images on U.S. Coins, Part 2." *Numismatist* 119:9 (September 2006): 56–63.

_____. "Native American Images on U.S. Coins, Part 3." *Numismatist* 119:10 (October 2006): 60–66.

Lott, Davis Newton. *The Presidents Speak: The Inaugural Addresses of the American President, from Washington to Clinton*. New York: Henry Holt, 1994.

Louderback, Jim. "The Disappearing Dollar?" *The Numismatist* 117:1 (January 2004): 101–102.

Lundstrom, Marjie. "Sacagawea dollar coin? Californians just aren't buying the idea." *Sacramento Bee* (September 21, 2002).

de Lys, Claudia. *A Treasury of American Superstitions*. New York: New York Public Library, 1990.

MacCannell, Dean. "Sights and Spectacles." *Iconicity: Essays on the Nature of Culture. Festschrift for Thomas A. Sebeok on His 65th Birthday*, ed. Paul Bouissac, Michael Herzfeld, Roland Posner. Tübingen: Stauffenberg Verlag, 1986. 421–35.

MacCash, Doug. "Message Money." *The Times–Picayune* (New Orleans, June 22, 2003). Sec E: 1–3.

MacGrane, Reginald Charles. *The Panic of 1837: Some Financial Problems of the Jacksonian Era*. Chicago: University of Chicago Press, 1924.

Mackay, Hugh, ed. *Consumption and Everyday Life*. London: Sage/Open University, 1997.

Madison, James. "To the People of the State of New York." *The Heath Anthology of American Literature*, ed. Paul Lauter et al. Volume 1. Lexington, MA–Toronto: D. C. Heath, 1990. 1013–18.

Maier, Pauline. *American Scripture: Making the Declaration of Independence*. New York: Knopf, 1997.

Malaby, Thomas. *Making Virtual Worlds: Linden Lab and Second Life*. Ithaca, NY: Cornell University Press, 2009.

Male, Roy R., ed. *Money Talks: Language and Lucre in American Fiction*. Norman: University of Oklahoma Press, 1980.

Mannheim, Bruce. "Iconicity." *Key Terms in Language and Culture*, ed. Alessandro Duranti. Malden, MA–Oxford, UK: Blackwell, 2001. 102–5.

Marcellus, Jane. "Nervous Women and Noble Savages: The Romanticized 'Other' in Nineteenth-Century US Patent Medicine Advertising." *Journal of Popular Culture* 41:5 (October 2008): 784–808.

Marotta, Michael E. "Short Snorters: Keeping the Tradition Alive." *The Numismatist* 115:11 (November 2002): 1302–1305.

Martin, David A. "The Changing Role of Foreign Money in the United States, 1782–1857." *Journal of Economic History* 37 (1997): 1009–1027.

Marx, Karl. *Capital*. Trans. Eden Paul and Cedar Paul. New York: Dutton, 1930.

_____. *A Contribution to the Critique of Political Economy* [1859]. Trans. W. I. Stone. Chicago: Charles H. Kerr, 1904.

_____. *Grundrisse: Foundations of the Critique of Political Economy* [1857–58], ed. David McLellan. London: Paladin, 1980.

_____, and Friedrich Engels, *The Communist Manifesto*. Trans. David McClellan. Oxford: Oxford University Press, 1992.

Marx, Leo. *The Machine in the Garden: Technology and the Pastoral Ideal in America*. Oxford: Oxford University Press, 1964.

Massey, J. Earl. *America's Money: The Story of Our Coins and Currency*. New York: Crowell, 1968.

Matusow, Allen J. *Nixon's Economy: Booms, Busts,*

Dollars, and Votes. Lawrence: University Press of Kansas, 1998.

McCullough, David. *The Part Between the Seas: The Creation of the Panama Canal, 1870–1914.* New York: Simon & Schuster, 1977.

McCusker, John J. *How Much Is That in Real Money? A Historical Price Index for Use as a Deflator of Money Values in the Economy of the United States.* Second revised edition. Worcester, MA: American Antiquarian Society/Newcastle, DE: Oak Knoll, 2001.

_____. *Money and Exchange in Europe and America, 1600–1775: A Handbook.* Second Edition. Chapel Hill: University of North Carolina Press, 1992.

_____, and Russell R. Menard. *The Economy of British North America, 1607–1789.* Chapel Hill: University of North Carolina Press, 1985.

McDonald, Forrest. *Alexander Hamilton: A Biography.* New York: W. W. Norton, 1979.

_____. E Pluribus Unum: *The Formation of the American Republic, 1776–1790.* Second edition. Indianapolis, IN: The Liberty Fund, 1979.

_____. *Novus Ordo Seclorum: The Intellectual Origins of the Constitution.* Lawrence: University Press of Kansas, 1985.

McGinley, Christina L. "Coining Nationality: Woman as Spectacle on 19th Century Currency." *American Transcendental Quarterly* 7 (1993): 247–69.

McIlvaine, Paul. "Short Snorters of World War II." *The Numismatist* 122:5 (May 2009): 39–42.

McLaughlin, Kevin. "Just Fooling: Paper, Money, Poe." *Differences: A Journal of Feminist Cultural Studies* 11:1 (Spring, 1999): 38–67.

_____. *Paperwork: Fiction and Mass Mediacy in the Paper Age.* Philadelphia: University of Pennsylvania Press, 2005.

McMurtry, Larry. *Sacagawea's Nickname. Essays on the American West.* New York: New York Review Books, 2001.

_____. "Separate and Unequal." *New York Review of Books* XLVIII (March 8, 2001): 20–22.

Meltzer, Allan H. *A History of the Federal Reserve.* Vol. 1, *1913–1951.* Chicago: University of Chicago Press, 2002.

Melville, Herman. *The Confidence-Man: His Masquerade.* New York: Oxford University Press, 1989.

_____. *Moby-Dick.* Everyman's Library. London: Dent/New York: Dutton, 1969.

Merk, Frederick. *Manifest Destiny and Mission in American History: A Reinterpretation.* New York: Random House, 1966.

Meyers, Jeffrey. *Edgar Allan Poe: His Life and Legacy.* New York: Cooper Square Press, 1992.

Meyers, Joe. "Back from the Brink." *The Numismatist* 121:3 (March 2008): 44–47.

Meyerson, Michael I. *Liberty's Blueprint: How Madison and Hamilton Wrote the Federalist Papers, Defined the Constitution, and Made Democracy Safe for the World.* New York: Basic Books, 2008.

Michaelis, Anthony R. "OVD: The Bank Note of the Future." *IBNS (International Bank Note Society) Journal* 32:3 (September 1993): 5–14.

Michaels, Walter Benn. *The Gold Standard and the Logic of Naturalism: American Literature at the Turn of the Century.* Berkeley: University of California Press, 1987.

Michener, Ron, and Robert E. Wright. "State 'Currencies' and the Transition to the U.S. Dollar: Clarifying Some Confusions." *American Economic Review* (June 2005): 682–703.

Mihm, Stephen. "The Almighty Dollar at Home and Abroad: Transnational History and the Currency Question." *Almighty Dollar: Papers from the Velden Conference,* ed. Heinz Tschachler, Eugen Banauch, and Simone Puff. Wien: LIT Verlag, 2010.

_____. *A Nation of Counterfeiters: Capitalists, Con Men, and the Making of the United States.* Cambridge, MA: Harvard University Press, 2007.

Milder, Robert. "Herman Melville." *Columbia Literary History of the United States,* ed. Emory Elliott. New York: Columbia University Press, 1988. 429–47.

Miller, Arthur H. "Railroad." *American Icons: An Encyclopedia of the People, Places, and Things That Have Shaped Our Culture,* ed. Dennis R. Hall and Susan Grove Hall. Westport, CT: Greenwood Press, 2006. III: 585–91.

Mitchell, Ralph A., and Neil Shafer. *Standard Catalog of Depression Scrip of the United States: The 1930s.* Iola, WI: Krause Publications, 1983.

Mitchell, W.J.T. *Iconology: Image, Text, Ideology.* Chicago: University of Chicago Press, 1986.

_____. *Picture Theory: Essays on Verbal and Visual Representation.* Chicago: University of Chicago Press, 1994.

_____. *What Do Pictures Want? The Lives and Loves of Images.* Chicago: University of Chicago Press, 2006.

Mitchell, Wesley Clair. *A History of the Greenbacks.* Chicago: University of Chicago Press, 1903.

Moran, Michael F. *Striking Change: The Great Artistic Collaboration of Theodore Roosevelt and Augustus Saint-Gaudens.* Atlanta, GA: Whitman Publishing, 2007.

Morant, Mack Bernard. *African Americans on Stamps.* Jefferson, NC: McFarland, 2001.

Morris, Charles R. *The Trillion Dollar Meltdown: Easy Money, High Rollers, and the Great Credit Crash.* New York: PublicAffairs, 2008.

Mossman, Philip. *Money of the American Colonies and Confederation: A Numismatic, Economic, and Historical Correlation.* Numismatic Studies, vol. 20. New York: American Numismatic Society, 1993.

Mudd, Douglas A. "Image and Republican Sovereignty: Negotiating the Numismatic Iconography of the Early Republic." *ANA (American Numismatic Association) Journal* 1:1 (Spring 2006): 29–41.

Muller, Marion. "Folding Money." *The Numismatist* 101:2 (February 1988): 254–60.

Mundell, Robert A. "A Theory of Optimum Currency Areas." *American Economic Review* 51 (1961): 657–665.

Münder, Peter. "Zu wertvoll für die Kunst." *Süddeutsche Zeitung* (January 23/24, 1999): vii.

Münz- und Papergeld in Österreich, 1816–1966 [exhibition catalog], ed. Österreichische Nationalbank. Wien: ÖNB, 1966.

Muscalus, John A. *The Extensive Use of Christ on Paper Money Circulated in the United States.* Bridgeport, PA: J. A. Muscalus, 1968.

Nelson, Dana D. *National Manhood: Capitalist Citizenship and the Imagined Fraternity of White Men.* Durham, NC: Duke University Press, 1998.

Nettels, Curtis P. *The Money Supply of the American Colonies Before 1720.* Madison: University of Wisconsin Press, 1934.

"New Laws Impact 2009 Coins." *The Numismatist* 121:2 (February 2008): 37.

Newman, Eric P. "The Dollar $ign: Its Written and Printed Origins." *America's Silver Dollars,* ed. John M. Kleeberg. Coinage of the Americas Conference, Proceedings No. 9. New York: American Numismatic Society, 1995. 1–49.

_____. "The Earliest Money Using the Dollar as an Official Unit of Value." *The Numismatist* 98:11 (November 1985): 2181–2187.

_____. *The Early Paper Money of America.* Fourth edition. Iola, WI: Krause Publications, 1997.

_____. "The Successful British Counterfeiting of American Paper Money During the American Revolution." *British Numismatic Journal* 29 (1958): 174–87.

_____. "Unusual Printing Features on Early American Paper Money." *Money of Pre-Federal America,* ed. John M. Kleeberg. Coinage of the Americas Conference Proceedings No. 7. New York: American Numismatic Society, 1992. 59–83.

Nicholson, Colin. *Writing and the Rise of Finance: Capital Satires of the Early Eighteenth Century.* Cambridge, UK: Cambridge University Press, 1994.

Niven, John. *Samuel P. Chase: A Biography.* New York: Oxford University Press, 2002.

_____, ed. *The Salmon P. Chase Papers: Correspondence, 1858–March 1863,* vol. 3. Kent, OH: Kent State University Press, 1966.

"No Change, Please." *Kansas City Star* (September 30, 2002).

Nora, Pierre. "Between Memory and History: Les lieux de mémoire [1984]." *Representations* 26 (Spring 1989): 7–25.

_____. *Realms of Memory: Rethinking the French Past.* 3 vols. New York: Columbia University Press, 1996.

Norman, Russell. *The Novelist and Mammon: Literary Responses to the World of Commerce in the Nineteenth Century.* Oxford: Clarendon Press, 1986.

Norris, Frank. *McTeague. A Story of San Francisco. Novels and Essays.* New York: Library of America, 1986. 261–573.

Nugent, Walter T.K. *Money and American Society, 1865–80.* New York: Free Press, 1968.

"Numismatic Narratives." *The Numismatist* 101:10 (October 1988): 1727–1728.

Nussbaum, Arthur. *A History of the Dollar.* New York: Columbia University Press, 1957.

Nygren, Edward J. "The Almighty Dollar: Money as a Theme in American Painting." *Winterthur Portfolio* 23 (Summer-Autumn 1988): 129–50.

Oakes, Dean, and John Schwartz. *Standard Guide to Small-Size U.S. Paper Money, 1928 to Date.* Iola, WI: Krause Publications, 1974. 6th edition 2005. Iola, WI: Krause Publications/KP Books, 2005.

Oakes, James. *The Radical and the Republican: Frederick Douglass, Abraham Lincoln, and the Triumph of Antislavery Politics.* New York: Norton, 2007.

O'Donnell, Chuck. *The Standard Handbook of Modern United States Paper Money.* 7th ed. Iola, WI : Krause Publications, 1982.

"Offenses Against the Currency, Coinage, etc." *Statutes at Large.* Vol.35, pt.1. Washington, DC: Government Printing Office, 1909. Ch.7. 1115–22.

O'Leary, Cecilia Elizabeth. *To Die For: The Paradox of American Patriotism.* Princeton, NJ: Princeton University Press, 1998.

Oliver, Nancy Y., and Richard G. Kelly. "Illicit Craft." *The Numismatist* 120:11 (November 2007): 52–56.

Olson, Lester C. *Emblems of American Community in the Revolutionary Era: A Study in Rhetorical Iconology.* Washington, DC–London: Smithsonian Institution Press, 1991.

O'Malley, Michael. "Specie and Species: Race and the Money Question in Nineteenth-Century America." *The American Historical Review* 99:2 (April 1994): 369–395.

Orsmby, W. L. *A Description of the Present System of Bank Note Engraving, Showing Its Tendency to Facilitate Counterfeiting; to Which Is Added a New Method of Constructing Bank Notes to Prevent Forgery.* New York–London: Willoughby, 1852.

Ovason, David. *The Secret Symbols of the Dollar Bill.* New York: HarperCollins, 2004.

Palley, Thomas. "Don't Bet Against the Dollar." *Foreign Policy* (December 18, 2007): 1–2.

Parry, Ellwood. *The Image of the Indian and the Black Man in American Art, 1590–1900.* New York: Braziller, 1974.

"Pass the Berk." *The Numismatist* 120:9 (September 2007): 36.

Passic, Frank. "The 1889–90 Albion College Currency." *The Mich-Matist* 37:1 (Winter 2001): 42–53.

Patrick, John Joseph. "John Sherman: The Early Years, 1823–1865." Ph.D. diss., Kent, OH: Kent State University, 1982.

Patterson, Richard S., and Richardson Dougall. *The Eagle and the Shield: A History of the Great Seal of the United States.* Washington, DC: Department of State, 1976.

Peterson, Peter G. "No Free Lunch." *The National Interest* 6:2 (July/August 2007): 19–22.

_____. *Running on Empty: How the Democratic and Republican Parties Are Bankrupting Our Future and What Americans Can Do About It.* New York: Farrar, Straus and Giroux, 2004.

Petrov, Vladimir. *Money and Conquest: Allied Occu-*

pation Currencies in World War II. Baltimore, MD: Johns Hopkins University Press, 1967.

Philpott, W.A., Jr. "Pin Holes in Paper Money." *The Numismatist* 65:10 (October 1952): 876–77.

Pick, Albert, and Rudolf Richter. *Papiergeld. Spezialkatalog Österreich, 1759–1986.* Dornbirn: Sedlmayer, 1986.

Pocock, J. G. A. *Virtue, Commerce and History. Chiefly in the Eighteenth Century.* Cambridge, UK: Cambridge University Press, 1985.

Poe, Edgar Allan. "The Gold-Bug." *Poetry and Tales.* New York: The Library of America, 1984. 560–96.

Poggi, Gianfranco. *Money and the Modern Mind.* Berkeley: University of California Press, 1993.

Pope, Alexander. *Epistle to Allen, Lord Bathurst. Epistles to Several Persons (Moral Essays).* Ed. F. W. Bateson. The Twickenham Edition. London: Methuen, 1951.

Porter, Kirk H., and Donald B. Johnson. *National Party Platforms.* Champaign: University of Illinois Press, 1966.

Potter, O. B. *The National Currency and Its Origins.* New York: J. J. Little, 1879.

Priddat, Birger P. "'Geist der Ornamentik,' Ideogrammatik des Geldes: Allegorien bürgerlicher Zivilreligion auf Banknoten des 19. und 20. Jahrhunderts." *Kapitalismus als Religion,* ed. Dirk Baecker. Berlin: Kadmos Verlag, 2003. 19–34.

The Prints of Roy Lichtenstein: A Catalogue Raisonné 1948–97. Manchester, VT: Hudson Hills Press, 2000.

Prown, Jules David. "Mind in Matter: An Introduction to Material Culture Theory and Method." *Winterthur Portfolio* 17:1 (1982): 1–20.

Purdy, Anthony, ed. *Literature and Money.* Amsterdam–Atlanta, GA: Rodopi, 1993.

Raitz, Jerri C. "Set in Stone." *Numismatist* 1119:11 (November 2006): 48–54.

Rathkolb, Oliver. *Die paradoxe Republik. Österreich 1945–2005.* Wien: Zsolnay, 2005.

Ravitch, Frank S. *Masters of Illusion: The Supreme Court and the Religion Clauses.* New York: New York University Press, 2007.

Records of the Bureau of Engraving and Printing. "Press Copies of Official and Miscellaneous Letters Sent, 1862–1912." Vol. 1 of 346. Record Group 318. Washington, DC: National Archives.

Redlich, Fritz. *The Molding of American Banking: Men and Ideas.* 1947, 1951; New York: Johnson Reprint Corporation, 1968.

Reed, Fred. *Abraham Lincoln: The Image of His Greatness.* Atlanta, GA: Whitman, 2009.

_____. "Paper Dolls." *The Numismatist* 120:11 (November 2007): 41–50.

_____. "Portrait of a President." *The Numismatist* 122:2 (February 2009): 45–50.

_____. *Show Me the Money! The Standard Catalog of Motion Picture, Television, Stage and Advertising Prop Money.* Jefferson, NC: McFarland, 2005.

Remini, Robert. *Andrew Jackson and the Bank War.* New York: W. W. Norton, 1967.

Reps, J. W. *Monumental Washington: The Planning and Development of the Capital Center.* Princeton, NJ: Princeton University Press, 1967.

Reynolds, David S. *Beneath the American Renaissance: The Subversive Imagination in the Age of Emerson and Melville.* Cambridge, MA: Harvard University Press, 1988.

Reynolds, Larry J. "American Cultural Iconography: Vision, History, and the Real." *American Literary History* 9 (1997): 381–95.

_____, and Gordon Hutner, eds. *National Imaginaries: The Cultural Work of American Iconography.* Princeton and Oxford: Princeton University Press, 2000.

Richards, Leonard L. *Shays's Rebellion: The American Revolution's Final Battle.* Philadelphia: University of Pennsylvania Press, 2003.

Richards, Thomas. *The Commodity Culture of Victorian England: Advertising as Spectacle, 1851–1914.* Stanford, CA: University of Stanford Press, 1990.

Richardson, Heather Cox. *The Greatest Nation of the Earth: Republican Economic Policies During the Civil War.* Cambridge, MA: Harvard University Press, 1997.

Ritter, Gretchen. *Goldbugs and Greenbacks: The Antimonopoly Tradition and the Politics of Finance in America, 1865–1896.* Cambridge, UK: Cambridge University Press, 1997.

Rockoff, Hugh. *The Free Banking Era: A Re-Examination.* New York: Arno Press, 1975.

_____. "*The Wizard of Oz* as a Monetary Allegory." *Journal of Political Economy* 98:4 (1990).

Rohrbough, Malcolm J. *Days of Gold: The California Gold Rush and the American Nation.* Berkeley: University of California Press, 1997.

Rosenzweig, Roy, and David Thelen. *The Presence of the Past: Popular Uses of History in American Life.* New York: Columbia University Press, 1998.

Rothbard, Murray N. *A History of Money and Banking in the United States: The Colonial Era to World War II.* Auburn, AL: Ludwig von Mises Institute, 2002.

Rothman, Hal. *Neon Metropolis: How Las Vegas Started the Twenty-First Century.* New York–London: Routledge, 2002.

Rowe, John Carlos, ed. *Post-Nationalist American Studies.* Berkeley: University of California Press, 2000.

Rulau, Russell. *Standard Catalog of United States Tokens, 1700–1900.* Fourth edition. Iola, WI: Krause Publications, 1997.

Ryzin, Robert A. Van. *Crime of 1873: The Comstock Connection; a Tale of Mines, Trade and Morgan Dollars.* Iola, WI: Krause Publications, 2001.

Sachs-Hombach, Klaus, ed. *Bildwissenschaft.* Frankfurt am Main: Suhrkamp, 2005.

Saldívar, José David. *Border Matters: Remapping American Cultural Studies.* Berkeley: University of California Press, 1997.

Samuel, Raphael. *Theatres of Memory: Past and Present in Contemporary Culture.* London: Verso, 1994.

Santos, Bob. *In God We Trust? A Guide to Personal*

Money Management in Today's World. Lima, NY: B.A.S.I.C. Books, 2003.

Sardar, Ziauddin, and Borin van Loon. *Introducing Cultural Studies.* London: Icon Books, 2004.

Schaaf, Bernard. "The Shrinking Dollar or The Decline and Fall of Beautiful American Banknotes." *International Bank Note Society Journal* 24:2 (June 1985): 38–40.

Schingoethe, Herb, and Martha Schingoethe. *College Currency: Money for Business Training,* ed. Neil Shafer. Port Clinton, OH: BNR Press, 1993.

Schlesinger, Arthur M., Jr. *The Age of Jackson.* Boston: Little, Brown, 1945.

_____. *The Age of Roosevelt.* Vol.II. *The Coming of the New Deal.* 1958; Boston, MA: Houghton Mifflin, 1988.

_____. *The Cycles of American History.* Boston: Houghton Mifflin, 1986.

_____. "History and National Stupidity." *New York Review of Books* LIII:7 (April 27, 2006): 14–15.

Schwan, C. Frederick and Joseph E. Boling. *World War II Remembered: History in Our Hands.* Port Clinton, OH: BNR Press, 1995.

Schwartz, Barry. *George Washington: The Making of an American Symbol.* New York: Free Press, 1987.

Scott, Kenneth. *Counterfeiting in Colonial America.* New York: American Numismatic Society, 1957.

Scroggs, William O. *A Century of Banking Progress.* Garden City, NY: Doubleday, Page, 1924.

Servet, Jean-Michel. *L'Euro au quotidien. Une question de confiance.* Paris: Desclée de Brouwer, 1998.

Shafer, Neil, and Colin R. Bruce II, eds. *Standard Catalog of World Paper Money.* 9th edition. Volume Two, *1368–1960.* Iola, WI: Krause Publications, 2000.

Sharkey, Robert P. *Money, Class, and Party: An Economic Study of Civil War and Reconstruction.* Baltimore: Johns Hopkins University Press, 1959.

Shell, Marc. *Art and Money.* Chicago: University of Chicago Press, 1995.

_____. *Money, Language, and Thought. Literary and Philosophic Economies from the Medieval to the Modern Era.* Baltimore, MD: Johns Hopkins University Press, 1982.

_____. *The Painting in the Trash Bin: Otis Kaye and the Perplexities of Art.* Chicago: University of Chicago Press, forthcoming.

_____. *Wampum and the Origin of American Money.* Champaign, IL: University of Illinois Press, forthcoming.

Sherman, John. *Recollections of Forty Years in the House, Senate and Cabinet.* Chicago: Werner, 1895.

Shumway, David R. *Creating American Civilization: A Genealogy of American Literature as an Academic Discipline.* Minneapolis: University of Minnesota Press, 1994.

Silverman, Kenneth. *A Cultural History of the American Revolution.* New York: Crowell, 1976.

Silvers, Robert B., and Barbara Epstein, eds. *Striking Terror: America's New War.* New York: New York Review Books, 2002.

Simmel, Georg. *The Philosophy of Money.* Third edition. Trans. Tom Bottomore and David B. Frisby. 1978; London–New York: Routledge, 2004.

Skaggs, David Curtis. "Postage Stamps as Icons." *Icons of America,* ed. Ray B. Browne and Marshall Fishwick. Bowling Green, OH: Bowling Green University Popular Press, 1978. 198–208.

Slaughter, Anne-Marie. *A New World Order.* Princeton, NJ: Princeton University Press, 2004.

Smidt, Corwin E., ed., *In God We Trust? Religion and American Political Life.* Grand Rapids, MI: Baker Academic, 2001.

Smith, Harry. *Anthology of American Folk Music.* Folkways, 1952; republished Smithsonian Folkways, 1997.

Smith, Lawrence Dwight. *Counterfeiting: Crime Against the People.* New York: Norton, 1944.

Smith, Walter Buckingham. *Economic Aspects of the Second Bank of the United States.* Cambridge, MA: Harvard University Press, 1953.

Snyder, Joel. "Picturing Vision." *Critical Inquiry* 6 (1980): 499–526.

Solomon, Raphel E. "Foreign Specie Coins in the American Colonies." *Studies on Money in Early America,* ed. Eric P. Newman and Richard G. Doty. New York: American Numismatic Society, 1976. 25–42.

Soosten, Joachim von. "Schwarzer Freitag: Die Diabolik der Erlösung und die Symbolik des Geldes." *Kapitalismus als Religion,* ed. Dirk Baecker. Berlin: Kulturverlag Kadmos, 2003. 121–43.

Soros, George. *The New Paradigm for Financial Markets: The Credit Crisis of 2008 and What It Means.* New York: PublicAffairs Books, 2008.

Spengler, Oswald. *Jahre der Entscheidung.* Munich: C.H. Beck, 1933. Trans. into English as *The Hour of Decision.* New York: Alfred A. Knopf, 1933.

Spillman, Lynette P. *Nation and Commemoration: Creating National Identities in the United States and Australia.* Cambridge, UK: Cambridge University Press, 1997.

Stahl, Alan M. "American Indian Peace Medals of the Colonial Period." *Money of Pre-Federal America,* ed. John M. Kleeberg. Coinage of the Americas Conference Proceedings, Number 7. New York: American Numismatic Society, 1992. 159–80.

Standish, David. *The Art of Money: The History and Design of Paper Currency from Around the World.* San Francisco: Chronicle Books, 2000.

Stearn, Gerald Emmanuel, ed. *Broken Image: Foreign Critiques of America.* New York: Random House, 1972.

Steel, Ronald. "Where it Began [Review of James Chace, *1912: Wilson, Roosevelt, Taft, and Debs—The Election That Changed the Country* (New York: Simon and Schuster, 2004)]." *New York Review of Books* LI: 14 (September 23, 2004): 58–61.

Steil, Benn. "The End of National Currency." *Foreign Affairs* (May/June 2007): 1–10.

Stevens, G. W. *The Land of the Dollar.* New York: Dodd, Mead, 1897.

Stiglitz, Joseph E., and Linda J. Bilmes. *The Three Trillion Dollar War: The True Cost of the Iraq Conflict.* New York: Norton, 2007.

Stryper. "In God We Trust." *In God We Trust.* Enigma Records, 1988.

Suetonius (Caius Suetonius Tranquillus). *De Vita Caesarum.* Trans. John C. Rolfe. Vol. 1. Cambridge, MA: Harvard University Press—London: Heinemann, 1920.

Sumner, William Graham. *A History of Banking in the United States.* New York: Journal of Commerce and Commercial Bulletin, 1896.

Swanson, Gerald J. *America the Broke: How the Reckless Spending of The White House and Congress Are Bankrupting Our Country and Destroying Our Children's Future.* New York: Doubleday/Currency Business Books, 2004.

Swanson, Guy R. "Agents of Culture and Nationalism: The Confederate Treasury and Confederate Currency." *The Banker's Art: Studies in Paper Money,* ed. Virginia Hewitt. London: British Museum Press, 1995. 132–39.

Syrett, Harold C., et al., eds. *The Papers of Alexander Hamilton.* New York: Columbia University Press, 1961–1987.

Tabbert, Mark A. *American Freemasons: Three Centuries of Building American Communities.* New York: New York University Press, 2005.

Talbott, John R. *Obamanomics: How Bottom-Up Economic Prosperity Will Replace Trickle-Down Economics.* New York: Seven Stories Press, 2008.

Talbott, Strobe, and Nayan Chanda, eds. *The Age of Terror: America and the World After September 11.* New York: Basic Books, 2002.

Taxay, Don. *The U.S. Mint and Coinage: An Illustrated History from 1776 to the Present.* New York: Arco, 1966.

Taylor, Mark C. *Altarity.* Chicago: University of Chicago Press, 1987.

_____. *Confidence Games: Money and Markets in a World Without Redemption.* Chicago: University of Chicago Press, 2004.

Taylor, Walter Fuller. *The Economic Novel in America.* Chapel Hill: University of North Carolina Press, 1942.

Temin, Peter. *The Jacksonian Economy.* New York: W. W. Norton, 1969.

Terkel, Studs. *Hard Times: An Oral History of the Great Depression.* 1970; New York: Pantheon Books, 1986.

Thayer, Theodore. "The Land Bank System in the American Colonies." *Journal of Economic History* 13 (1953): 145–59.

Théret, Bruno. "L'euro en ses tristes symboles. Une monnaie sans âme ni culture." *Le Monde diplomatique* (Décembre 2001): 4–5. An English version is available to subscribers at *http://mondediplo.com/2001/12/.*

Thomas, Dwight, and David K. Jackson. *The Poe Log: A Documentary Life of Edgar Allan Poe, 1809–1849.* Boston: G. K. Hall, 1987.

Thompson, Kenneth, ed. *Media and Cultural Regulation.* London: Sage/Open University, 1997.

Thoreau, Henry David. *Walden.* Boston: Houghton Mifflin, 1964.

Thornton, Tamara P. *Handwriting in America: A Cultural History.* New Haven: Yale University Press, 1996.

Thrift, N., and A. Leyshorn. "A Phantom State? The De-Traditionalisation of Money, the International Financial System and International Financial Centres." *Political Geography* 13 (1994): 229–37.

Timberlake, Richard H., Jr. *The Origins of Central Banking in the United States.* Cambridge, MA: Harvard University Press, 1978.

Tocqueville, Alexis de. *Democracy in America.* Abridged with an introduction by Thomas Bender. 1945; New York: Random House/Modern Library, 1981.

Tompkins, Jane. *Sensational Designs: The Cultural Work of American Fiction.* New York: Oxford University Press, 1985.

Trachtenberg, Alan, ed. *Critics of Culture: Literature and Society in the Early Twentieth Century.* New York: Wiley, 1976.

_____. *The Incorporation of America: Culture and Society in the Gilded Age.* New York: Hill & Wang, 1982.

Trachtenberg, Marvin. *The Statue of Liberty.* Harmondsworth: Penguin, 1977.

Trani, Eugene O. "Dollar Diplomacy." *Encyclopedia of American Foreign Policy,* ed. Alexander DeConde et al. New York: Scribner's, 1978. 268–74.

Travers, Len. *Celebrating the Fourth: Independence Day and the Rites of Nationalism in the Early Republic.* Amherst: University of Massachusetts Press, 1997.

Trithemius, Johannes. *In Praise of Scribes [De Laude Scriptorum].* Trans. Roland Behrendt. Lawrence, KS: Coronado Press, 1974.

Tschachler, Heinz. "Dollar Bill." *American Icons: An Encyclopedia of the People, Places, and Things That Have Shaped Our Culture,* ed. Dennis R. Hall and Susan Grove Hall. Westport, CT: Greenwood Press, 2006. 1: 205–12.

_____. "From 'Wildman' to 'True Native American': Images of American Indians on Paper Money." *ANA Journal: Advanced Studies in Numismatics* 2:1 (Spring 2007). 8–28.

_____. "'I send you 19 small flaggs': The Lewis and Clark Expedition and the Creation of an Imagined Community." *Holidays, Ritual, Festival, Celebration, and Public Display,* ed. Christina Sánchez Carretero, and Jack Santino. Alcalá de Henares: Universidad de Alcalá/Instituto Universitario de Estudios Norteamericanos, 2003. 105–20.

_____. "Louisiana DIX Notes and the Dixieland Myth." *The Numismatist* 121:11 (November 2008): 48–54.

_____. "'Sacred Emblems of Attachment': The Lewis and Clark Expedition, American Nationalism, and the Colonization of the West." *RAVEN: A Journal of Vexillology* 12 (2005): 55–78.

Turkle, Sherry, ed. *Falling for Science: Objects in Mind.* Cambridge, MA: MIT Press, 2008.

Tyler, Francine. "The Angel in the Factory: Images

of Women Workers Engraved on Ante-Bellum Bank Notes." *Imprint: Journal of the American Historical Print Collectors Society* 19:1 (Spring 1994). 107–18.

Unger, Irwin. *The Greenback Era: A Social and Political History of American Finance, 1865–1879.* Princeton, NJ: Princeton University Press, 1964.

U.S. Census Bureau. *Statistical Abstracts of the United States: 2008.* 127th Edition. Washington, DC, 2007.

U.S. General Accounting Office. "Financial Impact of Issuing the New $1 Coin." GAO/GGD-00-111R. Washington, DC: April 7, 2000.

_____. "New Dollar Coin. Marketing Campaign Raised Public Awareness but Not Widespread Use." GAO-02-896, Report to the Subcommittee on Treasury and General Government, Committee on Appropriations, United States Senate. Washington, DC: September 13, 2002.

U.S. House of Representatives. "Will Jumbo Euro Notes Threaten the Greenback?" Hearing before the Subcommittee on Domestic and International Monetary Policy, Committee on Banking and Financial Services, One Hundred Fifth Congress, second session, October 8, 1998. Washington, DC: General Printing Office, 1998.

Valenze, Deborah. *The Social Life of Money in the English Past.* New York: Cambridge University Press, 2006.

Veblen, Thorstein. *The Theory of the Leisure Class.* New York 1899; Boston: Houghton Mifflin, 1973.

Vendler, Helen. *Soul Says.* Cambridge, MA: Belknap Press of Harvard University Press, 1995.

Vermeule, Cornelius C. *Numismatic Art in America: Aesthetics of the United States Coinage.* Second Edition. Atlanta, GA: Whitman, 2007.

Vernon, John. *Money and Fiction: Literary Realism in the Nineteenth and Twentieth Centuries.* Ithaca, NY: Cornell University Press, 1984.

Wagnleitner, Reinhold. *Coca-Colonization and the Cold War: The Cultural Mission of the United States in Austria After the Second World War.* Chapel Hill, NC: University of North Carolina Press, 1994.

Wald, Kenneth D. *Religion and Politics in the United States.* Second edition. Washington, DC: Congressional Quarterly Press, 1992.

Wald, Priscilla. *Constituting Americans: Cultural Anxiety and Narrative Form.* Durham, NC: Duke University Press, 1995.

Waldstreicher, David. *In the Midst of Perpetual Fetes: The Making of American Nationalism, 1776–1820.* Chapel Hill: University of North Carolina Press, 1997.

Warhol, Andy. *The Philosophy of Andy Warhol.* New York: Harcourt Brace, 1975.

Watkins, T.H. *The Hungry Years: America in an Age of Crisis, 1929–1939.* New York: Holt, 1999.

Watts, Emily S. *The Businessman in American Literature.* Athens: University of Georgia Press, 1972.

Weatherford, Jack. *The History of Money: From Sandstone to Cyberspace.* New York: Crown, 1997.

Weber, Max. *The Protestant Ethic and the Spirit of Capitalism.* Trans. Talcott Parsons. New York: Scribner's 1958.

Weishaar, Wayne, and Wayne W. Parrish. *Men Without Money.* New York: Putnam's, 1933.

Weld, Isaac, Jr. *Travels Through the States of North America and the Provinces of Upper and Lower Canada.* Vol. 1. London: Stockdale, 1799.

Wells, David A. *Robinson Crusoe's Money; or, The Remarkable Financial Fortunes and Misfortunes of a Remote Island Community.* Ill. Thomas Nast. 1876; New York: P. Smith, 1931.

Wennerlind, Carl. "The Death Penalty as Monetary Policy: The Practice and Punishment of Monetary Crime." *History of Political Economy* 36 (2004): 131–61.

Wersich, Rüdiger B. "Pledge of Allegiance to the Flag." *USA Lexikon,* ed. the same. Berlin: Erich Schmidt Verlag, 1996. 569.

Wertheimer, Eric. *Underwriting: The Poetics of Insurance in America, 1722–1872.* Stanford, CA: Stanford University Press, 2006.

Weschler, Lawrence. *Boggs: A Comedy of Values.* Chicago: University of Chicago Press, 1999.

_____. "Money Changes Everything." *The New Yorker* (January 16, 1993): 38–41; *The New York Times* (December 6, 1992): 42.

Weyers, Christian. "Über die Herkunft des Dollarzeichens." *Zeitschrift für Semiotik* 13:3–4 (1991): 367–76.

Whalen, Terence. "Edgar Allan Poe and the Horrid Laws of Political Economy." *American Quarterly* 44:3 (September 1992): 381–417.

Whalin, W. Terry. "Disney Dollars: Legal Tender in the Magic Kingdom." *The Numismatist* 100:7 (July 1987): 1424–28.

Wilber, E. J., and E. P. Eastman. *A Treatise on Counterfeit, Altered, and Spurious Bank Notes.* Poughkeepsie, NY: published for the authors, 1865.

Williams, Raymond. *Culture and Society, Coleridge to Orwell.* 1958; London: Hogarth Press, 1990.

_____. *Television: Technology and Cultural Form.* London: Fontana, 1974.

Williamson, Judith. *Decoding Advertisements: Ideology and Meaning in Advertising.* London: Marion Boyars, 1978.

Wills, Gary. *Under God: Religion and American Politics.* New York: Simon & Schuster, 1990.

Wilson, Rob. *The American Sublime: The Genealogy of a Poetic Genre.* Madison: University of Wisconsin Press, 1991.

Wilson, Thomas. *The Power "To Coin Money": The Exercise of Monetary Power by the Congress.* New York: M.E. Sharpe, 1992.

Winthrop, John. "From *The Journal of John Winthrop.*" *Concise Anthology of American Literature,* ed. George McMichael. Fourth Edition. Upper Saddle River, NJ: Prentice Hall, 1998. 68–79.

Wodak, Ruth, Rudolf de Cillia, Martin Reisigl, and Karin Liebhart. *The Discursive Construction of National Identity.* Trans. Angelika Hirsch and Richard Mitten. Abingdon, UK: Marston Books, 1999.

Wolfe, Alan. *The Transformation of American Reli-*

gion: *How Americans Live Their Faith*. New York: Free Press, 2003.

Wood, Gordon S. "Alexander Hamilton and the Making of a Fiscal-Military State." *Revolutionary Characters: What Made the Founders Different*. New York: Penguin, 2006. 119–40.

_____. Apologies to the Iroquois. *The New York Review of Books* LIII: 6 (April 6, 2006): 50–53.

_____. *The Creation of the American Republic*. Chapel Hill: University of North Carolina Press, 1969.

_____. "Rambunctious American Democracy." *The New York Review of Books* XLIX (May 9, 2002): 20–23.

Woodmansee, Martha, and Mark Osteen, eds. *The New Economic Criticism: Studies at the Intersection of Literature and Economics*. New York–London: Routledge, 1999.

Woods, Stuart. *Two-Dollar Bill*. New York: Putnam, 2005.

Wright, Robert E. *The U.S. National Debt, 1785–1900*. 4 vols. London: Pickering and Chatto, 2005.

_____, and David J. Cowen. *Financial Founding Fathers: The Men Who Made America Rich*. Chicago: University of Chicago Press, 2006.

Yarrow, Andrew. *Forgive Us Our Debts: The Intergenerational Dangers of Fiscal Irresponsibility*. New Haven: Yale University Press, 2008.

Yeoman, R. S. *Guide Book of United States Coins*. The Official Red Book®, ed. Kenneth Bressett. 61st edition. Atlanta, GA: Whitman Publishing, 2007.

Zelinsky, Wilbur. *Nation into State: The Shifting Symbolic Foundations of American Nationalism*. Chapel Hill: University of North Carolina Press, 1988.

Zelizer, Viviana A. *The Social Meaning of Money: Pin Money, Paychecks, Poor Relief and Other Currencies*. New York: Basic Books, 1994; Princeton, NJ: Princeton University Press, 1997.

Zischka, Anton. *Der Dollar. Glanz und Elend der Weltwährung*. Third edition. Munich: Langen-Müller, 1995.

Internet Sources

123posters.com. "Al Pacino Posters." 05/28/09 <http://www.123posters.com/pacino.htm>.

50 Cent. 10/26/05 <http://www.50cent.com/>.

The American Bar Association. "Elk Grove Unified School District *v.* Newdow et al." March 2004. 04/13/04 <http://www.abanet.org/publiced/preview/briefs/march04.html#elk>.

Barnwell, Stephen. "Dream Dollars." 06/19/07 <www.dream-dollars.com>.

_____. "Dream Dollars." 04/20/07 <http://www.stephenbarnwell.com/press1.htm>.

Brouillet, Carol. "Unmasking the Big Deception [Mission Statement]." 13/11/06 <http://www.deceptiondollar.com/mission.htm>.

"Bush Notes." 07/04/07 <www.themillion.com>.

Cassanello, Robert. "INQ: OAH Magazine." Online posting. 2 May 2007. <H-AMSTDY@H-NET.MSU.EDU>.

Chao, Tom. "Known Replicas of Obsolete Notes." 02/07/07 <http://www.tomchao.com/replicas.html>.

The Coin Coalition. "Why a Dollar Coin?" 06/17/02 <http://www.coincoalition.org/why.htm>.

Confederate Currency: The Color of Money. 2001–2006. 10/29/08 <www.colorsofmoney.com>.

Davies, Roy. "Electronic Money, E-Money, and Digital Cash." 13 March 2007. 05/18/07 <http://www.ex.ac.uk/~RDavies/arian/emoney.html>.

_____. "The Word 'Dollar' and the Dollar Sign $." 11/08/06 <http://www.exeter.ac.uk/~RDavies/arian/dollar.html>.

Dictionary of Sexual Terms. Online edition. 2004 06/26/07 <http://www.sex-lexis.com/Sex-Diction ary/queer%20as%20a%20three-dollar%20bill>.

"Dollar is Dolor." 11/15/06 <http://www.geocities.com/levelwater/mathlies13.html>.

The Dude. "The Sticker Dude's Flux Bucks." n.d. 06/17/02 <www.raggededgepress.com>.

Edwards, Kathleen A. "Good Books to Teach Children about Money." *Amazon: Listmania!* May 15, 2006. 08/23/06 <www.amazon.com/gp/richpub/listmania>.

European Central Bank. "Images of Banknotes and Coins." 04/30/07 <http://www.ecb.int./bc/euro/banknotes/html/index.en.html>.

Federal Reserve Bank of San Francisco (FRBSF). "American Currency Exhibit." April 5, 2006. 08/25/07 <http://www.frbsf.org/currency/>.

The Federal Reserve Board. "The Twelve Federal Reserve Districts." December 13, 2005 <http://www.federalreserve.gov/otherfrb.htm>, accessed 03/30/07.

FoundMagazine. "France No Good." August 20, 2005. 09/12/07. <www.foundmagazine.com/comments/575>.

Franklin, Benjamin. "A Modest Enquiry into the Nature and Necessity of a Paper-Currency." Department of Humanities Computing, University of Groningen, The Netherlands, "From Revolution to Reconstruction: A Hypertext on American History from the colonial period until Modern Times." 03/07/07 <http://odur.let.rug.nl/~usa/D/1726-1750/franklin/paper.htm>.

Fuchshuber, Julia. "Financial Times— der US-Dollar und seine Repräsentation in der amerikanischen Kunst." *Deutsch-amerikanischer Almanach* 9 (2001). 02/13/97 <http://daa.amerikanistik.net/daa9/financialtimes.html>.

Fuselier, Pascal. "How Dixieland Got Its Name and Other French Influence Facts in the United States." 04/22/05 <http://www.geocities.com/old_time_time/dixieland.htm>.

Geoffrey of Monmouth. *Vita Merlini*. Trans. Basil Clarke. Cardiff, UK: University of Wales Press, 1973. 05/05/07 <http://www.geocities.com/bran waedd/merlini.html>.

Ginnie Mae. "Brain Food: Cool Facts: Money." 06/17/02 <http://www.ginniemae.gov/homezone/brainfood/coolfacts.html>.

Grand Rapids Art Museum Online. "American Masters: The Manoogian Collection." 2001. 06/28/07 <www.tfaoi.com/am/16am/16am98.jpg>.

GreatSeal.com. "The Great Seal of the United States."

2007, 04/20/07 <*http://www.greatseal.com/index.html*>.

Hall, Ed. "U.S. National Debt Clock." 09/20/06 <*http://www.brillig.com/debt_clock*>.

Harth, David Greg. "I am not afraid." 09/12/07 <*http://www.sptimes.com/News/122701/Weekend/Art_show_honors_terro.shtml*>.

Heritage Auction Galleries. "Heritage Sets World's Paper Money Record." Press Release December 16, 2006. 05/31/07 <*http://www.ha.com*>.

Holzer, Harold. "Beyond Face Value: Slavery Iconography in Confederate Currency." Civil War Center / Louisiana State University. *Beyond Face Value: Depictions of Slavery in Confederate Currency.* 1996–2007. 09/11/08 <*http://www.cwc.lsu.edu/BeyondFaceValue*>.

"Icon." *The American Heritage® Dictionary of the English Language.* Fourth Edition. Boston: Houghton Mifflin, 2000. 05/24/03 <*http://www.yourdictionary.com/ahd/i/i0015000.html*>.

Indian Humor. National Museum of the American Indian. 1995. 12/01/05 <*http://www.nmai.si.edu/exhibitions/indian_humor/exhibit/7.htm*>.

International Association of Millionaires. "I.A.M. Million Dollar Bill." 04/12/07 <*www.i-a-m.ws/bill.htm*>.

Irvin, Benjamin H. "Benjamin Franklin's '*Enriching Virtues*': Continental Currency and the Creation of a Revolutionary Republic." *Common-Place* 6:3 (April 2006). 04/17/09 <*http://www.common-place.org/vol-06/no-03/irvin/*>.

Irving, Washington. "The Devil and Tom Walker: Tales of a Traveller." *The Literature Network.* 2000–2009. 02/12/09 <*http://www.online-literature.com/irving/tales-of-a-traveller/*>.

_____. "The Great Mississippi Bubble." *The Crayon Papers.* February 27, 2000. 02/13/08 <*www.online-literature.com/irving/crayon-papers/2/*>.

Jurek, Richard. "The Jefferson Space Museum." 05/05/08 <*http://www.jefferson-in-space.blogspot.com/*>.

Kant, Immanuel. "Beobachtungen über das Gefühl des Schönen und Erhabenen" [1764]. *Vorkritische Schriften II, 1757–1777. Das Bonner Kant-Korpus.* Institut für Kommunikationsforschung und Phonetik der Universität Bonn, 01/03/2007 <*http://www.ikp.uni-bonn.de/Kant/aa02/253.html*>, accessed 02/10/07.

Kelly, Don C. "Paper Money." 06/04/07 <*http://www.donckelly.com*>.

Kenston High School. "Let us all remember." © 1998–2002 Kenston Local Schools. 05/05/02 <*http://www.kenston.k12.oh.us/khs/current/us_dollar_bill.htm*>.

Lichtenstein, Roy. *Ten Dollar Bill.* 05/05/02 <*www.cosmopolis.ch*>.

Lipschutz, Ronnie D. "In God We Trust. All Others Pay Cash." *Good Times,* July 18, 2002. 06/14/06 <*http://www.people.ucsc.edu/~rlipsch/god.html*>.

Little Lost Star. "Two dollar bill (2002)." 08/16/06 <*http://everything2.com/index.pl?node_id=97632&displaytype=printable&lastnode_id=97632*>.

Mann, John W. W. "The Lemhi Shoshone, Federal Recognition, and the Bicentennial of the Corps of Discovery." n.d. <*http://www.lemhi-shoshone.com/john_ww_mann.html*>, 12/13/07.

Maritz AmeriPol®. "Proud to Be an American: Patriotic Feelings Rate 7.8 on Ten-Point Scale." 06/21/00 <*www.maritz.com/mmri/apoll/release.asp*>.

Markstein, Donald D. "Unce Scrooge." 08/07/06 <*http://www.toonopedia.com/scrooge.htm*>.

The Max Hunter Folk Song Collection. "Two Dollar Bill." 08/16/06 <*http://www.missouristate.edu/folksong/maxhunter/1258/index.html*>.

McLarty, Mary Alice. "The Dollar Bill." 04/16/02 <*http://www.maryalice.com/DollarBill.html*>.

The Michigan Bar Association. "In God We Trust, All Others Pay Cash!" 06/14/06 <*http://www.michbar.org/publications/sbm_ppp/sld003.htm*>.

Museum of American Finance. "MAKING MONEY: Bank Note Engraving and the Fight Against Counterfeiting, Exhibit February — December 2006." 11/30/06 <*http://www.financialhistory.org/*>.

"My Fractional Notes." 10/18/06 <*http://www.myfractionalnotes.com/1STISSUE/FR1236.JPG*>.

National Flag Foundation. "Mission Statement." 2004. 05/09/07 <*http://www.americanflags.org/index.flash.html*>.

National Numismatic Collections. "Native Americans, Women, and African Americans on Early United States Bank Notes." 02/01/06 <*http://americanhistory.si.edu/collections/numismatics/survivin/112.htm*>.

_____. "U.S. One Dollar, 1882." 04/29/07 <*www.americanhistory.si.edu/collections*>.

Null, Christopher. "Review of *Twenty Bucks.*" 1999. 03/21/07 <*www.filmcritic.com*>.

ODD#III(a);pQ$:10Afm3155.p. (sic). "A Short Discourse on the Ancient and Accepted Discordian Practice of Fnording Dollar Bills." n.d. 06/17/02 <*http://jubal.westnet.com/hyperdiscordia/fnording_dollar_bills.html*>.

O'Malley, Michael. "Free Silver and the Constitution of Man: The Money Debate and Imigration at the Turn of the Century." *Common-Place* 6(2006). 04/17/09 <*http://www.common-place.org/vol-06/no-03/omalley/*>.

"The Origins of $, The Dollar Symbol." 11/14/06 <*http://www.pballew.net/dollar.html*>.

Orzano, Michele. "Learning the Language." 10/15/06 <*http://www.coinworld.com/news/111504/BW_1115.asp*>.

Österreichische Bundesforste. "Berge, Wälder, Seen: wichtigste Identifikationsfaktoren Österreichs [press release]." January 5, 2005. 01/11/05 <*http://www.oebf.at.index.php*>.

PageWise, Inc. "The new US currency—can you spot a fake?" 06/17/02 <*http://mi.essortment.com/currencyuspape_ramq.htm*>.

PollingReport.com. "Religion." 07/14/06 <*www.pollingreport.com/religion.htm*>.

PollingReport.com. "Religion, part 2." 07/01/03 <*www.pollingreport.com/religion2.htm*>.

Polsky, Richard. "Art Market Watch." 05/05/02 <*www.artnet.com*>.

Prusmack, Tim. "Money-Art." 01/24/06 <*www.money-art.com/index.html*>.

Reed, Richard J. "World Paper Money: Souvenir Cards." 2002. 06/21/07 <*www.misterbanknote. com/souvcards.html*>.

Ron Wise's World Paper Money. "Disney Dollars." 06/19/07 <*http://aes.iupui.edu/rwise/banknotes/ united_states/USADisneyPNL-1Dollar-2000_f.jpg*>.

_____. "Educational and Play Money." 07/04/07 <*http://aes.iupui.edu/rwise/banknotes/united_states /USAFantasy-100Dollars-SchoolMoney_f.jpg*>.

_____. "Fantasy Notes: Liberty." 07/04/07 <*http:// aes.iupui.edu/rwise/countries/united_states.html# fantasy*>.

_____. "Fantasy Notes: P-NL 2001." 07/04/07 <*http: //aes.iupui.edu/rwise/banknotes/united_states/Usa-Fantasy-2001(Dollars)-2001_f.jpg*>.

_____. "Liberty Dollars: Brochure Insert." 07/04/07 <*http://aes.iupui.edu/rwise/banknotes/united_states /USAFantasyPNL-100Years-LibertyBanknote-In sert-1986-donatedta.jpg*>.

Roosevelt, Theodore. "There can be no fifty-fifty Americanism in this country." *The Columbia World of Quotations*, ed. Robert Andrews et al. Columbia University Press, 2006. *eNotes.com*. 2006. 04/16/07 <*http://history.enotes.com/famous-quotes/ there-can-be-no-fifty-fifty-americanism-in-this*>.

Saint Louis Federal Reserve Bank. "The Fed's Regional Structure." 06/02/05 <*http://www.stlouis-fed.org/publications/pleng/structure.html*>.

Samuelson, Robert. "The Cashless Society has Arrived." June 2007. 08/15/07 <*www.realclearpolitics. com/articles/2007/06/the_cashless_society_has_arriv. html*>.

Slick Times. "Political Funny Money." 2007. 06/26/ 07 <*www.slick.com*>.

Smith, Sandra. "J.S.G. Boggs: Life Size and In Color." *Visible Language* 29:3/4 (1995). 11/07/05 <*http:// www.jsgboggs.com/whois.html*>.

Smithsonian Institution. "Improvised Money." 10/16/06 <*http://www.smithsonianeducation.org/ educators/lesson_plans/revolutionary_money*>.

Štraus, Stane. "Polymer Bank Notes of the World:" 05/09/08 <*www.polymernotes.org*>.

Theo, Kelly Sue. "Dollar bill pictures and what they mean." PageWise, Inc. 2001. 04/16/02 <*http://mi. essortment.com/dollarbillpict_rixh.htm*>.

Tin Signs USA. "Cash desk poster." 06/14/06 <*http:// www.tinsignsusa.com/index.html*>.

U.S. Civil War Center. "Beyond Face Value: Depictions of Slavery in Confederate Currency." 09/09/ 08 <*http://www.cwc.lsu.edu/cwc/BeyondFaceValue/ visit/navvisit.htm*>.

U.S. Department of the Treasury. "History of the Treasury: Treasurers of the U.S.: Mary Ellen Withrow." 10/18/06 <*http://www.ustreas.gov/education/ history/treasurers/mewithrow.shtml*>.

_____. "U.S. Currency and Coin Outstanding and in Circulation." 09/29/06 <*http://www.fms.treas.gov*>.

U.S. Department of the Treasury, Bureau of the Public Debt. "The Public Debt Online." 09/20/06 <*http://www.publicdebt.treas.gov/opd/opd.htm*>.

U.S. District Court, District of Columbia. "American Council of the Blind et al. *v.* O'Neill et al." Civil Action No. 2002-0864. 05/05/08 <*https://ecf.dcd. uscourts.gov/cgi-bin/Opinions.pl?2006*>.

U.S. Mint. "Coins Online." December 28, 2006. 01/ 23/07 <*http://www.usmint.gov/whats_new/Coins Online/index.cfm?flash=yes*>.

_____. "The First Spouse Gold Coin Program." 06/20/07 <*http://www.usmint.gov/mint_programs/ firstSpouse/*>.

_____. "H.I.P. Pocket Change." July 1999. 03/07/08 <*http://www.usmint.gov/kids/*>.

_____. "Historical Images Library." 02/13/07. <*http: //www.usmint.gov/about_the_mint/CoinLibrary/in dex.cfm*>.

_____. "The Presidential $1 Coin Program." December 28, 2006. 01/23/07 <*http://www.usmint.gov/ mint_programs/$1coin/index.cfm*>.

U.S. Supreme Court. "Elk Grove Unified School District and David W. Gordon, Superintendent, Petitioners v. Michael A. Newdow, et al." Docketed: May 9, 2003 Lower Ct: United States Court of Appeals for the Ninth Circuit. 04/13/04 <*http:// www.supremecourtus.gov/oral_arguments/argu ment_transcripts/02-1624.pdf*>.

U.S. Treasury Bureau of Engraving and Printing (USBEP). "Annual Production Figures." 08/21/06 <*http://www.moneyfactory.com/section.cfm/2/51*>.

_____. "The Bureau of Engraving and Printing's Western Currency Facility." 04/27/04 <*http:// www.moneyfactory.gov/newmoney/main.cfm/media/ western*>.

_____. "Cool Facts about Money." 06/17/02 <*http:// www.ginnimae.gov/homezone/brainfood/coolfacts. html*>.

_____. "Counterfeiting Laws." 11/07/06 <*http:// www.moneyfactory.gov/document.cfm/18/103*>.

_____. "Defacement of Currency." 11/07/06 <*http:// www.moneyfactory.gov/document.cfm/18/104*>.

_____. "The Great Seal of the United States on Paper Currency," 08/15/01 <*http://www.moneyfactory. gov/document.cfm/18/2233*>.

_____. "In God We Trust." 08/21/06 <*http://www. moneyfactory.gov/document.cfm/18/107*>.

_____. "International Training and Education." 09/28/04 <*http://www.moneyfactory.com/new money/main.cfm*>.

_____. "Money Facts: African Americans." 04/16/02 <*http://www.bep.treas.gov/document.cfm/18/97*>.

_____. "Money Facts: Bureau History." 11/07/06 <*http://www.moneyfactory.gov/document.cfm/18/101*>.

_____. "Money Facts: Fun Facts" 2006. 11/07/06 <*http: //www.moneyfactory.gov/document.cfm/18/106*>.

_____. "Money Facts: Origin of the $ Sign," 11/07/06 <*http://www.moneyfactory.gov/document.cfm/18/113*>.

_____. "Moneyfactory.Com. Large Denominations: One Hundred Thousand Gold Certificate." 02/14/ 07 <*www.moneyfactory.gov/print.cfm/5/42/1359*>.

_____. "The New Color of Money." 04/27/04 <*www. moneyfactory.com/newmoney*>.

_____. "New Money Information," 06/29/06 <*www. moneyfactory.gov/newmoney*>.

_____. "Redesign of the $5 Note (press release)." June 29, 2006. 06/29/06 <*http://www.moneyfac*

tory.gov/newmoney/main.cfm/media/releases0629 2006>.

_____. "The Redesigned $10 Note Starts Circulating Today," 03/02/06 <*http://www.moneyfactory.gov/ newmoney/main.cfm/partners/vipreTranscript_030 22006>.*

_____. "Reproduction of Currency." 11/07/06 <*http: //www.moneyfactory.gov/document.cfm/18/117>.*

_____. "Safer, Smarter, More Secure $50 Bill Issued (Press Release)." September 28, 2004. 04/28/04 <*http://www.moneyfactory.gov/newmoney/main.cf m/media/releases09282004>.*

_____. "Selection of Portraits and Designs Appearing on Paper Currency." 08/15/01 <*http://www. moneyfactory.gov/document.cfm/18/118>.*

_____. "Survey about New Web Site Features for Bureau of Engraving and Printing." October 6, 2008. 10/07/08 <*http://research.opinionguru.com/mrl Web/mrlWeb.dll?l.Project=a15057>.*

The University of Notre Dame. Department of Special Collections. "The Coins of Colonial and Early America." 06/11/07 <*http://www.coins.nd.edu/Col Coin>.*

The University of Virginia. Capitol Project. 2000. 04/16/07 <*www.xroads.virginia.edu>.*

The Warhol Museum in Pittsburgh. 05/05/02 <*http: //www.warhol.org/credits.html>.*

Warshauer, Matthew. "Who Wants to Be a Millionaire: Changing Conceptions of the American Dream." *American Studies Today Online* 9 (2002). 11/24/03 <*http://www.americansc.org.uk/Online/ American_Dream.htm>.*

Washington, George. "Farewell Address of 1796." The Avalon Project at Yale Law School. 1996. 04/ 16/07 <*http://www.yale.edu/lawweb/avalon/wash ing.htm>.*

Weeks, Albert L. "Customer Comment on Brian Burrell, *The Words We Live By: The Creeds, Mottoes, and Pledges That Have Shaped America* (New York:

Free Press, 1997)." January 1, 1998. 10/05/04 <*www. amazon.com>.*

"Wheresgeorge." 03/19/07 <*www.wheresgeorge.com/ press>.*

Wikipedia. "Coin Coalition." 08/21/06 <*http://en. wikipedia.org/wiki/Coin_Coalition>.*

_____. "Currency Bill Tracking." 03/21/07 <*http:// en.wikipedia.org/wiki/Currency_bill_tracking>.*

_____. "Fake Denominations of United States Currency." May 26, 2007. 06/26/07 <*http://en.wiki pedia.org/wiki/Fake_denominations_of_United_ States_currency>.*

_____. "In God We Trust." 06/14/06 <*http://en. wikipedia.org/wiki/In_God_We_Trust>.*

_____. "Save the Greenback." 08/21/06 <*http://en. wikipedia.org/wiki/Save_the_Greenback>.*

_____. "Scrooge McDuck," 04/14/06 <*www.wiki pedia.org/wiki/Scrooge_McDuck>.*

_____. "Second Life." 02/22/07 <*http://en.wikipedia. org/wiki/second_Life>.*

_____. "United States Two Dollar Bill." 08/16/06 <*http://en.wikipedia.org/wiki/United_States_two-dollar_bill>.*

Wilson, John and Nancy. "The History and Collecting of Large Size Notes & Deuces." *FUN-Topics* 44:3 (Fall 1999). 04/20/06 <*www.funtopics.com/ fun_topics_v44n3_wilson.html>.*

"Wo ist mein Geld." 03/19/07 <*www.wo-ist-mein-geld.de>.*

Wocka. User Submitted and Ranked Jokes. "The Two Dollar Bill." 08/16/06 <*http://www.wocka.com/ 12767.html>.*

Wolff, Edward N. "The Rich Get Richer: And Why the Poor Don't." *The American Prospect* 12:3 (February 12, 2001). 02/20/07 <*http://www.prospect. org/print-friendly/print/V12/3/wolff-e.html>.*

Yale University Art Gallery. New Haven, CT. Trumbull Collection. 01/16/07 <*http://artgallery.yale. edu>.*

Index

Numbers in **bold italics** indicate pages with photographs.